# Long-Term Trends IN THE Well-Being OF Children AND Youth

D1571518

ISSUES IN CHILDREN'S AND FAMILIES' LIVES

Edited By

Roger P. Weissberg

Herbert J. Walberg

Mary Utne O'Brien

Carol Bartels Kuster

The University of Illinois at Chicago Series
on Children and Youth

CWLA Press • Washington, DC

CWLA Press is an imprint of the Child Welfare League of America. The Child Welfare League of America is the nation's oldest and largest membership-based child welfare organization. We are committed to engaging people everywhere in promoting the well-being of children, youth, and their families, and protecting every child from harm.

CHILD WELFARE LEAGUE OF AMERICA, INC.
HEADQUARTERS
440 First Street, NW, Third Floor, Washington, DC 20001-2085
E-mail: books@cwla.org

CURRENT PRINTING (last digit)
10 9 8 7 6 5 4 3 2 1

Cover and text design by Jennifer R. Geanakos

Printed in the United States of America

ISBN # 0–87868–824–2

Library of Congress Cataloging-in-Publication Data

Long term trends in the well-being of children and youth / edited by
Roger P. Weissberg ... [et al.].
        p. cm.
Includes bibliographical references and indexes.
  ISBN 0-87868-824-2
  1. Children--United States--Social conditions. 2. Youth--United
States--Social conditions. 3. Children--Health and hygiene--United
States. 4. Youth--Health and hygiene--United States. 5. Child
welfare--United States. 6. Child development--United States. 7. Social
indicators--United States. 8. Health status indicators--United States.
I. Weissberg, Roger P., 1951-
  HQ792.U5 T75 2001
  305.23'0973--dc21
                                    2001035014

*As we focus on trends that influence the well-being of children and youth, we think of our parents with love and gratitude.*

*The editors dedicate this book to*
*Snooks and Ned Weissberg*
*Helen B. and Herbert J. Walberg, Sr.*
*Anne, Robert, Edith, and Henry*
*Diane and Robert Bartels*

# Contents

## PART I: VOLUME OVERVIEW AND AN INTRODUCTION TO SOCIAL INDICATORS

## PART II: BEHAVIORAL INDICATORS

# PART III. FAMILY INDICATORS

# PART IV. BROADER CONTEXTUAL AND POLICY ISSUES

## TABLES

## FIGURES

# Foreword

Several years ago, our university's Center for Urban Educational Research and Development and our Prevention Research Training Program in Urban Children's Mental Health cosponsored a series of planning meetings for an interdisciplinary group of faculty whose scholarship focused on children, families, schools, and communities. The group generated a variety of collaborative projects through which our university might improve the lives of children and youth. One of these projects—led by Herb Walberg and Roger Weissberg—was to establish the current University of Illinois at Chicago (UIC) Book Series on Children and Youth, of which this book is a part. Under the auspices of the UIC Great Cities Institute, the book and conference program has been sustained by continuing funds from the university's central administration.

The first book in the UIC Series was called *Children and Youth: Interdisciplinary Perspectives.* It provided diverse views of child development and intervention with an emphasis on families, education, and health care. A second volume, titled *Promoting Positive Outcomes,* highlighted school- and community-based strategies for enhancing positive youth development. This current effort, *Long-Term Trends in the Well-Being of Children and Youth,* examines several decades of indicators that reflect changes in children's behavior as well as social-environmental factors that influence their development. The contributors provide new perspectives on how today's children are functioning in educational and health domains, why their performance has improved or worsened, and what implications these findings have for programs and policies to benefit children and families. We are delighted that UIC faculty and this series are actively advancing research, theory, and scholarship about risk and protective factors that influence child development and multidisciplinary strategies to promote young people's successful participation in society.

For their continuing effort, I am grateful to Herb and Roger. In two senses, the series they lead represents well UIC's important mission: First, as is the case of many research universities, UIC seeks to break the barriers among traditional departments, colleges, and other units within our institution. The series and the present book exemplify such effort. The chapters derive from the disciplines of history, psychology, and sociology; the professions of criminal justice, education, medicine, public health, and social work; and community, media, policy, prevention, and social indicators studies, the last group of which are themselves crossdisciplinary. The UIC and national advisory committees, moreover, have guided the series and the present volume. The members represent such fields as African American studies, child development, economics, disabilities, English, kinesiology, nursing, pediatrics, psychiatry, political science, physical therapy, public affairs, public health, social policy, and urban planning. Also included is the highest administrative officer of the University of Illinois system of universities, James Stukel, whose continuing support from the series inception—including membership on the advisory committee—is gratefully acknowledged.

Second, the series and this book represent an important UIC effort to relate university research directly to social policy and practice. Not only is the series interdisciplinary, but it addresses problems and opportunities that challenge policymakers and child and youth service workers in cities and elsewhere. In behalf of UIC, I thank the Child Welfare League of America and particularly its chief editorial advisor Thomas Gullotta for cooperation in the production and distribution of the series to precisely such readers.

*—Elizabeth Hoffman*

President, University of Colorado

Provost and Vice Chancellor for Academic Affairs
University of Illinois at Chicago, 1997–2000

# Issues in Children's and Families Lives: An Annual Book Series

**Senior Series Editor**
Thomas P. Gullotta, Child and Family Agency of Southeastern Connecticut

**Editors, The University of Chicago at Illinois Series on Children and Youth**
Arthur J. Reynolds, University of Wisconsin-Madison
Herbert J. Walberg, University of Illinois at Chicago
Roger P. Weissberg, University of Illinois at Chicago

Drawing upon the resources of the Child and Family Agency of Southeastern Connecticut, one of the nation's leading family service agencies, **Issues in Children's and Families' Lives** is designed to focus attention on the pressing social problems facing children and their families today. Each volume in this series will analyze, integrate, and critique the clinical and research literature on children and their families as it relates to a particular theme. Believing that integrated multidisciplinary approaches offer greater opportunities for program success, volume contributors will reflect the research and clinical knowledge base of the many different disciplines that are committed to enhancing the physical, social, and emotional health of children and their families. Intended for graduate and professional audiences, chapters will be written by scholars and practitioners who will encourage readers to apply their practice skills and intellect to reducing the suffering of children and their families in the society in which they live and work.

*—Thomas P. Gullotta*

Chief Executive Officer
Child and Family Agency of
Southeastern Connecticut

# University Advisory Committee for the University of Illinois at Chicago Series on Children and Youth

# National Advisory Committee for the University of Illinois at Chicago Series on Children and Youth

# Preface

The University of Illinois at Chicago (UIC) Series on Children and Youth is published as a part of the annual book series Issues in Children's and Families' Lives, edited by Thomas P. Gullotta. Drawing on multiple academic disciplines and the full range of human service professions, its goal is to inform and stimulate policymakers and professionals that serve children and youth. From such academic disciplines as psychology and sociology as well as such professions as education, medicine, nursing, and social work, the contributors draw on basic and applied research aimed at uncovering both "the truth" and "the good." Thus, the goal of the series is to bring together pertinent knowledge about children and youth as well as to identify policies, programs, and practices that benefit them.

—*Herbert J. Walberg*
—*Roger P. Weissberg*

Editors
University of Illinois at Chicago
Series on Children and Youth

# PART I

## VOLUME OVERVIEW AND AN INTRODUCTION TO SOCIAL INDICATORS

# ONE

# Contributions and Complexities of Studying Trends in the Well-Being of Children and Youth

*Mary Utne O'Brien, Roger P. Weissberg, Herbert J. Walberg,*
*and Carol Bartels Kuster*

For those who study, provide services, and advocate for children and young people, the advent of a new century prompts examination of the status of what we hold most important. It is a time that stimulates consideration and assessment of where we have been and where we are now, that our future scholarship, service, and advocacy will be effective and fruitful.

Efforts to improve the well-being of children and youth must be based on a deep understanding of current indicators of well-being as well as historical patterns in the statistics that underlie them. Following Duncan (1974, p. 5096), we define *indicators* as "quantitative descriptions of social conditions that are intended to inform public opinion and national policymaking." An indicator, then, is not simply a statistic or data set. Rather, it is selected data intended to bring insights to various audiences about social problems and achievements. In recent years, there has been substantial improvement in indicators of well-being among children and youth and in their accessibility to users.

In 1995, the National Research Council declared that federal statistics on children were highly fragmented: "Policy toward children in the U.S. is best portrayed as an accumulation of responses to problems that are rarely viewed as interrelated, and the lack of a coherent, logically integrated system of data reflects that" (1995). Since that time, however, several activities have moved federal statistical agencies toward improved ongoing measurement and indicators of the well-being of children, and some states have undertaken improvements as well (Hauser et al., 1997). In particular, in 1997, the Federal Interagency Forum on Child and Family Statistics (the forum) was signed into being, and it continues to work to foster coordination, collaboration, and integration of federal data collection on children and reporting of children's conditions. In April 1997, an executive order was signed to require from the forum an annual report to the President of the United States on the conditions of children. This report, titled *America's Children: Key National Indicators of Well-Being*, is available on the Internet at http://childstats.gov and updated annually. The

*America's Children* report measures the condition of children and challenges the federal statistics system to improve and expand the array of available measures. The indicators are organized into five categories: demographics, economic security, health, behavioral and social environment, and educational status. Although many criteria might be employed to select from the dozens of indicators available, the forum wisely settled on the following:

- easy to understand in a variety of settings,
- objectively based on substantial research and reliable data,
- balanced so that no single area of a child's life dominates the report,
- measured regularly so that they can be updated and show trends over time, and
- representative of large segments of the population rather than of one particular group.

Simultaneous with the government's efforts to improve indicators, a number of private organizations made great strides in creating and maintaining indicators and bringing them to national attention. Perhaps the most ambitious of these is the Annie E. Casey Foundation's *KIDS COUNT Data Book*, produced and distributed free of charge for the last 10 years. The book provides data on 10 key indicators for children in all 50 states, as well as national statistics for the same indicators, and national-only data on seven other dimensions. In selecting indicators, measures were identified to:

- reflect a wide range of factors affecting children's well-being (such as health, adequacy of income, and educational attainment),
- reflect experiences across a range of developmental stages from birth to early adulthood, and
- permit legitimate comparisons because they are consistent across states and over time.

Other scholarly initiatives undertaken in recent years to develop and report indicators of youth well-being include *The Social Health of the Nation* (Miringoff & Miringoff, 1999), a product of the Working Group on Social Indicators; *The State of Americans* (Bronfenbrenner et al., 1996); *The Index of Leading Cultural Indicators* (Bennett, 1999); *Indicators of Children's Well-Being* (Hauser et al., 1997); the Centers for Disease Control and Prevention (2000) *Fact Sheet: Youth Risk Behavior Trends* (annually reported in *Mortality and Morbidity Weekly* and at www.cdc.gov); and *The State of America's Children Yearbook* (Children's Defense Fund, 2000). In addition to the *KIDS COUNT Data Book*, the Annie E. Casey Foundation commissioned the organization Child Trends to produce a Web-based inventory of projects that focus on the development or use of indicators of child, youth, and family well-being. This inventory contains over 80 projects and can be found at www.childtrends.org. These and many other indicator data sources are described in greater detail in another chapter (Brown and Corbett, this volume), which delves deeply into the limits and strengths of indicator data and the various purposes to which these data can appropriately be put as tools of social policy.

The indicator reports provide a detailed picture of many aspects of the lives of children and youth today. However, if we are to develop and strengthen our knowledge of the forces affecting children's lives, target resources effectively, and draw public attention to the related issues and problems, more is needed. We need a better understanding of:

- how child and youth well-being has changed over the last century,
- how these changes vary by the domain of inquiry and population subgroup,
- the causal factors involved in these changes, and
- the implications of these changes for the future.

This volume in the University of Illinois at Chicago Series on Children and Youth, *Long-Term Trends in the Well-Being of Children and Youth,* provides an important addition to the timely status reports offered by the indicator sources noted above. The authors assembled in this book were asked to adopt an ambitious long-term perspective of at least 50 years (when data availability permitted) in their examination of indicators of the educational, social, and physical functioning of America's young people. They look back over much of the last century to examine changes in the wide variety of domains that together add up to the complex picture of our children's overall well-being—including educational attainment, drug use, sexual behavior, health, family composition and supports, economic security, child care, government policies and programs, media, and even the communities in which our youth live. We asked the authors to describe the extent to which things are getting better or worse for children in their particular domain of focus, and the trends in the environmental factors that influence the development of children and youth (birth to age 21). We also asked them to consider the implications of the data for programs and social policies for young people and discuss the adequacy of current policies and programs in light of the documented trends. As editors, we appreciate how effectively each contributor responded to our set of challenging requests.

## Summary of Book Organization, Chapters, and Themes

This volume consists of four parts. The first examines the principal tool of this book: Social indicators in the trends of well-being of children and youth. In

Part I, this chapter and the one that follows discuss the value, complexities, and possibilities for appropriate and effective use of social indicators to monitor well-being and understand and improve program impacts. The second section brings us to the concrete particulars of long-term trends in four key realms of child and youth behavior for which strong cross-time indicator data are available: educational attainment, substance use, sexual behavior, and health. The third section examines indicators relating to the most important social unit affecting children, their families. Chapters in this section examine trends in family composition and circumstances; trends in one form of family pathology, child maltreatment; and, finally and more broadly, trends in child care and family supports. The fourth and final section of this volume provides a framework for understanding trends in children's well-being by describing broader contextual and policy issues that affect children and their families: the communities in which they live, the changing media environment, and historical and current policy trends.

### Part I: Volume Overview and an Introduction to Social Indicators

*Chapter 1: Contributions and Complexities of Studying Trends in the Well-Being of Children and Youth* (Mary Utne O'Brien, Roger P. Weissberg, Herbert J. Walberg, and Carol Bartels Kuster). In this introductory chapter, we present a brief summary of the book's organization and the individual chapters. We next provide a summary of the authors' data, as well as some additional indicators from other sources in a single table, for a broad overview of key trends in and current status of child and youth well-being in the United States. We conclude with a summary of the picture that emerges and generalizations that can be forged from the cross-time and cross-domain data and offer our views on the contributions and complexities of the emerging picture.

*Chapter 2: Social Indicators as Tools of Public Policy* (Brett V. Brown and Thomas Corbett). The essential theme of this volume is to delineate changes in the welfare of children over the past century. Obviously this task requires the ability to identify and track indicators of well-being. We need to be confident about our information, able to recognize when changes are occurring, and skillful enough to monitor trends. Brett Brown and Thomas Corbett describe some of the ways that social indicators have been used for monitoring the well-being of children and families, including description, monitoring, goal-setting, outcomes-based accountability, and evaluation. The authors provide concrete examples of these uses at the local, state, and federal levels.

Despite the promise of social indicators as tools for creating the most effective social policy, the ways in which these tools are used may depend in large part on the purpose and motivation of policymakers. Brown and Corbett describe the characteristics of a good social indicator system and outline the technical, practical, and political challenges faced in developing such a system. Finally, they describe ways that government at all levels, private foundations, and researchers can contribute to the development of good measures and the ability to understand and use them effectively. They warn that "good measures, good data, the skills to use them well, and the will to use them wisely, we believe, are prerequisites for their success" (page 48).

## Part II: Behavioral Indicators

The behavioral domains examined in Part II are those that provide a glimpse of the broader social fabric of children's lives and well-being. Thus, the chapters in Part II describe changes in indicators of children and youth's educational activity and attainment (Stedman); use and abuse of licit and illicit drugs (Johnston and O'Malley); sexual behavior and its consequences, for example, pregnancy, childbirth, and sexually transmitted diseases (Abma); and, more broadly, the physical health of children and youth (Klerman).

*Chapter 3: U.S. Educational Achievement in the 20th Century: Brilliant Success and Persistent Failure* (Lawrence C. Stedman). At a time when our national public education system is increasingly questioned and doubted, and the educational performance of today's students is popularly believed to be substantially inferior to students of yesteryear, Lawrence Stedman's chapter provides a clear and concise accounting of the facts regarding what our schools do well and how they fall short of the mark. Stedman confronts the myths and suppositions regarding public education with a thoughtful and careful reading of the evidence. He documents the great success of our educational system—the nearly universal enrollment of students from all social classes, races, and geographical locations—while detailing the persistent problems engendered by the mass educational bureaucracy—notably, poor mastery of subjects by the great majority of students, both past and present.

Criticism of the public school system is not a new phenomenon. Neither are efforts at reform. Using academic achievement data from the mid-1800s to the present, Stedman creates a comprehensive analysis and history of U.S. public education. He describes several common measurement problems and popular misinterpretations of the extant data-misinterpretations that frequently lead to condemnation of the modern educational system and its students. He provides a rational and factual discussion of academic trends that indicate the good news that our schools are matriculating more students from more diverse backgrounds than ever before. The bad news is that many schools still fail to engage students in anything but the poorest and most shallow learning. Yet there is reason to be hopeful. Some schools and school districts have reorganized and redesigned themselves to successfully engage and challenge students in an intellectually rich environment. Stedman concludes by providing several concrete recommendations for changing schools from institutions of mediocrity to institutions of excellence.

*Chapter 4: Tobacco, Alcohol, and Other Drug Use in Adolescence: Modern - Day Epidemics* (Lloyd D. Johnston and Patrick M. O'Malley). Although psychoactive substances have been used for centuries in many cultures, licit and illicit drug use has reached its zenith in the latter half of this century, emerging as one of the major threats to modern public health. As Lloyd Johnston and Patrick O'Malley make clear, the United States has one of the highest rates of illicit drug use in the world, particularly among adolescents and young adults. This is certainly no surprise to those concerned with reducing drug initiation and use. However, as these authors demonstrate, there are some important lessons to be drawn from a study of trends in drug use. Notably, their analysis indicates that increased drug use among youth has not followed a steadily inclining course over time. Rather, there have been many peaks and valleys in the rate of adolescent drug use across time; across different classes of substances; and across racial, gender, and geographical lines.

So how can we make sense of such variability, and more important, how can we put this understanding to work for us in the war against drugs today? Johnston and O'Malley have researched carefully the relationship between varying rates of drug use and relevant social conditions and provide several thoughtful and plausible explanations. In doing so, they explore the roles that changes in families, schools, media, and other institutions have played in influencing rates of drug use. These authors offer insight into policies that have worked in the past and that can be applied in the future. They remind us that despite the current high rates of use, the fight against drug use has not been a losing battle. We need to fight it on many fronts, however. Through accurate description of the connections between social conditions and rates of drug use, Johnston and O'Malley lay the groundwork for the development of sensible policy that addresses the many facets of drug use among youth. They remind us that drug use can be reduced if we have the will to apply what we know.

*Chapter 5: Sexual Activity Among Teenagers in the United States* (Joyce C. Abma). Given the negative consequences and increased risk associated with early sexual activity and childbearing, sexual behavior and pregnancy rates among youth are of longstanding concern to researchers and policymakers interested in children's well-being. Joyce Abma describes the rather complex picture across time of rates of sexual initiation, sexually transmitted diseases, pregnancy, and childbirth among heterosexual teens. For example, rates of birth for all teens (married and unmarried) today are nearly identical to the birthrate among teens in the 1940s. However, there are clear differences in rates of sexual activity and marital status that influence the outcomes of these births.

The United States has experienced profound changes in economic conditions, educational requirements, and social norms that have resulted in later ages at entry into full-time work, marriage, and other adult roles. Though initiation of these behaviors reserved primarily for adults has been occurring at later ages, however, initiation of sexual behaviors and first intercourse has been occurring at earlier ages in the past few decades. This has resulted in a youth cohort that is unmarried, economically dependent, and sexually active for longer periods than ever before, all of which translates into higher risk for negative outcomes. Abma provides a thorough description and discussion of many facets of youth sexual behavior. She describes and explains trends in this important aspect of children's health and provides suggestions for helping youth to successfully make the transition to healthy and responsible adulthood.

*Chapter 6: Trends in the Health of Children in the United States* (Lorraine V. Klerman). Few things are more central to a child's well-being than good physical health. By many indicators, children in the United States today are healthier and will live longer lives than at any time previously. As a nation we have made terrific gains in protecting children from the threats of contagious illness, lead poisoning, anemia, and sudden infant death syndrome. Lorraine Klerman writes that these improvements testify to the positive effect of the public health initiatives that targeted these conditions. Today there is perhaps greater recognition than ever before that many of the most prevalent threats to children's health cannot be prevented or cured by traditional medical health services. Instead, improving child health requires changes in health behavior and in the physical and social environment.

Klerman describes several public health initiatives and traces their positive effects in the decreased prevalence and incidence rates among children. She makes it clear that improved understanding of causality combined with clear commitment to a goal can create substantial improvements in the health of millions of children. She also makes it clear that our work is not yet done. Child abuse, asthma, AIDS, premature birth, and obesity are a few of the worst threats to children's health today, particularly among our most vulnerable children— children of color living in or near poverty, or without a regular source of health care. So how do we use this knowledge to initiate change? Klerman gives recommendations for addressing these problems through social policy that

- reduces absolute and relative poverty rates;
- encourages behavior change through education;
- uses legislation, regulation, and taxation to promote the health of children; and
- improves access to quality medical care.

## Part III: Family Indicators

The three chapters of Part III focus on aspects of the proximal social unit in the lives of children—their families. Taken together, these chapters explain how the well-being of children and youth is affected by the interrelated issues of family circumstances and family functioning (Hernandez), child maltreatment (Cicchetti and Toth), and child care and family support (Cahan and Bromer).

*Chapter 7: Changing Family Circumstances* (Donald J. Hernandez). Donald Hernandez reminds us that there have always been children and families in poverty; there have always been children of single parents, divorced parents, unemployed parents, and working mothers; in short, a variety of diverse family structures have always existed in U.S. society. But as Hernandez demonstrates, these family structures have changed dramatically during the past century. Hernandez uses census and survey data to document the timing, magnitude, and reasons for the extraordinary changes in family composition, parents' education, mothers' work, and family income experienced by children over the last 100 to 150 years. He also illustrates how and why these changes matter to the well-being of children, showing how such changes in family circumstances affect family functioning and resources and parents' ability to care for and nurture their children.

Many of these changes are shaped and often constrained by social and economic policies and conditions that are beyond individual control. For example, Hernandez describes the rapid decline in the proportion of children raised in two-parent farm families, from 70% in 1830 to less than 30% in 1930, whereas the proportion of nonfarm families with fathers who worked outside the home and stay-at-home mothers jumped from only 15% to a majority of 55%. An equally dramatic drop in family size accompanied this change: from 7.3 siblings per family in 1865 to only 2.6 by 1930. In little more than a human lifetime, therefore, the nature of childhood was transformed from one in which all family members worked side-by-side to one in which children were separated from working fathers while staying home with mothers who were not employed outside the home, and with at least five fewer siblings competing for parental time, attention, and resources. Examining more recent decades, Hernandez describes similarly powerful effects on childhood well-being of the large growth in mother-only families and the rise in rates of divorce.

He also chronicles trends in poverty and income inequality, aging, immigration, and welfare policy and explains their implications for the well-being of children. Of particular importance, Hernandez describes the differential impact that changing societal conditions and economic and social policies have had on black, white, and Latino families. His analysis of the past lays the groundwork for improving family functioning in the future. He provides thoughtful projections for the ways in which families will likely change as well as careful recommendations for public policies that address increasing poverty—policies that include welfare, employment, immigration, child care and education, and parental leave.

*Chapter 8: Child Maltreatment: Past, Present, and Future Perspectives* (Dante Cicchetti, Sheree L. Toth). Dante Cicchetti and Sheree Toth confront us with a number of deeply troubling inconsistencies in our nation's approach to child welfare. Consider that recent estimates of child maltreatment indicate that 1 out of every 43 children in the United States has experienced some form of maltreatment at the hands of a parent or primary caregiver. Consider also that the estimated number of seriously injured children rose nearly 300% between 1986 and 1996. Then consider that the percentage of children whose maltreatment was officially investigated by Protective Services *declined* by 18% during those same years. How do we make sense of these trends that are in direct opposition to rhetoric proclaiming that our children are our greatest national treasure?

Cicchetti and Toth describe the complexity of understanding, treating, and preventing child maltreatment in the United States. On the basis of an increasingly sophisticated model of the causes and outcomes of child maltreatment, these authors present a framework for understanding how different levels of a child's environment (e.g., the macrosystem of beliefs, values, culture; the exosystem of community characteristics; the microsystem of family factors; and individual developmental factors) influence whether that child will suffer at the hands of a parent or caregiver. They describe interventions at each level that can influence how well a child will survive maltreatment.

Despite increased awareness of child abuse and neglect and the establishment of agencies and systems designed to intervene in such cases, children continue to experience maltreatment at the alarming rates described above. On the basis of research evidence and their own years of experience with child welfare systems, Cicchetti and Toth describe and analyze our failure to stem the increase in the occurrence of child maltreatment and the relationship between this failure and our continued focus on parental rights. The authors emphasize that children's rights must be at the forefront of all efforts designed to protect children.

*Chapter 9: Trends in the History of Child Care and Family Support: 1940 to 2000* (Emily D. Cahan, Juliet Bromer). Through much of our nation's history, attitudes toward child care and the use and provision of child care services outside the home have changed along with changes in women's need and desire to participate in the workforce, and with the popularization of various scientific views of early childhood development. Emily Cahan and Juliet Bromer begin their discussion in the industrial era and take us to World War II, through to Head Start in 1965, and up to the late-1990s findings on the critical importance of early childhood development for long-term cognitive functioning. In the mid-1800s, when men left home to work in new industries and family farms gave way to urban homes, "child care" and "work" became separate spheres of responsibility for women and men, respectively. The culture became, and for over a century, stayed hostile to group child care outside the home: The belief among professionals and mothers themselves was that young children should not be separated from their mothers (the limited child care that did exist was linked to the needs of poor mothers who worked of necessity).

Social, scholarly, and economic trends in the 1960s through the 1990s have brought about a transformation in our views of child care, if not in the supply and quality of care. Early childhood education came to be understood as critical to the development of full social and intellectual development. In early 1965, Project Head Start was created, merging child care, preschool education, and family support into one service for our nation's "disadvantaged" children. Cahan and Bromer document that since that time there has been a decline in federal support, increases in state control over programs, and an increase in use of child care programs across economic lines. In the 1990s, changes in the U.S. family and workforce and welfare reform policies increased demand for child care. Recent research reports demonstrating no direct negative effects of child care on children, the importance of the first three years of life in cognitive development, and the need for more and better quality child care nationwide have solidified the changes in U.S. approaches to child care. The authors find some hope in the fact that debates about whether child care is good for our children have given way to questions of how to make child care work for our children and families.

## Part IV: Broader Contextual and Policy Issues

In the chapters that constitute Part IV, experts on current programmatic responses to children's well-being argue in behalf of a number of measures in response to the trends evidenced in the earlier sections. Leventhal and Brooks-Gunn make the case for critical contextual elements related to the community in considering the development of programs and identifying their effects on children. Next, Donald Roberts chronicles the changing media environment to which children and youth have been exposed, and the evidence on media effects on children. The book concludes with two chapters on policy and children's outcomes, which taken together illuminate the historical origins of the current policy landscape within which programs and other responses are crafted (Hawes and Lindenmeyer) and suggest how an understanding of the current policy environment can enable us to act effectively in behalf of children (Wilcox and Barone).

*Chapter 10: Indicators of Children's Well-Being in a Community Context* (Tama Leventhal, Jeanne Brooks-Gunn). Many of the chapters in this book describe the importance of how children and their families live and the effect on their overall well-being. But what about where children live? How much does community matter to the well-being of children? According to a thoughtful analysis by Tama Leventhal and Jeanne Brooks-Gunn, it may matter very much. The authors describe ways in which communities have been defined and studied and outline the community characteristics that are most influential in determining outcomes for children. Many would agree that growing up in a poor neighborhood limits children's opportunities and chances for achievement. Yet even poor neighborhoods can produce successful and responsible adults. So what aspects of neighborhoods and communities are most influential for children's optimal development? These authors examine the evidence for a variety of community characteristics, such as residential stability, income and socioeconomic status, collective efficacy, and racial/ethnic heterogeneity.

Community and neighborhood aspects of children's lives are often overlooked in studies of child health and well-being and by policymakers attempting to address child health concerns. The evidence presented by these authors suggests that these efforts could be greatly improved through enhanced monitoring and understanding of the role of communities in children's lives. To this end, the authors provide an expanded conception of community and a framework of the most influential facets of community life.

*Chapter 11: Children and the Changing Media Environment: From Plato's Republic to Hillary's Village* (Donald F. Roberts). What are the media messages that our children receive about the world and about themselves? How have these messages changed over the years? What is their influence on children's development? Donald Roberts illustrates that these questions are not unique to our time. For centuries, the influence of media stories on children has been of concern in many societies. From ancient storytellers; to fairy tales; to comic books, television, and the Internet, people have been concerned about the ways media influence and impress children—and legitimately so. Today's technological advances mean that media messages reach children more frequently and more vividly than ever before. We are all aware that the content of much of this media programming is violent, sexual, or otherwise inappropriate for children and the overwhelming evidence is that media content does influence children's thinking and behavior. Roberts examines the evidence regarding the various types of messages targeted at children, including violence, sexuality, commercial appeals, and attitudes about substance use, and provides a thoughtful analysis regarding their likely effect on children.

As parental ability to block offensive or inappropriate material decreases with advances in technology, many parents and concerned citizens are left wondering what can be done to protect, inform, and successfully socialize our children. Based on his analysis of past efforts and on the difficulties inherent in censorship efforts, Roberts describes the roles that parents, schools, media, and the government can play in assuring that children are protected from the negative effects of media exposure while still obtaining the benefits.

*Chapter 12: Historical Overview of Children and Childhood in the United States in the 20th Century* (Joseph M. Hawes, Kriste Lindenmeyer). Historians Joseph Hawes and Kriste Lindenmeyer provide a context for reflecting on many of the changes in conditions described in this volume as they identify broad trends in the United States in approaches to children and the major social and political developments affecting children. They trace the influences of intellectual movements in the social and psychological sciences, changes in the economy, two world wars, and the creation and dismantling of major political structures and legislation (e.g., Social Security) on public attitudes toward children and the role of the broader society in protecting children and promoting their healthy physical and emotional development. For example, Hawes and Lindenmeyer demonstrate that a direct effect of the discovery that World War I conscripts were by and large dismally prepared for the mental and physical demands of the military encouraged the scientific study of children and shifted attention from "problem children" to an emphasis on normal children and their development.

Hawes and Lindenmeyer's review begins with the important contextual observation that over the last 150 years, children have gone from constituting 52% to less than 25% of the U.S. population—a drop of more than half. This datum may go some way toward an explanation of the phenomenon that even as calls to action in behalf of children have increased, direct measures to improve the well-being of children have regularly fought uphill battles in the political arena. The authors' description of the push and pull of events on measures to provide for child welfare illustrates also the tension this country has experienced between the government's contribution to the safety and well-being of its citizens, especially its children, and the fear of invading parental rights. Finally, Hawes and Lindenmeyer's political history includes descriptions of decades of turf wars within the federal government, the effect of which has been to undercut coordinated efforts to support children and families, continuing through to today.

*Chapter 13: Policy Trends Affecting Children and Youth* (Brian L. Wilcox, Charles Barone). In the concluding chapter in this volume, Brian Wilcox and Charles Barone move us from the past to a focus on the present as they describe the broad trends that shape the current policymaking process, along with the policies themselves, that in turn affect the well-being of children and youth. Returning to the observation made by Hawes and Lindenmeyer that the age structure of the U.S. population has changed dramatically, Wilcox and Barone argue that this demographic trend, more than any other, affects national policy. The corollary to the fact of proportionately fewer youth in our population is the fact of a large and growing population of older Americans, millions of whom will soon retire and look to those relatively few remaining in the workforce for support in the form of Social Security and Medicare. These individuals thus represent an enormous potential drain of national resources away from child welfare. Declaring that "budget policy is social policy," the authors expand on this point, describing a number of additional constraints on the nation's finances—large debt payments; increasing middle-class entitlements for retirement, disability, and health (currently 55% of federal revenues); and state budget pressures. Even now, before the retirement boom, children and youth have not fared as well as the elderly in federal spending. Children have little political clout, Wilcox and Barone argue, and poor children in particular are inadequately represented.

Wilcox and Barone focus on another strand in the policy process that appears throughout this volume, namely, the debate around the degree to which responsibility for children's welfare should be ascribed to government (at every level) versus other entities—charities, churches, businesses, and, of course, the family. They argue that this ongoing argument continues to undercut the development of effective policy approaches to youth and is illustrated by case studies of legislation.

Finally, Wilcox and Barone caution that the current policy temperament toward downsizing of government roles, devolution of authority from the center, and deregulation—relaxing oversight and simplifying rules for programs—make progress toward comprehensive child and youth policy in the United States unlikely. They suggest that advocates become informed by research on the developmental and contextual factors affecting youth well-being, work to generate and wield high-quality data on the issues they care about, and use this information to educate and inform policymakers. These data can also be used to influence the contexts themselves, such as school characteristics, neighborhood quality, residential segregation, and the economic health of communities.

We find that a number of topics and themes recur among the chapters in this volume, above and beyond those the authors were explicitly asked to address. One is the conflict between the role of government versus the role of the family. Several of these authors address what are described as the persistent conflict in policy circles and public debate in beliefs about the role of government and family authority and primacy in ensuring and attending to the well-being of children. The tension is between a government role in ensuring the safety and well-being of its citizens, especially its children, and a fear of invading parental rights. A related issue discussed in these chapters is the conflict between supporters of family preservation and policies and laws protecting "parental rights" versus child-focused interventions. The result, they say, is limited funds and fragmented policy.

Other authors point to a long history of turf wars within the federal government as responsible for policy fragmentation, the effect of which has been to undercut efforts to support children and families, continuing today. For example, there is no single authority at the federal, state, or local level addressing child care. Over 90 separate federal programs in 11 federal agencies fund child care, which is just one aspect of child welfare (U. S. General Accounting Office, 1997).

A number of authors argue that to respond adequately to the needs of children requires an appreciation for and understanding of broader contexts. Many of these broader contexts—levels of violence in neighborhoods, for example, or community efficacy, or changes in area immigrant populations—set the terms within which children will or will not attain measures of health and well-being. To attempt to change aspects of the lives of children without taking into account these contextual factors may strongly mitigate or undercut the effectiveness of those attempts.

## Overview of Trends Across Behavioral and Environmental Domains

The single most frequent theme among the chapters in this book is the authors' testimony to the power and value of indicators and other data to educate the public and policymakers. Although the power of data to influence policy is only indirect and often complex, the authors in this volume repeatedly show the necessity of accurate and in-depth description of conditions of our children and youth. Such indicators are described as a critical tool in formulating appropriate policy solutions and in attracting attention and support to causes. In this section, therefore, we present a summary table of indicators. These indicators capture trends in a variety of behavioral and environmental or contextual domains related to children's well-being. Our goal is to identify some general conclusions and implications.

Table 1–1 presents data on aspects of the changing demographics of children in the United States, some of the the domains addressed in this volume (changing family circumstances, poverty, substance use, health, and education), as well as trends in crimes affecting and involving children. For each element in the table, we show the earliest and latest data available to us on that variable.

The data in the table suggest that any initial lack of certainty about an overall trend in well-being is justified: The trends shown by some indicators give us reason to be greatly encouraged, whereas other trends are disheartening. None of the long-term trends, however, justifies a pronouncement of relentless decline in youth well-being, or conversely, unremitting improvement. In fact, the single pattern that best describes several trends in the indicators in Table 1–1 is that of a wave—steadily worsening from the 1960s through the early 1990s then more gradually improving during the remainder of the decade.

The first section of the table (demographics) provides some basic orientation to the youth population (under 18) in the United States. The population of children has grown along with the U.S. population as a whole, increasing almost 50% since mid-century. But their increase in numbers has not been proportional; as a percentage of the total population, children have dropped, from 31% in 1950 to 26% in 1998, a near-20% decline. The racial makeup of the child population has also changed. Two decades ago almost three-quarters of children in America were white. Because of increases in immigration and different rates of reproduction among different groups, today fewer than two-thirds of America's children are white, and the U.S. Census predicts that this number will fall further, to 55%, by the year 2020. In related data not shown, 30 years ago, only 1 in 100 children born was of mixed race; today that number is 1 in 19, and in states like California and Washington, it is closer to 1 in 10 (Federal Interagency Forum, 1999). These changes give many young people a chance to challenge old notions of race, but the changes bring with them tensions as well, around issues of identity, for example.

The block of indicators on family circumstances shows relatively substantial changes in indicators of family life that have concerned many policy analysts and child advocates, although changes in many are not inherently either positive or negative. For example, the two-parent farm family has virtually disappeared since 1950, and labor-force participation among women increased from 20% in 1900 to 60% in 1998. Declining though still substantial percentages of children live with two parents. Divorce rates more than doubled between 1960 and 1980 but have since leveled off and begun a slow decline. Over the same period, the marriage rate has steadily declined, from 73.5 per 1,000 in 1960 to only 49.4 per 1,000 in 1997, indicating that a portion of the decline in divorce is due to the decline in marriages (Bennett, 1999).

The poverty indicators in the family circumstances section of Table 1–1 show a worrisome but not entirely grim pattern. The percentage of children living with at least one working parent has risen (and post–welfare reform data not yet available in this format will show even greater increases). The proportion of children with housing problems has increased by a fifth since 1978 (from 30% to 36%). The enormous gains in real incomes and standards of living between the 1940s and 1973 also saw a sharp drop in the proportion of children living in poverty, from almost 27% in 1960 to about 18% in 1980. That proportion has remained relatively flat since then, at roughly 20%. In the face of nearly a decade of economic expansion and improvements in the well-being of the rest of the U.S. population, the persistence of a core 20% of children in poverty—with much higher rates among children of color—leads to the sense that things are now even worse for this group of children than before.

The trends in child maltreatment lend credence to this perception. Data on child maltreatment are quite limited, relative to that available in the other domains, but one national time series data set shows that from 1979 to 1996

**Table 1–1: Recent trends in youth indicators for U.S. children**

| INDICATOR | PERIOD | EARLIEST | LATEST | CHANGE |
|---|---|---|---|---|
| No. of children in millions | 1950–1998 | 47.3 | 69.9 | 22.6 |
| Children under age 18 as percentage of the population | 1960–1998 | 36.0 | 26.0 | –10.0 |
| Children under age 18 as percentage of dependent population | 1960–1998 | 79.0 | 67.0 | –12.0 |
| White, non-Hispanic children under age 18 as a percentage of children | 1980–1998 | 74.0 | 65.0 | –9.0 |
| Percentage of children ages 5 to 17 who speak another language at home | 1979–1995 | 8.5 | 14.1 | 5.6 |
| Percentage of children ages 5 to 17 who have difficulty speaking English | 1979–1995 | 2.8 | 5.1 | |
| Percentage of children under age 18 living with two parents | 1980–1998 | 77.0 | 68.0 | –9.0 |
| Births per 1,000 to unmarried women 15 to 44 years old | 1980–1997 | 29.4 | 44.0 | 14.6 |
| Teen birth rate (births per 1,000 teenagers ages 15 to 17) [1] | 1985–1996 | 31.0 | 34.0 | 3.0 |
| Percentage of children under age 18 living in poverty | 1980–1997 | 18.0 | 19.0 | 1.0 |
| Percentage of children under age 18 living w. at least one employed parent | 1980–1997 | 70.0 | 76.0 | 6.0 |
| Percentage of children under age 18 with housing problems | 1978–1995 | 30.0 | 36.0 | 6.0 |
| Percentage of children under age 18 with insufficient food | 1989–1997 | 4.7 | 3.4 | –1.3 |
| Percentage of children under age 18 with health insurance | 1987–1997 | 87.0 | 85.0 | –2.0 |
| Percentage of children under age 18 in very good or excellent health | 1984–1996 | 78.0 | 81.0 | 3.0 |
| Percentage of children under age 18 with chronic health conditions | 1984–1996 | 5.0 | 6.0 | 1.0 |
| Percentage of low birthweight births | 1980–1997 | 6.8 | 7.5 | 0.7 |

| | | | | |
|---|---|---|---|---|
| Infant mortality per 1,000 births within first year of life | 1980–1997 | 12.6 | 7.1 | -5.5 |
| Child death rate per 100,000, children ages 5 to14 | 1980–1998 | 30.6 | 20.7 | -9.9 |
| Rate of teen death by accident, homicide, and suicide, ages 15 to 19 [2] | 1985–1996 | 63.0 | 62.0 | -1.0 |
| Child immunization ages 19 to 35 months | 1994–1997 | 69.0 | 76.0 | 7.0 |
| Daily cigarette smoking among 12th graders [3] | 1980–1998 | 21.3 | 22.4 | 1.1 |
| Heavy drinking during past two weeks by 12th graders | 1980–1998 | 41.2 | 31.5 | -9.7 |
| Illicit drugs during past 30 days by 12th graders | 1980–1998 | 37.2 | 25.6 | -11.6 |
| Victims of violent crimes ages 12 to 17 per 1,000 [4] | 1980–1997 | 37.6 | 27.1 | -10.5 |
| Serious violent crime involving youth ages 12 to 17 per 1,000 [5] | 1980–1997 | 34.9 | 30.7 | -4.2 |
| Percentage 3- to 4-year-olds in early childhood education | 1980–1997 | 30.0 | 48.0 | 18.0 |
| Mathematics achievement score, age 13 | 1982–1996 | 269.0 | 274.0 | 5.0 |
| Reading achievement score, age 13 | 1980–1996 | 259.0 | 259.0 | 0.0 |
| Percentage 18- to 24-year-olds completed high school | 1980–1997 | 84.0 | 86.0 | 2.0 |
| Percentage of youth age 16 to 19 neither working nor in school | 1985–1997 | 11.2 | 8.1 | -3.1 |

Source: Except where indicated otherwise, Federal Interagency Forum on Child and Family Statistics (1999). pp. 67–105.

1. Annie E. Casey Foundation (1999).
2. Snyder & Sickmund (1999). p. 19.
3. Johnston, O'Malley, & Bachman (1999).
4. Federal Bureau of Investigation (2000).
5. Office of Juvenile Justice and Delinquency Prevention (1999).

the number of children abused, neglected, or endangered almost tripled. More maltreatment was reported among lower-income families, and children of single parents were at higher risk. Maltreatment reports from another source that collects state child protection agency reports suggests a flatter but still disturbingly high level of child abuse in this country.

The indicators in the next domain in the chart, health, show primarily improvements over time. Childhood immunizations increased from 69% in 1994 to 77% in 1996 and have been fairly steady since then. Decreases in the rate of infant mortality have occurred among all racial groups since the early 1980s, declining almost 35% overall—from 9.2 to 6.0 per 1,000 births—in the period 1983 to 1997. Child death rates (among 5- to 14-year-olds) also declined by a third over this period. The only health-related indicators in Table 1–1 showing little or no improvement over this time period are health insurance coverage (holding steady since 1987 at about 86%), and the rate of low-birthweight births, which has increased almost 10% in the last two decades. Recent research indicates that this drop in birthweight is almost entirely attributable to the increase in multiple births due to fertility-enhancing drugs. Finally, although teenagers' reports of considerations of suicide have declined (from 29% to 19% in less than a decade), actual suicide rates among teens have increased, doubling from 1960 to 1990 but declining somewhat since that time.

Substance use patterns vary considerably depending on the substance examined. Whereas cigarette smoking among teens has remained at about one-third of the 12th-grade population for a quarter of a century, marijuana smoking and other illicit drug use have shown a U shape since 1975, when about 30% of youth used these substances, dipping to a low point in 1990, and rising to near–historically high levels again in 1999. Drinking among high school seniors has shown a gradual downward trend since 1975, when over two-thirds reported drinking alcohol in the last 30 days, to just over one-half doing so in 1999.

Trends in crimes affecting children exhibit a somewhat similar pattern. Violent crime at the societal level rose sharply through the 1960s, 1970s, and 1980s but declined steadily throughout most of the 1990s. Although the rate of violent crime has decreased by one-sixth since 1990, it is still at almost four times the level found in 1960. The rate of violent crime victimization among 12- to 17-year-olds increased from 1980 to 1990 then dropped substantially in the 1990s. The rate of children as perpetrators of violent crime showed the same pattern: a large increase followed by an even steeper decline in the 1990s. Even rates of domestic violence, a crime with strong negative effects on the young children in the home who frequently witness the events (40% of homes with domestic violence have children under 12) have declined since the mid-

1970s. The decline has been especially substantial in black households (e.g., domestic homicides against black males dropped 74% from 1976 to 1998; black females killed by intimates dropped 45% in the same period; domestic homicides against white males dropped 44%; the trend was unchanged with regard to white females killed by intimates [Rennison & Welchans, 2000]).

The final section of Table 1–1 presents data related to education. Those items representing aspects of educational performance, namely, reading achievement scores for 13-year-olds, show relative stability over time (achievement trends for mathematics are similar). The percentage of young children attending preschool increased dramatically in the last decades of the 20th century, however, while the percentage of older teens neither working nor in school declined. In fact, in the areas of enrollment and completion of high school, remarkable improvements have been made since the start of the 20th century: high school attendance and completion have increased from a rate of only about 1 in 10 children in 1900 to 9 in 10 children today.

Taken as a whole, the data in Table 1-1 show areas of strong improvement, especially in children's health and their access to education. Also apparent are areas in which things have gone very wrong for some period but are now improving, as in exposure to domestic and community violence and direct criminal victimization. Nevertheless, the absolute levels of many events and conditions—out-of-wedlock births, substance use, child maltreatment, even educational attainment—indicate that there is considerable need for efforts to improve the well-being of children in this country.

## Conclusions

Is it possible to make an accurate summary statement about the trends in child and youth well-being in this country? We have struggled to identify a primary common strand, explanation, or observation among the many chapters in this volume, as well as the most recent indicator data, and conclude that characterizing and understanding the well-being of children and youth in the United States is complex. Great variation by domain exists in both the long-term trends and the current indicators of child and youth well-being, and no single factor—poverty, for example, or race—adequately explains the variations.

The variability in improvements across domains (education, substance use, sexual behavior, health, etc.) and subgroups of children and young people indicates that there is a great deal going on, and that it is more than a simple story of economic improvements. The case of infant mortality clearly illustrates this point. Infant mortality in the United States is 50% higher for children born to poor families (13.5 per 1,000 births versus 8.3 per 1,000) (Kiely, 1988). This difference is usually invoked to explain why blacks, a group with a high poverty rate, have more than twice the infant mortality rate of whites (14.2 versus 6.1). But the infant mortality rate for Latinos, who have a slightly higher poverty rate than blacks, is only 6.1, indicating that the link to poverty is more complicated than it at first may seem.

Is race, then, the key explanatory factor in these trends? Once again, the answer is not so simple as a single factor. For example, the gap in educational achievement between Latinos and whites is even larger than that between blacks and whites and has not decreased in the last decade. Yet when we look to health status the picture is not the same: Latino and white youth show similar levels of health and have far better health on a number of indicators than do blacks (infant mortality being just one of these).

Another dimension of complexity is geography. In selecting and presenting indicators that permit state-by-state comparisons of child well-being as well as a national portrait, the *KIDS COUNT Data Book* (Annie E. Casey Foundation, 1999) also underscores a fact of children's well-being not visible in the federal indicators: There is considerable variability by state. The state-specific data thus make possible examination of the variations in state policies that could be responsible for the differences in child well-being (although *KIDS COUNT* does not itself do that) and permit the monitoring of possible effects of new state policies as they are introduced.

At least four factors, therefore, must be considered simultaneously in a full accounting of children's well-being in any domain: trends over time, by race, by income group, and by geographic region.

In the face of these realities, several recommendations are either indicated or directly advocated by the authors in this volume. First, child advocates must continue and expand efforts to generate and wield high-quality data on the issues of most concern for educating and informing policymakers and the public. Thus, we need indicator data to inform the public about the magnitude and consequences of well-being and problems of children and youth. The caution that we must add, however, is that indicators are rarely self-explanatory. Simple indicators may be easy for the public to understand but are frequently misleading without controls for race or income, for example. Yet such transformation of the data adds to complexity and renders data less easy to be broadly understood. Nevertheless, properly used, indicators can provide an understanding of the complexities, ensuring that policies that attempt to tackle the wrong problem do not proceed.

Adding to the complexity of indicators is the fact that the populations of greater concern may vary by the substantive area under review. Chronically ill children may be needed for health surveys, or children of non-English-speaking parents for studies of preschool and early school years. More longitudinal data on youth are also needed to help identify precursors of serious problems in middle school and adolescence. And the changing demographics of the childhood population require new strategies for oversampling currently unrepresented subgroups.

We also need more data on the organization and distribution of resources (e.g., health care, early education, and school experiences) across subgroups (e.g., race and geography). Better state and local estimates are also needed, because that is where so many policy actions and programmatic responses are to be found.

A number of the authors in this volume recommend that instead of competing over diminishing resources on an issue-by-issue, program-by-program basis, child and youth advocates must unite and adopt a broader agenda. Their data also suggest that the strategies adopted to change the circumstances of children should be multidimensional. A mentoring program here, sex education there, afterschool programs over there—these piecemeal responses do not add up to much impact; they rarely change lives. The most vulnerable families and children face multiple, not singular, problems. For example, the *KIDS COUNT Data Book* presents data on the relationship between a number of indicators and poor long-term outcomes for children. The indicators or risk factors examined are

- not living with both parents,
- household head is a high-school dropout,
- family income is below poverty line,
- parents do not have steady, full-time employment,
- family is receiving welfare benefits, and
- child does not have health insurance.

The presence of any one of these factors makes coping a challenge, but research shows that in combination they significantly increase the threats to children's long-term well-being (for example, increasing the likelihood of failing to complete high school, and unwed teenage pregnancy). Although in 1999, 47% of U.S. children experienced none of these risk factors, in that same year, 13%, or more than nine million children, were growing up with a combination of four or more of these disadvantages, and another 14.5 million experienced two to three of them.

The implications of these data are that to improve the well-being of children and youth, solutions must be

- multidimensional;
- family-focused, that is, grounded in child's family context and in context of family's surroundings;

- comprehensive and coordinated (e.g., parent education, family support, crisis support, drug treatment, job training, and housing assistance);
- long-term, because it may take years to nurture the skills, resources and relationships that will enable impoverished and isolated families; and
- able to engage entire communities.

This is hardly a simple agenda, but according to the authors in this book, it is one more likely than short-term, issue-specific initiatives to bear fruit in the face of today's policymaking realities.

## Authors' Note

We appreciate the financial support provided by the University of Illinois at Chicago (UIC) for this book series, and also the intellectual support and guidance of our UIC and national advisory committees. We also appreciate the effective work of all the volume authors for their scholarly contributions. Finally, we express our heartfelt gratitude to Rebecca DuLaney Beyer for her support in helping us organize and finalize this chapter and the entire volume.

## References

Annie E. Casey Foundation. (1999). *Kids count data book: 1999.* Baltimore: Author.

Bennett, W. J. (1999). *The index of leading cultural indicators.* New York: WaterBrook Press.

Bronfenbrenner, U., McClelland, P., Wethington, E., Moen, P., & Ceci, S. J. (1996). *The state of Americans.* New York: Free Press.

Centers for Disease Control and Prevention. (2000). *Fact sheet: Youth risk behavior trends, 1991-1999.* Retrieved in 2000 from www.cdc.gov/nccdphp/dash/yrbs/trend/htm.

Children's Defense Fund. (2000). *The state of America's children yearbook 2000.* Washington, DC: Author.

Duncan, O. D. (1974). Developing social indicators. *Proceedings of the National Academy of Science, 71,* 5096-5102.

Federal Bureau of Investigation. (2000). *Uniform crime reports 1999 preliminary annual report.* Washington, DC: Author.

Federal Interagency Forum on Child and Family Statistics. (1999). *America's children: Key national indicators of well-being.* Washington, DC: U.S. Government Printing Office. Available from http://childstats.gov.

Hauser, R. M., Brown, B. V., & Prosser, W. R. (Eds.). (1997). *Indicators of children's well-being.* New York: Russell Sage Foundation.

Johnston, L. D., O'Malley, P. M., & Bachman, J. G. (1999). *National survey results on drug use from the Monitoring the Future Study, 1975-1997. Volume I: Secondary school students.* Rockville, MD: National Institute on Drug Abuse.

Kiely, J. L. (1988, December 15). Poverty and infant mortality—United States, 1988. *Morbidity and Mortality Weekly Report, 44,* 922–927.

Miringoff, M., & Miringoff, M. L. (1999). *The social health of the nation: How America is really doing.* New York: Oxford University Press.

National Research Council, Institute of Medicine. (1995). *Integrating federal statistics on children.* Washington, DC: National Academy Press.

Office of Juvenile Justice and Delinquency Prevention, U.S. Department of Justice. (1999). *Juvenile arrests 1998.* Washington, DC: U.S. Government Printing Office.

Rennison, C. M., & Welchans, S. (2000). *Intimate partner violence* (U.S. Department of Justice, NCJ 178247). Washington, DC: U.S. Government Printing Office.

Snyder, H. N., & Sickmund, M. (1999). *Juvenile offenders and victims: 1999 national report.* Washington, DC: U.S. Department of Justice, Office of Justice Programs, Office of Juvenile Justice and Delinquency Prevention.

U. S. General Accounting Office. (1997). *Welfare reform: Implications of increased work participation for child care* (GAO/HEHS-97-75). Washington, DC: U.S. Government Printing Office.

# TWO

# Social Indicators as Tools of Public Policy

*Brett V. Brown and Thomas Corbett*

Powerful themes in U.S. social policy are converging to increase the importance of social indicators as tools of public policy. The 1990s witnessed a significant devolution of power and responsibility over public policy from the federal government to the states and, increasingly, from states to local communities. This increased responsibility, and the greater flexibility that goes with it, has encouraged states and communities to begin reinventing the ways in which they coordinate, plan, produce, and evaluate the policies they pursue and the services they render, moving from a focus on process and inputs (what organizations and programs do) to a focus on outcomes (what they accomplish). Social indicators for tracking the well-being of children and families are becoming increasingly important tools of governance in this age of devolution and reinvention.

But growing interest in the use of social indicators has engendered a number of challenges that must be addressed if states and communities are to take full advantage of their potential as tools for effective governance. The need for social indicators is fast outstripping the available stock of data and measures and the resources available to develop them. The rules for the appropriate application of these indicators are unclear. The knowledge to use them well and wisely is often lacking, and the opportunities for their misuse are considerable.

In this chapter, we consider the nature of these challenges that states and communities must address and strategies that can be pursued to meet these challenges. We begin by briefly describing the emerging forces of devolution and reinvention, and their relation to social indicators. We then put forward a simple typology of the ways in which social indicators are used in governance, including monitoring and planning, goal setting, accountability, and, in rare cases, evaluation. The next section discusses the characteristics of a good system of social indicators of child and family well-being and identifies some of the technical and political challenges facing states and localities in the development and proper use of social indicator data. Finally, we make recommendations regarding the complementary roles that states, the federal government, research institutions, and private foundations may adopt to support states and local communities in furthering their capacities to develop and use social indicator data.

## Devolution, Reinvention, and the Rise of Social Indicators

*Devolution* may be broadly defined as the transfer of responsibility for social program design and implementation from higher to lower levels of government. The handing down of responsibility for the partial funding of such programs is also a common part of devolution, in which greater control over programs is ceded to the lower level of government with the understanding that fewer dollars will be transferred from above over the long term. The United States has gone through several cycles of devolution and centralization during the 20th century (Brown & Corbett, 1997).

In the 1990s, we entered a devolutionary phase, which is being implemented through two approaches that we have termed *incremental* and *structural* devolution. *Incremental* devolution is exemplified by the proliferation of federally approved welfare waiver experiments that were granted over a decade beginning in the mid-1980s, waivers that became both more numerous and more complex over time. *Structural* devolution involves the formal transfer of control over selected social service functions to the states, most often including the block granting of funds for such services. The most recent welfare reform law, the Personal Responsibility and Work Opportunity Act of 1996, exemplifies this approach. Other service areas in which this approach has been recently considered include Medicaid and Youth Services.

Devolution provides states with greater flexibility in the design and implementation of social programs, and with greater responsibility for planning and for achieving results. In addition, fiscal pressures resulting from reduced levels of federal funding provide additional incentives to design programs and policies that will be both efficient and effective. In response, states are adopting a number of policy tools related to the government reinvention movement including comprehensive and integrated service planning and design at the state and local levels (e.g., state benchmarking and local comprehensive community initiatives), a shift toward outcomes-based accountability both within agencies and between state and local governments, and the pursuit of competitive market-driven models of service delivery (e.g., welfare service privatization efforts in Texas and Wisconsin). All of these strategies depend heavily on the use of social indicators for their successful implementation.

## The Uses of Social Indicators for Social Policy

Emerging forms of social policymaking involve distinct demands on the characteristics of the social indicators used and the expertise of those who use them;

therefore, policymakers must develop a common understanding and language regarding social indicators. The goal of this section is to lay the foundation for this common understanding and common language.

We identify five basic policy-relevant uses of social indicators:

- description, for the sake of knowledge about society;

- monitoring, to track outcomes that may require policy intervention and to aid in planning;

- setting goals, to focus and coordinate activities across agencies, between higher and lower levels of government, and between public and private groups at all levels of government;

- outcomes-based accountability, to hold managers, agencies, governments, and even whole communities responsible for improving social well-being; and, in limited circumstances,

- evaluation, to determine which programs and policies are effective (or destructive) and, where possible, to determine the reasons for success or failure.

These uses are organized into a typology according to the progressively exacting demands of each. The result is a sort of Russian doll format: Description forms the outermost shell, evaluation the core, and the three intermediate levels share some characteristics of those outside in addition to their own particular characteristics.

When there is active interest in some dimension of social well-being, a dimension that might require a government response, the task of description becomes one of monitoring. When social indicators become associated with active policies intended specifically to improve social well-being, monitoring becomes goal setting. When there are consequences associated with failure or success in meeting specified social goals, goal setting becomes outcomes-based accountability. Finally, when those held accountable are asked to demonstrate scientifically the relation between their activities and the social outcomes they are intended to affect, accountability becomes evaluation.

## Description

The most basic function of a social indicator of child and family well-being is to describe the condition of children and families. Social indicators are used for descriptive purposes to enhance our knowledge of society. Unlike the other functions described here, however, there is no necessary or implied relation to a social action agenda.

The U.S. Interagency Forum on Child and Family Statistics, for example, has been working to improve the quality, coverage, and availability of child well-being indicators collected by the federal statistical system. Forum members are working to identify and fill data gaps by developing new measures and incorporating them into existing surveys. The forum has supported the efforts of one of its members, the Assistant Secretary for Planning and Evaluation (DHHS/ASPE) to produce and disseminate an annual report on over 90 indicators of child well-being at the national level titled *Trends in the Well-Being of America's Children and Youth*. In addition, the forum has produced its own annual report on the condition of children, mandated by the President, titled *America's Children: Key National Indicators of Well-Being*. This report focuses on 25 indicators of well-being.

## *Monitoring*

Social indicators used for monitoring purposes provide a means for identifying emerging, waning, and continuing needs of children and their families, needs that may be amenable to change through intentional intervention. The primary consumers of social indicator data for this purpose are governments, political and advocacy groups, and citizens. Policymakers at the national, state, and local levels are increasingly using such information to prioritize and guide government action.

For organizations with a broad social agenda for promoting the well-being of children, the list of monitoring indicators can be similar in size and scope to one defined for descriptive purposes. Several private organizations now produce reports containing a broad set of national child well-being measures, including the Annie E. Casey Foundation's *KIDS COUNT Data Book* (1996), the Children's Defense Fund's *The State of America's Children Yearbook* (1994), and William Bennett's *Index of Leading Cultural Indicators* (1993). State-level organizations that are part of the Annie E. Casey Foundation project produce annual reports about children in nearly every state and the District of Columbia.

Government agencies also monitor well-being for a variety of purposes. Some monitoring efforts are very specific. For example, the Centers for Disease Control and Prevention's (CDC) communicable disease surveillance system tracks a variety of communicable diseases and works with state and local health departments to respond to outbreaks.

Other federal monitoring efforts are broader and intended to inform policy in a more general way. Both the CDC and the National Center for Education Statistics work with states and cities to field surveys that provide state- and, in some cases, local-level indicators related to health behaviors and academic achievement among children and their families, including:

- The Youth Risk Behavior Survey, currently fielded in public high schools in some 39 states, 16 cities, and four U.S. possessions, tracks trends in a variety of health risk behaviors like drug use, sexual practices, diet and exercise, and the use or nonuse of safety equipment.
- The National Immunization Survey provides annual estimates of immunization rates among 2-year-olds for each of the 50 states.

- The Pregnancy Risk Assessment Monitoring System, currently fielded in 19 states, provides information on prenatal care, pre- and postnatal maternal behaviors, infant health, and well-baby care.
- The National Assessment of Educational Progress (NAEP) has periodically fielded assessments in math, reading, and science to students in the fourth and eighth grades in participating states. In 1994, 44 states and the District of Columbia participated in the survey.

A number of local areas have developed their own geographic information system databases that measure well-being at the neighborhood level. These databases usually include both direct measures of child well-being and neighborhood characteristics known or believed to affect the well-being of children. Cleveland, Atlanta, Boston, Chicago, Denver, Oakland, and Providence are working with researchers from the Urban Institute to improve methodologies for building such systems (Urban Institute, 1995). These data systems are used extensively for local services planning.

## Goals

Another basic function of social indicators is the monitoring of progress toward the social goals adopted by governments, agencies within governments, and whole communities. Goals serve as focal points around which to organize social action in an effective and coordinated manner. Unlike simple monitoring, goals are associated with an active plan to improve social well-being along one or more specified dimensions. Even broad, general goals (e.g., all children will be healthy) are typically related to concrete, measurable objectives to be reached over a specified period of time, like these from Minnesota Milestones:

> By the year 2000, 90% of all 2-year-olds will be fully immunized, only 3.5% of newborns will be born with low birthweight, and only 35% of 12th grade students will report using alcohol or illegal drugs within the previous month.

Goals often serve as management tools for focusing activities within particular agencies, for coordinating activities across governmental agencies and between those agencies and community nongovernmental organizations. Goal setting can also function to create consensus among stakeholders whose cooperation will be needed for effective social action. Indeed, this is often a necessary step for effective management. In such cases, goals must be identified from the ground up rather than imposed from the top down.

The jump from social indicator as monitoring tool to social goal is a large one. Goals are intended to affect the distribution of budgetary resources, the design and implementation of program strategies, and the formation of basic policy, often across many agencies and organizations. To be effective, they require the active cooperation of many stakeholders. As a result, the lists of social indicators that are used as goals tend to be considerably shorter than those compiled for monitoring or descriptive purposes. In addition, because the consequences associated with their use are more profound, it is particularly important that such measures be valid, sensitive, and accurate barometers of the conditions of interest.

The federal government launched and sustained several major goals' projects, including Healthy People 2000 (U.S. Department of Health and Human Services 1990, 1994) and Education Goals 2000. Healthy People 2000 was a 10-year plan to improve the health of the U.S. population. The plan consisted of 298 health objectives with specific target levels for each objective. One objective was to reduce the proportion of 20- to 24-year-olds who smoke from 30% in 1987 to 15% by the year 2000 (National Center for Health Statistics, 1995). The U.S. Public Health Service, the 50 state health departments, and over 270 national organizations participated in a three-year process to develop these objectives. States and communities were encouraged to adopt their own year 2000 objectives modeled on the national effort and to develop systems for monitoring progress toward meeting state and national health goals. This initiative led to the development or enhancement of numerous data collection efforts designed to track progress toward these goals at the national, state, and local levels. Plans are currently under way to extend this program into the next decade as Healthy People 2010.

In 1989, President George H. W. Bush and the 50 state governors adopted six National Educational Goals. These goals, plus two others, were adopted into law in 1994 as part of the Goals 2000: Educate America Act. Although state participation in the program is strictly voluntary, federal grants were available to all states submitting approved plans for improving education outcomes related to these goals, and for developing, field-testing, and evaluating state assessments to measure progress toward the goals. As in Healthy People 2000, states set their own target levels for each specific goal.

Many states have developed their own goal-oriented programs independent of, though often encompassing, these national efforts. Two of the most comprehensive and well-known state plans are Oregon's Benchmarks (outcomes) program and Minnesota's Milestones, both of which set goals encompassing well-being for the entire state population. Some states have comprehensive programs targeted specifically toward children. The National Center for Children in Poverty (1996) mapping and tracking project has identified such programs in eight states. The more active of these programs include Vermont's Success by Six and Ohio's Family and Children First.

Local municipal governments and community organizations are encouraged to participate in the benchmarks process. For example, the Oregon

Commission on Children and Families was founded in 1993 with the mission of empowering local communities to improve the lives of their own children through comprehensive community planning efforts guided by a concrete set of benchmarks adopted by each community. State and local commissions have jointly identified and adopted 10 core benchmarks. In addition, most local commissions have identified their own child benchmarks to guide planning efforts.

## Outcomes-Based Accountability

Social indicators used for accountability are essentially goals with attached consequences. There is a contractual element (explicit or implicit, voluntary or involuntary) in which one party holds the other responsible for achieving specified, socially desirable goals. For example, the federal government may hold states accountable for achieving preselected goals in a program area; states similarly may hold counties accountable; counties may hold service providers accountable, and so forth. Consequences may include sanctions for failure, rewards for success, or both.

Relationships of accountability can be based on measures of process (e.g., how well one executed the intended action or program), on measures of outcomes (on the dimensions of social well-being that the programs or policies are ultimately intended to affect), or on systems of measurement that include both. Relationships of accountability based on outcomes have the advantage of providing the actors with programmatic flexibility while still holding them accountable for results (Schorr et al., 1995). The devolution revolution, as we have described it, has been motivated in part by the belief that providing such flexibility to actors at the state and local levels is one key to improving the effectiveness of social programs and policy.

This flexibility of process has a price, however, in terms of the knowledge that is generated. Outcomes-based accountability that does not also include an explicit evaluation component cannot produce certain knowledge of the best practices, and of what works, though it may be used to identify best practitioners, persons, or organizations who build up successful track records over time. It can also be used to flag approaches that may be particularly promising or particularly damaging, which can be targeted for formal evaluation.

The additional burdens placed on accountability measures relative to goals substantially shape both the types of measures chosen for such purposes and the target levels. A social goal may be broad, requiring the work of many actors over a long period of time. An accountability measure, on the other hand, must be defined such that the actions of an individual actor, agency, or government can be reasonably expected to produce changes in the measure, usually in a relatively short period of time. Furthermore, the measure requires that the impact of other influences can be factored out in some way, either statistically or through careful definition. As a result, good outcomes-based accountability measures can be far more difficult to identify and operationalize than goals.

Accountability measures tend for several reasons to set more conservative targets than do goals. Goals often express a society's more lofty and ambitious desires for the future: For example, "By the year 2010 every child will come to school ready to learn." Accountability measures, by contrast, must pay greater attention to what is realistically achievable. It is one thing to condition state education financial assistance on improving high school graduation rates, and quite another to condition aid on 100% graduation rates. In addition, those held accountable have a strong interest in minimizing expectations, and since they often help shape definitions and set target levels for such measures, they are frequently able to negotiate targets that fall short of what might be achieved.

*Federal-state relationships.* One result of devolution has been that account-ability measures are shifting away from those assessing process or effort to those reflecting outcomes or results. (At the same time, there has been a move in the direction of less accountability of any sort.) For example, under the old Aid to Families with Dependent Children (AFDC) system, states were held accountable for how accurately they applied the rules in making eligibility determinations. Poor execution could result in reductions in federal funds to the state. Under the Temporary Assistance for Needy Families Block Grant, which replaces AFDC, states are to be held accountable, through a combination of budgetary sanctions and positive incentives, for results ranging from reaching target employment lev-els among assistance recipients to lowering the state's nonmarital birthrate.

*State-local relationships.* Devolution is also being pursued in many state capitals, and is likely to move forward even more rapidly in light of the new welfare reform laws. Examples include block-granting funds to local govern-ments, and the establishment of local commissions to coordinate child and family services across agencies and between local agencies and private com-munity organizations (see Gold & Watson, 1996). Efforts to enhance local accountability and performance typically require the reporting of selected indi-cators of child and family well-being to the state, as well as their use for pur-poses of goal identification, planning, and program design by the localities. As of yet there are few cases in which explicit sanctions are attached to poor per-formance as measured by the social indicators, though clearly these relation-ships are being structured with the assumption that localities will be held responsible for achieving results.

For example, the state of Oregon has set up local commissions on children and families in every county. These commissions receive funding and technical assistance from the State Commission on Children and Families. Each com-mission identifies a minimum of 11 child well-being benchmarks (outcomes) that they will target.

The commissions are charged with
- conducting needs assessments,
- planning and coordinating local and state services,
- distributing and coordinating funding streams,
- encouraging citizen involvement, and
- promoting services integration and systems reforms (Bruner et al.).

At present, failure to meet benchmark standards will result in additional technical assistance from the state commission. Eventually, however, county commissions may face financial consequences for long-term failure to achieve goals.

The Massachusetts Department of Education has proposed regulations that would allow the state to take over individual schools or entire school districts judged to be underperforming. Schools could be classified as underperforming based on one or more of the following conditions:
- student academic performance below minimum standards,
- high dropout rates,
- low attendance rates,
- loss of accreditation,
- operational deficiencies, or
- noncompliance with state or federal laws.

Other state-local initiatives using outcomes accountability are designed to improve local service provision through enhanced market-style competition among such groups. For example, under Wisconsin's W-2 welfare program, local government agencies will compete with each other and with private service providers to administer the welfare program in their county. The contractor will be given broad discretion in administering the program and will be judged by broad outcome or performance criteria set at the state level. It is unclear whether these criteria will include measures related to the well-being of children, though this has been under discussion.

Several states have taken steps to implement a performance-based budgeting process in which agencies are held accountable for results, and in which ineffectiveness or failure to perform results in lost revenues or program termination or both. For example, Texas has developed a statewide strategic plan called Texas Tomorrow. Under this plan, state agencies will be held accountable for advancing specified state goals and funded according to demonstrated agency performance in obtaining outcomes specified in their agency strategic plans. Statewide goals for children and families were developed in consultation with the relevant state agencies, advocacy groups, and with the input of public testimony (see Council of Chief State School Officers, 1996).

*Citizen-politician relationships.* In a democracy, the notion of accountability is inherent in the relationship between citizens and elected officials at all levels of government, with the ballot box as the ultimate accountability mechanism. The accountability measures that define that relationship are often, though not always, vague and can change over time with the shifting concerns of the electorate.

Private organizations are working to increase citizen access to child well-being data for their own communities and states, and for the nation. For example, the Annie E. Casey Foundation's KIDS COUNT Data Books, produced nationally and in all but 1 of the 50 states, are intended to serve multiple purposes, including providing citizens with the information they need to hold state and local officials accountable for improving the well-being of children. Massachusetts KIDS COUNT is organizing community groups across the state to use local data provided by KIDS COUNT for this purpose (Children's Advocacy Board, 1994).

## Evaluation

Causal evaluations of programs and policies are our only means of building a knowledge base of the approaches that work and the reasons why they work. This knowledge is essential if governments and communities are to take advantage of their own past experience and the experience of others to identify and adopt the best practices. In addition, systems of accountability are greatly strengthened by providing a scientific basis for linking efforts to outcomes.

Traditionally, social indicators have played a limited role in the formal evaluation of programs and policies. They have functioned primarily as early warning systems, identifying potentially promising (or potentially dysfunctional) programs deserving rigorous evaluation. This is an important role, and one whose significance would increase under devolution as the number and type of policy experiments at the state and local level expands.

Social indicators have rarely served as evaluation tools in the approaches that have been developed over the last 30 years such as the experimental method, pre-post and comparative models, and multivariate analyses of national data. These methods have usually relied on microanalytic techniques using individual-level data, rather than macroanalytic approaches using aggregate data. Social indicators are, by contrast, typically used in the form of aggregate measures reflecting the condition of population subgroups.

Furthermore, these traditional evaluation techniques rely on the identification of a *counterfactual* to measure the effects of a program or policy. A counterfactual is what would have happened in the absence of the program or policy being evaluated. Such tools are difficult to use when evaluating policies that entail comprehensive changes to the entire social service system, a common characteristic of government reinvention efforts. First, such efforts are designed so that all members of the target population are to be affected, precluding experimental evaluation designs. Second, there are multiple, interrelated program changes that are intended to produce changes along many dimensions of social well-being. The nature of the changes is likely to differ substantially from site to site, complicating the identification of a counterfactual.

In response, theorists have been developing an alternative method of evaluation that does not require a counterfactual and that is more appropriate to the multiple inputs–multiple outputs nature of these initiatives (Chen, 1990; Connell & Kubisch, 1996; Weiss, 1995). This theory-driven or theories of change approach depends on the development of an explicit model relating the complex programmatic changes to intermediate and long-term changes in the well-being of the target population. Each element of programmatic change is linked causally to the outcomes it is expected to affect. The theories of change underlying the model are judged according to the cumulative evidence of actual outcomes for the many hypothesized linkages in the model (see Connell & Kubisch, 1996).

Although this approach may seem foreign to those well-versed in counterfactual methods, Connell points out that theory-driven models are well established in the physical sciences (J. P. Connell, personal communication, 1996). In addition, it has some methodological similarities to social science–based approaches to microsimulation modeling (see Citro & Hanushek, 1991). A weakness of the approach, however, is the lack of a strong theory of community dynamics, the presence of which would seem to be a prerequisite for the successful application of such models in evaluations. Nevertheless, it is hoped that the implementation of such approaches will build the theoretical knowledge over time.

Aggregate social indicators of well-being are integral tools of this approach to evaluation. They represent the intermediate and long-term goals of each initiative and are the ultimate measuring sticks for the initiative's success or failure. The outcomes are identified through a process that includes all relevant stakeholders in the community, in consultation with the evaluator, who draws on knowledge of scientific theory. A similar process is undertaken to identify the expected linkages between program change and the social outcomes. Thus the model is grounded in science and in the community's expectations. The proper relationship between these two forces is a matter of ongoing debate within the literature.

The Cleveland Community Building Initiative is an example of a comprehensive community initiative that is attempting to use this theory-driven approach to evaluation (Center on Urban Poverty and Social Change, 1996). The initiative began in 1994 and involves four Cleveland neighborhoods. Village councils made up of residents, business interests, and representatives of local social service agencies identify neighborhood goals and the local resources and strategies that can be used to meet these goals. The Center for Urban Poverty and Change at Case Western Reserve University is working with the councils to identify their underlying theories of change, assisting them to make underlying assumptions explicit and testable. In addition, they have produced a substantial neighborhood database that assists neighborhoods in identifying assets and that will be used to evaluate their programs over time.

### Different Uses of Social Indicators: An Example

To clarify the distinctions among the various uses of social indicators described above, we look at a familiar data item, the child poverty rate.

- Descriptive use. Data on the child poverty rate (trends over time, differences across population subgroups) can give us meaningful information about children's lives. Used in conjunction with other indicators, such data can even enhance our understanding of how society functions. If these data are used in a purely descriptive manner, however, they will not be expected to have any direct impact on policies for helping children.

- Monitoring use. The child poverty rate can be observed with the idea that society is interested in and capable of lowering that rate if it reaches a certain level (though that level may not be commonly agreed upon). It may also be used in planning and allocating program resources. The use of indicators to inform policy at such a general level is best described as monitoring.

- Goal-setting use. As a matter of policy, we can take the monitoring function a step further by setting a normative goal to be achieved. Goal setting can be explicit or subtle. It is not inconceivable that a political body would establish the objective of cutting child poverty in half by a certain date, or set a goal of not permitting child poverty to worsen as welfare reform is being introduced.

- Accountability use. The stakes are raised when success in meeting a goal is rewarded or failure punished or both. States that reform welfare and reduce child poverty might receive more federal dollars; those states in which child poverty increases by some amount might be subject to fiscal penalties and bad publicity.

- Evaluative use. We can hold a state, county, agency, or program accountable for performance even if we do not know for sure they are responsible for success or failure for child poverty going up, down, or staying the same. However, when we go beyond responsibility to understanding whether a particular policy approach actually lowered the poverty rate that we have been tracking, we have moved to a level where we wish to establish causal links between policy initiatives and outcomes.

## Summary

Moving from level to level—from describing to monitoring, from monitoring to setting goals—increases the importance of actual numbers or rates (e.g., the child poverty rate) to the policymaking and public-management processes. Not surprisingly, the need for quality numbers, or indicators, is critical. If an indicator is used merely in a descriptive sense, some flaws in the way it is conceptualized and measured may be of interest but not of great social importance. But when we use an indicator to hold entities responsible or decide whether programs are useful or not, we had better know what we are measuring and be confident that it is what we think it is.

## Effective Social Indicator Data Systems: Technical and Practical Challenges

Social indicators hold great promise as powerful tools of social policy. Although the promise of social indicators may be great, governments at all levels face considerable challenges in developing the appropriate data sources, the training to use them well, and the political will to use them wisely. In this section, we briefly consider the nature of the challenges facing states in each of these three dimensions.

Good indicators should be

- grounded in scientific theory and existing research;
- measured regularly and in a timely fashion;
- easily understood;
- available at the local level and for policy-relevant population subgroups; and whenever possible,
- measured comparably across local areas and population subgroups (Moore, 1997).

The discussion of these criteria (which draws substantially from Moore [1997]), and some of the difficulties which states face in meeting them, are discussed below.

*Grounded in theory and research.* Any system of social indicators should be well grounded in social theory. Systems of child well-being indicators should be based on comprehensive models of well-being to ensure that all relevant dimensions of well-being as well as key measures of children's environments (e.g., the family and community) are adequately covered. In addition, they should incorporate a developmental perspective, which recognizes that well-being is defined differently at different stages in the child's development. Examples of such models include the ecological model of child development (Bronfenbrenner, 1979), the social capital approach (Coleman, 1988), choice-investment theory (Haveman & Wolfe, 1994), and a general resource framework that draws from all these models (Brooks-Gunn et al., 1995).

Empirical research plays a key role in defining the contents of this conceptual framework. Research helps us identify which dimensions of child well-being are important by demonstrating their relationship to other valued dimensions of child well-being (e.g., good physical health promotes cognitive development), to well-being in adulthood (e.g., academic achievement in high school is strongly related to earnings in adulthood), and to the well-being of other members of society (e.g., low rates of juvenile violent crime lead to greater safety for all members of society). In addition, empirical research is needed to identify elements of social context that have the largest overall impact on the well-being of children.

Empirical research is also needed to verify the validity and reliability of particular measures, demonstrating that each measure adequately reflects the concept it is meant to represent, and that it provides comparable measures across groups (e.g., between counties within a state) and over time.

*Regular and timely.* Virtually all uses of social indicators require data that are regularly measured so that trends can be tracked over time. This means that important social indicators must be incorporated into data sources that can provide fresh estimates on a regular basis, such as an annual survey or a continuously updated administrative database. Measures that are expected to change more slowly can be measured less frequently without loss of utility. It is equally important that social indicator data be available on a timely basis. Estimates that are three to four years old are too far removed from the current policy environment to be of much use.

*Easily understood.* The people who work with social indicators—whether in the public or private sector—have widely varying levels of statistical sophistication. Social indicators of children's well-being should always be easily and immediately understood by those who will be using them. An indicator that is technically superior but difficult to understand is, for most purposes, not preferable to one that may be slightly less accurate but whose meaning is transparent.

*Available at the local level and for population subgroups.* Separate estimates for localities and population subgroups are needed to efficiently plan and target resources and to assess whether progress is being made across different populations. Important subgroups may differ somewhat from indicator to indicator but will commonly include such fundamental social characteristics as poverty status, race and ethnicity, family structure, age, and gender.

## Challenges for Existing State and Local Data Systems.

State and local governments face a number of challenges in building their data systems to meet the criteria described earlier. First, there are many important aspects of child well-being that cannot be tracked at any level because the research has not been done to develop good operationalized measures for them, or because the data simply have not been gathered. Even at the national level, where social indicator data are comparatively plentiful, a recent federal report identifies many such areas in which adequate data have not been gathered or in which good operationalized measures have not been developed, including child abuse, child mental health, parent-child interaction, youth criminal activity, neighborhood quality, and positive or assets-based measures of all sorts (Brown & Stagner, 1997).

Often, indicators that are gathered at the national level are not available at the state and local levels. Most states are heavily dependent on the federal data system for data on their own population.

A recent review of federal sources of state and local data on children identified substantial gaps in coverage below the national level (Brown & Botsko, 1996). A number of states and communities field their own surveys to fill these gaps, and more have additional health- and education-related administrative data that can be used to construct child indicators. (Oregon, for example, has fielded its own state population survey, and Wisconsin its own annual state health survey. Every three years, Minnesota fields a youth risk behavior survey covering approximately 90% of all public high schools.) Even within the most active states, however, large gaps remain, particularly at the local level.

For data that are available, problems with data quality are a common concern. The measures themselves may be problematic (i.e., there are problems with the validity and reliability of the measures), or the data may be gathered improperly. This is more often the case with administrative data, but can also be an issue with survey data. Among the 39 states that fielded the Youth Risk Behavior Survey in 1995, over 40% failed to draw a representative sample, making the resulting data virtually useless for tracking trends in the well-being of adolescents in those states.

When the need for an indicator is great, pressure can be strong to use whatever is available, regardless of the quality of the indicator. Further, budgetary pressures can foster the continued use of low-quality measures because of the increased costs associated with proper measurement. However, the negative consequences of using poor-quality measures can be great. Inadequate measures can fail to pick up changes in well-being or, worse, indicate change when no change has occurred. The use of poor measures for planning can lead to the inefficient allocation of resources; for goals tracking, the failure to identify actual progress; for accountability, the unjust penalizing or erroneous reward of persons, agencies, or whole levels of government; for evaluation, the misidentification of effective and ineffective policies and programs. The more serious the consequences associated with using indicators, the more important it is that they be measured accurately.

*Training.* Social indicators are tools, and like most tools require some knowledge and skill to use properly. As devolution progresses, many people will be asked to make responsible use of tools for which they have little training. Lack of training could lead to frustration among the users, and to inefficient use or misuse of the data, with negative consequences for the social policy efforts that depend on them.

The state of Oregon acknowledged early on the importance of proper training as a prerequisite for the success of its benchmarks program. The state's Commission on Children and Families helps to set up local commissions in each county to coordinate the design and delivery of services to children and their families. The state also provides thorough and ongoing training and technical assistance to the local commissions to help them plan and then to develop and use social indicators to track their progress toward both state and local goals (Oregon Commission on Children and Families, 1994, 1996). This training and ongoing support is considered crucial to the success of the benchmarks effort.

*Political challenges.* Political challenges to the successful employment of social indicators as policy guides are substantial and increase as one moves from less to more politically sensitive uses in our typology (i.e., from monitoring to goals setting, accountability, and evaluation). The pressures to use goals and accountability for partisan or self-interested purposes rather than as tools of good government are great. In addition, devolution itself has increased the pressure to adopt such approaches to governance quickly, with the possible result that they will be employed haphazardly and supported by inadequate measures and inadequate training. Finally, even the successful employment of these strategies can produce problems that must also be addressed. We will address each issue in turn.

The partisan and competitive nature of politics can easily undermine efforts to rationalize the policy process through the dispassionate use of social indicators. The competitiveness inherent in the process often leads to exaggerated claims regarding proposed policies; such claims are much more difficult to put forward and sustain where, for example, strong accountability frameworks are in place. The partisan or ideological component of policymaking can also be threatened by strong systems of accountability and evaluation whose results may run counter to ideologically derived policy platforms. These political pressures can lead to using social indicators as weapons rather than as tools for public management. Consequent responses can include attempts to minimize their power and importance or, alternatively, to control them. We characterize these responses as muddling, gaming, misrepresentation, and manipulation.

- Muddling. Politicians may well speak enthusiastically of the need for accountability, the establishment of social goals, and the importance of monitoring social well-being but fail to follow through in any sustained manner to establish such programs.

- Gaming. Those who define social goals and measures of accountability set the terms by which political success is judged. There are strong interests in defining the terms of success in ways that will be friendlier to particular political agendas. Also, a bureaucratic interest exists in defining success in ways that can be easily met by those held accountable.

- Misrepresentation. It is common for political agents to use a trend in a social indicator to make claims about the effectiveness or failure of particular policies. Often these claims go considerably beyond what can reasonably be inferred from the data. The chances for active misrepresentation are strongest in relationships of accountability in which the consequences of failure to perform are substantial, and can be particularly strong when those held accountable are also the ones responsible for collecting the data, a common arrangement under devolution.

- Manipulation. There are many ways to manipulate the collection and presentation of social indicators to one's advantage. These can range from the selective presentation (or nonpresentation) of data for certain years or for certain population subgroups, to the deliberate manipulation of the data collection process.

Finally, devolution creates its own pressures to reinvent the delivery of government services in ways that require intensive use of social indicators. Such pressure can easily result in the adoption of accountability frameworks, goal-driven program coordination, and evaluation strategies without the time, training, technical assistance, or data development necessary to make them successful. Devolution, if it proceeds too quickly, could become its own worst enemy.

## Recommendations

Devolution both encourages and demands that state and local governments reinvent the ways in which their work is carried out. The challenges outlined in the previous section, however, are substantial, and the clock is ticking. There is much work to be done in the development of good measures and good data to support these efforts, and for increasing the capacities of all actors (legislators, government managers, citizens) to understand and use them effectively. We make specific recommendations to the federal government, state and local governments, private foundations, and the research community.

### *Federal Government*

The growing need for state- and local-level social indicators is fast outstripping what is currently available. Although some of these data needs will be unique to each locality, a large proportion of the required measures are the same across many or all jurisdictions. Furthermore, there are important benefits to having comparable measures across jurisdictions, for purposes of accountability and the identification of best practices. It makes sense, therefore, that devolution will be best served through some central coordination of data collection and measurement development activities by the federal government. Such an approach can take advantage of economies of scale, and is necessary to produce data that are comparable across jurisdictions.

Under devolution, federal agencies will need to work closely with states and localities to develop and expand federal data collection efforts in ways that will meet evolving state and local data needs. Federal agencies have developed a number of models for producing such data, which include more or less direct input from state and local users. (See Brown and Botsko [1996] for a recent review of these data sources.) Of these, the approach taken by the CDC to monitor health indicators within states may serve as a model for data generation efforts under devolution. The Behavior Risk Factor Surveillance System is an annual health survey of adults, with representative samples fielded in every state and the District of Columbia. Each survey consists of the common core questions developed jointly by the CDC and state health departments. In addition, states may include optional topical modules. The state health departments field all surveys, with strong technical assistance from CDC staff. The CDC also provides funding to support the collection of data. The survey is designed to ensure some comparability across states, while providing each state with maximum flexibility to adapt the survey to its own needs.

Federal agencies can open up national survey efforts to states willing to pay to have special surveys in their state. The CDC is considering opening up its National Immunization Survey (NIS) to states wishing to pay for health- and welfare-related surveys in their state. The NIS is a telephone survey of families with 2-year-old children. To identify these families, the CDC screens a very large number of households each year. This screening process could be used as a low-cost means of identifying representative state samples that can be used for other surveys, allowing states to produce surveys much more cheaply than if they started from scratch. (Though based on the screener for the NIS, the effort itself is known as State and Local Area Integrated Telephone Surveys, or SLAITS.) The Census Bureau is considering a similar arrangement when it begins fielding the American Community Survey. This is a possible replacement for much of the decennial Census and is designed to contact approximately 700,000 households per year beginning in 2000, expanding further when becoming fully implemented in 2003.

Federal agencies can also support states and localities by providing technical assistance as these entities develop their own administrative and survey data. Moreover, they might focus additional and sustained resources to improve the quality of existing social indicators and to develop new measures in important areas where good indicators do not currently exist. In addition, federal agencies should work to adapt existing measures so that states and localities can gather them cheaply, perhaps through existing administrative data systems. At present, both the Assistant Secretary for Planning and Evaluation and the National Institute for Child Health and Human Development (NICHD), both of the U.S. Department of Health and Human Services, have been funding efforts to produce new social indicators of child well-being from existing data, and conceptualizing new measures that could easily be included in existing surveys. The National Education Goals Panel Goal 1 Technical Planning Group has long been interested in the appropriate assessment of children's early learning and development.

## State Governments

Devolution is giving states new responsibilities for policy development and service delivery, and new opportunities to reinvent the ways they deliver those services. The individual states will need to understand and make provisions for the new data requirements they are generating, and for the training required to develop the requisite skills to use social indicators effectively. Both data development and skills training will cost money at a time when budgets are expected to be tight. The pressures to underinvest in these activities will be strong when funds are needed to support basic services. The ultimate cost of underinvestment in these areas, however, will be reduced effectiveness and possible failure.

Although each state will follow its own path, each will benefit by forging links with other states, with the federal government, and with research institutions. Under devolution, the diffusion of knowledge and the promotion of cooperative relationships across states will come less from the top down, and more from horizontal links among the states themselves. States have much to gain by creating these links. For example, a new consortium of seven Midwestern states (Illinois, Indiana, Iowa, Michigan, Minnesota, Ohio, and Wisconsin) has been meeting regularly to discuss welfare reform to learn from each other and, possibly, to coordinate activities across states. They have identified as a top priority discussions on how to define and measure success under welfare reform.

States should, as a group, work with federal agencies to define the federal role of data development for social indicators. Federal agencies represent a great resource for states, and close cooperation and dialogue can define a role to help states meet their emerging data needs in a more efficient manner.

Finally, state governments should pursue working relationships with academic institutions, particularly state universities. Oregon and California have already made strong links with their universities for benchmark development and administrative data integration activities, respectively.

## Local Governments

Because many states are considering how to devolve responsibilities to local communities, local governments will need to work closely with state agencies to develop the social-indicator data they need, and the skills to use them effectively. In addition, localities that are being particularly aggressive in developing comprehensive approaches to service delivery will need to look beyond the state to forge links with other localities pursuing a similar course.

## Foundations

Private foundations have played a critical role in raising the profile of social indicators as public policy tools. Through its national and state KIDS COUNT projects, the Annie E. Casey Foundation has fostered the use of social indicators to monitor child well-being by groups inside and outside of government at all levels. KIDS COUNT data have become a part of direct government planning in several states, and figure prominently in the policy discourse of many states and localities.

Other foundations have been working to develop the information and the techniques required for policy-related applications of social indicators, and to actively encourage their adoption. The Improved Outcomes for Children Project is a joint effort by the Center for the Study of Social Policy and the Harvard Project on Effective Services; its funders include the Lilly Endowment, the Pew Charitable Trusts, the Danforth Foundation, and the Carnegie Corporation. This effort has focused on the implementation of goal-identification and outcomes-based accountability strategies by states and local communities to improve outcomes for children. Another effort, by the Aspen Institute Roundtable on Comprehensive Community Initiatives, focuses on a broad range of implementation and assessment issues related to such comprehensive local efforts. The roundtable has focused on developing a theory-driven approach to managing and evaluating these initiatives. Roundtable members are preparing a list of social-indicator measures to be used for such initiatives. Over half a dozen foundations have funded this effort.

We strongly recommend that foundations continue to fund efforts of this sort, because their importance will only grow as devolution and reinvention advance. In addition, we suggest several complementary areas in which foundations can play a facilitating role. First, as the need for cooperation and information exchange across states and localities increases dramatically under devolution, the mechanisms to accomplish these functions must also evolve. Foundations can provide initial funds to establish these important links across jurisdictions. The Midwestern consortium described above, funded by the Joyce Foundation, is a concrete example of the horizontal linkages states must make.

Second, we recommend that foundations help the academic community and the policy community to forge stronger links. Developing and refining social indicators where good measures are currently lacking requires basic research. Another important task is the development of cost-efficient means by which states and localities can measure and track these indicators. Academics and policymakers must develop theories and models to direct the use of social indicators for various purposes.

### The Research Community

The research community has a crucial role in refining existing indicators, developing new measures, and supporting basic research.

As an area of academic interest, social indicators received a moderate amount of attention in the 1960s and 1970s before virtually disappearing during the 1980s. Recently, social indicators have been experiencing something of a renaissance in academic circles, beginning with a major national conference on social indicators of children's well-being in the fall of 1994 (see Hauser et al., 1997). The work has been carried forward by researchers affiliated with the NICHD Child and Family Research Network, who have been working with federal agencies through the Interagency Forum on Child and Family Statistics to create new measures for the federal statistical system. In addition, researchers affiliated with the Aspen Institute's Comprehensive Community Initiative have been working to identify social indicator measures that can be used at the community level (see Connell et al., 1995).

Possible strategies for increasing academic involvement include the establishment of research networks or institutes to focus specifically on social indicators, the development of a cross-disciplinary journal on the subject, and the establishment of specific links between interested academics and policymakers with individual states and localities.

## Summary

Devolution is creating new opportunities and new pressures to reinvent the ways in which government at all levels serves its people. Many of the emerging strategies of reinvention (outcomes-based accountability, system-wide coordination and integration, benchmarking, the competitive awarding of service contracts) make substantial use of social indicators. Good measures, good data, the skills to use them well, and the will to use them wisely are, we believe, prerequisites for their success.

We have identified the major technical and political challenges that must be met if social indicators are to be implemented and used effectively for public administration. There is much work to be done, and the clock is ticking. All of the actors discussed—the federal government, state and local governments, academics, and foundations—must invest and engage in a serious and sustained collaborative effort to meet these challenges and truly reinvent the ways we do the public's business. It will not be cheap, nor will it be easy. But this approach is almost certainly our best alternative for safeguarding and improving the well-being of children.

## Authors' Note

Development of this chapter was made possible with funding from the Pew Charitable Trusts.

## References

Annie E. Casey Foundation. (1996). *Kids count data book.* Washington, DC: Annie E. Casey Foundation and the Center for the Study of Social Policy.

Bennett, W. J. (1993). *The index of leading cultural indicators* [Brochure]. Washington, DC: Published jointly by Empower America, the Heritage Foundation, and Free Congress Foundation:

Bronfenbrenner, U. (1979). *The ecology of human development: Experiment by nature and design.* Cambridge, MA: Harvard University Press.

Brooks-Gunn, J., Brown, B., Duncan, G. J., & Moore, K. A. (1995). Child development in the context of family and community resources: An agenda for national data collections. In *Integrating federal statistics on children: Report of a workshop* (pp. 27–97). Washington, DC: National Academy Press.

Brown, B., & Corbett, T. (1997). *Social indicators and public policy in the age of devolution: Special Report Series No. 71.* Madison, WI: Institute for Research on Poverty.

Brown, B. V., & Botsko, C. (1996). *A guide to state and local-level indicators of child well-being available through the federal statistical system.* Washington, DC: Child Trends, Inc.

Brown, B. V., & Stagner, M. (Eds.). (1997). *Trends in the well-being of America's children and youth: 1997.* Washington, DC: Child Trends, Inc.

Bruner, C., Both, D., & Marzke, C. (1996). *Steps along an uncertain path: State initiatives promoting comprehensive community-based reform.* Des Moines, IA: National Center for Service Integration.

Center on Urban Poverty and Social Change. (1996). *Cleveland community-building initiative measurement of long-term outcomes.* Cleveland, OH: Center on Urban Poverty and Social Change.

Chen, H. (1990). *Theory-driven evaluations.* Newbury Park, CA: Sage.

Children's Advocacy Board. (1994). *All our children: The Massachusetts agenda.* Boston: Children's Advocacy Board.

Children's Defense Fund. (1994). *The state of America's children yearbook 1994* (2nd ed.). Washington, DC: Children's Defense Fund.

Citro, C. F., & Hanushek, E. A. (Eds.). (1991). *Improving information for social policy decisions: The uses of microsimulation modeling.* Washington, DC: National Academy Press.

Coleman, J. (1988). Social capital in the creation of human capital. *American Journal of Sociology, 94* (Suppl. 94), S95–S120.

Connell, J. P., & Kubisch, A. C. (1996). *Applying a theories-of-change approach to the evaluation of comprehensive community initiatives: Progress, prospects, and problems.* Unpublished manuscript.

Connell, J. P., Kubisch, A. C., Schorr, L. B., & Weiss, C. H. (Eds.). (1995). *New approaches to evaluating community initiatives: Concepts, methods, and contexts.* Queenstown, MD: Aspen Institute.

Council of Chief State School Officers. (1996). *Changing decision making to improvements results for children and families: How ten states are tackling tough governance issues.* Washington, DC: Author.

Gold, S. D., & Watson, K. (1996). *The other side of devolution: Shifting relationships between state and local governments.* Washington, DC: Urban Institute.

Hauser, R., Brown, B., & Prosser, W. (1997). *Indicators of children's well-being.* New York: Russell Sage.

Haveman, R., & Wolfe, B. (1994). *Succeeding generations: On the effects of investments in children.* New York: Russell Sage.

Moore, K. A. (1997). *Criteria for indicators of child well-being.* In R. Hauser, B. Brown, & W. Prosser (Eds.), *Indicators of children's well-being* (pp. 36–44). New York: Russell Sage.

National Center for Children in Poverty. (1996). *Map and track: State initiatives for young children and families.* New York: Columbia University.

National Center for Health Statistics. (1995). *Healthy People 2000 review, 1994.* Washington, DC: U.S. Government Printing Office.

Oregon Commission on Children and Families. (1994). *Comprehensive planning guide: Communities investing in the future.* Salem, OR: Author.

Oregon Commission on Children and Families. (1996). *Outcomes measure notebook, 1995-1997.* Salem, OR: Author.

Schorr, L., Farrow, F., Hornbeck, D., & Watson, S. (1995). *The case of shifting to results-based accountability.* Washington, DC: Center for the Study of Social Policy.

Urban Institute. (1995). *The Urban Institute's 1995 annual report.* Washington, DC: Author.

U.S. Department of Health and Human Services. (1990). *Healthy People 2000.* Washington, DC: U.S. Government Printing Office.

U.S. Department of Health and Human Services. (1994). *Healthy People 2000 review 1994.* Washington, DC: U.S. Government Printing Office.

Weiss, C. H. (1995). Nothing as practical as good theory: Exploring theory-based evaluation for comprehensive community initiatives for children and families. In J. P. Connell, A. C. Kubisch, L. B. Schorr, & C. H. Weiss (Eds.), *New approaches to evaluating community initiatives: Concepts, methods, and contexts* (pp. 65–92). Queenstown, MD: Aspen Institute.

# PART II
## BEHAVIORAL INDICATORS

# THREE

# U.S. Educational Achievement in the 20th Century: Brilliant Success and Persistent Failure

*Lawrence C. Stedman*

During the 20th century, U.S. schooling underwent a remarkable transformation. In a globally unprecedented fashion, our high schools became a mass institution and the familiar modern features of education were established: multipurpose comprehensive high schools, standardized testing, ability grouping and tracking, child-centered elementary programs, junior high and then middle schools, and expanded curricular electives.

Educators have long debated how these changes affected academic achievement. Two broad formulations have dominated—one historical, one contemporary. Several scholars have contended there was a decline in excellence across the century as schools shifted their focus from academics to social and personal development to accommodate the new masses of students (Bestor, 1985; Hirsch, 1987). The classic curriculum of Latin, algebra, and ancient history was shed for a modern program of social studies, general math, and life skills. Child-centered education, emphasizing students' interests over traditional subject matter, took hold of the schools while the social efficiency movement promoted vocational education and tracking and thus limited access to serious academic knowledge. The watershed document was *Cardinal Principles of Secondary Education Report,* which stressed social adjustment and deemphasized academic knowledge and college preparation (Commission on the Reorganization of Secondary Education, 1918). According to this scenario, the subsequent curriculum revision movements of the 1920s and 1930s and the life-adjustment movements of the 1940s and 1950s produced the decline. In *Why Johnny Still Can't Read*, Flesch (1981) blamed the decline on the abandonment of phonics.

This historical explanation contrasts with one focused on a contemporary decline of excellence. This second account holds there was a major downturn in achievement beginning in the mid-1960s. The Reagan administration's report *A Nation at Risk* popularized the notion of a modern decline with its exhortation about a "rising tide of mediocrity that threatens our very future as a Nation and people" (National Commission on Excellence in Education, 1983, p. 5). This claim continues to be echoed, as in *The Decline of Intelligence in America* by Itzkoff (1994).

53

Many analysts link the modern decline to political-social forces, particularly to liberalism and the romantic education of the 1960s. They argue that schools shifted from excellence to equity and moved away from traditional values and standards. A student-centered, soft pedagogy became the norm. Curriculum and textbooks were "dumbed down" to meet the needs of an increasingly diverse student body, discipline was relaxed, and multiculturalism replaced the traditional academic canon. The result was a deep pervasive achievement decline that affected rich children and poor, suburban and urban students, and top achievers in particular.

A refined version of this formulation holds that the decline ended around 1980 and that schools are slowly recovering, thanks to A Nation at Risk and the reimposition of standards (Ravitch, 1995). Although often attributed to conservatives, the concern over the decline crosses the conservative-liberal and traditional-progressive divides.

It was inevitable that such dramatic formulations would produce a counterreaction. In the 1990s, a group of researchers dubbed the "revisionists" challenged the conventional view of decline and failure of U.S. schools (see, e.g., Bracey, 1991). They argued that there never really was a test score decline and that the educational crisis had been manufactured by right-wing forces wishing to discredit public schooling and either impose a regimen of tough standards and discipline or privatize education through vouchers. The revisionists contend there has been a steady improvement in student achievement throughout the century, which has now reached record levels. This case is described well by Berliner and Biddle (1995) in The Manufactured Crisis (see review in Stedman, 1996).

The revisionists' claims have circulated widely in teachers' union reports, syndicated columns, and articles in The New York Times and Better Homes and Gardens. The National Council of Teachers of English (1996) pronounced that "students today read better and write better than at any other time in the history of the country" (p. 5).

What does the record tell us? Do modern students perform as well as those of prior generations? Have literacy and achievement declined in recent decades? How well informed were students in earlier eras? Unfortunately, commentators often have misrepresented the evidence and ignored measurement problems and contradictory data (Stedman, 1996).

The evidence has important implications for school reform. If performance truly has been declining, then it may make sense to resurrect the traditional policies of an earlier era—old-fashioned teaching, tough standards, and no-nonsense discipline. On the other hand, if the schools really are performing "better than ever," it suggests that sweeping reforms—such as radical restructuring and school vouchers—are unnecessary and that we would be better off targeting those with lower achievement such as inner-city children, minority students, and slower learners.

In this chapter, I assemble a record of U.S. achievement and assess the competing accounts. I first describe the data on school participation. Then, to assess the historical formulation, I look at long-term achievement comparisons from the earliest decades of the century. To judge the claims of a contemporary decline, I next focus on the evidence from the 1960s through the 1990s, including trends by race and urban-rural status. I conclude with a discussion of the quality of achievement across the 20th century, particularly how much students learned in different eras, and its implications for reform.

## Participation Trends

Enrollment grew at a staggering rate during the century. In 1900, high schools enrolled about 630,000 students; by the late 1990s, they enrolled over 14 million (National Center for Education Statistics, 1999, p. 69). The proportion of the 14- to 17-year-old age group enrolled grew from only 10% in 1900 to more than 70% by 1940. By the 1970s, high school enrollment had become nearly universal, with more than 90% enrolled (Figure 3–1).

The population's educational attainment soared. In the 1930s, the typical adult age 25 and older had received only an elementary school education. By 1980, median school years had increased to over 12. Racial equality also improved greatly. In 1940, nonwhite adults lagged several years in attainment. By 1990, parity had almost been achieved. Among young adults, 25 to 29, blacks and other races had completed 12.8 years compared with 12.9 for whites.

The United States clearly succeeded in expanding school participation during the 20th century, but what were the consequences? Did the creation of a modern, mass institution produce a decline in achievement?

## Historical Comparisons of Achievement: 1840s to the 1940s

Educators have repeatedly used then-and-now studies to judge how changes in school practices affect achievement. In these studies, researchers test students on a test given years or decades earlier. One of the first showed that 1906 ninth-graders in Springfield, Massachusetts, outperformed their 1846 counterparts in spelling, arithmetic, and geography.

Although seductively simple, then-and-now studies have problems. Many involve small, local samples, so it is difficult to determine national trends. Few researchers accounted for changing student composition or the changing relevance of test material. Lower dropout rates and older test formats frequently disadvantaged contemporary groups. Despite these difficulties, a rough portrait of the trends has emerged in three areas: reading, subject matter achievement, and adults' general knowledge. These long-term comparisons span the decades from the middle of the 19th century through the 1980s.

**Figure 3–1: 9th to 12th grade enrollment as a percentage of 14- to 17-year-olds**

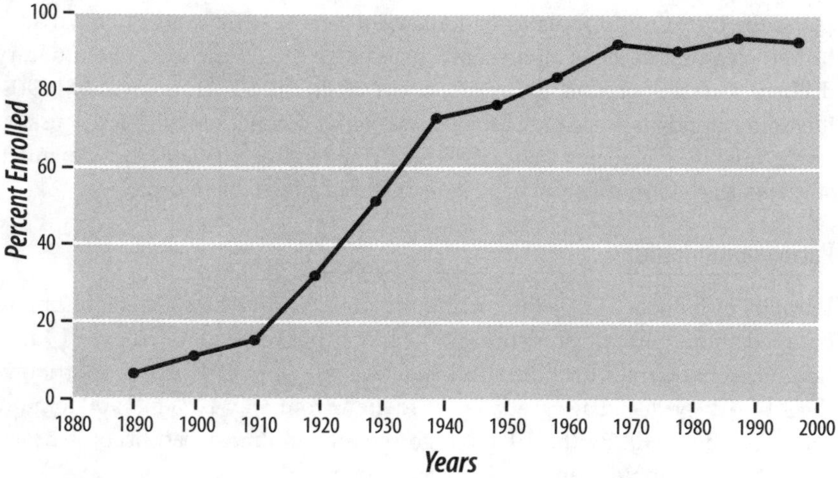

The data for Figure 3–1 are from the National Center for Education Statistics (1999), p. 69.

## Reading Achievement

After reviewing then-and-now reading studies, Farr, Tuinman, and Rowls (1974) concluded that each generation has been better-skilled than the last. They contended that "anyone who says that *he knows* that literacy is decreasing is...at best unscholarly and at worst dishonest" (p. 140). A subsequent study showed that Indiana students in 1976 outperformed those of 1944 to 1945 once age differences were accounted for. This suggested that, even in the trough of the modern decline, students were doing as well as those of a prior generation.

In the 1980s, Stedman and Kaestle updated this review and expanded it to functional and job literacy, trends on the National Assessment of Educational Progress (NAEP), and renorming studies (1991). The authors found that reading performance had been generally stable during the 20th century. Overall, more studies showed gains than declines, but the gains were small, usually half a year or less—well within the margin of errors in the studies. There is little hard evidence, therefore, that the increase of child-centered education or the supposed abandonment of phonics over the century harmed *national* reading achievement.

## Subject Matter Achievement

Then-and-now studies in nonreading areas uniformly showed that elementary school achievement was higher in the first decades of the 20th century than it had been in the 1840s to 1860s. These studies covered diverse areas such as arithmetic, spelling, grammar, geography, and history.

Trends within the 20th century were also positive but not as consistent. Elementary school students generally made progress in the 1920s through the 1940s, but had mixed performance in arithmetic and spelling. Secondary students generally maintained or improved achievement, although there was a major exception. Sligo (1955) found that Iowa high school students did more poorly in the mid-1950s in algebra, U.S. history, and English correctness than they had in the early 1930s. They performed comparably in science. The declines, however, were relatively modest, generally five to seven percentage points over 20 years, and the 1930s students had several advantages. The tests were then part of a statewide academic contest. The high schools coached directly for the tests and students grew familiar with the tests' content and unusual formats. The curricula also were better aligned with the tests. The 1930s English curriculum, for example, focused heavily on the skills on the English correctness test whereas the 1950s curriculum emphasized literature and speech skills. What is striking, though, is the poor performance in both periods. Even in the 1930s, students correctly answered only 24% of the algebra items, 33% of the English items, and slightly over 40% of the science and history items.

Other studies suggested improvement during the period (Stedman & Kaestle, 1991). A national renorming study of the General Educational Development (GED) examination showed that seniors (in predominately white public high schools) improved their achievement slightly between 1943 and 1955 in social studies, composition, natural science, literature, and math. Another study of 60 communities in seven states (about 230,000 students) showed gains of four months to two years in reading, math, and vocabulary from the late 1930s to the mid-1940s.

Whittington (1991) found that different generations of high school students had similar U.S. history knowledge from 1915 to 1986. Although one assessment of comparable questions had limitations (it involved only 43 items and combined results from earlier periods), the overall research was compelling because it used several different methods and national samples from the 1930s through the 1980s. Whittington concluded:

> The perception of a decline in the "results" of American education is open to question. Indeed, given the reduced dropout rate and less elitist composition of the 17-year-old student body today, one could argue that students today know more American history than did their age peers of the past. (p. 778)

## Adults' General Knowledge

Then-and-now studies of adults' general knowledge show similar patterns. Political scientists, who have repeated survey questions, have found that civics knowledge remained stable, though at modest levels, from the 1940s through the 1980s. World War II draftees, given a version of the Word War I Army Alpha test, showed a striking gain of 33%. The test covered general knowledge as well as number patterns, verbal analogies, and synonyms. Geography knowledge may have gotten worse, however. A Gallup study showed that adults could identify fewer European countries in 1988 than they could in 1947 (Stedman, 1993). No doubt, the recently-concluded Second World War helped to raise the 1947 scores.

Although any given period has limited evidence, much of the historical record suggests that student achievement has been roughly stable across the 20th century, at least into the 1970s. The transformation of the high school into a mass institution and the adoption of life-adjustment education apparently did not worsen academic achievement. Still, we must not overlook the low levels of achievement that repeatedly show up in national assessments, a serious problem discussed later in this chapter.

## Modern Achievement Trends: 1960s to the Present

In this section, I assess the claims that a decline of excellence began in the mid-1960s. First, I describe the quality of the modern achievement measures and review data from the National Assessment of Educational Progress (NAEP), our best barometer of contemporary trends. Next, I examine the leading evidence for a modern test score decline and its possible educational causes. I finish the section by examining racial and urban-rural achievement trends.

### Contemporary Achievement Measures

NAEP is our best measure because it tests nationally representative samples of students at ages 9, 13, and 17 every few years in the major academic areas. The tests involve authentic materials—real literature, newspaper articles, and poetry—and complex tasks such as explaining responses, interpreting graphs and tables, and evaluating passages. NAEP repeats items to establish trends.

This test has distinct advantages over the other indicators used in discussions of a national achievement decline such as Scholastic Aptitude Test (SAT) scores, test renormings, and state data. For example, the SAT gauges the performance of a self-selected, changing sample of college-bound students (mostly from the top half of their classes), not the typical student. It judges aptitude, not achievement. Students have to answer more than one question a minute (over 200 problems in three hours). Such rapid-fire processing of analogies and math conundrums is a poor way of judging our students' learning and thoughtfulness. Even the College Board has warned educators not to use the SAT to assess national educational quality.

Test renorming data are also limited. Publishers redesign tests roughly every seven years. So that districts can compare results, publishers conduct renorming studies in which samples of students are given both the new and old tests. Problems abound. The samples are usually not nationally representative—only a few districts are tested. Sometimes two different groups take the tests or only parts of the tests are given. Trends are confounded by district familiarity and teaching-to-the-test behavior. Publishers themselves have cautioned against using the data to infer national trends, citing changing samples and the changing relevance of content.

State trends are also subject to test familiarity problems and are not nationally representative. Data for the 1960s and 1970s were limited to a handful of states. Iowa was often used as a barometer, for example, but it is predominately rural and has few minority students.

## NAEP Achievement Trends

What does NAEP reveal about achievement trends? The general pattern is one of stability (Stedman, 1993, 1998). I start with literacy because it undergirds academic performance and is a perennial concern of educators. Both reading and writing have been remarkably level for several decades (Figure 3–2). Given the central role they play in learning and schoolwork, such constancy is important and directly contradicts assertions about a decline of literacy.

Students at all three ages also maintained their math performance over this past generation. Nine- and 13-year-olds even improved their math and science scores some during the 1980s, although their scores since then have been generally level.

Seventeen-year-olds' science and civics achievement, however, declined somewhat in the 1970s. The science decline amounted to about seven percentage points in 13 years, but performance has much recovered since 1982.

The evidence for a decline at the top is mixed. On the SAT, there was a drop in verbal scorers above 600 in the early 1970s (from 11% to 8%), but trends have been flat since. In contrast, the American College Tests (ACT) showed little change in top scorers over the past several decades, although there was a small drop in 1997 (National Center for Education Statistics, 1999, p. 152). The percentage of 17-year-olds achieving the highest level (350) on NAEP also has remained roughly stable.

There are other indications that performance has been level or improving. High school completion rates among young adults, including receiving the GED, have held steady in the 82% to 86% range for a generation. Math and science enrollments increased during the 1980s and 1990s (National Center for Education Statistics, 1999, p. 156). Given the major changes in school populations and societal conditions over the past generation, such stable trends on key

## Figure 3–2: Reading achievement, 1971–1999

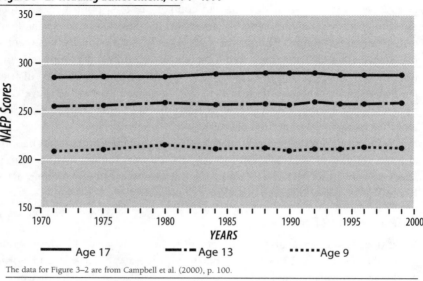

The data for Figure 3–2 are from Campbell et al. (2000), p. 100.

indicators represent an enormous school resilience, one that deserves greater recognition.

### A Great Test Score Decline?

The case for a major decline has rested on the less reliable measures of national trends: college entrance examinations, renormings, and state data. Although achievement was essentially stable in the 1960s, declines were pervasive on these indicators during the 1970s, at least at the high school level (Koretz, 1987; Stedman, 1998; Stedman & Kaestle, 1991). The decline in SAT scores has received the most publicity. A huge apparent decline occurred in SAT scores—verbal scores decreased over 50 points and math scores decreased over 30 points between the mid-1960s and 1980. The size of the declines has been expressed dramatically. Copperman (1979) argued that high school students of the late 1970s ranked at only the 39th percentile of their 1965 counterparts. On several tests, 11th and 12th graders lost an apparent year or more in achievement during the 1970s.

Such stark descriptions are problematic, however. Standardized tests are constructed in such a way that small shifts in performance can produce large changes in grade equivalents and percentiles. On the Science Research Associates test, for example, 12th graders dropped a full grade level in reading during the 1970s, but this was only from 72% to 68% correct, a four percentage point drop. Other tests showed similar or even smaller changes. Such declines do not seem that worrisome. Even the SAT decline was more modest than has been portrayed. Each question corresponds to about 10 points in the middle of the scale. The overall drop of about 50 verbal points was thus a loss of approximately five questions or about six to seven percentage points over 17 years.

Compositional changes also caused much of the decline. The SAT, for example, was originally normed in 1941 on about 11,000 mostly white, male, middle-class students headed to Ivy League colleges. As a result of expanded opportunities in the 1960s and 1970s, more minority, lower ability, and poor students now go to college. The pool broadened to students going to less selective universities and two-year colleges. Today, SATs are taken by over a million students, almost a third are minorities, a majority are women, and more have lower socioeconomic status and high-school rank.

Still, the SAT decline was not entirely compositional. The increase in minority students who are test takers cannot explain the large decline in *white* students' scores during the 1960s and 1970s. The most comprehensive analysis—by the College Board's special advisory panel (Wirtz, 1977)—suggested that up to 75% of the 1960s decline and up to 30% of the 1970s decline was due to demographic changes. If one adds age and birth order effects (younger students and siblings score lower), up to 50% of the 1970s decline may have been compositional. This suggests that the overall SAT raw score decline amounted to only a couple of questions or three to four percentage points.

Compositional changes also affected scores on the standardized tests given to the average high school student. Families were larger, there were more single-parent households, immigration from low-scoring groups increased, and fewer African American students dropped out. These factors likely explained as much as 30% to 50% of the secondary score decline (Koretz, 1987; Stedman & Kaestle, 1991).

We also should put the decline into its historical context and consider the contradictory evidence. Even after decreasing during the 1970s, scores on several major high school tests remained around or above early 1960s levels. When compared to the gains in educational attainment during the past generation, the decline seems less substantial. The population's median educational level increased two full years between 1960 and 1980. Between 1940 and 1980, it increased nearly four years, from 8.6 to 12.5 years of schooling. A decline of only a few percentage points or a half year (adjusting for compositional changes) appears modest compared with these impressive gains.

The evidence contradicting a decline in the 1970s was extensive. Secondary students gained five months to a year in reading and math comparisons of the Metropolitan and Stanford Achievement Tests. NAEP scores held steady in several areas, including reading. Seventeen-year-olds improved their functional literacy and several writing skills. Juniors and seniors raised their scores between 1973 and 1982 on the Stanford Achievement Test in reading, spelling, math, and science.

Those who cite the SATs rarely mention the College Board's achievement tests. During the worst decline in SAT scores, college-bound students made progress on six major tests: English composition, the three high school sciences (biology, chemistry, and physics), and the two major foreign languages (French and Spanish). Even though these students had lower verbal SAT scores than their predecessors, they still had higher achievement scores. Intriguingly, the *average* high school student did not lose ground on SAT skills. A short version, the Preliminary Scholastic Aptitude Test, given to nationally representative samples of juniors, showed that scores in the early 1980s matched those of the 1960s. ACT natural science scores also remained stable.

Finally, whatever declines occurred ended on most indicators some time in the late 1970s, and several scores had reversed themselves by the early 1980s. Composite scores on the Iowa Test of Basic Skills, for example, reached all-time highs by 1984, just a year after the *Nation at Risk* report (National Commission on Excellence in Education, 1983). Instead of a "rising tide of mediocrity," the report should have proclaimed a "rising tide of test scores." Our best evidence, therefore, suggests that there was only a modest decline in the 1970s and that, given the historical context and contradictory data, it was less troubling than depicted.

### Educational Causes and Consequences of the Decline

Many educators attributed the decline to the spread of open classrooms, the shopping mall high school, or a loss of respect for authority. Others blamed general social factors such as increased television watching, family breakdown, or a decline in the work ethic.

Such explanations may often seem convincing but do not account for the timing of the score declines, the variations in achievement by grade and subject, and the scores that improved. Several analysts found little evidence that these factors caused the decline. At the elementary school level, open education was never that widely adopted and students were not adversely affected—their achievement scores were generally stable; their reading scores even increased. At the high school level, the *Nation at Risk* authors (National Commission on Excellence in Education, 1983) argued the curriculum had become "homogenized, diluted, and diffused" (p. 18), although the nationally representative transcript data showed an increase, not a decrease, in academic course enrollments.

Two studies for the advisory panel on the SAT score decline suggested that it was not linked to school changes or innovation (appendix to Wirtz, 1977). One compared changes in high schools with stable SATs and high schools with declines worse than the nation's. Principals in the two sets of schools reported similar increases in discipline problems, pass-fail grading, and nontraditional offerings. English curricula and academic course enrollments were similar. The second study showed that SAT scores had declined similarly in traditional and experimental high schools.

Researchers have vigorously debated the consequences of the decline. Several economists argued it greatly worsened the nation's productivity, but their estimates mistakenly assumed a lengthy, deep decline and ignored the demographic changes in test takers. Researchers have found that test scores have little relation to job proficiency, so whatever declines occurred would not have had much economic impact. Indeed, even as more lower-scoring workers entered the workforce, labor productivity increased faster in the 1980s than at any time since World War II. Given the contradictory evidence, the decline was probably too limited to have had any significant lasting consequences.

## Racial and Urban-Rural Achievement Trends

Equal opportunity has been a persistent concern of U.S. educators. Unfortunately, racial and ethnic achievement gaps remain large. Although black students have made major strides in reading, course taking, and high school completion, recent NAEP assessments show that black high school juniors and seniors are performing at or below the level of white middle-schoolers in each academic area (Figure 3–3). Latino high school students are doing better than black students in math and science, but also generally lag three to four years behind white high school students.

The trends are striking. Black students gained much in the 1980s, but their progress generally slowed or ceased in the late 1980s and early 1990s. This pattern shows up across subject areas and ages. Reading trends are representative (Figure 3–4).

There is little cause for optimism in the data (Campbell et al., 2000, p. 39). In reading, the race-related achievement gaps at ages 13 and 17 are even larger than they were in 1988. Nine-year-old black students are as far behind white students as they were in 1980. In math, about a third of the gap was bridged during this past generation, but the gap remains large and has been increasing among older students in the 1990s. In science, the gaps are as large as they were in the early 1980s; they are even increasing for 17-year-olds. The concerns go well beyond the schools as a national report on the condition of black education makes clear:

> *Black children are at an educational disadvantage relative to white children for a number of reasons, including lower average levels of parental education, a greater likelihood of living with only one parent, fewer resources in their communities as a result of income-based residential segregation, and, especially, a greater likelihood of experiencing poverty. In*

## Figure 3–3: Racial gaps in achievement by subject, 1994–1999

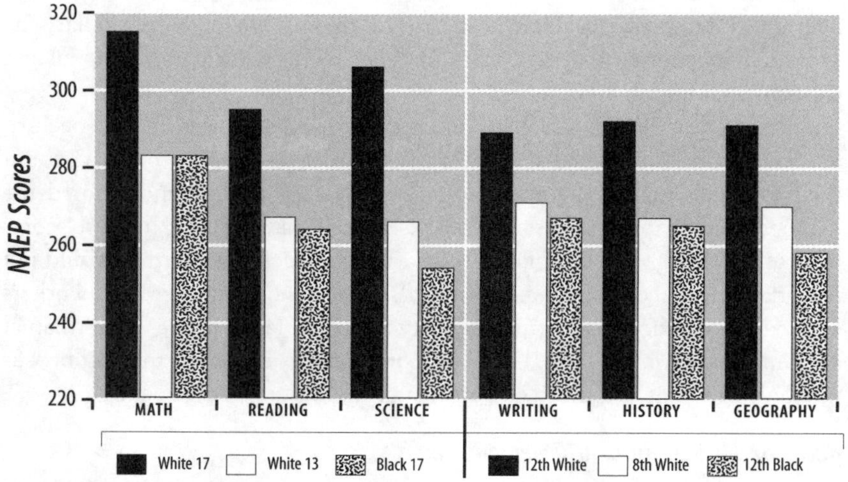

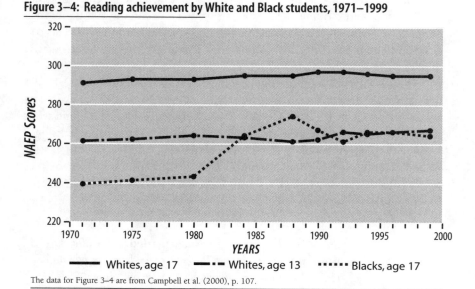

Math, reading, and science data for Figure 3–3 are for 13- and 17-year-olds in 1999. These data are from Campbell et al. (2000), pp. 107–109. Writing data are for 8th and 11th graders in 1996. History and geography data are for 8th and 12th graders in 1994. These data are from the National Center for Education Statistics (1999), pp. 136, 138.

## Figure 3–4: Reading achievement by White and Black students, 1971–1999

The data for Figure 3–4 are from Campbell et al. (2000), p. 107.

*1992, 46% of black children, as opposed to 16% of white children, lived in*
*a family with an income level below the poverty line.* (Smith, 1995, p. 1)

Latino students made even less progress than black students did during this
past generation (Campbell et al., 2000, pp. 40, 107–109). Like black students,
their progress generally came to a halt in the 1990s. In most cases, the white-
Latino gaps are as large as they were more than a decade ago. The most striking
exception is in science, in which 17-year-old Latino students have been improving fairly steadily, but even in that subject, younger students' scores have leveled
off and the gaps are similar to or worse than they were 15 to 20 years ago.

NAEP also has tracked achievement in urban and rural schools.
"Advantaged urban" schools were in major cities and suburbs in which many
parents were professionals and managers. "Disadvantaged urban" ones were in
metro areas in which a large fraction of parents were on welfare or were not regularly employed. "Extreme rural" schools were in communities of under
10,000 in which many parents were farmers or farm workers.

These definitions have proved problematic because they confounded geographical and occupational indicators and used principals' estimates. NAEP
eventually redefined the categories without regard to occupations, but did not
report such data in its 1999 trend report. Nevertheless, the earlier trend data
for 17-year-olds are revealing (Mullis et al., 1991). In each assessment, advantaged urban schools performed best, followed by extreme rural, and then disadvantaged urban schools. The achievement gaps among these schools generally grew smaller during the 1980s. Extreme rural schools, in particular, gained
on advantaged urban ones. In science, despite a national downturn, advantaged urban schools held their own (Figure 3–5). This may have been due to
better science teachers, resources, and equipment. Science achievement in disadvantaged urban schools paralleled national trends, with a substantial decline
followed by recovery.

Overall, advantaged and disadvantaged urban schools remain separated by
four or more years in achievement (Mullis et al., 1991). Although they have
made some gains, disadvantaged schools stopped improving in reading in 1988
and lagged as far behind in science as they did in the late 1970s. The conclusion is distressing but unavoidable. In most cases, the progress toward equal
educational opportunity has stalled.

## Persistent Achievement Problems

The brilliant success of U.S. schools—creating a mass system of education
without a general achievement decline—should not obscure a more fundamental problem: the persistent weak performance by students.

**Figure 3–5: Science achievement by 17-year-olds in schools in different communities, 1977–1990.**

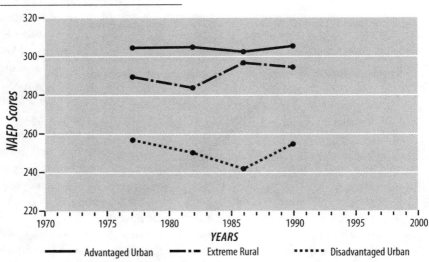

The data for Figure 3-5 are from Mullis et al. (1991), p. 227. The definition of community type changed after 1990, and the data were not included in the 1999 trend report.

## Contemporary Achievement Problems

Only about 50% of our high school students reach the 300 level in the NAEP assessments and very few—5% to 10%—reach the 350 level, the levels purportedly needed for higher education, business, and government (Campbell et al., 2000; Stedman, 1993). Performance has also fallen short on three new levels used in the 1990s: basic, proficient, and advanced (Table 3–1). Senior data provide the best overall gauge of K-12 performance. Although a growing percentage of students has achieved proficiency in reading, now up to 40%, approximately 25% still remain below the basic level and only 6% have reached the advanced level. Writing performance is substantially poorer, with fewer than 25% of students having achieved proficiency. In math, few students achieved proficiency, whereas almost a third failed to reach the basic level, which reflects only *partial* mastery of fundamentals. Students also struggled in civics and geography. Performance was poorest in history. Over half the seniors scored below the basic level. These data indicate a serious educational problem.

The validity of these levels has been questioned, however. Their predictive validity is undetermined—the connection to future academic and economic success is likely more tenuous than claimed in NAEP reports. The original 300 and 350 levels were arbitrarily set at one and two standard deviations above the mean, which initially predetermined that only a small percentage would reach the 350 level. A 1992 General Accounting Office report questioned the relia-

## Table 3–1: 12th-grade achievement on NAEP, 1994–1998
### (Percentage at given levels)

| SUBJECT | YEAR | BELOW BASIC | AT BASIC | PROFICIENT OR BETTER | ADVANCED OR BETTER |
|---|---|---|---|---|---|
| Reading | 1998 | 23 | 37 | 40 | 6 |
| Writing | 1998 | 22 | 56 | 22 | 1 |
| Math | 1996 | 31 | 53 | 16 | 2 |
| Civics | 1998 | 35 | 39 | 26 | 4 |
| Geography | 1994 | 30 | 43 | 27 | 2 |
| History | 1994 | 57 | 32 | 11 | 1 |

"Proficient or better" includes students at the "advanced or better" level. "At basic" calculated from "Below basic" and "Proficient or better." The reading data are from Donahue et al. (1999), p. 20; the writing data are from by Greenwald et al. (1999), p. 25; the math data are from Reese et al. (1997), p. 47; the civics data are from the National Center for Education Statistics (1998), p. 8; and the geography and history data are from the National Center for Education Statistics (1999), pp. 137–138. Science data were not included because these levels did not appear in the 1996 science report.

bility of the new levels. The extent of these problems, however, has been vigorously disputed. Both the Commissioner of the National Center for Education Statistics and NAEP's governing board believe the levels are "useful and valuable" in reporting achievement (Reese et al., 1997, p. 8).

There are good reasons for taking NAEP findings seriously. It is troubling that few students do well when the problems defining the upper levels are not that difficult. The problems at the 350 level in math include routine fractions and percentages, whereas many in history require nothing more than recognition of basic information. The percentage of students at the top level, though limited at first, has not grown for several decades. Finally, item reviews have avoided many scaling problems and confirmed serious achievement problems in each subject (Stedman, 1993, 1996). In what follows, I review findings in the major areas.

### Math, History, and Geography

Math educators have reported "superficial learning" and "major deficiencies" at all ages. High school juniors and seniors struggle with material they covered in seventh- and eighth-grade general math courses—simple algebra and basic math such as estimations, finding area, and percentages.

Many of these students do not know elementary yet important information from U.S. history courses such as the purpose of the Monroe doctrine, the names of leading muckrakers, or that the Scopes trial dealt with evolution. In the 1994 assessment, fewer than half realized that preventing the spread of communism dominated U.S. foreign policy in the postwar period, recognized the Camp David accords, or could date a newspaper report about the Civil War destruction of Charleston. In the late 1980s, the vast majority of high school students did not know that Jim Crow laws segregated blacks; many were unaware of *Plessy v. Ferguson* and *Brown v. Board of Education.*

Their geographical knowledge is also limited, as NAEP studies in the late 1980s and 1990s showed. Many seniors—over a third—had trouble with the concepts of latitude and longitude. Most could not interpret a graph of birth and death rates. Given our country's Vietnam experience, it is unsettling that almost two-thirds could not locate Southeast Asia on a world map. About two-thirds did not know where Saudi Arabia was. Most students had trouble identifying the Pyrenees, Japan, the Mediterranean, and the Persian Gulf. Fewer than half knew slavery was a major reason many Caribbean people are of West African descent. These are disturbing findings for an increasingly diverse, multicultural society.

The problems show up beyond the K-12 level. In 1988, a Gallup assessment of college seniors found "significant gaps" in history and literature knowledge. A majority could not identify the Federalist Papers, the Missouri Compromise, Reconstruction, or major works by Shakespeare and Jane Austen. They also did not know the authors Ralph Ellison and Richard Wright, nor were they familiar with Martin Luther King's "Letter from the Birmingham Jail." Another Gallup survey showed that U.S. adults ages 18 and older could identify only four countries in Europe, three in South America, and fewer than 6 of 10 U.S. states.

## *Literacy*

Although literacy has not declined, it too remains at low levels. Many students lack critical reading skills and are not well read. They are unfamiliar with major women and African American writers and with classics by Shakespeare, Joseph Conrad, and Walt Whitman. NAEP's writing assessments have provided some of the clearest evidence because they use criterion-referenced scoring as well as scaling. Few students have done well. In 1990, most persuasive papers by 17-year-olds were rated unsatisfactory or minimal; informative writing was better, but many papers were still inadequate (Mullis et al., 1991). In 1998, only about a quarter of the 12th grade students tested achieved the top two marks, whereas younger students did substantially worse (Greenwald et al., 1999, p. 132). In 1992, the first national assessment of classroom portfolios showed that even our students' best writing—done with consultation, revision, and choice of topics—is not that good. Only 4% to 12% of the eighth graders' papers achieved high marks (5 or 6) on the six-category scale. One-fourth to almost half received low marks (1 or 2), differing by informative and narrative tasks.

Three decades of national studies have revealed serious adult literacy problems (Stedman & Kaestle, 1991). Much of the population—from 15% to 30%—has trouble reading common materials such as news articles, maps, report cards, tax tables, and medicine directions. Although minorities, the elderly, and those without a high school diploma are the most severely affected, the problem is general. A national assessment in the early 1990s showed that 16% to 20% of the nation's high school *graduates* struggle with everyday materials; 14% to 16% of whites also fell in the lowest level.

A highly technical debate has flourished about the validity of such findings, yet few researchers deny that millions of adults are seriously hampered by literacy problems. Such semiliterate adults need special assistance, but it is too late for K-12 school reforms to help them. In *Illiterate America*, Kozol (1985) called for a national literacy corps to empower these adults educationally and politically.

## Perspectives on Low Achievement

It is easy to be critical of 17-year-olds' current lack of knowledge. Many of us acquired much of our knowledge after high school—reading biographies, traveling, taking college courses, and following the news. Still, the material we are talking about is basic. Most people would reasonably expect high school seniors to have mastered seventh-grade math and basic social studies information, but they have not.

To be sure, there have been bright spots. High school students know elementary math operations such as addition and how to read a line graph. Most are competent with basic writing mechanics—spelling, grammar, and punctuation—and so additional whole-class drill is considered unnecessary. They are familiar with some major documents from U.S. history and with major countries such as Canada and Germany. Outright illiteracy is rare. But, on the whole, achievement is at troubling low levels.

Student motivation to do well may be a factor. If the NAEP tests were high stakes, performance probably would be better, but placing NAEP items into moderate-stakes settings—such as the Georgia assessment program—has not changed the results. Compared to the marathon performance required on the SATs, the NAEP testing burden is light, only 45 to 50 minutes.

Achievement also may be worse than the data imply. The NAEP results do not include dropouts who presumably would score lower. To reach a given level, students only had to answer correctly 65% to 80% of its problems—a low standard of competence. NAEP is increasingly using performance assessment—the science test now includes drawing, writing, and open-ended questions. Students, however, often do even worse on open-ended items. In 1992, reading performance declined markedly on such items—from around two-thirds correct on multiple-choice problems to a third or less on extended response questions. This suggests that as we probe students' understanding, we are likely to find that achievement is even poorer than we thought. Although the evidence should be interpreted cautiously, it seems reasonable to conclude that much of the curriculum is not being learned.

## Achievement Problems, 1940s–1960s

Examining knowledge levels in the pre-1965 period provides a historical perspective on the contemporary decline of the standards argument. How much was learned at a time when many feel our schools focused on excellence, the traditional canon was solidly in place (before the supposed distractions of multiculturalism), the atmosphere more disciplined, textbooks demanding, grades not yet inflated, and students more select?

The first international assessment, given in 1964, provides some answers. It tested seniors in 12 developed countries who were taking college-preparatory math (Husén, 1967). In the United States, this was an exclusive club of 18%. Even though they had attended school from 1953 to 1964, a supposed heyday of U.S. education, they performed poorly—under 20% correct and last by a large margin. Our 13-year-olds also did poorly, ranking next to last, at only about half the level of top-ranking Japan. Neither our college-bound or average students were apparently learning math very well in the 1950s and early 1960s.

In 1960, Project TALENT studied a national sample of over 400,000 high school students. Researchers tested students' ability to read leading periodicals and novelists (Flanagan, 1962). Twelfth graders averaged 78% on passages from film magazines such as *Silver Screen* and 67% on writings from Louisa May Alcott, but performance dropped off rapidly. Material from *Time* was understood at only 35%; *Atlantic Monthly and Saturday Review* at only 28%. Passages from Jules Verne garnered 45% correct, Joseph Conrad 40%, and Jane Austen 33%. The typical senior knew little about art and the Constitution. Only half knew who painted the Mona Lisa; only about a sixth knew what "double-jeopardy" or "indictment" mean. Students did know popular culture information such as what the acronym 'UFO' signifies and the opening words to the national anthem (75%).

National polling in the 1950s and 1960s suggests that general knowledge has been weak for decades. In the late 1950s, high school graduates, ages 25 to 36, averaged only 65% correct on public figures and events, history, humanities, geography, and science. There were surprising gaps. In politics, only about a third knew their member of Congress; fewer than half which party controlled Congress. In foreign affairs, only about a third knew Adenauer and about half Nehru. In literature and art, only 8% knew Rubens was a painter, only one in five knew who composed "The Messiah," and only 37% knew who wrote *A Midsummer Night's Dream*. In geography, only about half knew Montana bordered Canada or that Mt. Everest was the highest mountain.

The problem with historical knowledge goes back at least half a century (Stedman, 1993). In the midst of World War II, *The New York Times* surveyed 7,000 first-year students in 36 colleges and found a "striking ignorance of even the most elementary aspects of United States history" ("Ignorance of U.S.

History," 1943, p. 1). Even though these students were an elite—college attendance remained relatively rare until the mid-1960s (see data in Snyder & Shafer, 1996, p. 70)—they knew "almost nothing about many important phases of this country's growth and development" ("Ignorance of U.S. History," 1943, p. 1). Only 16% could name two contributions by Thomas Jefferson. Only 20% could name two figures connected with trusts, and only 13% knew James Madison was president during the War of 1812.

These findings were startling and produced congressional calls for an investigation of the nation's schools. In 1944, the independent Committee on American History in Schools and Colleges found that high school seniors were also doing poorly, answering correctly only about a third of the items.

The geography problem likewise is not recent. Although a then-and-now study showed adults knew more in the 1940s than in the 1980s, performance was weak then. Although it was just after World War II, respondents could locate only half the European countries asked for. Geography knowledge was also poor on the 1943 *Times* survey of first-year college students.

### Pre–World War II Achievement Problems

The record of low achievement dates to the earliest years of the 20th century, well before the life-adjustment education movement of the 1950s, and even before the curricular changes of the 1920s and 1930s. Performance was poor even during the years when a highly select minority attended high school and college. This suggests that the achievement problems have historical and structural roots and were not caused by contemporary changes in school standards or the historical transformation of the high school into a mass institution. Here are several snapshots of the historical evidence:

- About half the students failed their college board examinations in the first two decades of the century and this was with a low standard—a score of only 60 out of 100. About two-thirds failed their history examinations during the 1910s. These much vaunted "essay" examinations required only short paragraph answers; specimen papers suggest grading was not excessively tough.

- In World War I, a large national group of literate white draftees scored only 32% correct on the Army Alpha test of historical, literary, scientific, and popular culture information.

- High school students routinely did poorly on the early standardized tests in history, geography, and civics during the 1910s and 1920s (for history, see Whittington, 1991). These were often curriculum- and textbook-based and designed to measure how much was learned, not to force scores into a bell-shaped curve.

- As part of a 1923 to 1924 inquiry, the American Historical Association tested students in 36 high schools in six states. It found that the typical junior or senior who had completed a history/civics course averaged only around 40% correct (55% on traditional material).

- A large-scale 1928 to 1932 longitudinal study in Pennsylvania showed that high school and college performance was poor (Learned & Wood, 1938). High school seniors averaged only 23% correct in algebra and 34% in U.S. history. College students performed best in English basics (55% to 60%), but did poorly in math, literature, and general culture (science, fine arts, and history), averaging a third correct or less.

It was widely recognized at the time, by testing supporters and critics alike, that students simply were not learning fundamental information. The poor results helped galvanize the push for progressive education because they demonstrated that traditional education, with its emphasis on facts and memorization, was not succeeding.

## Summary of Trends and Implications for Reform

Looking across the 20th century, one finds a pattern of persistent failure. Although U.S. schools succeeded in becoming a modern, mass institution, they have yet to develop high-achieving, well-informed students and citizens generally. Students struggle in the major academic areas and lack important political knowledge and literacy skills. In a society torn by debates over affirmative action, it is alarming how poorly informed our students are about our country's tortured racial history. A complex, democratic society needs a well-read and knowledgeable citizenry, yet we are far from accomplishing this.

For too long, the educational debate has focused on whether achievement has been declining. Although there were some minor downturns in the 1970s, achievement and general knowledge have remained at roughly the same low levels for most of the 20th century. There is little in the record that would lead to projecting different results for the future. Even in the few areas in which scores improved, such as in math, progress has slowed. At current rates, it will take another generation before all seniors reach the basic math level and until the year 2132 before even half achieve proficiency (Stedman, 1998). Despite some gains in the 1980s, black and Latino students and disadvantaged urban schools remain far behind academically. The real issue, therefore, is not the decline of excellence, but the historical lack of excellence.

Fifty or more years of low achievement implicates the traditional teaching practices and the bureaucratic school structures that have dominated education for much of the 20th century. Tweaking the system at the margins or trying to return to a supposed golden age of education is not likely to be successful. In the 1980s, the major reform reports exaggerated the decline and called for a return to old-fashioned standards and practices. Yet back-to-basics policies have not restored academic quality. Math educators attribute students' poor problem-solving skills to an overemphasis on computation. Reading specialists worry that the basal-reader approach has neglected real literature and contributed to aliteracy—people who know how to read but do not. Our students' poor performance in the pre-decline, pre-1965 period suggests that simply restoring old standards (credits, homework, and examinations) will not be enough; we need fresh approaches to teaching and school organization.

To be successful, reform will have to transform the deep structure of schooling that has sustained low achievement: hierarchical bureaucratic organization, tracked programs, and the historic pattern of assembly-line curriculum and teaching. Reformers increasingly point out that schools are organized more for administrative convenience than for learning—obsessively concerned with testing, classifying, and tracking students. Madcap 40-minute periods and excessive teacher workloads—120 to 140 students in high schools—sustain dull, mechanized teaching. NAEP surveys show that our teaching has been textbook- and test-driven and dominated by chalk-and-talk methods for decades. We rarely find small group work, extended projects, or lengthy research and writing assignments. The Third International Math and Science Study showed that the United States has a fragmented curriculum and shallow teaching. Over the past decade, thought-provoking profiles have portrayed a system in crisis. Particularly in high schools, students are often disengaged, teachers' work factory-like, and intellectual life poor.

If we continue organizing schools and teaching the same way, we will get the same poor results. If we want students to read widely on their own and take an active interest in learning, then we must captivate them and not just command them. To reach students personally, educators will have to break down large-scale, impersonal bureaucratic schools. Simply raising external standards will be insufficient. In fact, the current push for high-stakes testing and state and national outcome standards, although it may superficially raise some test scores, is likely to exacerbate the problems. The movement ignores the underlying structure of schooling, narrows the curriculum to what is tested, and gives short shrift to the importance of creating opportunity-to-learn standards, engaging students, and ensuring equitable school funding.

In his *In the Name of Excellence,* Toch (1991) documents how schools and districts have put on the trappings of higher standards, but have not fundamentally changed the conditions of learning or the relationships among students, teachers, and administrators. He looks across several decades of reform and reminds us of the importance of humanizing our institutions. He writes:

*Though the excellence movement was in part spawned by the excesses of the 1960s educational philosophy, the observations that led reformers of two decades ago to their radical prescriptions are still valid and remain largely unaddressed...their criticisms that the public schools were repressive, impersonal places that promoted conformity at the expense of personal expression and rendered learning boring and lifeless were and remain essentially accurate.* (p. 272)

Toch (1991) concludes that we now need to blend the 1960s reformers' call to humanize the schools with contemporary reformers' push for rigorous standards. Such an approach would be more likely to develop reflective, well-informed students than current practice does. There has been a common call across the educational and political spectrum to develop an engaging and challenging academic curriculum, end tracking, and emphasize writing. Conservative as well as progressive educators have decried the pernicious effects of skills-based multiple-choice testing. The advocates for intellectually demanding programs include such diverse educators as Chall, Jencks, Ravitch, Shanker, and Sizer.

The achievement problem, however, represents only part of the picture. Reformers worry about other issues as well. Is the school environment safe and supportive? Are students developing healthy attitudes and being prepared well for democracy? Do they have a sense of ethics, activism, and social responsibility? These may seem like quaint notions, but reform should not be a mere quest for higher test scores.

The most promising approach is that of the Coalition of Essential Schools—a national network of restructuring high schools whose principles Sizer (1984) describes in *Horace's Compromise* and subsequent books. These schools emphasize standards, knowledge, and excellence, but do so through personalization, coaching, and exhibitions of mastery.

The educational crisis, however, originates deep within the society. It is not solely the schools' fault nor can it be solely the schools' responsibility to fix. We must make our educational efforts part of a broader social and political agenda, one that challenges the vested interests that care more about profits and coarse entertainment than nurturing learning and the welfare of communities. Families and students need to resist the commercial onslaught and reorder their priorities. Reading books, being involved with the community and hands-on projects, and doing schoolwork should take precedence over MTV, video games, and aimless Internet surfing. We must fight the economic stresses and displacements that disrupt family life, produce violence, and undermine student development. We need new state and federal initiatives to address the large, lingering socioeconomic inequalities and racial and urban achievement gaps. We have to dismantle powerful, entrenched bureaucracies and overhaul school-financing systems that underfund education and shortchange poorer communities. In short, only if we combine deep social reform with systematic school change can we hope to achieve a truly successful mass educational system in the 21st century.

## Author's Note

Achievement evidence is reviewed by Berliner and Biddle (1995), Bracey (1991), Farr et al. (1974), Koretz (1987), Ravitch (1995), Stedman and Kaestle (1991), and Stedman (1993, 1996, 1998). The October 1996 issue of *Research in the Teaching of English* presented a collection of articles by authors with different perspectives on literacy trends. Then-and-now studies are reviewed by Farr et al. (1974), Sligo (1955), and Stedman and Kaestle (1991).

Part of this research was funded by a National Academy of Education Spencer Foundation postdoctoral fellowship. Much thanks to my talented and hardworking graduate assistants: Debra Dushko, Joshua Glantz, Lisa Higgins, Christopher Lopez, Tama Mann, Kelly O'Sullivan, Lisa Schrot, and Eileen Spardutti.

## References

Berliner, D., & Biddle, B. (1995). *The manufactured crisis: Myths, fraud, and the attack on America's public schools.* New York: Addison-Wesley.

Bestor, A. (1985). *Educational wastelands: The retreat from learning in our public schools* (2nd ed.). Chicago: University of Illinois Press.

Bracey, G. (1991). Why can't they be like we were? *Phi Delta Kappan, 73,* 105–117.

Campbell, J., Hombo, C., & Mazzeo, J. (2000). *NAEP 1999 trends in academic progress: Three decades of student performance.* Washington, DC: U.S. Department of Education.

Commission on the Reorganization of Secondary Education. (1918). *Cardinal principles of secondary education* (Bulletin No. 35). Washington, DC: U.S. Bureau of Education.

Copperman, P. (1979). The achievement decline of the 1970s. *Phi Delta Kappan, 60,* 736–739.

Donahue, P., Voelkl, K., Campbell, J., & Mazzeo, J. (1999). *NAEP 1998 reading report card for the nation and the states.* Washington, DC: U.S. Department of Education.

Farr, R., Tuinman, J., & Rowls, M. (1974). *Reading achievement in the United States: Then and now* (ERIC Document Reproduction No. ED 109 595). Bloomington, IN: Indiana University.

Flanagan, J. (1962). Maximizing human talents. *Journal of Teacher Education, 13,* 209–215.

Flesch, R. (1981). *Why Johnny still can't read: A new look at the scandal of our schools.* New York: Harper & Row.

Greenwald, E., Persky, H., Campbell, J., & Mazzeo, J. (1999). *NAEP 1998 writing report card for the nation and the states.* Washington, DC: U.S. Department of Education.

Hirsch, E. D. (1987). *Cultural literacy.* Boston: Houghton Mifflin Company.

Husén, T. (Ed.). (1967). *International study of achievement in mathematics: A comparison of twelve countries* (Vol. 2). New York: John Wiley & Sons.

Ignorance of U.S. history shown by college freshmen. (1943, April 4). *The New York Times,* p. 1.

Itzkoff, S. (1994). *The decline of intelligence in America: A strategy for national renewal.* Westport, CT: Praeger.

Koretz, D. (1987). *Educational achievement: Explanations and implications of recent trends.* Washington, DC: Congressional Budget Office.

Kozol, J. (1985). *Illiterate America.* New York: Anchor Press, Doubleday.

Learned, W., & Wood, B. (1938). *The student and his knowledge.* New York: The Carnegie Foundation for the Advancement of Teaching.

Mullis, I., Dossey, J., Foertsch, M., Jones, L., & Gentile, C. (1991). *Trends in academic progress* (ERIC Document Reproduction Service No. ED 338 720). Washington, DC: U.S. Government Printing Office.

National Center for Education Statistics. (1998). *NAEP 1998 civics report card highlights.* Washington, DC: U.S. Department of Education.

National Center for Education Statistics. (1999). *Digest of education statistics 1999.* Washington, DC: U.S. Department of Education.

National Commission on Excellence in Education. (1983). *A nation at risk.* Washington, DC: U.S. Government Printing Office.

National Council of Teachers of English. (1996). *Standards for the English language arts.* Urbana, IL: Author.

Ravitch, D. (1995). *National standards in American education: A citizen's guide.* Washington, DC: The Brookings Institution.

Reese, C., Miller, K., Mazzeo, J., & Dossey, J. (1997). *NAEP 1996 mathematics report card for the nation and the states.* Washington, DC: U.S. Department of Education.

Sizer, T. (1984). *Horace's compromise.* Boston: Houghton Mifflin.

Sligo, J. (1955). *Comparison of achievement in selected high school subjects in 1934 and 1954.* Unpublished doctoral dissertation, State University of Iowa.

Smith, T. (1995). *The educational progress of black students.* Washington, DC: U.S. Department of Education.

Snyder, T., & Shafer, L. (1996). *Youth indicators 1996.* Washington, DC: U.S. Department of Education.

Stedman, L. (1993). The condition of education: Why school reformers are on the right track. *Phi Delta Kappan, 75,* 215–225.

Stedman, L. (1996). Respecting the evidence: The achievement crisis remains real. *Education Policy Analysis Archives, 4.* http://epaa.asu.edu/v4n7.html. Retrieved March 15, 2000.

Stedman, L. (1998). An assessment of the contemporary debate over U.S. achievement. In D. Ravitch (Ed.), *Brookings papers on education policy: 1998,* (pp. 53-121). Washington, DC: The Brookings Institution.

Stedman, L., & Kaestle, C. (1991). Literacy and reading performance in the United States from 1880 to the present. In C. Kaestle, H. Damon-Moore, L. Stedman, K. Tinsley, & W. Trollinger (Eds.), *Literacy in the United States* (pp. 75–128). New Haven: Yale University Press.

Toch, T. (1991). *In the name of excellence: The struggle to reform the nation's schools, why it's failing, and what should be done.* New York: Oxford University Press.

Whittington, D. (1991). What have 17-year-olds known in the past? *American Educational Research Journal, 28,* 759–780.

Wirtz, W. (1977). *On further examination.* Report of the Advisory Panel on the Scholastic Aptitude Test Score Decline. New York: College Board.

# FOUR

# Tobacco, Alcohol, and Other Drug Use in Adolescence: Modern-Day Epidemics

*Lloyd D. Johnston and Patrick M. O'Malley*

## Background and Introduction

Psychoactive substance use has existed in human societies throughout the millennia. Opium was used in Asia Minor as early as 5000 B.C.; cannabis was brewed in a tea in ancient China; coca leaves have been chewed in South America for centuries; and some Native American populations have a long tradition of using peyote in religious rituals (Maisto et al., 1991). With the exception of alcohol, early use often was medicinal or religious in nature. During the 20th century, advances in pharmacology dramatically increased the purity of the naturally occurring pharmacopoeia and added many new substances through the development of synthetic chemical compounds, most of which were developed originally for medicinal purposes.

Whereas the use of psychoactive substances has a long history, illicit drug use as a major social problem has been more recent, beginning around the 16th century, and certainly it has reached new heights in the second half of the 20th century. The extent and nature of the social problems vary across time and across cultures as a function of

- the particular drugs being used to alter mood and consciousness,
- the segments of the population who use them,
- how many individuals use them, and
- the situations and reasons for which they are used.

Many factors can cause changes in the patterns of use over time, including

- the extent to which people are aware of the psychoactive potential of various substances,
- the proportion of the population that has access to the substances,
- the role of substances in social rituals,

- the norms and laws in the society regarding the use of each substance,
- willingness in the population (or in particular segments) to violate predominant laws and norms about use,
- beliefs about the benefits and hazards associated with use, and
- other social connotations of use (Johnston, 1991).

The legal status of a particular drug has a major impact on what forces can be brought to bear on use. When the manufacture and sale of a substance is legal, advertising, promotion, and an industry's ability to lobby for favorable policies (and against unfavorable policies) can become powerful factors. Even when a drug is illegal, marketing forces can be brought to bear; however, in this case the options are more limited, and "lobbying" may take the form of illegal bribes of government officials.

Presently, the prevalence of use of legal and illegal drugs varies widely among nations, with the United States having one of the highest rates of illicit drug use in the world, particularly among its adolescents and young adults. The situation is not static, however; considerable change occurs over time in the levels of use in many countries, and in the United States in particular (Johnston, et al., 1998a, 1998b; Substance Abuse and Mental Health Services Administration [SAMHSA], 1998).

## Differentiating Licitly and Illicitly Used Drugs

Drugs, whether natural or synthetic, are inherently neither good nor evil. They acquire particular connotations as a result of various factors, including the extent to which they are seen to be addictive or otherwise damaging to the user and to others in society. Religious prohibitions, such as those in the Islamic and Mormon religions, also can play an important role in attaching meaning to drug use.

In the United States, drugs are regulated under the Comprehensive Drug Abuse Prevention and Control Act of 1970. A drug is placed in one of five schedules, depending on its potential for abuse and its potential medical uses. Drugs with high potential for abuse and no legitimate medical use are placed in Schedule I; marijuana, LSD, other hallucinogenic drugs, and heroin are examples. It is illegal to manufacture, distribute, or possess these substances. Drugs with high abuse potential, but with some legitimate medical uses, are placed in Schedule II; amphetamines, cocaine, morphine, methadone, and some barbiturates are examples. Other schedules include substances with less potential for abuse and some legitimate medical uses; these include tranquilizers, sedatives, and some barbiturates. There is considerable standardization across countries in the classification of these drugs as a result of various international treaties ratified during the 20th century.

The availability of the drugs on Schedules II through V is controlled through the use of physicians' prescriptions, with more stringent requirements ordered according to the schedule (lower numbers require more stringent procedures). Although this control system can be quite rigorous, a number of these controlled substances can be diverted into the illegal market in this country; moreover, in many other countries (particularly developing countries) the controls are often very weak to begin with.

Inhalants are a class of substances that are not specifically dealt with under the controlled substances act, but they are sometimes used for psychoactive purposes. Young adolescents, in particular, use them largely because they are readily available, cheap, and legal to buy and possess. They include such things as glues, aerosols, butane, gasoline, nitrous oxide, and various solvents.

Currently, the legal status of psychoactive substances and their actual public health impact are in serious misalignment; for example, the least controlled—tobacco—incurs one of the highest rates of morbidity and mortality. It is estimated that approximately one-third of all regular smokers will die prematurely from the use of that substance and an even higher proportion will become seriously ill. Such misalignment in large part can be explained by historical accident: The use of cigarettes became widespread before the health consequences were fully recognized. Because a significant proportion of the population was already using (and addicted) by the time the health consequences were fully understood, prohibition was no longer a viable alternative from either a political or an efficacious public policy perspective. Furthermore, the perception that the attempt at alcohol prohibition early in the 20th century was a policy failure has discouraged any such similar steps for tobacco. Because of the increased recognition of the severe health effects of tobacco, however, social norms against use have strengthened considerably and legal restrictions on use have grown. It is estimated that currently nearly 500,000 U.S. citizens die prematurely each year as a result of tobacco use and that between 100,000 and 200,000 die from factors related to alcohol use.

## Interconnections with Other Deviant Behaviors

At the individual level, there is a fairly strong association between drug use of all kinds and other problem behaviors addressed in this volume, such as truancy, interpersonal aggression, property crime, and precocious sexual behavior. In general, when a new illicit drug becomes available or popular, such as crack cocaine in the mid-1980s, it is the more deviance-prone individuals in the population who are most at risk of initiating use of the drug.

Because of this strong association, some have suggested that the increase in illicit drug use among youth in the latter half of the 20th century was a reflection of a more general increase in overall delinquency. However, empirical data from the Monitoring the Future Study refute this notion: Aggregate measures of nondrug delinquent behaviors among high school seniors showed no covariation over time with illicit drug use in the last two decades (Johnston et al. 1998a).

### Interconnections Among the Different Drugs

There is a high degree of positive association in the use of nearly all of the psychoactive drugs, whether legal or controlled. Even the use of over-the-counter drugs such as stay-awake pills, diet pills, and sleeping aids is correlated with the use of other drugs. Some of this correlation can be explained by an underlying deviance proneness as a common cause of many of these behaviors. Another possible explanation is that there could be a general proneness to use chemicals to alter mood, regardless of their legal or normative status in the society—a proneness that may be biological or psychological or both.

We know from our own studies of U.S. adolescents that although usage rates for the various substances at any given time tend to be positively correlated, they do not necessarily covary across time. Indeed, tobacco, alcohol, marijuana, inhalants, tranquilizers, and cocaine, as well as certain other drugs, have all shown very different trends from one another over the past 20 years. Although there may be some common determinants to trends in the use of a number of drugs, there also are some very important influences—such as attitudes and beliefs—that are specific to individual classes of drugs, which drive the trends in their use.

There also tends to be a sequential pattern of involvement in use of the various drugs. Most youngsters who initiate marijuana use previously have used cigarettes or alcohol or both. And most youngsters who use any of the other controlled or illegal drugs previously have used marijuana (Kandel et al., 1992). This sequential orderliness to young people's involvement with drugs no doubt reflects in part a natural tendency to venture into dangerous territory gradually—beginning with the drugs that are seen as least socially disapproved and least dangerous to use. Some researchers have argued that the impressive degree of sequential association also reflects a causal role for each stage in the sequence, a view sometimes described as the "stepping stone theory." Thus, the fact that cigarette smokers are so much more likely to try marijuana than nonsmokers may be the result of some causal connection; for example, a cigarette smoker may have learned how to ingest marijuana (which also is smoked), or the cigarette smoker may have been reinforced for inhaling smoke, or the smoker's brain may have been altered in a way that smoking marijuana can be more reinforcing. More research will be needed to test these hypotheses.

### The Importance of Adolescence

Although certain patterns of drug use may be more prevalent in adulthood, in recent decades use has been very high among U.S. adolescents. Furthermore, for a number of drugs, the majority of people who are ever going to initiate use do so in adolescence. This is particularly true for the legal drugs, alcohol and cigarettes. In the 1990s, the lifetime prevalence for having tried alcohol by the senior year in high school averaged around 85% of all students, and for cigarettes the comparable number was about 63% (Johnston et al., 1998a).

Most of the controlled substances and illegal drugs show high rates of initiation in adolescence. In the case of marijuana, for example, a follow-up survey of high school seniors in the classes of 1977 to 1979 showed that 56% of them had started marijuana use in adolescence, and "only" 21% more had done so by age 32 (Johnston & O'Malley, 1997). Because of the sequential nature of drug involvement, it is clear that nearly all of those who will eventually become involved in using the most dangerous drugs—such as heroin and crack cocaine—already have begun their pattern of involvement with the drugs that come earlier in the sequence by the time they leave adolescence.

## Societal Conditions of Relevance to Drug Use

Why U.S. young people have such high levels of illicit drug use compared with adolescents in most other countries is an often-asked question. Our answers are several and remain conjectural rather than established facts.

### Affluence

One factor is that the relatively great affluence of the United States allows many to afford drugs, providing drug producers with an enormous market. For example, the majority of the world's cocaine, virtually none of which is produced in the United States, is consumed in North America. This large market for drugs has provided newer generations of U.S. young people with access to, and awareness of, the many psychoactive substances being used. Those who grew up in the 1940s and 1950s, for example, had far less access to and awareness of illicit drugs than youngsters who have grown up in subsequent decades.

In addition, U.S. young people themselves have a great deal of discretionary money, and thus can afford to purchase legal and illegal drugs. In addition, they also have easy access to automobiles, which many can afford, allowing escape from adult monitoring and supervision.

### Structural Changes in Socialization and Social Control

A number of structural changes in society also have reduced the monitoring and individual support and influence youngsters receive from caring adults.

These changes include:
- the increased mobility of families and the resulting separation of children from extended family members and long-term neighbors;
- the increasing size of secondary schools, with the accompanying potential for anonymity within that key institutional setting;
- the reconfiguration of the nuclear family because of an increasing divorce rate as well as an increasing rate of childbirth outside of marriage;
- the decline in involvement in organized religions; and
- the increasing concentration of the population in large, urban, impersonal communities.

In addition, the proportion of mothers working outside the home has increased dramatically in recent decades, with a resulting reduction in adult monitoring.

As U.S. adolescents have had diminishing contact with nurturing and personally involved adults, through default the popular media have tended to fill much of the void. Radio, television, and movie consumption by U.S. teens is very great today. Yet these sectors are controlled by organizations that do not have among their goals the constructive education and socialization of young people. Their primary goals are to attract audiences—whatever it takes—and thus to maximize profits. The net effect has been to shift some of the role of socializing and educating children away from involved caregivers who are motivated to have a constructive impact on children, to other institutions that have little inherent motivation to fulfill this role. We believe that these changes have helped create fertile conditions in the 20th century for the spread of drug use among adolescents, partly as a result of less adult social control exercised in the lives of youngsters and partly as a result of less constructive role modeling and value transmission.

Drug use correlates strongly with
- academic grades and school truancy,
- number of evenings spent in the home, and
- the young person's degree of religious involvement.

In other words, attachment or bonding to constructive, adult-run socializing institutions is associated with a lower level of smoking, drinking, and illicit drug use.

## Social Alienation

The U.S. epidemic of illicit drug use among youth, which emerged in the 1960s, was influenced heavily by the Vietnam War, the youth alienation the war caused, and the resulting emergence of a counterculture movement. The use of certain illicit drugs—marijuana and hallucinogens in particular—was strongly associated with exhibiting counterculture values and behaviors. Indeed, passing a marijuana joint became a symbolic ritual within the movement, simultaneously expressing contempt for the predominant societal norms and solidarity with others in the movement. Although there may have been an upsurge in mind-expanding drugs during this period in any case, the war in Vietnam and the alienation to which it gave rise had a substantial catalytic effect on the epidemic. That rebellion against particular norms in society was uncorrelated with delinquency—even though both were strongly correlated with illicit drug use (Johnston, 1973).

## Sources of Information on Trends

Reliable and systematic scientific information on the use of licit and illicit substances did not appear until the latter half of the 20th century, primarily because scientific surveys of representative samples of adolescents on these subjects did not exist. What is known from the available data will be summarized briefly at the beginning of each of the following sections on tobacco, alcohol, and illicit drugs, respectively.

The earliest nationwide survey series on substance use among adolescents were launched in the 1970s. The National Household Survey on Drug Abuse (SAMHSA, 1998) was begun in 1972 and continues today. It includes a national sample of 12- to 17-year-olds, as well as samples of older age groups. In 1975, the Monitoring the Future Study was launched; funded by the National Institute on Drug Use, it has conducted annual surveys of students in school each year since then. In 1990, another school-based survey series—the biennial Youth Risk Behavior Study—was launched by the Centers for Disease Control and Prevention (Kann et al., 1996). Most of the trend data presented in this chapter covering recent decades derive from the Monitoring the Future Study (Johnston et al., 1998a, 1998b), which is widely viewed as one of the most reliable sources of trend information on youth substance use. However, the other two survey series have produced long-term trend results that are quite consistent with those presented here, although the household surveys tend to produce lower absolute prevalence rates, most likely due to greater concealment in reporting in the home setting.

The Monitoring the Future Study involves confidential, self-administered questionnaires completed in school by about 16,000 students in approximately 140 schools at each grade level surveyed. The considerable evidence for the reliability and validity of the substance abuse measures is discussed in Johnston et al. (1998a). Table 4–1 provides data from selected years in this series to provide an overview of the trends that have occurred in recent decades.

## Table 4–1: Prevalence and trends in use of various drugs for 8th, 10th, and 12th graders

| | LIFETIME | | | | ANNUAL | | | | 30-DAY | | | |
|---|---|---|---|---|---|---|---|---|---|---|---|---|
| | 1975 | 1980 | 1991 | 1996 | 1975 | 1980 | 1991 | 1996 | 1975 | 1980 | 1991 | 1996 |
| **Cigarettes** | | | | | | | | | | | | |
| 8th grade | • | • | 44.0 | 49.0 | • | • | • | • | • | • | 14.3 | 21.0 |
| 10th grade | • | • | 55.1 | 61.2 | • | • | • | • | • | • | 20.8 | 30.4 |
| 12th grade | 73.6 | 71.0 | 63.1 | 63.5 | • | • | • | • | 36.7 | 30.5 | 28.3 | 34.0 |
| **Alcohol** | | | | | | | | | | | | |
| 8th grade | • | • | 70.1 | 55.3 | • | • | 54.0 | 46.5 | • | • | 25.1 | 26.2 |
| 10th grade | • | • | 83.8 | 71.8 | • | • | 72.3 | 65.0 | • | • | 42.8 | 40.4 |
| 12th grade | 90.4 | 93.2 | 88.0 | 79.2 | 84.8 | 87.9 | 77.7 | 72.5 | 68.2 | 72.0 | 54.0 | 50.8 |
| **Been drunk** | | | | | | | | | | | | |
| 8th grade | • | • | 26.7 | 26.8 | • | • | 17.5 | 19.8 | • | • | 7.6 | 9.6 |
| 10th grade | • | • | 50.0 | 48.5 | • | • | 40.1 | 40.1 | • | • | 20.5 | 21.3 |
| 12th grade | • | • | 65.4 | 61.8 | • | • | 52.7 | 51.9 | • | • | 31.6 | 31.3 |
| **Any illicit drug including inhalants** | | | | | | | | | | | | |
| 8th grade | • | • | 18.7 | 31.2 | • | • | 11.3 | 23.6 | • | • | 5.7 | 14.6 |
| 10th grade | • | • | 30.6 | 45.4 | • | • | 21.4 | 37.5 | • | • | 11.6 | 23.2 |
| 12th grade | 55.2* | 65.4* | 44.1 | 50.8 | 45.0* | 53.1* | 29.4 | 40.2 | 30.7* | 37.2* | 16.4 | 24.6 |
| **Marijuana** | | | | | | | | | | | | |
| 8th grade | • | • | 10.2 | 23.1 | • | • | 6.2 | 18.3 | • | • | 3.2 | 11.3 |
| 10th grade | • | • | 23.4 | 39.8 | • | • | 16.5 | 33.6 | • | • | 8.7 | 20.4 |
| 12th grade | 47.3 | 60.3 | 36.7 | 44.9 | 40.0 | 48.8 | 23.9 | 35.8 | 27.1 | 33.7 | 13.8 | 21.9 |
| **Inhalants** | | | | | | | | | | | | |
| 8th grade | • | • | 17.6 | 21.2 | • | • | 9.0 | 12.2 | • | • | 4.4 | 5.8 |
| 10th grade | • | • | 15.7 | 19.3 | • | • | 7.1 | 9.5 | • | • | 2.7 | 3.3 |
| 12th grade | • | 11.9 | 17.6 | 16.6 | • | 4.6 | 6.6 | 7.6 | • | 1.4 | 2.4 | 2.5 |
| **LSD** | | | | | | | | | | | | |
| 8th grade | • | • | 2.7 | 5.1 | • | • | 1.7 | 3.5 | • | • | 0.6 | 1.5 |
| 10th grade | • | • | 5.6 | 9.4 | • | • | 3.7 | 6.9 | • | • | 1.5 | 2.4 |
| 12th grade | 11.3 | 9.3 | 8.8 | 12.6 | 7.2 | 6.5 | 5.2 | 8.8 | 2.3 | 2.3 | 1.9 | 2.5 |
| **Cocaine** | | | | | | | | | | | | |
| 8th grade | • | • | 2.3 | 4.5 | • | • | 1.1 | 3.0 | • | • | 0.5 | 1.3 |
| 10th grade | • | • | 4.1 | 6.5 | • | • | 2.2 | 4.2 | • | • | 0.7 | 1.7 |
| 12th grade | 9.0 | 15.7 | 7.8 | 7.1 | 5.6 | 12.3 | 3.5 | 4.9 | 1.9 | 5.2 | 1.4 | 2.0 |
| **Amphetamines** | | | | | | | | | | | | |
| 8th grade | • | • | 10.5 | 13.5 | • | • | 6.2 | 9.1 | • | • | 2.6 | 4.6 |
| 10th grade | • | • | 13.2 | 17.7 | • | • | 8.2 | 12.4 | • | • | 3.3 | 5.5 |
| 12th grade | 22.3 | 26.4 | 15.4 | 15.3 | 16.2 | 20.8 | 8.2 | 9.5 | 8.5 | 12.1 | 3.1 | 4.1 |
| **Heroin** | | | | | | | | | | | | |
| 8th grade | • | • | 1.2 | 2.4 | • | • | 0.7 | 1.6 | • | • | 0.3 | 0.7 |
| 10th grade | • | • | 1.2 | 2.1 | • | • | 0.5 | 1.2 | • | • | 0.2 | 0.5 |
| 12th grade | 2.2 | 1.1 | 0.9 | 1.8 | 1.0 | 0.5 | 0.4 | 1.0 | 0.4 | 0.2 | 0.2 | 0.5 |

* In 1975 and 1980, this index does not include inhalants, but this omission has very little effect on prevalence rates.

## Tobacco: Trends and Determinants in Use

Our discussion of tobacco will focus on cigarette smoking, simply because it is the most common and most damaging form of tobacco consumption in the United States. Epidemiological research has clearly established that the great majority of eventual smokers initiate this behavior in childhood or adolescence. The research has also shown that (a) the behavior is a highly stable one, and (b) once a particular birth cohort establishes a higher or lower rate of smoking in adolescence, relative to other birth cohorts, that cohort will retain its relative position throughout the life cycle. Individual and cohort stability are explainable by the highly addictive nature of nicotine, which is why the rate of smoking attained in adolescence is so pertinent for the eventual health and longevity of each birth cohort.

### *Overall Trends*

Systematic surveys specific to tobacco use by U.S. youth began in 1968. However, by using data collected in the National Health Interview Surveys, the 1994 Surgeon General report was able to reconstruct prevalence of regular smoking among U.S. youth ages 10 to 19 for the years from 1920 to 1980 (USDHHS, 1994). These rough estimates showed that smoking among white males increased fairly steadily but fairly slowly from approximately 16% in 1920 to 20% in 1975. Smoking among white females increased much more dramatically, from approximately 1% in 1920 to 20% in 1975. The rates of smoking among young African American males, which were consistently lower than among young white males, increased from approximately 13% in 1920 to 16% in 1950, then began decreasing very gradually back to approximately 13% in 1975. Smoking among African American females, as with white females, increased dramatically, from approximately 2% in 1920 to 12% in 1975; unlike African American males, smoking continued to increase among African American females throughout the six decades.

Figure 4–1 shows the trends in smoking among U.S. adolescents from 1975 to 1995. It shows the proportion of students who reported having one or more cigarettes during the prior 30 days (that is, the 30-day prevalence of smoking).

The trend curve in Figure 4–1 shows a peak in smoking among seniors in 1976, a substantial decline over the following five years, then a leveling in use for more than a decade (even though use among adults continued to decline during this period as a result of increased quitting). Then, in the 1990s, there was a fairly dramatic change in the situation as smoking rates among U.S. teenagers began to increase sharply.

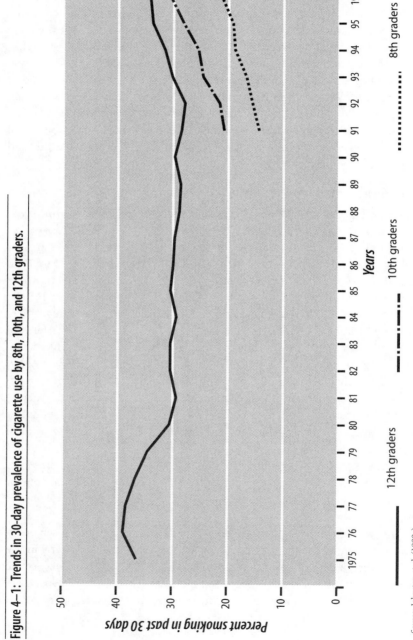

Figure 4–1: Trends in 30-day prevalence of cigarette use by 8th, 10th, and 12th graders.

Source: Johnston et al. (1998a).

The declines in smoking prevalence among high school seniors in the late 1970s actually reflect earlier declines in initiation that occurred when these cohorts were in elementary school. (The evidence for this is based on retrospective reports from those seniors.) This pattern reflects the lasting cohort differences noted earlier. The pattern of cohort differences is important because it means that the factors that caused the downturn exhibited by seniors in the late 1970s actually affected them when they were much younger, in the early 1970s. We will return below to a consideration of what those factors may have been.

## Subgroup Differences in Levels and Trends

For a long period of time, smoking was more prevalent among males than among females, but with the advent of the feminist movement and the tobacco industry's successful association of smoking with female liberation, young women caught up to and passed young men in their rates of smoking. Among high school seniors this occurred by 1976, lasting through 1991, at which point the smoking rates for males—perhaps spurred by the Joe Camel advertising campaign—once again exceeded that for females.

Race/ethnicity is another important dimension on which subgroup differences in smoking emerged in recent decades—particularly between African American and white adolescents. Among 12th graders in 1975, whites were only a little more likely to be smokers than African Americans or Latinos, but over the next two decades a large difference emerged. Smoking by African American and Latino students decreased more between 1977 and 1981 than it did among whites. Furthermore, the long-term decline among African Americans continued after 1981, whereas use among white students stabilized. (In the 1990s, smoking rates among African American and Latino students increased, along with those of whites, but the large differences still remain.) Clearly, smoking assumed a different social meaning with the African American adolescent subculture, but how and why this occurred is not yet fully understood. Between 1995 and 1996, the 30-day prevalence was 14% among African American seniors, 25% among Latino seniors, and 38% among white seniors.

Those students who are not bound for college have far higher smoking rates than those who are, and this relationship between eventual educational attainment and smoking has existed among U.S. young people for at least two decades. The differential pattern is established in childhood and adolescence and then holds through later stages in the life cycle.

To the extent that there have been rural-urban differences in adolescent cigarette smoking in recent years, they are quite modest, with rural areas having slightly higher smoking rates than urban areas.

## Likely Explanations for the Levels and Changes in Smoking Rates

As indicated above, awareness and access are two important explanatory factors for substance use. Virtually all young people are aware that cigarettes can be smoked for psychoactive effect, and access by minors has been close to universal. (In 1996, some 77% of all eighth graders said they could get cigarettes fairly easily, if they wanted to.) Thus, awareness and access help to explain the high prevalence rates for smoking. Efforts to reduce youth access are now being implemented around the nation, but the success of these efforts, both in reducing access and ultimately in reducing actual use, is yet to be determined.

The laws regarding sale to or use by minors have seldom been enforced. Furthermore, the societal norms communicated to children have been extremely mixed, because society has winked at the sale of cigarettes to minors and because it has permitted the ubiquitous advertising and promotion of cigarettes. Many children also have parents who smoke, although this known risk factor has changed for the better in recent years as smoking among adults has declined.

Surprisingly, not all youth consider smoking to be dangerous. In recent years, only approximately 50% of all eighth graders think that smoking a pack or more of cigarettes daily poses a "great risk" of harm to the user. Although the proportion who see great risk grows to more than two-thirds by 12th grade, by that time many students already have established a pattern of regular use and report that they have tried to quit without success. It is clear from the way that cigarettes are marketed that the social symbolism of smoking is a very important part of why people smoke. Boys can fancy themselves as the rugged Marlboro cowboy or the suave Joe Camel by smoking the appropriate brand; girls are offered the emancipated, stylish, and slender Virginia Slims image; and so on. But another part of the symbolism for children and adolescents is more generic. By simply smoking any brand, they can feel more "grown up," or precocious, and perhaps more independent, venturesome, rebellious, or tough. When teens are asked whether smoking makes a boy or girl their age seem more grown up, few say that it does, but the majority say that they think it makes smokers look like they are trying to appear more grown up. These generic connotations of smoking probably have always provided important motivators for minors, so they may not explain the trends in use, but there is evidence that some of the additional connotations created by the highly sophisticated marketing and promotion of various brands may well have contributed to the trends in use.

Along these lines, the downturn in smoking observed among 12th graders in the late 1970s, and among younger teens in the early 1970s, may well have had its origins in the withdrawal of cigarette advertising from radio and television in 1971. It took the tobacco industry some time to compensate for the loss of these powerful marketing outlets, which may have allowed initiation rates among teens to drop for a few years as a result of all the other antismoking forces that were then gaining momentum. With massive increases in advertising and promotion budgets, and the adoption of images attractive to youth, the decline was soon terminated among the nation's young people (even though adult use continued to decline).

Another form of social learning and social influence, which we believe contributed to the subsequent increase in smoking in the 1990s, was the behavior of popular cultural role models, including in their media portrayals and in their "real life" behavior. There appears to have been a dramatic increase in the portrayal of smoking in movies and in television programming. Some of it has been clearly traceable to paid brand placement by the cigarette companies in movies such as *Superman II*. In more recent years, placing cigarette smoking in movies and the association of smoking with the image of particular actors seem to have become fads within the entertainment industry. The impact of this fad is extended in time as these movies are rerun on television.

## Alcohol: Trends and Determinants in Use

Alcohol, like tobacco, is a legal substance that is age-regulated to purchase. In the United States, the minimum purchasing age is now 21 in all states, although before 1987 there was some variation among states, with a number of states allowing alcohol purchase at age 18. Also like tobacco, alcohol is heavily advertised and promoted, with many messages appealing particularly to young people. Although alcohol use is not as stable as tobacco use, it is nevertheless a habitual behavior that starts in adolescence in almost all cases. Occasional consumption of large quantities of alcohol (e.g., five or more drinks in a row) is quite common among U.S. adolescents, and reaches peak rates in the early 20s.

### Overall Trends

Blane and Hewitt (1977) conducted a survey of the existing literature on alcohol use by youth, covering the years 1940 to 1975. They concluded:

> *Analysis of 120 surveys about junior and senior high school drinking practices conducted between 1941 and 1975 reveals that prevalence and other characteristics of drinking rose steadily from World War II until about 1965. [Between 1965 and 1975] drinking behaviors have remained relatively constant* (p. xii-1).

Figure 4-2 shows the trends in use of alcohol (the proportion who say they have consumed alcohol on one or more occasions in the prior 30 days) among U.S. teens from 1976 to 1996. The figure shows a peak in 30-day prevalence

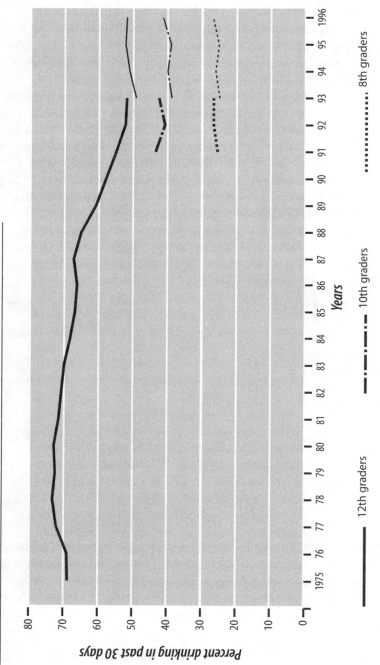

**Figure 4–2: Trends in 30-day prevalence of alcohol use by 8th, 10th, and 12th graders.**

In 1993, the question text was changed slightly in half the forms to indicate a "drink" meant "more than just a few sips." In 1994, the remaining forms were changed. The thinner lines connect percentages based on the revised questions.

Source: Johnston, O'Malley, & Bachman (1998a).

of alcohol use at about 72% among seniors in the period 1978 to 1980. During the 1980s and the early 1990s, there was a considerable decline in use, with prevalence dropping to 51% by 1993, a relative decline of 30%. Some of this decline was a result of raising the minimum drinking age in those states that had allowed drinking before age 21. However, even in states that had a consistent minimum drinking age of 21, some decline occurred over that same period, reflecting a general secular trend toward less drinking (O'Malley & Wagenaar, 1991).

In 1993, the alcohol question in the Monitoring the Future study was reworded to eliminate the reporting of use of "just a few sips" of a drink in order to delineate more clearly inappropriate drinking behavior; therefore the data for recent years are not entirely comparable to the data prior to 1993. Between 1993 and 1996 there was rather little change in monthly prevalence at any of the three grade levels.

### Subgroup Differences in Levels and Trends

Monthly prevalence of alcohol use is only slightly higher among boys than girls in the eighth grade. By senior year, however, a considerable gap emerges, with boys reporting greater use.

There also are important racial/ethnic subgroup differences in alcohol use. African American youngsters report considerably lower alcohol use than do white or Latino youngsters. From 1995 to 1996, 18% of African American eighth graders reported some alcohol use in the prior 30 days, compared with 27% for white eighth graders and 30% for Latino eighth graders. Among 12th graders, the corresponding figures are 37%, 55%, and 48%. (The fact that the rates for Latino students are lower than whites in 12th grade, but slightly higher in eighth grade, is likely due to the considerably higher dropout rates among Latinos.) At both grade levels, white students are about 50% more likely to report alcohol use than African American students. The relative rankings have not changed among seniors over the last two decades.

Seniors who are planning to attend college have slightly lower prevalence rates of alcohol use than those who are college bound (in 1996, the percentages were 49% and 55%, respectively), and this relationship has also been evident for two decades. The difference between the college bound and those not college bound is more pronounced at the lower grades. Among 1996 eighth graders, 24% of the college bound reported drinking in the past 30 days, compared with 42% of those not college bound. The latter group contains most of those who will eventually drop out of school, which may account for the greater difference in the younger grades. (It should be noted that relatively few youngsters today say that they are not planning to go to college.)

Although substance abuse is sometimes viewed as more of an urban problem than a rural problem, adolescent alcohol use is far from that. Among 8th, 10th, and 12th graders, alcohol is as prevalent among those not living in metropolitan areas as among those who are.

## Likely Explanations for the Levels and Changes in Alcohol Use

As with tobacco, nearly universal awareness and access can help to explain the high prevalence rates for alcohol use. In 1996, some 75% of all eighth graders said they could get alcohol fairly easily, if they wanted to. Attempts to reduce youth access to alcohol have been partially successful, judging by the effects attributable to the increases in minimum drinking ages. But as with cigarette smoking, the societal norms communicated to children have been mixed, at best, both because society has tolerated the use of alcohol by minors and because it has permitted the ubiquitous advertising and promotion of alcohol, particularly advertising with a strong attraction to youth. Alcohol advertising frequently utilizes sexually attractive models and party situations, sports figures and scenes, and animal characters such as Spuds Mackenzie and the Budweiser frogs—all of which seem likely to be particularly effective with adolescents.

Heavier use, particularly to the point of intoxication, is potentially very dangerous. In 1996, 10% of 8th graders (who are 13 or 14 years old), 21% of 10th graders (15 or 16 years old), and 31% of 12th graders (17 or 18 years old) reported having been drunk at least once in the prior 30 days.

The subgroup differences in prevalence of alcohol use described above pertain as well to the prevalence of getting drunk, with the differences between groups generally being stronger. For example, among 1995 to 1996 seniors, 37% of white students reported having been drunk at least once in the past 30 days, compared with about one-third as many African American students (13%) and two-thirds as many Latino seniors (26%).

Although most adults might assume that all youngsters perceive the dangers in drinking to excess, the data are not so reassuring. In 1996, only 50% of seniors saw a great risk of harm in having five or more drinks once or twice each weekend—the type of heavy party drinking that is most common among adolescents. The corresponding figures for 8th- and 10th graders are about the same.

During the earlier period of decline in drinking, the proportion of seniors reporting great risk in weekly binge drinking rose considerably, from 35% in 1979 to 49% in 1991. Disapproval of this behavior also increased, from 56% of seniors saying they disapproved in 1980 to 71% in 1992. After 1992, disapproval fell to 65% by 1996, but perceived risk changed rather little. These trends in attitudinal factors very likely help account for the changes in actual use patterns.

## Illegal Drugs and Controlled Substances: Trends and Determinants in Use

As noted above, there is a wide range of psychoactive substances that are legally controlled or prohibited from manufacture, distribution, and possession. By far the most widely used of these substances among U.S. adolescents over the past 30 years has been marijuana, which contains the active ingredient tetrahydrocannabinol or THC. It is usually smoked as a marijuana cigarette or "joint," but it can also be eaten or smoked in a water pipe or "bong." Young people who cross the line into using a controlled substance outside of medical regimen usually start with marijuana, which is seen as one of the least dangerous and least socially disapproved of these drugs. A significant proportion of these young people then go on to use one or more of the so-called hard drugs, like hallucinogens, stimulants, cocaine, sedatives, tranquilizers, or opiate-type drugs.

### *Overall Trends*

Figure 4–3 shows the long-term trends in the use of various illicit drugs among U.S. high school seniors. It shows that there has been a wide fluctuation in the proportion of U.S. youth who engaged in these behaviors over the past two decades. (Table 4–1 provides exact prevalence rates for these drugs, along with additional ones.) And, if we had the data going back a decade earlier to 1965, before the illicit drug epidemic burgeoned, it would show even greater fluctuation, because illicit drug use was at negligible levels within the general population before the epidemic emerged in the late 1960s. But from the late 1960s on there was a steady and dramatic increase in the proportions of U.S. young people willing to cross some lines that were previously considered taboo to cross. Norms against the use of marijuana and LSD, in particular, eroded—first among college students and then among secondary school students—as Timothy Leary intoned "tune in, turn on, drop out" and as the Vietnam War, Watergate, and other historical events of the period alienated a significant portion of the youth population.

Marijuana use increased dramatically in the late 1960s and 1970s, before beginning a long decline that lasted into the early 1990s. Cocaine use increased in the late 1970s among adolescents, remained at historically high levels for the first half of the 1980s, and then plummeted after 1986. In the 1990s, cocaine use among adolescents increased modestly, as did the use of a number of the other illegal and controlled substances, but marijuana use showed the greatest increase during this period.

One of the interesting features of the upturn in illicit drug use in the 1990s is that it began among the younger teens (8th graders after 1991) and then showed up among the older teens (10th and 12th graders after 1992). This dynamic stands in stark contrast to the original epidemic, which began among

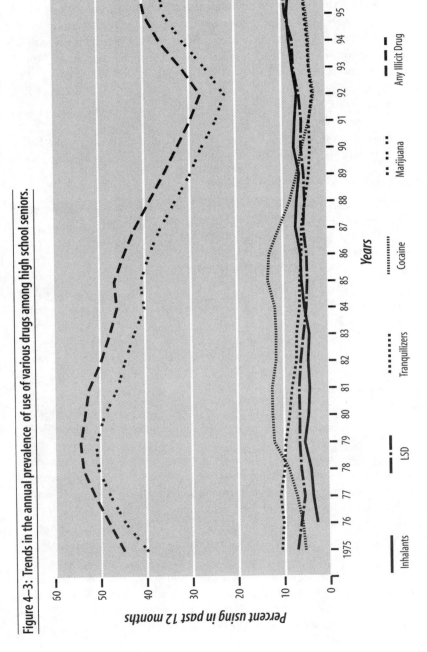

Figure 4–3: Trends in the annual prevalence of use of various drugs among high school seniors.

Source: Johnston, et al. (1998a).

young adults and then radiated down the age spectrum. In fact, illicit drug use among adults did not increase at all in the first half of the 1990s; it increased only among U.S. adolescents. As those more drug-experienced adolescents become college students and young adults through the process of generational replacement, they are bringing their habits with them, and prevalence rates are beginning to increase in the older groups (Johnston et al., 1998b). This pattern of change suggests that, for the first time in recent years, lasting cohort differences account for most of the change in illicit drug use—not the more typical secular trends simultaneously observable in all age groups. This in turn suggests that there is something different about growing up in the United States in the 1990s than in the preceding years—something different having to do with socialization and learning about these drugs. We will return to this point.

### Key Subgroup Differences in Levels and Trends

There are few gender differences in drug use at the 8th- and 10th-grade levels, but some differences begin to emerge by 12th grade, when boys start to show higher prevalence rates, particularly for the frequent use of drugs (such as daily marijuana use). The fact that younger girls tend to date older boys may help to explain the parity in use in the lower grades.

There are some important racial/ethnic differences in the use of illicit drugs, with African American students reporting lower prevalence rates at all grade levels on virtually all of the illicit drugs. Latino students report quite high rates in 8th grade, but usually fall between whites and African Americans by 12th grade. (This decline in their relative position very likely reflects the higher dropout rate among Latinos.)

While still in high school, those students who are college bound (and attaining higher grades on average) are less likely to be using illicit drugs than those not expecting to go to college. Interestingly enough, after high school, those in college tend to catch up, in part because more of them move out of their parents' home into a peer-living environment, and in part because many more of them defer marriage, which has a moderating effect on use (Bachman et al., 1997).

By the middle 1990s there was not much difference in illicit drug use existed between rural and more urban areas. (Marijuana use is slightly positively correlated with urbanicity, amphetamine use slightly negatively correlated, and use of most of the other drugs is uncorrelated.) But this similarity conceals a more complicated dynamic. For a number of drugs, including marijuana and cocaine, urbanicity differences have tended to be greatest when usage levels were at their peak. In other words, an epidemic tends to bloom more fully in urban areas and then the differences subside as rates decline. New drugs sometimes are first introduced in urban areas, as was the case for crack cocaine, but use quickly spreads to communities of all sizes.

## Likely Explanations for Levels and Trends in Use

As noted earlier in this chapter, contemporary U.S. youngsters are quite aware of the psychoactive potential of a broad array of drugs, and it seems that new drugs are continually added to the smorgasbord. Furthermore, because of the size of the U.S. demand for drugs, a highly sophisticated and differentiated underground marketing system has emerged, making many drugs readily available. For over two decades, 80% to 90% of high school seniors have said they could get marijuana fairly or very easily if they wanted some. In 1996, roughly 60% said they could get amphetamines, and roughly 50% said they could obtain LSD and cocaine. Even for heroin and crack cocaine, the proportions were over 40%.

In addition to the widespread awareness and availability of these drugs among U.S. adolescents, many do not think that experimenting with them is dangerous (many more think that regular use is dangerous), and significant minorities do not disapprove of their use. To illustrate, only 16% of seniors in 1996 thought experimental use of marijuana entailed great risk (though this rose to 26% for occasional use and 60% for regular use). Even for heroin, which carries a serious risk of addiction, only about half (53%) saw trying it once or twice as carrying great risk. With regard to personal disapproval, only about half of all 1996 seniors (53%) disapproved of trying marijuana (80% disapproved of regular use). For most of the remaining illicit drugs, much higher proportions disapproved of their use, which helps to explain why the use of these drugs is much less prevalent than the use of marijuana. For amphetamines, LSD, or powdered cocaine, about 80% of the seniors disapproved of even trying them once or twice. For crack cocaine, barbiturates, and heroin, between 85% and 92% disapproved of trying them.

Changes in the degree of risk perceived and disapproval have proven to be very important determinants of levels of actual use. Figure 4–4 shows how the use, perceived risk of use, and disapproval of use have covaried over time for marijuana. It also presents the perceived availability measure to show that availability appears to have played little role either in bringing about the decline in use from the late 1970s to the early 1990s, or in the increase in use since then. On the other hand, attitudes and beliefs (sometimes referred to as "demand side factors," as contrasted to "supply side factors") have played a very significant role (see Bachman et al., 1990, 1998). This has been true for a number of other drugs, as well, including cocaine, which plummeted in use after 1986 when the media reached a veritable frenzy on the issues of crack and cocaine, including

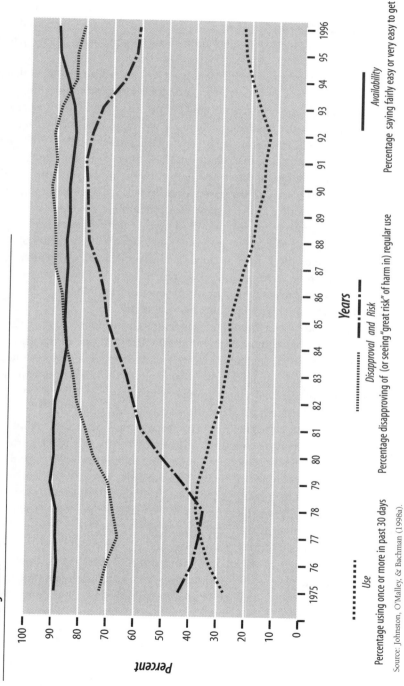

Figure 4–4: Marijuana—Trends in perceived availability, perceived risk and disapproval of regular use, and prevalence of use in past 30 days for 12th graders.

Years

Availability
Percentage saying fairly easy or very easy to get

Disapproval and Risk
Percentage disapproving of (or seeing "great risk" of harm in) regular use

Use
Percentage using once or more in past 30 days

Source: Johnston, O'Malley, & Bachman (1998a).

the widely reported death of Len Bias (a first-round draft pick for professional basketball) after his first experience with cocaine. The risks perceived to be associated with cocaine soared after 1986, as did disapproval, and use fell precipitously.

The evidence on the links between perceived risk, disapproval, and actual use of a drug is extensive—most of it coming from the Monitoring the Future Study. Covariation at the aggregate level, sometimes with a shift in perceived risk a year prior to the change in actual use, has been documented for many years (Johnston et al., 1998a, and previous volumes in that series). When asked their reasons for not using marijuana, students listed concerns about adverse physical and psychological effects as the top two reasons; furthermore, their mentions of these reasons increased over time as use began to decrease (Johnston, 1985). Other analyses have shown that there was no decline in use among young people at any given level of perceived risk (for example, "moderate risk"); rather, an increasing proportion of students migrated to the higher levels of perceived risk during the downturn in marijuana use (Bachman et al., 1990, 1998). These same analyses showed that cross-time changes in key lifestyle correlates, such as religiosity or conservatism, could not account for the observed changes in either marijuana or cocaine use.

There also have been important changes in the symbolism of drug use over the three decades of the most recent epidemic. Early on, use of marijuana and use of LSD were social statements as well as hedonistic behaviors. After the Vietnam War and the counterculture movement faded from memory, the social symbolism disappeared for young people, which may also help to explain the long decline in adolescent drug use that began in the late 1970s.

As with cigarettes, the behavior of important role models also can influence young people's propensity to use illicit drugs. Sometimes there are gurus, like Timothy Leary, but much more common are entertainers and sports figures who influence by example and by the messages they give. At the beginning of the epidemic many rock groups were quite overt about their own use of drugs, and they also literally sang their praises. These included the Beatles, who were particularly influential in their day. During the 1980s, far fewer entertainers extolled the supposed virtues of drug use, and to a certain degree the country spoke with one voice to its children about drugs. By the 1990s, however, as concern about the issue subsided, prodrug voices were once again raised, especially among rap, grunge, and hard rock bands. In the late 1980s, many young people already believed that drug use was condoned and widely practiced among those in the entertainment and professional sports communities, but this belief grew during the 1990s. Even the fashion industry came out with the "heroin chic" style. Fortunately the fashion and music industries, at least, appeared to be retreating from the issue by 1997, albeit more likely out of concern for the tragedies that have befallen so many in their own industries than out of concern for the country's children.

## Summary

In this chapter, we have shown that use of licit and illicit substances by U.S. young people has fluctuated widely over time. Illicit drug use expanded rapidly in the late 1960s and early 1970s in what can only be described as a national epidemic, eventually becoming a pandemic reaching the far corners of the world. As societal tumult of the 1960s and early 1970s faded into history, and as the adverse consequences of various forms of drug use came to be more fully appreciated by young people, a long decline in drug use began, starting in the late 1970s and ending by the early 1990s. That epidemic rendered some semipermanent changes that place future generations of U.S. youth at continuing risk. Awareness of the psychoactive potential of a great many drugs became widespread and lasting, and extensive systems for supplying drugs throughout the country became well established. As young people's concerns about the hazards of drugs subsided—partly as a result of the contraction of the epidemic and partly as a result of various social institutions diminishing their efforts to reduce substance abuse—a new generation of young people became susceptible to the lure of drugs. Thus, in the 1990s, we saw a considerable relapse in illicit drug use, specific to adolescents. By the late 1990s, however, evidence existed that the important erosion in perceived risk and peer norms related to illicit drug use may have been ending or beginning to reverse. Young people have once again been exposed to the negative consequences of drug use and a number of societal institutions have increased their attention toward actively confronting the problem.

Cigarette use among young people increased through the late 1970s, before decreasing briefly, then leveling between the early 1980s and the early 1990s. Smoking among adolescents increased sharply in the 1990s, but late in the decade there were indications of leveling, as the issue of adolescent tobacco use came into sharp public focus and debate.

Finally, alcohol use, which for some decades has been very high among U.S. adolescents, increased during the height of the illicit drug epidemic. Use then declined appreciably in the 1980s (as the perceived risks of heavy drinking grew) and remained relatively stable in the 1990s.

What the future holds for these various classes of abusable substances depends very much on society's responses to adolescent use of such drugs. Major initiatives are under consideration with regard to underage tobacco use—including substantial price increases, restrictions on advertising, counter-advertising, and the setting of national targets for reducing use. If some or all of these initiatives are enacted, the impact could be quite dramatic. Similar considerations may also be raised in the coming years with regard to alcohol use, although the tobacco and alcohol industries are highly resistant to such reforms. We expect the problem of illicit drug use to remain widespread for some years to come, although a number of initiatives now under way, including a national antidrug media campaign and the formation of thousands of community coalitions devoted to preventing drug use by young people, may make an important difference. Furthermore, largely ineffective prevention curricula in schools throughout the United States are being replaced by programs of demonstrated effectiveness. With or without these social programs, however, we expect to see a cyclical process of increases in use, followed by decreases among the following birth cohorts who have the opportunity to observe firsthand the ravages of that increased use.

## Implications for Policies and Programs

One very important lesson from the data reviewed in this chapter is that these behaviors among U.S. young people—smoking, drinking, and illicit drug use—can be changed substantially over time when the appropriate forces are brought to bear. Perhaps we have largely lost the "war on drugs" on the battlefield of supply reduction, considering the extensive availability that exists today after 30 years of costly efforts to close down the supply. But the country has had considerable success on the demand-reduction battlefield, as the long decline in illicit drug use from the late 1970s through the early 1990s amply illustrates. To the extent that the attitudes and beliefs of young people about the dangers and social acceptability of drug use can be changed, use can be contained.

The second lesson to be drawn from this history derives from what happened in the 1990s. After a long period of declining use, use of the illicit drugs rebounded in what we have called a "relapse phase" in the epidemic. Just as drug addiction is a chronic, relapsing disease for the individual, popular drug use can be a chronic, relapsing problem for society. But, if one takes seriously our interpretation of the causes of the relapse—namely, reductions in perceived risk and disapproval of drug use among young people because they heard fewer cautions, observed fewer drug-related tragedies, and eventually received more encouragement to use—then the solution to preventing future relapses becomes obvious. We must institutionalize prevention to be sure that even those cohorts of youngsters who grow up during the periods of low use (the most naive and vulnerable cohorts) know why they should avoid drugs. They will continue to have an awareness of the psychoactive potential of a broad array of drugs; they will continue to be tempted by the unending introduction of new drugs, each of which starts with its own allure; and they will have easy access to many drugs for the foreseeable future. But what they will not have, unless it is built into the system for the long run, are the educational and socialization experiences that provide the knowledge, motivation, and social skills to stay away from substances that can so severely damage them physically, psychologically, and socially. To achieve that, the country needs effective prevention programs woven into the curriculum of most schools—most likely programs that cut across kindergarten through senior year—with age-appropriate modules building upon and reinforcing the lessons learned at earlier stages. We also need a system to alert, inform, and guide every generation of parents about the hazards of drugs, and what they can do to help protect their own children. Finally, we need to continue to use the mass media as a vehicle for constructive messages (the antidrug spots) and to persuade those in the mass media and other entertainment industries to begin to own up to their responsibilities, derived from their enormous influence on the nation's children.

# References

Bachman, J. G., Johnston, L. D., & O'Malley, P. M. (1990). Explaining the recent decline in cocaine use among young adults: Further evidence that perceived risks and disapproval lead to reduced drug use. *Journal of Health and Social Behavior, 31*, 173–184.

Bachman, J. G., Johnston, L. D., & O'Malley, P. M. (1998). Explaining the recent increases in students' marijuana use: The impacts of perceived risks and disapproval, 1976 through 1996. *American Journal of Public Health, 88*, 887–892.

Bachman, J. G., Wadsworth, K. N., O'Malley, P. M., Johnston, L. D., & Schulenberg, J. (1997). *Smoking, drinking, and drug use in young adulthood: The impacts of new freedoms and new responsibilities.* Mahwah, NJ: Lawrence Erlbaum Associates.

Blane, H. T., & Hewitt, L. E. (1977). Alcohol and youth: An analysis of the literature, 1960-1975. *Report to the National Institute on Alcohol Abuse and Alcoholism.* (NTIS No. PB-268 698).

Johnston, L. D. (1973). *Drugs and American youth.* Ann Arbor, MI: Institute for Social Research.

Johnston, L. D. (1985). The etiology and prevention of substance use: What can we learn from recent historical changes? In C. L. Jones & R. J. Battjes (Eds.), *Etiology of drug abuse: Implications for prevention* (NIDA Research Monograph No. 56, pp. 155-177). Washington, DC: National Institute on Drug Abuse.

Johnston, L. D. (1991). Toward a theory of drug epidemics. In R. L. Donohew, H. Sypher, & W. Bukoski (Eds.), *Persuasive communication and drug abuse prevention* (pp. 93–132). Hillsdale, NJ: Lawrence Erlbaum.

Johnston, L. D., & O'Malley, P. M. (1997). The recanting of earlier-reported drug use by young adults. In L. Harrison & A. Hughes (Eds.), *The validity of self-reported drug use: Improving the accuracy of survey estimates* (NIDA Research Monograph No. 167; pp. 59–80; NIH Publication 97-4147). Washington, DC: National Institute on Drug Abuse.

Johnston, L. D., O'Malley, P. M., & Bachman, J. G. (1998a). *National survey results on drug use from the Monitoring the Future Study, 1975-1997. Volume I: Secondary school students.* (NIH Publication No. 98-4345). Rockville, MD: National Institute on Drug Abuse.

Johnston, L. D., O'Malley, P. M., & Bachman, J. G. (1998b). *National survey results on drug use from the Monitoring the Future Study, 1975-1997. Volume II: College students and young adults* (NIH Publication 98-4346). Rockville, MD: National Institute on Drug Abuse.

Kandel, D. B., Yamaguchi, K., & Chen, K. (1992). Stages of progression in drug involvement from adolescence to adulthood: Further evidence for the gateway theory. *Journal of Studies on Alcohol, 53,* 447–457.

Kann, L., Warren, C. W., Harris, W. A., Collins, J. L., Williams, B. I., Ross, J. G. et al.. (1996). Youth Risk Behavior Surveillance-United States, 1995. *Morbidity and Mortality Weekly Report, 45*(SS-4), 1–84.

Maisto, S. A., Galizio, M., & Connors, G. J. (1991). *Drug use and misuse.* New York: Holt Rinehart & Winston.

O'Malley, P. M., & Wagenaar, A. C. (1991). Effects of minimum drinking age laws on alcohol use, related behaviors, and traffic crash involvement among American youth: 1976-1987. *Journal of Studies on Alcohol, 52,* 478–491.

Substance Abuse and Mental Health Services Administration. (1998). *National Household Survey on Drug Abuse Main Findings 1996.* (DHHS Publication No. [SMA] 98-3200) Rockville, MD: Author.

U.S. Department of Health and Human Services. (1994). *Preventing tobacco use among young people: A report of the Surgeon General.* Atlanta, GA: USDHHS, Public Health Service, Centers for Disease Control and Prevention, Office on Smoking and Health.

# FIVE

# Sexual Activity Among Teenagers in the United States

*Joyce C. Abma*

Sexual activity among youth has been of concern to researchers, practitioners, and policymakers for decades. Important long-term changes have occurred in the transition from childhood to adulthood that have altered the context in which sexual activity begins. The result is a lengthening of the period of time during which youth are at risk of early pregnancy and other negative consequences of sexual activity, consequences that can compromise the transition from childhood to adulthood. These consequences have entered the public and policy arena as priority issues related to the personal well-being of youth and society at large. Currently, policies, programs, and legislation reflect intensified efforts toward counteracting the negative effects of sexual activity among youth. The Welfare Reform Act of 1996 characterizes the current rate of childbearing among teens as a national crisis and proclaims that reducing this rate is a "very important government interest" (Personal Responsibility and Work Opportunity Reconciliation Act of 1996, P.L. 104-193, 101[10]).

Changes in economic conditions, educational requirements, and social norms have resulted in later ages at entry into full-time work, marriage, and other adult roles. Although the average age at first marriage has increased, and the average number of years of schooling has increased, the average age at first intercourse has been declining. Thus, there has been a lengthening of the period during which youth are unmarried, economically dependent, and sexually active. For example, in 1960, when the average age at first marriage was at a record low, 14% of women age 15 to 19 were married. Since then, the average age at marriage has increased dramatically, and in 1992, only 5% of women age 15 to 19 were married (Bachrach et al., 1997). The modern late-marriage regime is unique from a longer term perspective as well, especially for young black women. In 1870, the median age at first marriage was just under 20 among black women, whereas in 1990 it was almost 28 (Fitch & Ruggles, 2000).

At the same time, sexual intercourse has been occurring at earlier ages, and this has been accompanied by slightly younger ages at puberty. In the mid-1950s, just over one-quarter of females had become sexually active before the age of 18, whereas in 1988, over half had done so (Alan Guttmacher Institute, 1994). In 1890, the average interval between menarche and first marriage was 7.2 years; in 1988, the average interval between menarche and first marriage was 11.8 years—an increase of 4.6 years, or more than 50% (Alan Guttmacher Institute, 1994). Another way of depicting the change is in the increasing frequency of premarital sex. For women married between 1965 and 1974, 2% first had sexual intercourse five or more years before their first marriage. For women married between 1990 and 1995, 56% had first sex this long before first marriage (Abma et al., 1997).

Younger ages of puberty and first sex translate to higher risks of both pregnancy and sexually transmitted diseases (STDs). Young women who have sexual intercourse at earlier ages are more likely to suffer pelvic infections and have higher rates of gonorrhea than any other age group (Hatcher et al., 1998). Those with earlier first intercourse have higher numbers of both recent and lifetime sexual partners, more frequent sexual activity, and a lower likelihood of using contraception at first intercourse (Abma et al., 1997; Abma & Sonenstein, 2001; Kost & Forrest, 1992; Mosher & McNally, 1991; Seidman et al., 1994; Sonenstein et al., 1991). Adolescents are more vulnerable to STDs than adults not only because of their higher likelihood of unprotected sex, but because they are biologically more susceptible to infection (Institute of Medicine, 1997).

Longer intervals between first sex and first marriage mean longer periods of exposure to the risk of nonmarital pregnancy. This in turn has implications for disruption or disadvantage, particularly for young women, in the increasingly long and demanding postchildhood period of preparation for economic independence. Compared with those who have their first birth at age 20 or older, young women who have a birth during the teen years complete less education and are more likely to be single parents. The extensive research that has been conducted to help understand this pattern shows that the causes of disadvantages for teen parents are not clear-cut. Economic and social disadvantages such as poverty and low educational attainment render early childbearing more likely. Many of the disadvantages that teen mothers have, therefore, originate in their backgrounds. Most research also shows, however, that some negative effects are indeed a result of the burdens of early childbearing (Maynard, 1997). The children of teen parents, in turn, tend to have poorer health, worse educational outcomes, more behavior problems, and higher rates of early childbearing themselves. Since the 1980s, public concern with these personal and social costs has grown. This concern has been the impetus for the development of programs and policies whose mission is to reduce teen pregnancy (see Kirby,

2001, for an evaluation of such programs). For example, state policies mandated by the 1996 welfare reform legislation include a requirement that states outline plans for reducing the rate of nonmarital teen pregnancies, and bonuses to states that achieve the greatest reductions in nonmarital births without increases in abortion (Wertheimer & Moore, 1998).

Information on levels of sexual activity among adolescents was not available on a national level before the early 1970s. At this time, the large baby boom cohort was reaching the early childbearing ages. The need to track and develop explanations for the childbearing of young, unmarried women provided an incentive for the collection of such sensitive data on a national level. Thus, the first national survey of the sexual behavior of teenage girls took place in 1971 (Zelnik et al., 1981). Since then, surveys have been ongoing, responding to continuing needs to understand early pregnancy and also responding to needs to understand more recent phenomena such as HIV. As surveys have evolved, their usefulness for understanding sexual activity has continued to improve. Thus, this chapter focuses on some of the most recent data on sexual activity among youth during contemporary times, drawing on information about longer term changes where possible. Sexual activity among the youngest adolescents and preadolescents is described where sample sizes permit. It is useful to begin with an understanding of the trends in and current prevalence of problems that stem from sexual risk-taking.

## Pregnancy and Childbearing Among Youth

### Pregnancy

In 1997, the most recent year for which estimates are available, there were approximately 870,000 pregnancies among women age 15 to 19, including 358,000 among those under age 18 (Ventura et al., 2001). These pregnancies are more likely to be unintended (too early or not wanted at any time) than those occurring to adults (Brown & Eisenberg, 1995; Henshaw, 1998). Pregnancies can end in live birth, abortion, stillbirth, or miscarriage. More pregnancies to teens result in abortions than among any other age group. In 1996, 30% of pregnancies to teens ended in abortion. Of the remaining pregnancies, 483,000 ended in live births and 134,000 in miscarriage or stillbirth (Ventura et al., 2001).

The teen pregnancy rate is the number of pregnancies per 1,000 females age 15 to 19. At this writing, estimates of teen pregnancy rates are available from 1976 to 1997. Generating estimates of pregnancy requires data on the three possible outcomes of pregnancy, namely, live birth, induced abortion, and fetal loss (miscarriage and stillbirth). Pregnancy rates are available only since 1976 because that is the earliest time point for which fetal loss data can be estimated for unmarried teens, and because abortion data before this time are less reliable (Bachrach et al., 1997). The most recent pregnancy data is for 1997 because that is the most recent year for which abortion data are available.

In the two decades prior to 1990, teen pregnancy rates fluctuated somewhat, but generally increased (mostly due to an increase in the proportion of teens who had had sexual intercourse; The Alan Guttmacher Institute, 1994) until 1991. As shown in Figure 5–1, from the mid-1970s to 1980 there was a steady increase, from 101 to 110 pregnancies per 1,000 female teens, followed by a slow decrease to a low of 105 in 1986 and 1987. The fact that this period (1980 to 1987) was relatively stable despite increases in sexual activity probably reflects better contraceptive use among teens. This notion is supported by data that show that the percentage of women who were teens at first premarital intercourse who used a contraceptive method at first intercourse increased between 1980 and 1990, from 53% to 71% (Peterson, 1995). Following 1987, the rate shot up, reaching a peak in 1991 at 117 pregnancies per 1,000 female teens. This is an overall increase of 15% between 1976 and 1991. After 1991, however, the rate began to decrease, and by 1997 it had reached the lowest recorded level in two decades, at 99 per 1,000 teen females.

## Abortion

Figure 5–1 also shows trends in the abortion rate among teens (number of abortions per 1,000 females age 15 to 19) for the period from 1976 through 1996. The abortion rate among teens increased in the years following its legalization in 1973 then stabilized and began a decrease in the 1980s that is ongoing. In 1976, the rate of abortions among teens was 34 per 1,000 females age 15 to 19. After increasing to 43 in 1980, the rate remained relatively constant until about 1988, after which it declined to 28 per 1,000 in 1997 (Ventura et al., 2001). Figure 5-1 shows this rate, along with the teen pregnancy rate (number of pregnancies per 1,000 females age 15 to 19) and birthrate (number of births per 1,000 females age 15 to 19). The birth rate will be discussed in the next section in more detail and across a longer time period, but it is useful to examine the three rates together to see what contributions the changes in the number of abortions and the changes in the number of pregnancies have made to the trends in the birthrates. The recent decline in the birthrate, beginning in 1991, occurred despite a continuing decrease in the abortion rate and in tandem with a decrease in the pregnancy rate.

## Births

Vital statistics data allow us to examine longer term trends in childbearing and to consider data for more recent years than in the case of pregnancy and abortion. Figure 5–2 shows trends for the period from 1940 through 2000, for all

## Figure 5–1: Estimated pregnancy, birth, and abortion rates for teens (United States)

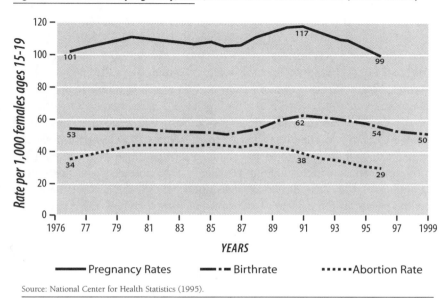

Source: National Center for Health Statistics (1995).

## Figure 5–2: Birthrates for all teens and unmarried teens (United States)

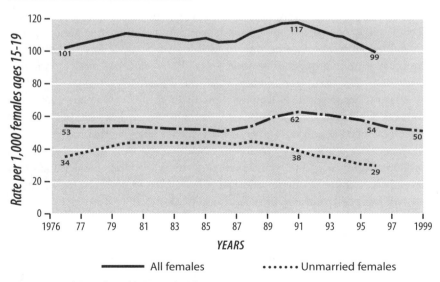

Source: National Center for Health Statistics (1995).

teenage females for unmarried teen females. It is useful to consider the birthrate not only among teens as a whole, but also among unmarried teens, since early childbearing and out-of-wedlock childbearing are both of interest.

Between 1991 and 1999, the birthrate among teens declined from 62.1 to 49.6 births per 1,000 females age 15 to 19, a decline of 22% (Ventura et al., 2001). This decline has been received as good news by policymakers, researchers, and the general public. The current teen birthrate is actually lower than the rate in 1940, when it was 54.1 per 1,000 women age 15 to 19. After 1940, teen birthrates showed patterns characteristic of overall birthrates during this baby boom era. The rate increased from 1945 to 1957, when it peaked at 96 per 1,000 women age 15 to 19. The teen birthrate then declined gradually and remained stable throughout the late 1970s and most of the 1980s. Beginning in 1987, the rate increased until 1991, at which point the recent decline began. In the context of the larger picture, therefore, the current teen birthrate is much lower than the high level reached during the baby boom and has recently dropped slightly below the comparatively low level that was maintained through most of the 1980s.

Although the birthrate among *all* teens has fluctuated somewhat since 1940, the trend in the birthrate to *unmarried* teens has varied less dramatically: It increased consistently up to 1994 (Ventura & Bachrach, 2000). The birthrate to unmarried teens in 1940 was only 7 per 1,000 women age 15 to 19. The rate began to stabilize in 1991, reached a peak of 46 in 1994, and then declined to 40.4 by 1999. Thus the recent trend in unmarried birthrates resembles the recent trend in overall teen birthrates and the trend in pregnancies, that is, a decline following a period of increase. It is important to note that although teen nonmarital birthrates have been generally increasing, teens do not account for the bulk of nonmarital childbearing. Only about one-third of all nonmarital births in 1998 were to teen mothers (Ventura & Bachrach, 2000).

Despite recent declines among teens in pregnancy rates, birthrates, and unmarried birthrates, these rates remain higher than those among teens in other developed countries. The available evidence suggests that rates of sexual experience are not appreciably different between the United States and other developed countries. Thus, the difference between the United States and other developed countries in these rates stems from U.S. adolescents' less frequent use and less effective use of birth control (Hatcher et al., 1998).

## STDs Among Youth

Each year, about three million teenagers acquire an STD (Institute of Medicine, 1997). One quarter of all sexually transmitted infection cases in the United States are among teens. Rates of chlamydia, gonorrhea, vaginitis, and pelvic inflammatory disease are all highest in adolescents and decline dramatically with increasing age (Hatcher et al., 1998).

Gonorrhea and chlamydia are the two most common curable STDs among teenagers. Gonorrhea rates have been relatively constant among teens between the 1980s and the 1990s. Between 1995 and 1999, rates declined. Among both the youngest males, age 10 to 14, and among males age 15 to 19, the rate declined 32%.[1] The gonorrhea rate declined for females as well during that time period. Among females age 10 to 14, it declined by 24%, and among females age 15 to 19, it declined by 22% (Division of STD Prevention, 2000).[2] It is possible that such declines reflect the effectiveness of recent programs designed to increase awareness of HIV and STD prevention among youth.

For female adolescents, the rate of chlamydia infection is estimated to be two to four times that of gonorrhea infection. In 1999, the rate among females age 15 to 19 was 2,484 per 100,000 (compared with 738 reported gonorrhea cases per 100,000), whereas the rate of reported cases among males was about the same as their rate of gonorrhea in 1999 (Division of STD Prevention, 2000). Incidences of herpes infection, genital warts, and asymptomatic cervical human papillomavirus (HPV) infection all increased dramatically from the mid-1960s to 1995 (Hatcher et al., 1998).

Since HIV has a long latency period before manifestation as AIDS, a good indication of the incidence of HIV among teens is found in the incidence of AIDS among those having just aged out of the teen years. During the period 1996 to 2000, there were 1,722 reported cases of AIDS among those aged 13 to 19, whereas there were 36,252 cases of AIDS among those aged 20 to 29 (Centers for Disease Control and Prevention [CDC], 2001).

## Sources of National Data on Sexual Activity Among Teenagers

This section describes some key sources of national data on estimates of sexual activity among youth in the United States. These surveys are designed to help explain teenage pregnancy rates and birthrates, the risk of HIV, and health or reproductive health in general. Each survey occupies a unique niche in helping to understand teen sexual activity, its antecedents, and its consequences. Estimates from the surveys can be compared, but there are limits to this comparability because of differences in the surveys' purposes, the populations they cover, and the methodology employed (for example, see Santelli et al., 2000). This is not an exhaustive list.

John Kantner and Melvin Zelnik, researchers at Johns Hopkins University in Baltimore, conducted the first National Survey of Young Women in 1971. The survey was undertaken to remedy what was then a complete absence of information at the national level on teen sexual behavior and contraceptive use (see Zelnik et al., 1981). The 1971 and 1976 rounds included females ages 15 to 19. In 1979, the survey included both young women age 15 to 19 and young men age 17 to 21, but only those young men residing in standard metropolitan statistical areas. Sample sizes were 4,341 and 2,178 for the 1971 and 1976 female surveys, and 1,717 and 917 for the female and male metropolitan-area samples in 1979. The surveys were designed to collect information on sexual activity, contraceptive use, and premarital pregnancy and its resolution and to provide data for trends in these events over time. The National Survey of Family Growth (NSFG) took over this function when it began interviewing teens in 1982. The Kantner and Zelnik surveys are the source of the data from the 1970s, the earliest data presented in the following sections of this chapter.

The NSFG is a principal source of estimates of sexual activity among females. The NSFG collects information on sexual behavior in the context of its primary purpose, which is to provide data on factors related to birth and pregnancy rates among women ages 15 to 44 in the United States. Therefore, as of the most recent data collection, the NSFG data has included information only on heterosexual vaginal intercourse and selected characteristics of the woman's male partner. The NSFG was conducted in 1973, 1976, 1982, 1988, and 1995. The population interviewed included only ever-married females in the first two surveys but expanded to include never-married females in the 1982, 1988, and 1995 surveys. The 1995 survey included more aspects of sexual experience and activity than in past cycles and also kept the time series intact (see Abma et al., 1997).

Because of the scarcity of national data on the study of the sexual behavior of teen males, the National Survey of Adolescent Males (NSAM) was designed to provide national information on adolescent males' sexual activity and related topics (for methodology, see Sonenstein et al., 1998; Sonenstein et al., 1997; Sonenstein et al., 1989). The NSAM's data collection timing parallels that of the NSFG, with rounds in 1988 and in 1995, enabling the comparison of estimates for females and males from two independent samples for the same points in time. The 1988 NSAM included 1,880 never-married males age 15 to 19, and the 1995 round included 1,729 males age 15 to 19 of all marital statuses.

The National Longitudinal Study of Adolescent Health, also referred to as Add Health and initiated in March 1994, provides data on a wide range of health behaviors and health-related characteristics of adolescents in grades 7 through 12 (see Bearman et al., 1997). It employs an innovative design including variables measuring the individual, family, peer group, school, and community. The primary sample consisted of 90,000 students in 7th through 12th grades from 160 schools, during the 1994 to 1995 school year. Researchers also conducted in-home interviews with a subsample of 20,000 of these students and their parents in 1995 and again in 1996. They interviewed school administrators of the subsample of adolescents as well. The topics addressed by the survey include sexual behavior, STDs, number of sexual partners, forced sexual intercourse, and contraceptive use. Both young men and women were represented in the sample, and the design involved oversamples of special sub-groups defined by race/ethnicity, socioeconomic status, and physical disability. To extend the investigation of risk behaviors beyond the early teenage years, a follow-up survey was designed, which began in August 2001.

The Youth Risk Behavior Surveillance System (YRBSS) is conducted by the CDC and provides data on health-risk behaviors among high school students through surveys conducted at the national, state, and local levels (see Kann et al. 1993). It has been conducted in 1990, 1991, 1993, 1995, 1997, and 1999, employing a cross-sectional, three-stage, cluster sample of students in grades 9 to 12 in schools nationwide. Samples have ranged from approximately 11,600 to approximately 16,300 respondents. Oversampling of schools with high pro-portions of African American and Latino students enables separate analyses of these special groups. The behaviors addressed by the survey are those that increase risks of social problems, morbidity, and mortality among adolescents.

Because it is biennial, the YRBSS provides timely data on sexual risk-tak-ing indicators among students at the national level. Through its surveys admin-istered in 33 states, it is also useful for providing such information at the state level. The YRBSS provides measurement of basic demographic information such as age, grade, gender, and race, but lacks any more detailed background information on youth. By virtue of being a school-based sample, it does not include the subpopulation of youth that, for whatever reason, are not in school at a particular point in time.

## Trends and Differentials in Sexual Behavior Among Youth

### *What Fraction of Youth Are Sexually Experienced?*

Since the early 1970s, more and more youth in their teenage years have become sexually experienced, that is, had sex at least once by the survey date. Figure 5–3 shows this trend and represents the full time series that is covered by national data on sexual activity among the total population of youth. Note that data for males are available only since 1979 and are restricted to metro-politan-area, never-married males age 17 to 19 at each of the three time points. This is because the 1979 National Survey of Young Men included only metro-politan areas and interviewed men age 17 to 21. The percentages in Figure 5–3 represent a snapshot or a cross-section at each survey point; that is, they show how many teens have had sex, at whatever age they happened to be at the time of the survey (15, 16, 17, 18, or 19).

At the beginning of the 1970s, about one-third of never-married teen girls had had sexual intercourse at least once. A decade later, nearly half had had sex-ual intercourse. The proportion peaked in the late 1980s, when a little more than half of never-married teen girls reported having had sex. This pattern is

## Figure 5–3: Percentage of teens who have ever had sex

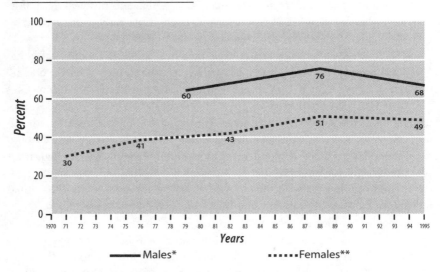

* Never-married metropolitan males age 17 to 19. Sources: 1979—Sonenstein et al., 1989; 1988 and 1995—National Survey of Adolescent Males

**Never-married females age 15 to 19. Sources: 1971 and 1976—Zelnick et al., 1981; 1982, 1988, and 1995—National Survey of Family Growth, Cycles 3,4, and 5.

echoed by the males, but more males report sexual experience than females at every point. At the end of the 1970s, two-thirds of never-married, metropolitan teen males had had sex at least once. Ten years later, this climbed to 76% of such males. However, this increase appears to be stopping in more recent years. Among females, the proportion stabilized, and among males, a slight decline actually occurred between 1988 and 1995. Since this pattern is so important, it is discussed below for the larger sample of all never-married teen males and never-married teen females.

As Table 5–1 demonstrates, the proportion of never-married males who had ever had sex declined from 60% to 55% between 1988 and 1995, a decrease that is statistically significant (Sonenstein et al., 1998). The most recent trend data that have been compiled and presented in detail from the YRBSS reinforce the evidence for a decline. Between 1991 and 1997, the percentage of high school males who ever had sex declined by 11% (CDC, 1998). Among females, the data show no statistically significant changes in percentages who are sexually experienced since the late 1980s (also see Singh & Darroch, 1999).[3] In the larger context, this absence of change is actually an encouraging departure from the trend of steady increases in sexual experience among teen females since the 1970s.

This pattern in sexual activity may be reflecting fluctuations over the decade in conditions that shape the attitudes of youth, through influences that

Table 5–1: Percentage of never-married males and females ages 15–19 who have ever had sexual intercourse, by age at interview, race, and ethnicity.

| | NEVER-MARRIED MALES | | NEVER-MARRIED FEMALES | | |
| --- | --- | --- | --- | --- | --- |
| | 1988 | 1995 | 1982 | 1988 | 1995 |
| Total ages 15 to 19 | 60% | 55% | 43% | 51% | 49% |
| Age at interview | | | | | |
| 15 | 33 | 27 | 18 | 28 | 22 |
| 16 | 50 | 45 | 29 | 34 | 38 |
| 17 | 66 | 58 | 40 | 50 | 50 |
| 18 | 72 | 67 | 54 | 69 | 63 |
| 19 | 86 | 84 | 66 | 75 | 73 |
| Black | 81 | 80 | 58 | 60 | 58 |
| White | 57 | 50 | 40 | 51 | 48 |
| Latino | 60 | 61 | 40 | 46 | 53 |

Source: 1982, 1988, and 1995 National Survey of Family Growth, and 1988 and 1995 National Survey of Adolescent Males.

include peers, parents, adults, and the media. There is evidence that attitudes have indeed changed. The percentage of teen males believing that it is okay to have sex even if one doesn't plan to marry the partner has decreased parallel to the trend in sexual behavior (Ku et al., 1998).

The proportion of teens who are sexually experienced at any given time varies dramatically depending on exact age. By age 19, the majority of teens have had sex. In 1995, 84% of males and 73% of females age 19 reported having had sex (Table 5–1).[4] Sexual experience is rarer among 15-year-olds. In 1995, 22% of never-married females and never-married males age 15 reported having had sex.

Since the earliest available data, studies have documented differences between young white and black females in sexual activity. Black females are more likely than white females to be sexually active, especially during the earliest teen years, a difference that persists to the present day. Table 5–1 shows that in 1995, higher proportions of black male and female youth had had sex than was the case for the white males and females. In the case of the females, it appears that the rates for white and black youth have become slightly more similar over time, because of increases among white female youth. (The change in the proportion of sexually experienced Latino females is based on small sample sizes and is not statistically reliable.)

## Age at Initiation of Sexual Activity

Study of the initiation of sexual activity is important for many reasons. It marks the beginning of potential exposure to STDs and pregnancy. Its timing is strongly associated with other aspects of sexual behavior that increase risks, such as frequency of intercourse and number of partners (Abma et al., 1997; Kost & Forrest, 1992; Seidman et al., 1992).

*What are the long-term trends in early initiation of sex?* Our knowledge of the trends in sexual activity among youth is limited by the relative recentness of data collection on the subject, but recent data can nonetheless shed light on earlier time periods. If surveys collect information from older women and men about their experiences when they were teenagers, the behavior of these older cohorts can be compared with that of the younger cohorts. Trends based on retrospective data should be interpreted with care due to possible recall error that may increase with the length of time between first intercourse and the interview. Nonetheless, what such data suggest is consistent with available cross-sectional data, that is, that young men and women have been initiating sexual activity earlier. For example, among women who turned 20 four decades ago (between 1958 and 1960), only 3% reported having had sex sometime before the age of 15, whereas among those who turned 20 in the early 1990s, 15% had had sex by this age (Moore et al., 1995; National Center for Health Statistics, 1995).

*Who has sex before age 15?* Many contemporary programs and messages geared toward youth encourage the delay of sexual intercourse. It is important to know which teens are beginning sexual activity earliest, both to target programs accordingly and to understand the process leading to initiation of sex. Table 5–2 shows that overall, in 1995, 19% of teen females had sex before age 15. About twice as many young black females (31%) initiated sex before age 15 as did young white females (16%). Because these differences are so large, these two groups are presented separately in the table, allowing us to examine whether characteristics and features of their lives operate differently on their behavior.

The family living situations that children experience makes a difference for early sexual initiation. Young female teens who grew up with both parents always present are less likely to have had sex by age 15, compared with those who grew up experiencing other family forms. This pattern holds for both black and white young women. The family form in which early sex is most common is the single parent from birth: For black teen females with this background, the proportion having had sex before age 15 was twice that of those who had grown up with two parents (42% compared with 21%).

This association of family structure with early sexual initiation is well documented. Whether a child grows up with two birthparents from birth to the time of leaving home, compared with growing up in any other type of parental arrangement, influences whether the child begins sex early, becomes pregnant, and/or has a birth during the teen years (Abma et al., 1997; Moore et al., 1998;

## Table 5–2:  Percentage of females ages 15–19 who had sexual intercourse before age 15, by selected characteristics.

|  | TOTAL | WHITE | BLACK |
|---|---|---|---|
| *Total* | *19%* | *16%* | *31%* |
| *Family background: Lived with …* | | | |
| Both (natural or adoptive) parents from birth | 11 | 10 | 21 |
| Single parent from birth | 34 | — | 42 |
| Both parents, then one parent | 23 | 18 | 34 |
| Ever lived with a stepparent | 25 | 22 | 36 |
| *Mother's education* | | | |
| Less than high school | 29 | 28 | 41 |
| High school degree | 18 | 15 | 31 |
| College | 14 | 12 | 24 |
| *Median family income of community*** | | | |
| $0–19,999 | 37 | — | 42 |
| $20,000–49,000 | 20 | 19 | 29 |
| $50,000 or more | 11 | 11 | — |
| *Unemployment rate (female) of community** | | | |
| 0–4% | 16 | 16 | 26 |
| 5–9% | 18 | 15 | 26 |
| 10% or higher | 31 | 21 | 38 |
| *Percentage of females separated or divorced in community*** | | | |
| 0–12 | 15 | 14 | 28 |
| 13–18 | 24 | 22 | 26 |
| 19 or higher | 32 | 23 | 35 |

— Figure omitted due to small number of cases
Source: 1995 National Survey of Family Growth.
* Community characteristics represent 1995 values and are measured at the level of the block group. This is a geographic unit smaller than a census tract, which is smaller than a county.

Wu & Martinson, 1993). The reasons that the type of family in which children grow up makes a difference for their sexual activity, pregnancy, and childbearing are the subject of much public debate and scientific research. An important focus of research is clarifying the relative importance of the different dimensions of childhood experience, for example, the family's economic and material resources, whether both parents are present in the household, and the stability or turbulence with respect to their presence. These factors are all highly interconnected. Many studies find that family income is strongly related to premarital birth among youth. However, one study showed that the number of changes in parents' marital status also made a significant impact, regardless of family income (Wu, 1996).

Obtaining measures of family income for youth is difficult because younger respondents to surveys do not usually know what their parents' income is. One way to examine the effect of family socioeconomic status is to use a substitute that is highly related to it, such as the education of the mother or father. Studies over the past decade have shown very consistently that mothers with higher educations have children who are less likely to begin sex early, have unprotected sex, become pregnant, and have a birth at a young age (Cooksey et al., 1996; Hayward et al., 1992; Moore et al., 1998). It is likely that this relationship is reflecting the effect of greater economic resources in the family. It could also be that more highly educated mothers have higher expectations for their children's education and this influences the emphasis they place on helping to avoid early pregnancy. In addition, more highly educated mothers may have better skills at conveying how to obtain and use contraceptives, perhaps reinforcing sex education taught in schools.

Table 5–2 demonstrates this pattern. Female youth whose mothers have more education are less likely to initiate sex early. Among young females whose mothers had less than a high school education, almost one-third had sex before age 15, compared with 14% of those whose mothers had attended some college.

One important line of analysis that has been applied to the understanding of socioeconomic status, family structure, and racial differentials in sexual behavior concerns the neighborhood context in which youth mature (Brewster, 1994a, 1994b; Lauritsen, 1994; Sucoff & Upchurch, 1998). Local socioeconomic factors may provide a setting in which early sexual activity and pregnancy are seen by youth as beneficial rather than costly. The fewer the opportunities for advancement and achievement of adult status through economic means, the lower are costs associated with behavior leading to (the possibility of) early pregnancy and childbearing. Sexual activity may take on more prominence and importance as a marker of the transition into adulthood in such a setting.

Table 5–2 is consistent with findings that the community in which children become teenagers is associated with their timing of sexual activity. Generally, female youth of both races were more likely to have intercourse before age 15 if they were in communities with fewer socioeconomic opportunities and more family disruption. Those with lower median family incomes, higher unemployment rates among females, and higher percentages of females separated or divorced had higher percentages of teens having had sex before age 15. As a specific example, 37% of teen females from communities with a median family income below $20,000 in 1995 had had sex before age 15. On the other hand, only 11% of those from communities with a median family income of $50,000 or more had had sex before age 15. This association between the characteristics of the community and relatively early initiation of sexual activity is apparent for both black and white female adolescents. Brewster (1994b) suggests that the absence from these communities of adults who exemplify rewards from stable unions and the communities' shortage of attainable economic adult roles may shape youth perceptions about their own future prospects.

## Multiple Sexual Partners

Individuals who have multiple sexual partners increase the chances that they will encounter a partner with an STD. Compared with older men and women, adolescents are more likely to have multiple partners in a given time period because most are not married. Much of the published data on the number of partners adolescents have is confined to the group of teens who have had sex in the three months prior to the survey, or the "sexually active" teens. This group of teens will have higher numbers of partners than the general population of teens, the majority of whom are not sexually active. Among sexually active teens, the number of sexual partners appears to be increasing. In the early 1970s, 38% of sexually active female teens living in metropolitan areas had had more than one partner in their lifetime. By 1988, 61% had had more than one partner, and in 1995, 70% (Kost & Forrest, 1992; National Center for Health Statistics, 1995). However, the most recent data indicate a decline in multiple sex partners among high school students between 1991 and 1999 (CDC, 2000).

*Who has multiple sexual partners?* Do the same factors that affect the age at first sex affect the chances of having multiple partners? Recent data show that the answer is yes. Table 5–3 demonstrates a clear pattern between a clear pattern between the age at which females' first intercourse occurs and the likelihood of having three or more partners in the year prior to the survey. Among those who were 13 or younger at first intercourse, 38% had three or more partners in the past year. In comparison, among those who were 17 or older at first sex, only 15% had three or more partners. This pattern—that is, increasing percentages with three or more recent partners at younger ages of first intercourse—is the most pronounced for the younger adolescent females (age 15 to 17) and for black teen females.

For all teen females, and for each subgroup (younger teen females, white, and black teen females), coming from a two-parent household rather than any other family type means fewer sexual partners in the recent past.

Young adolescent females from communities that are poorer have higher numbers of sexual partners. Of females age 15 to 17 who were living in locales with low family incomes (median family income under $20,000), 21% had three or more partners in the past year, compared with only 4% among those surrounded by families who were better off economically (median family income of $50,000 or more). Those living in areas in which unemployment and divorce were more prevalent also had higher numbers of partners.

## Table 5–3: Percentage of females ages 15–19 who had three or more male sexual partners in the past year, by selected characteristics.

| | AGES 15–19 | AGES 15–17 | WHITE | BLACK117 |
|---|---|---|---|---|
| *Total* | 12 | 9 | 11 | 19 |
| *Age at first intercourse* | | | | |
| Before age 14 | 38 | 41 | 37 | 45 |
| 14 | 31 | 26 | 28 | 36 |
| 15 | 23 | 17 | 28 | 19 |
| 16 | 11 | — | 9 | 12 |
| 17–19 | 15 | — | 14 | 29 |
| *Family (lived with)* | | | | |
| Both (natural or adoptive) parents from birth | 7 | 4 | 9 | 14 |
| Single parent from birth | 20 | 20 | 18 | 24 |
| Both parents, then one parent | 17 | 13 | 13 | 23 |
| Ever lived with a stepparent | 13 | 11 | 13 | 22 |
| *Median family income of community** | | | | |
| $0–19,999 | 22 | 21 | 15 | 24 |
| $20,000–49,000 | 12 | 9 | 10 | 22 |
| $50,000 or more | 6 | 4 | 5 | 11 |
| *Unemployment rate (female) of community** | | | | |
| 0–4% | 10 | 7 | 10 | 16 |
| 5–9% | 9 | 7 | 7 | 18 |
| 10% or higher | 19 | 16 | 15 | 26 |
| *Percentage of females separated or divorced in community** | | | | |
| 0-12 | 9 | 5 | 8 | 18 |
| 13-18 | 15 | 13 | 12 | 27 |
| 19 or higher | 17 | 16 | 15 | 17 |

— Figure omitted due to small number of cases

Source: 1995 National Survey of Family Growth.

* Community characteristics represent 1995 values and are measured at the level of the block group. This is a geo-graphic unit smaller than a census tract, which is smaller than a county.

## *First Sexual Intercourse: Voluntary or Nonvoluntary?*

The ongoing need for research designed to help understand sexual initiation has resulted in better information on an important topic directly related to the well-being of youth, namely, the incidence of nonvoluntary intercourse. The data and analyses usually focus on females, although surveys have generated important information on this topic for males as well (see, for example, Laumann et al., 1994). This information makes it clearer that becoming sexually active is not always a deliberate decision. A small but important minority of youth have first sexual experiences that are nonvoluntary. Nonvoluntary first intercourse is more likely among younger teen females (Abma et al., 1997; Abma et al., 1998; Moore et al., 1989), so the issues associated with nonvoluntary intercourse and early intercourse are interrelated. The negative consequences of nonvoluntary sex for females include a lower likelihood of contraceptive use, higher frequency of subsequent sexual activity, greater numbers of partners, and diminished psychological well-being and adjustment, compared with women whose first sexual intercourse was voluntary. Table 5–4 shows that in 1995, about 8% of teen females reported that their first intercourse was nonvoluntary.[5] For those whose first intercourse occurred before age 14, 21% had a nonvoluntary experience, compared with 3% among those age 17 to 19.

Higher percentages of black teen females and those from disrupted families (lived with two parents, then just one parent) had nonvoluntary first intercourse. This ties in with the aforementioned pattern of earlier sexual initiation among young women from nonintact family types. Parental supervision may be an important mechanism affecting teen sexual activity (Thomson et al., 1992), therefore it may be one factor underlying this pattern of greater early and nonvoluntary intercourse among female adolescents from households with fewer parents/parent-figures. Family environment deserves further careful study if we are to understand its role in the susceptibility of young teens to nonvoluntary intercourse.

One positive development in assessing nonvoluntary sex is capturing the wantedness of the experience on a continuum rather than relying completely on classifications as voluntary or not voluntary. When given an opportunity to rank first-sex wantedness on a scale of 1 to 10, with 10 representing *most* wanted experiences, teen females most often reported values of 5 or higher (68%, not shown in table). However, sometimes they reported values of 4 or lower even if they reported first intercourse as "voluntary." This combination of reporting (voluntary but relatively unwanted) is shown in the second column of Table 5–4. One-quarter of sexually experienced teen females characterized their first intercourse this way, and it was more common among females who were younger at first sex. This may be reflecting a large amount of ambivalence surrounding first sexual intercourse and a willingness to go through with an experience that they do not feel entirely positive about. Pregnancy prevention programs that help youth develop interpersonal skills (such as communication, negotiation, and refusal) and understand and cope with social pressures (see Kirby, 1997) may be particularly suited to addressing this type of experience.

The National Center for Health Statistics contains information on nonvoluntary first sex for the full age range of women in the National Center for Health Statistics survey (ages 15 to 44). This offers a glimpse into events as far

## Table 5–4: Percentage of females ages 15–19 who had sexual intercourse whose first intercourse was not voluntary, voluntary but unwanted, and voluntary and wanted.

| | NOT VOLUNTARY* | VOLUNTARY, UNWANTED** | VOLUNTARY, WANTED*** |
|---|---|---|---|
| *Total* | 8 | 25 | 67 |
| *Age at first intercourse* | | | |
| Younger than age 14 | 21 | 40 | 40 |
| 14 | 8 | 28 | 65 |
| 15 | 9 | 20 | 71 |
| 16 | 3 | 19 | 79 |
| 17 through 19 | 3 | 19 | 78 |
| *Race/Ethnicity* | | | |
| White | 7 | 22 | 71 |
| Black | 13 | 33 | 54 |
| Latino | 9 | 26 | 66 |
| *Family background: Lived with ...* | | | |
| Both (natural or adoptive) parents from birth | 7 | 25 | 69 |
| Single parent from birth | 8 | 29 | 63 |
| Both parents, then one parent | 12 | 22 | 67 |
| Ever lived with a stepparent | 8 | 22 | 70 |

Source: 1995 National Survey of Family Growth.

* First intercourse was reported as "rape" or "not voluntary."
**First intercourse was reported as "voluntary" and value on scale of wantedness was between 1 and 4.
***First intercourse was reported as "voluntary" and value on scale of wantedness was between 5 and 10.

back as the late 1950s. Among women whose first intercourse was between 1958 and 1974, 10% reported that it was nonvoluntary. This is in contrast to 6% among women whose first intercourse was between 1990 and 1995 (Abma et al., 1997). Thus, it would appear that women report a slightly decreasing amount of nonvoluntary first sex over the years. However, definitive conclusions about this trend should not be made on the basis of this evidence alone. It is possible that different age groups interpret their experiences differently depending on prevailing mainstream and subcultural norms at the time of the event. In addition, the amount of time that has passed since the event can affect respondents' ability to recall their thoughts at the time of the event.

### Females' First Sex: How Old Are Their Partners?

In recent years, there has been heightened concern over the age gaps between young females and the males with whom they have sex and especially conceive pregnancies. Some believe that most pregnancies to teens are caused by much older males. One example of a result of this concern is Section 906 of the 1996 Welfare Reform Act, which focuses attention on enforcing statutory rape laws as a means of curbing teen pregnancy. Part of the reason for the impression of a high and increasing prevalence of younger-female/older-male partnerships lies in the way figures are presented. For example, many statistics show percentages of females age 15 to 19 who had births with men age 20 or older. This grouping includes some age pairings that would not necessarily be seen as objectionable, and would not violate states' statutory rape laws. A more important question for addressing the well-being of children and youth is how often young adolescent females have sex with significantly older males. The role of older men in this regard, including long-term trends, must remain speculative, due to a paucity of data.

As Table 5–5 demonstrates, in 1995, among the teens who had had first intercourse at the age of 15 or younger, 13% had first male partners who were age 20 or older. Very few of these situations involved males age 25 or older; most were in their early 20s. The majority of teen females who were 15 or younger at first sex had partners who were 17 or younger (66%). Most teens follow this pattern, with the majority having first partners younger or older by about two years, echoing the age difference patterns among adult women.

Although most female teens have first sexual partners their own age or within two years of their own age, the large age gaps that do occur between female youth and their male partners have important implications for youth well-being. Larger age gaps tend to be associated with lower likelihood of contraceptive use and less-wanted intercourse on the part of females (Abma et al., 1998) and a higher likelihood of pregnancy and childbearing (Darroch et al., 1999).

## Contraceptive Use

Although the long-term trend has been toward greater proportions of young people being sexually experienced, it has been paralleled by a general trend toward greater use of contraception. Clear improvements are evident in teens' contraceptive use at first sex, but relatively high proportions still use no method of contraception at their most recent sex (Abma & Sonenstein, 2001; Manlove & Terry, 2000).[6]

Since the Food and Drug Administration's approval of oral contraceptives in 1960, the pill has become one of the two most common methods of birth control among teens. Most recently, however, teens are relying less on oral contraceptives. In 1988, among never-married teens who were sexually active, 43% used the pill at their last sex, but only 25% did so in 1995 (Abma & Sonenstein, 2001). The oral contraceptive is considered an effective method for preventing pregnancy, but its efficacy depends on teens adhering to a daily regimen. The

**Table 5–5: Percentage of females ages 15–19 who have had voluntary sexual intercourse, by age of first male partner, according to age at first intercourse.**

| | | | AGE OF PARTNER (YEARS) | | | | |
|---|---|---|---|---|---|---|---|
| CHARACTERISTICS | TOTAL | YOUNGER THAN 16 | 16–17 | 18–19 | 20–22 | 23–24 | 25 OR OLDER |
| *Total* | *100* | *18* | *43* | *24* | *11* | *2* | *1* |
| *Females' age at first intercourse* | | | | | | | |
| Younger than age 16 | 100 | 22 | 44 | 21 | 7 | 2 | 4 |
| 16 | 100 | 2 | 42 | 35 | 14 | 4 | 4 |
| 17 | 100 | 1 | 28 | 42 | 19 | 5 | 6 |
| 18 | 100 | 1 | 8 | 37 | 33 | 10 | 9 |
| 19 | 100 | — | 2 | 24 | 46 | 11 | 17 |

— Figure omitted due to small number of cases
Source: 1995 National Survey of Family Growth.
Note: Percentages may not add to 100 due to rounding.

other most commonly used method among sexually active youth is the condom, and its popularity has been growing. Over the past decade, the threat of STDs and HIV/AIDS became publicly recognized and addressed. This provided impetus for much more widespread and easier access to condoms and school, and media-based messages about the importance and proper use of this method. Education on how to obtain and use birth control methods has become nearly universal among youth. In 1995, 88% of girls and 79% of boys received formal instruction on methods of birth control before they were 18 years old (Lindberg et al., 2000).

Most recently, hormonal methods have become available that require less concerted effort to be used effectively, which may be especially important for teens' contraceptive use. Among black female teens who were using some method in 1995, 23% were using Norplant implants or Depo-Provera injections, as were 9% of white teens (Abma et al., 1997).

The trend in overall contraceptive use and condom use at first sex is depicted for females in Figure 5–4. Judging by reports of women age 15 to 44 in 1995, there has been a large increase in the use of a method at first sex over approximately the past two decades. Contraceptive use increased from 50% for those having first sex before 1980 to 76% for those having first sex between 1990 and 1995. The condom in particular has become an increasingly common method at first sex. Eighteen percent of females used the condom at first intercourse before 1980, whereas triple that percent (54%) used it at first intercourse in the early to mid-1990s.

**Figure 5–4: Percentage of females ages 15–44 who used any method of contraception at first premarital sex, and percent who used a condom.**

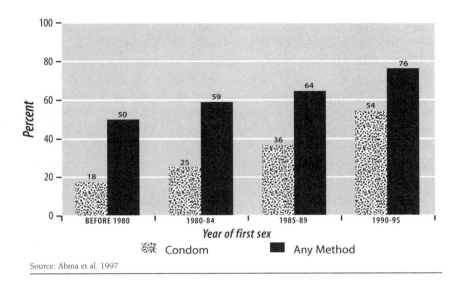

*Year of first sex*

Condom          Any Method

Source: Abma et al. 1997

Young males are also doing a better job of protecting themselves and their partners. A decade ago, about 60% of sexually experienced teen males used a condom at last sex, whereas in 1995, 67% did so. Even the youngest males have shown improvements in using the condom. Among those age 15, 60% used a condom at last sex in 1988, compared with 69% in 1995 (Sonenstein et al., 1998). Recent data for high-school students shows a continuation of this trend through 1997 (CDC, 1998). Young adolescent males in particular (age 15 to 17), are using contraception in general—that is, using any method at all at last sex—to a greater degree today than was the case a decade ago (Sonenstein et al., 1998).

## Conclusion

Children making the transition to adolescence and adulthood are in a uniquely challenging position, historically and demographically speaking. The amount of time between puberty, on one hand, and marriage and economic independence, on the other, has been increasing. Youth are not responding by delaying sexual activity but instead become sexually active sooner than in the past. Although many sexually active youth avert negative consequences by practicing contraception, others become pregnant and in some cases become parents at an early age, before reaching their educational and job preparation goals. About half of teens age 15 to 19 have had sex at least once, and about one-fifth have had sex before age 15. Approximately 10% of teen females become pregnant each year, amounting to about 900,000 pregnancies per year. About half of the pregnancies result in a live birth. In 1999, 50 out of every 1,000 teen females had a birth. The vast majority of teen births are nonmarital.

Rates of sexually transmitted infections among teens increased during the 1960s and 1970s and remained high through the 1980s and 1990s. About a quarter of all sexually transmitted infection cases are among teenagers. Sexually active teens are especially vulnerable to certain STDs such as chlamydia and gonorrhea.

Thus, the current circumstances for youth are far from problem-free, and certain groups of youth are at greater risk than others. Black youth, those from low-income families, those from neighborhoods with lower socioeconomic status, and those from single-parent or disrupted-parent families tend to have sex earlier, tend to be at greater risk of nonvoluntary sex, and tend to have a greater number of sexual partners. This background may render them less likely to successfully overcome burdens associated with the consequences of the risk behaviors, such as early childbearing.

The local neighborhood in which children are raised has an impact on their sexual risk behaviors as teens and the likelihood of teenage pregnancy and childbearing. Some social scientists predict that geographic concentration of poverty will intensify in the future (Massey, 1996). This extreme geographic concentration of poverty would imply a lesser chance of overcoming negative effects of sexual risk behaviors among economically disadvantaged subgroups in the future.

There are some indications, however, that efforts to curtail the negative effects of sexual activity have not been futile. Some of the evidence shows a reduction in sexual risk behaviors among teens. Overall, a smaller percentage of teens reported having had sex in 1995 than a decade earlier, and this trend seems to be continuing through 1999 (Abma & Sonenstein, 2001; CDC, 2000; Sonenstein et al., 1998). When they do become sexually active, teens use contraception more often than in the past. Since 1991, rates of teen pregnancy have declined (Ventura et al., 2001). Teen birthrates have also declined, most notably among the group at highest risk, namely, young black females (Ventura et al., 2000). In 1995, 96% of females age 18 to 19 had received formal instruction on sex education topics (Lindberg et al., 2000). Thus, not only are today's youth more likely to delay having sexual intercourse, they are better prepared when it does occur. These positive developments could be due to messages and efforts that cut across racial and socioeconomic subgroups. Messages emphasize the need to promote safe sexual practices, thus may foster a greater openness about sexuality. Positive efforts have resulted in the development of new effective contraceptive technology and the creation of programs aimed directly at teens teaching negotiating and communication skills, the benefits of delaying sex, and the benefits of practicing contraception. Developments such as these could be setting the stage for behavior that is less likely to jeopardize the adjustment of adolescents as they exit childhood.

## Endnotes

1. Among males age 10 to 14, the gonorrhea rate declined from 12 per 100,000 to 8 per 100,000 between 1995 and 1999. Among males age 15 to 19, it declined from 503 per 100,000 to 341 per 100,000.

2. For females age 10 to 14, the gonorrhea rate declined from 72 per 100,000 to 55 per 100,000 between 1995 and 1999, and among females age 15 to 19 it decreased from 848 per 100,000 to 738 per 100,000.

3. According to the National Survey of Family Growth (NSFG), percentages of never-married teen females who were sexually experienced declined slightly, from 51% to 49% between 1988 and 1995, but this change falls short of statistical significance. For female high school students, the Youth Risk Behavior Survey data showed only small fluctuations between 1991 and 1997 in the percentage who had ever had sex, none of which reached statistical significance. Thus, the most recent data are consistent with the notion of a recent leveling among female teens in the proportion experiencing sexual intercourse.

4. Estimates in all tables were calculated separately for Latino, non-Latino white, and non-Latino black teenagers. Thus, these three groups are mutually exclusive.

5. In the NSFG, respondents were asked to indicate on a scale from 1 to 10 how much they wanted first sex to happen, with 10 meaning "really wanted it to happen at the time" and 1 representing "really didn't want it to happen at the time." They were also asked if first sex was voluntary or not voluntary. Thus, their first intercourse can be classified as "voluntary and wanted," "voluntary but not wanted," and "not voluntary." The figures corresponding to "nonvoluntary" refer to those who responded that their first sex was a "rape" or reported that it was "not voluntary."

6. This measure, the percentage of teens that used contraception at the most recent sex in the three months prior to the survey, is a commonly used measure of "current" risk. Another measure is based on contraceptive use at any time during the month of the interview. The estimate of the percentage of teens having unprotected sex varies somewhat depending on which measure is used and on which subpopulation, or denominator, is examined: In 1995, out of all teen females, 7% were sexually active and had not used any form of contraception in the month of interview (Piccinino & Mosher, 1998).

## References

Abma, J., Chandra, A., Mosher, W., Peterson, L., & Piccinino, L. (1997). Fertility, family planning, and women's health: New data from the 1995 National Survey of Family Growth. *Vital and Health Statistics, 23.* Hyattsville, MD: National Center for Health Statistics.

Abma, J., Driscoll, A., & Moore, K. (1998). Differing degrees of control over first intercourse and young women's first partners: Data from the 1995 National Survey of Family Growth. *Family Planning Perspectives, 30,* 12-18.

Abma, J., & Sonenstein, F. (2001). Sexual activity and contraceptive practices among teenagers in the United States, 1988 and 1995. *Vital and Health Statistics, 23.* Hyattsville, MD: National Center for Health Statistics.

Alan Guttmacher Institute. (1994). *Sex and America's teenagers.* New York: Author.

Bachrach, C., Newcomer, S., Mosher, W., & Ventura, S. (1997). What is happening to teen nonmarital childbearing? In D. Besharov, F. Stewart, K. Gardiner, & M. Parker (Eds.), *Why have births among unmarried teens increased?* (pp. 1–42). Menlo Park, CA: The Henry J. Kaiser Family Foundation.

Bearman, P., Jones, J., & Udry, R. (1997). *The National Longitudinal Study on Adolescent Health: Research design.* Chapel Hill, NC: Carolina Population Center.

Brewster, K. (1994a). Contextual effects on the sexual behavior of adolescent women. *Journal of Marriage and the Family, 56,* 387-404.

Brewster, K. (1994b). Racial differences in sexual activity among adolescent women: The role of neighborhood characteristics. *American Sociological Review, 59,* 408-424.

Brown, S. S., & Eisenberg, L. (1995). *The best intentions: Unintended pregnancy and the well-being of children and families.* Washington, DC: National Academy Press.

Centers for Disease Control and Prevention. (1998). Trends in sexual risk behavior among high school students: United States, 1991–1997. *Morbidity and Mortality Weekly Report, 47,* 749–752.

Centers for Disease Control and Prevention. (2000). Youth risk and behavior surveillance—United States, 1999. *Morbidity and Mortality Weekly Report, 49,* 1–96.

Centers for Disease Control and Prevention. (2001). HIV and AIDS—United States, 1981-2000. *Morbidity and Mortality Weekly Report, 50,* 430–434.

Cooksey, E., Rindfuss, R., & Guilkey, D. (1996). The initiation of adolescent sexual and contraceptive behavior during changing times. *Journal of Health and Social Behavior 37,* 59-74.

Darroch, J., Landry, D., & Oslak, S. (1999). Age differences between sexual partners in the United States. *Family Planning Perspectives, 31,* 160–167.

Division of STD Prevention. (2000). *Sexually transmitted disease surveillance, 1999.* Atlanta, GA: Centers for Disease Control and Prevention.

Fitch, C., & Ruggles, S. (2000). Historical trends in marriage formation, United States 1850-1990. In L. Waite, C. Bachrach, M. Hindin, E. Thomson, & A. Thornton (Eds.), *The ties that bind: Perspectives on marriage and cohabitation* (pp. 59–88). New York: Walter de Gruyter, Inc.

Hatcher, R., Trussell, J., Stewart, F., Cates, W., Stewart, G., Guest, F., et al. (1998). *Contraceptive technology.* New York: Ardent Media, Inc.

Hayward, M., Grady, W., & Billy, J. (1992). The influence of socioeconomic status on adolescent pregnancy. *Social Science Quarterly 73,* 750–772.

Henshaw, S. (1998). Unintended pregnancy in the United States. *Family Planning Perspectives, 30,* 24–29.

Institute of Medicine. (1997). *The hidden epidemic.* Washington, DC: National Academy Press.

Kann, L., Kolbe, L., & Collins, J. (Eds.). (1993). Measuring the health behavior of adolescents: The Youth Risk Behavior Surveillance System. *Public Health Reports, 108,* (Suppl. 1), 1–96.

Kirby, D. (1997). *No easy answers.* Washington, DC: Task Force on Effective Programs and Research of the National Campaign to Prevent Teen Pregnancy.

Kirby, D. (2001). *Emerging answers: Research findings on programs to reduce teen pregnancy.* Washington, DC: National Campaign to Prevent Teen Pregnancy.

Kost, K., & Forrest, J. D. (1992). American women's sexual behavior and exposure to risk of sexually transmitted diseases. *Family Planning Perspectives, 24,* 244–254.

Ku, L., Sonenstein, F., Lindberg, L. D., Bradner, C., Boggess, S., & Pleck, J. H. (1998). Understanding changes in teenage men's sexual activity: 1979 to 1995. *Family Planning Perspectives, 30*, 256–262.

Laumann, E. O., Gagnon, J. H., Michael, R. T., & Michaels, S. (1994). *The social organization of sexuality: Sexual practices in the United States.* Chicago: University of Chicago Press.

Lauritsen, J. L. (1994). Explaining race and gender differences in adolescent sexual behavior. *Social Forces, 72*, 859–884.

Lindberg, L., Ku, L., & Sonenstein, F. (2000). Adolescents' reports of reproductive health education, 1988 and 1995. *Family Planning Perspectives 32,* 220–226.

Manlove, J., & Terry, E. (2000). *Trends in sexual activity and contraceptive use among teens.* Washington, DC: National Campaign to Prevent Teen Pregnancy.

Massey, D. (1996). The age of extremes: Concentrated affluence and poverty in the twenty-first century. *Demography, 33*, 395–412.

Maynard, R. (1997). *Kids having kids: Economic costs and social consequences of teen pregnancy.* Washington, DC: The Urban Institute Press.

Moore, K., Driscoll, A., & Lindberg, L. D. (1998). *A statistical portrait of adolescent sex, contraception, and childbearing.* Washington, DC: National Campaign to Prevent Teen Pregnancy.

Moore, K., Miller, B., Glei, D., & Morrison, D. (1995). *Adolescent sex, contraception, and childbearing: A review of recent research.* Washington, DC: Child Trends, Inc.

Moore, K., Nord, C., & Peterson, J. (1989). Nonvoluntary sexual activity among adolescents. *Family Planning Perspectives, 21,* 110–114.

Mosher, W., & McNally, J. (1991). Contraceptive use at first premarital intercourse: United States, 1965-1988. *Family Planning Perspectives, 23,* 108–116.

National Center for Health Statistics. (1995). 1995 National Survey of Family Growth [Unpublished data]. Hyattsville, MD: Author.

Peterson, L. (1995). Contraceptive use in the United States: 1982-1990. *Advance data from Vital and Health Statistics, 189.* Hyattsville, MD: National Center for Health Statistics.

Piccinino, L., & Mosher, W. (1998). Trends in contraceptive use in the United States: 1982-1995. *Family Planning Perspectives, 30*, 4–10.

Santelli, J., Lindberg, L. D., Abma, J., McNeely, C. S., & Resnick, M. (2000). Adolescent sexual behavior: Estimates and trends from four nationally representative surveys. *Family Planning Perspectives, 32,* 156–165.

Seidman, S., Mosher, W., & Aral, S. (1992). Women with multiple sexual partners: United States, 1988. *American Journal of Public Health, 82,* 1388–1394.

Seidman, S., Mosher, W., & Aral, S. (1994). Predictors of high-risk behavior in unmarried American women: Adolescent environment as a risk factor. *Journal of Adolescent Health, 15,* 126–132.

Singh, S., & Darroch, J. (1999). Trends in sexual activity among adolescent American women: 1982-1995. *Family Planning Perspectives, 31,* 212–219.

Sonenstein, F., Ku, L., Lindberg, L. D., Turner, C., & Pleck, J. (1998). Changes in sexual behavior and condom use among teenage males: 1988 to 1995. *American Journal of Public Health, 88,* 950–959.

Sonenstein, F., Ku, L., & Pleck, J. (1997). Measuring sexual behavior among teenage males in the United States. In J. Bancroft (Ed.), *Researching sexual behavior: Methodological issues.* (pp. 87–105). Bloomington: Indiana University Press.

Sonenstein, F., Pleck, J., & Ku, L. (1989). Sexual activity, condom use and AIDS awareness among adolescent males. *Family Planning Perspectives, 21,* 152–158.

Sonenstein, F., Pleck J., & Ku, L. (1991). Levels of sexual activity among adolescent males. *Family Planning Perspectives, 23,* 162–167.

Sucoff, C., & Upchurch, D. (1998). Neighborhood context and childbirth risk for black adolescents. *American Sociological Review, 63,* 571–585.

Thomson, E., McLanahan, S., & Curtin, R. (1992). Family structure, gender, and parental socialization. *Journal of Marriage and the Family, 54,* 368–378.

Ventura, S., & Bachrach, C. (2000). Nonmarital childbearing in the United States, 1940–1999. *National Vital Statistics Reports, 48.* Hyattsville, MD: National Center for Health Statistics.

Ventura, S., Mathews, T. J., & Hamilton, B. (2001). Births to teenagers in the United States, 1940-2000 *National Vital Statistics Reports, 49.* Hyattsville, MD: National Center for Health Statistics.

Ventura, S., Mosher, W., Curtin, S., & Abma, J. (2001). Trends in pregnancy rates for the United States, 1976-97: An update. *National Vital Statistics Reports, 49.* Hyattsville, MD: National Center for Health Statistics.

Wertheimer, R., & Moore, K. (August 1998). Childbearing by teens: Links to welfare reform. *New federalism: Issues and options for states.* Series A, No. A-24. Washington, DC: The Urban Institute.

Wu, L. (1996). Effects of family instability, income, and income instability on the risk of a premarital birth. *American Sociological Review, 61,* 386–406.

Wu, L., & Martinson, B. (1993). Family structure and the risk of a premarital birth. *American Sociological Review, 58,* 210–232.

Zelnik, M., Kantner, J., & Ford, K. (1981). *Sex and pregnancy in adolescence.* Beverly Hills, CA: Sage.

# SIX

# Trends in the Health of Children in the United States

*Lorraine V. Klerman*

B y many conventional measures, most children in the United States are physically healthy. Moreover, and again by the most frequently used measures, their health is improving. But the picture is not quite as bright as it might seem for several reasons. The first, although not the most important reason, is that this country does not have a sufficient number of ways to measure child health and, therefore, we really do not know how many children are healthy. We are better able to count those who are sick, injured, or disabled. A more important cloud over the picture is the discrepancy between the health status of white children and children of color, and the related differences by economic status. And finally, it is clear to the professionals who serve children that many children are experiencing unnecessary pain and suffering that statistics do not reveal. This chapter will address these issues within the context of trends over time in the health of children. (Substance abuse, including smoking, and fertility-related issues will not be reviewed because they are considered in the chapters in this volume by Johnston and O'Malley and Abma.)

After sections on monitoring and measurement, this chapter will review important indicators of health and examine overall trends; differences among racial, ethnic, and economic groups; other countries' experiences; and possible reasons for the trends. The chapter will then examine trends in the use of health services by children, again looking at racial, ethnic, and economic differences. Finally, the chapter will consider some actions that might be taken to improve the health of children.

## Importance of Monitoring Health

Monitoring the health of children over time is essential to their continued well-being. This monitoring can determine how changes in the physical or social environment or medical discoveries are influencing child health. Monitoring also provides the information necessary for the development of policies and programs and for their evaluation.

## Changes in the Physical and Social Environment

Children are particularly vulnerable to environmental insults, even in utero. Levels of toxins that would have minimal or no effect on adults can cause major damage to children. Lead is an example of this phenomenon. Studies of rates of lead poisoning in children have revealed that they dropped dramatically when legislation was passed requiring the removal of lead from gasoline. The removal of lead from interior paint further reduced blood lead levels in children. Other examples of how monitoring has led to improvements in child health include studies of outbreaks of food- and water-borne diseases that have pinpointed problems in sanitation at various levels of the food delivery system and drug surveillance that has detected the dangers to the fetus of thalidomide.

Changes in the social environment also affect children and need to be monitored. High rates of unemployment may lead to increased levels of child abuse and neglect. Neighborhood deterioration may cause disease and injury. Welfare reform may result in unanticipated changes in child health status.

## Medical Discoveries

One of the major reasons for the reduction of infant mortality in the last 10 years has been the discovery that surfactant increases lung maturity among premature infants and the development of ways to administer natural and artificial surfactant to these infants. As a result of this and other interventions in the period immediately before and after birth, the infant mortality rate has been markedly reduced. The effectiveness of vaccines against childhood diseases, such as diphtheria, whooping cough, measles, mumps, rubella (German measles), and polio, has also been shown by monitoring.

## Development and Evaluation of Policies and Programs

Monitoring can reveal stability or deterioration in indices of child health and alert the public health and medical communities to the need for new policies and programs. The failure of the low-birthweight rate to decline in recent years has clearly indicated gaps in our knowledge of the causes of preterm labor. The increase in adolescent homicide and suicide in the late 1980s and early 1990s pinpointed areas that needed attention. Such monitoring can trigger the development of federal, state, and local policies and programs whose goal is to favorably influence child health. A variety of measures are then needed to determine the impact of these policy initiatives. For example, favorable changes in the receipt of prenatal and child health care, and even improvements in pregnancy outcomes and child health, are believed to be at least partially because of the passage of Medicaid and its expansion over time. This program has brought health care to millions of poor pregnant women and children. (The potential impact of the 1997 State Child Health Insurance Program will be discussed in a subsequent section.) Even when the policies are not aimed directly at child health, as in the case of the welfare reform legislation to be discussed later, they often influence it.

## Measuring Children's Physical Health, Risk Factors, and Use of Health Services

Federal, state, and local governments, as well as private groups, collect data about the health of children; about factors that put them at risk for poor health, including health behaviors and environmental contaminants; and about their use of health services.

### *Federal Data Sources*

The federal government is the largest source of data about children's health, risk factors, and health care utilization. The National Center for Health Statistics (NCHS) not only compiles, analyzes, and publishes national and state data on births and deaths but also conducts both ongoing and periodic studies. One of the NCHS's continuing surveys is the National Health Interview Survey (NHIS), which asks a sample of U.S. families about many aspects of their health and health service use. Children are included in this survey, and analyses often focus on children. In addition, every few years, the NHIS adds a supplement on child health to its basic survey instrument. The National Hospital Discharge Survey is conducted every year and includes information on children's hospitalization.

Surveys that are conducted less frequently include the National Survey of Family Growth, a major source of information about fertility-related behavior; the National Health and Nutrition Examination Survey (NHANES), based on physical examinations, laboratory tests, and other data collected in the course of the examination; and the National Ambulatory Medical Care Survey and the National Hospital Ambulatory Medical Care Survey, which analyze data from office-based physicians and hospital outpatient and emergency departments, including information about child patients. There are also specialized surveys that are conducted less often, such as the National Maternal and Infant Health Survey.

The Agency for Healthcare Policy and Research conducts studies focusing on medical care use and cost. The Bureau of the Census' Current Population Survey collects information on health insurance, child care, and other child-related matters. The Centers for Disease Control and Prevention (CDC) sponsor the Pregnancy Risk Assessment Monitoring System (PRAMS) in several states and the Youth Risk Behavior Surveillance System (YRBSS) surveys. The Departments of Agriculture and Education also collect data on aspects of child health. The Environmental Protection Agency (EPA) monitors environmental contaminants that may affect child health.

## State and Local Data Sources

All states collect and analyze data on births and deaths and some environmental contaminants and also provide these data to the federal government. In addition, they may choose to participate in federally sponsored surveys such as PRAMS or the YRBSS that provide data on health behaviors and health care utilization. Many states have their own survey research units or contract with such units for household surveys in person or by phone or mail. Most states also maintain hospital data sets. Only the largest cities and counties, however, can afford to collect data on children's health, risk factors, and health care utilization.

## Private Groups

The Urban Institute is conducting the National Survey of America's Families, a major source of data on health care access. The Survey Research Center at the University of Michigan conducts the Panel Study of Income Dynamics, which has some child health–related data, and Monitoring the Future, a study of high school youth. Some of these studies are federally funded, and others are supported by one or more of the foundations with special interest in maternal or child health, such as the Commonwealth Fund, the Kaiser Family Foundation, and the Robert Wood Johnson Foundation.

## Problems with Current Data Sources

There are three major problems with many current data sources.

*Focus on ill health.* Most data collection efforts focus on ill health rather than health. They study deaths, diseases, disabilities, and use of services for health problems. There are a limited number of survey items or other data collection procedures that examine health, for example, as defined by the World Health Organization: "A state of complete physical, mental, and emotional well-being." Researchers are developing such indicators, but few have yet been used in large samples or on a national basis.

*Shortage of state and local data.* Federal surveys are the largest source of data about children, but aside from statistics on births and deaths (vital statistics), the federal information can seldom be analyzed by state or by localities within states. Thus, for example, although information is available about changes in the national rate of dental disease, the rates in particular states or counties can only be estimated. States have difficulty in regularly collecting data that is county- or city-specific, with the exception of birth and death certificates and sometimes hospital records. Because few counties and cities can afford such data collection, they must rely on the occasional state survey that includes local identifiers. Thus, there is a shortage of state- and local-specific information on the health of children. (In 2000, the federal Health Resources and Services Administration, in collaboration with the Association of State and Territorial Health Officials, the National Association of County and City Health Officials, and the Public Health Foundation, published community health status reports for all counties in the United States. These reports are available online at www.communityhealth.hrsa.gov. Unfortunately, they provide little information that is not available from birth and death certificates.)

*Underrepresentation.* Birth and death certificates are probably as likely to be completed for poor people or people of color as for the nonpoor and whites, but minority status may not be correctly recorded, and there is no good indicator of economic status on these certificates. Other data collection methods, however, may undercount people of color and the poor. Interviewers may be reluctant to visit homes in poor neighborhoods because of fear of violence and, even when they do, the person who answers the door may refuse to be interviewed. Such reluctance is higher in poor areas. Alternatively, the interviewer may not speak the respondent's language. Phone surveys face similar problems, in addition to the absence of phones in many poor households. Minorities and poor households often ignore mail surveys. Surveys conducted in classrooms do not include children who have dropped out of school or who are chronically absent. The Children's Defense Fund (1998) estimated that more than half of the net undercount of four million in the 1990 census was children and that this undercount was particularly high among children of color—possibly 7% of black children, 6.2% of Native American children, 5% of Latino children, and 3.2% of Asian American children. Thus, even though attempts are made to correct for undercounts by statistical methods, this country may not accurately know the extent of health and ill health among people of color and the poor.

## Children's Physical Health

Despite these problems, this country is fortunate to have much information that has been collected in a uniform way over a large number of years and, therefore, shows trends in children's health. Describing the trends in all indicators would take a book in itself, thus only selected indicators will be reviewed in this chapter. For more comprehensive reviews and updates on the information in this chapter, readers are referred to the most recent editions of the U.S. Department of Health and Human Services' (USDHHS's) annual volume *Trends in the Well-Being of America's Children and Youth* (2000); the Federal Interagency Forum of Child and Family Statistics' (2000) annual reports on *America's Children: Key National Indicators of Well-Being,*; the federal Maternal and Child

Health Bureau's (2000) annual reports on *Child Health USA*; NCHS's (1999) annual reports on *Health, United States*; and the EPA's (2000) *America's Children and the Environment*. These volumes provided much of the data in the review that follows, which examines trends in the physical health of infants, children, and adolescents.

## Infants

In the health field, infancy refers to the period between birth and 1 year. This period is further divided into the neonatal period (birth through 27 days) and the postneonatal period (28 to 365 days).

*Deaths.* There has been a remarkable decrease in infant mortality beginning practically with the publication of valid data. The infant mortality rate (deaths of infants per 1,000 live births) dropped from 47.0 in 1940 to 7.2 in 1998, the neonatal mortality rate dropped from 28.8 to 4.8, and the postneonatal mortality rate dropped from 18.3 to 2.4 (Murphy, 2000).

But in 1998, infant mortality rates were over twice as high among blacks as whites, 14.3 deaths per 1,000 live births as compared with 6.0. National data on Latinos have been available only since 1983. They show a decrease in infant mortality among all Latino groups from 9.5 to 5.9 in 1998, with sizeable differences among Latino subgroups (Murphy, 2000). In 1996, for example, Puerto Ricans had an infant mortality rate of 8.6, whereas the rate for Central and South Americans was only 5.0. In 1996, the infant mortality rate for Native Americans and Alaskan Natives was 10.0 deaths per 1,000 live births, and for all Asian and Pacific Islanders combined, it was 5.2 (NCHS, 2000). Death certificates do not provide information on economic status, but many studies linking deaths to measures of economic status, such as receipt of Medicaid or welfare benefits or the economic status of the infant's census tract, have shown an inverse relationship between economic status and infant mortality.

In 1996, the United States ranked 26th among industrialized nations in terms of its infant mortality rate (7.3). Japan had the lowest rate, 3.8. Seven other countries had rates less than 5 deaths per 1,000 live births, and eight had rates between 5 and 6 (Maternal and Child Health Bureau, 2000).

Much of the decline in infant mortality is probably due to advances in medical care, but the improvement in living standards in this country has certainly also contributed to the decline. Scientists have developed techniques to save the lives of premature infants, but not to reduce the percentage of infants born prematurely—and prematurity is one of the main causes of infant deaths. There was actually a 4.0% increase in deaths because of prematurity (disorders relating to short gestation and unspecified low birthweight) between 1979 and 1998. The other main cause of infant mortality, birth defects, dropped to 1.6 per 1,000 live births in 1998, a decline of 38.3% since 1979. The decline in birth defects is due to primary prevention, such as increased intake of folic acid before conception, as well as improvements in, and increased use of, prenatal diagnosis; the use of pregnancy termination services after a prenatal diagnosis of a serious defect; and the development of surgical techniques that increase survivorship among infants with defects (Murphy, 2000). Deaths from sudden infant death syndrome (SIDS) dropped 52.6% between 1979 and 1998 to 0.72 in 1998. Much of the credit for this is given to the "Back to Sleep" educational campaign (Murphy, 2000). The increasing availability and utilization of prenatal care have probably also contributed to the decline in infant mortality, but the maximum effect may not be realized until there is a better understanding of the causes of prematurity and congenital anomalies and preventive measures are developed.

   *Other measures of ill health.* Infants born weighing less than 2,500 grams are considered to be of low birthweight. Not only is their likelihood of dying higher than that of heavier infants, but their likelihood of requiring an extended period of hospitalization after birth, of being rehospitalized, and of long-term disability is higher, particularly for those less than 1,500 grams (very low birthweight). Low birthweight may be because of being born too early (usually defined as less than 37 weeks gestation), born too small for gestational age (defined as intrauterine growth retarded), or both. The percentage of low-birthweight infants has not declined appreciably in the last quarter century. Since 1970, the percentage of infants born at low birthweight has never been below 6.8, and in 1999 it was 7.6% (Ventura et al., 2001). As with infant mortality, the rates vary by racial and ethnic groups. In 1998, Native Americans/Alaskan Natives, Asian/Pacific Islanders, Latinos, and whites had rates between 6.4% and 7.4%, whereas blacks had a rate of 13% (Maternal and Child Health Bureau, 2000). The development of neonatal intensive care units with sophisticated equipment for monitoring and caring for very small babies, surfactant to increase lung maturity, and corticosteroids have all contributed to the survival of small infants, but no intervention to date has been able to significantly reduce the percentage who are born too early or too small.

### Children and Adolescents

Federal data sets often categorize children into four age groups: ages 1 to 4, 5 to 9, 10 to 14, and 15 to 19—and, when the numbers are small, further group them into ages 1 to 4, 5 to 14, and 15 to 24.

   *Deaths.* The death rate drops dramatically after the first year of life, so much so, in fact, that the number of deaths per 100,000 children in the specified age group is counted instead of the number of deaths per 1,000 live births. The death rate for children 1 to 4 years of age dropped from 139.4 per 100,000 in 1950 to 34.6 in 1998. Among children 5 to 14 years of age, it dropped from

60.1 to 19.9 (5 to 9 years: 17.7; 10 to 14 years: 22.1). Among youth 15 to 24 years of age, the mortality rate in 1950 was 128.1, and in 1998 it was 82.3 (15 to 19 years: 70.6; 20 to 24 years: 95.3). In all three age groupings, rates among males were higher than rates among females. Rates among black males were almost double those among white males, but the differences among females were not as great (Murphy, 2000). Again, special studies show an inverse relationship between mortality and economic status. And again, in all three age groupings, death rates in the United States are higher than in many other industrialized nations, largely because of our high rates of injuries.

Singh and Yu (1996) studied trends in childhood mortality from 1950 through 1993 and noted substantial declines, primarily because of decreases in unintentional injuries, cancer, pneumonia and influenza, and congenital anomalies. They also noted a twofold increase in suicide and homicide rates since 1968 and increased risk of death among people of color and those in the lower socioeconomic strata.

In 1998, the principal causes of death among 1- to 4-year-olds were unintentional injuries, congenital anomalies, homicide (largely because of child abuse), malignant neoplasms, diseases of the heart, and pneumonia and influenza. This rank order is largely unchanged since 1980, except for homicide rising from the fifth to the third cause. Among 5- to 14-year-olds, the leading causes were unintentional injuries, malignant neoplasms, homicide, congenital anomalies, and diseases of the heart. This rank order is also largely unchanged since 1980, again except for homicide, which rose from the fourth to the third cause. Among 15- to 24-year-olds, the leading causes were unintentional injuries, homicide, and suicide, a rank order that is unchanged since 1980 (Federal Interagency Forum on Child and Family Statistics, 2000; Murphy, 2000).

Rivera and Grossman (1996) compared rates of traumatic death in children less than 20 years of age in 1978 and 1991. They found that deaths from all injuries decreased by 26.5%, from 40.22 to 29.58 per 100,000 children. Unintentional deaths decreased by 38.9%, but intentional deaths (deaths from child abuse or neglect) actually increased by 47.1%. The largest decreases in rates were for poisoning because of gases and vapors and for motorcyclist and pedestrian injuries. Deaths because of homicide and suicide rose, largely because of increases in firearm deaths for these causes.

According to the CDC (2001), overall injury death rates (excluding adverse event–related deaths) are continuing to decrease: from 28.5 in 1981 to 18.3 in 1998 for those younger than 5 years of age, from 15.0 to 8.7 for 5- to 9-year-olds, from 17.0 to 12.2 for 10- to 14-year-olds, and from 71.1 to 55.0 for 15- to 19-year-olds. Death rates for motor-vehicle-related injuries have declined from 9.6 per 100,000 children 10 to 14 years of age in 1970 to 5.4 in 1998; for those ages 15 to 19, the rate has declined from 43.6 to 26.4 per 100,000 children. Homicide rates  increased and then began to decline over the same period. In 1970, the rate per 100,000 10- to 14-year-olds was 1.2; in 1993, it was 2.5; and in 1998, 1.5. For youth 15 to 19, death rates fluctuated from 8.1 in 1970 to 20.7 in 1993 to 11.8 in 1998. The rates among black males were much higher but are also decreasing (USDHHS, 2000).

Youth deaths because of injury by firearms increased from 2.4 per 100,000 children ages 10 to 14 in 1980 to 3.8 in 1993 and then decreased to 2.3 in 1998. Among those ages 15 to 19, the rates increased from 14.7 in 1980 to 28.2 deaths per 100,000 children in 1994 and then declined to 16.3 in 1998. The rates for black males are much higher. Suicide rates have begun to slowly decline after an increase from 0.6 to 1.7 deaths per 100,000 children ages 10 to 14 between 1970 and 1992. The rate was 1.6 suicides per 100,000 children in 1998. Among youth ages 15 to 19, the suicide rate was 5.9 in 1970, 11.1 in 1990, and in 1998, 8.9 per 100,000 children. White males had the highest rates (USDHHS, 2000).

International comparisons are revealing. Between 1992 and 1995, the motor vehicle traffic injury death rate among males 15 to 24 years of age was 41 per 100,000 in the United States. Among a group of 11 industrialized nations, only New Zealand was higher and only France about equal; all others were substantially lower. The rates in the Netherlands, Norway, England and Wales, and Scotland were about half those in the United States. Similarly, the firearm injury death rate in the same group over the same period was 54 per 100,000 in the United States. The highest rate in the other countries was 12.2 and the lowest 0.8 (NCHS, 1997).

The overall decline in childhood mortality is partially due to legislation and regulation aimed at reducing unintentional injuries, for example, better design of highways, fire-retardant clothing, automobile restraints, and window guards, and because of the decline in deaths from infectious diseases, which were a major cause of death in the early part of the century. Infectious diseases now contribute relatively little to the overall death rate, because of immunizations that prevent some childhood infections and antibiotics that cure others. Trend data showing that deaths from infectious diseases began to decline even before the availability of these preventive and therapeutic interventions, however, suggest that improvements in living conditions and better nutrition, including fortified foods, were also major contributors.

Part of the reason for the effectiveness of immunizations in reducing childhood illnesses and deaths has been the legislation that made immunizations a requirement for entry into schools and even child care. The epidemics of measles and other diseases in 1989 and 1990 were largely among preschool children, and this country is still struggling to raise the levels of immunization in this very vulnerable group.

The obvious exception to the decline in infectious disease is HIV/AIDS. This disease was unknown until the early 1980s. In 1998, it was the cause of death for 14 infants, 32 children between 1 and 4, 54 children between 5 and

14, and 194 youth between 15 and 24. (Murphy, 2000). The death rate among infants and children because of HIV/AIDS is declining, however.

Another example of a trend toward health improvement is in sickle cell disease. For black children with sickle cell disease, mortality rates decreased 41% between 1968 and 1992 for 1- to 4-year-olds, 47% for 5- to 9-year-olds, and 53% for 10- to 14-year-olds. Although this is a significant achievement for the medical profession and for the families of sickle cell patients, the small numbers involved (114 children between the ages of 1 and 14 in the earlier period and 63 in the later period) preclude this from having a major impact on mortality data (Davis et al., 1997).

*Other measures of health and ill health.* But health during childhood and adolescence is measured by ways other than deaths. One indicator of health status is parents' perceptions of the health of their children. The NHIS asks parents to rate their children's health as excellent, very good, good, fair, or poor. The percentage of children less than 5 years of age and 5 to 17 reported to be in excellent or very good health remained fairly constant, at around 80% between 1984 and 1996. Black children were more likely to be reported as being in fair or poor health than were white children. The percentage reporting fair or poor health at any age declined as family income rose (US DHHS, 2000).

Several measures of ill health have shown improvement. As noted earlier, the common infectious diseases of childhood such as diphtheria, whooping cough, measles, mumps, rubella (German measles), and polio are now relatively rare because of immunization. According to the Pediatric Nutrition Surveillance System, which collects data on children served by federally funded programs, and thus from children who are more likely to be of low income and of color, the prevalence of short stature (low height for age) among children younger than 2 declined from 10.5% in 1989 to 9.7% in 1997. During the same period, the prevalence among children 2 to younger than 5 declined from 7.5% to 5.7%. The rate was approximately twice as high among poor children (Lewit & Kerrebrock, 1997). Over the same time period, the prevalence of being underweight among those 2 to 5 decreased from 2.8% to 1.9%. The overall prevalence of anemia also declined in this time period among children 2 and younger from 19.4% to 18.4% and among those ages 2 to younger than 5 from 19.0% to 16.9%. The rate for black children younger than 2, however, increased (CDC, 1998). The declines are probably because of the federal Special Supplemental Nutrition Program for Women, Infants, and Children, which provides food to infants and children up to age 6 and to pregnant and lactating women. Vitamin-deficiency diseases are rarely seen in this country because of the addition of Vitamin D to milk and of B vitamins to grain products.

Nevertheless, national surveys suggest that not having enough food or an adequate diet is a problem in many low-income households. In 1995, 13.3%

of children younger than age 18 lived in households experiencing food insecurity without hunger, 5.1% in households experiencing food insecurity with moderate hunger, and 1.0% in households experiencing food insecurity with severe hunger. The percentages for 1999 were 13.1, 3.3, and 0.5. The rates for children below poverty were over double these. In 1994, 11% of children ages 2 to 5 were judged to have a poor diet, 12% of those 6 to 12, and 23% of those 13 to 18. In 1996, the percentages were 8, 13, and 20. Again, the percentages were higher among those in poverty (Federal Interagency Forum on Child and Family Statistics, 2000).

Lead poisoning, which in its most severe forms actually results in death, and even when less acute can cause neurological problems and learning deficiencies, has also been reduced, although it remains a problem. The CDC recommends that lead poisoning prevention activities reduce children's blood lead level to less than 10 micrograms per deciliter. NHANES has shown that the incidence of lead poisoning among children 1 to 5 years of age has decreased from 88.2% with blood lead levels equal to or more than 10 micrograms per deciliter in 1976 to 1980 to 4.4% in 1991 to 1994. Elevated blood lead levels are more common among black children, those from low-income families, and those who live in housing built before 1973 (USDHHS, 1999). The reduction is because of the outlawing of lead in gasoline and in interior paints, as well as lead abatement measures. High blood lead levels currently are mostly because of deteriorated lead paint in older homes and contaminated dust and soil. Small children play in these materials and then place their hands in their mouths.

Tooth decay is a common chronic childhood disease which is more prevalent among poor children. Dental problems cause children to lose a significant number of days from school and this number is much higher among poor families. Dental caries have decreased because of fluoridation of the water supply, dental sealants, and other preventive measures, but use of dental services by low-income populations is lower than that among the more affluent. The 1989 to 1991 NHANES found that 62.1% of children 2 to 9 years of age were caries-free in their primary dentition and 54.7% of children 5 to 17 years of age were caries-free in their permanent dentition (Kaste et al., 1996). Between 1971 to 1974 and 1988 to 1994, the percentage of 2- to 5-year-olds with at least one untreated dental caries declined from 24.4 to 18.7, and among 6- to 17-year-olds, from 55.0 to 23.1 (NCHS, 1999). In the 1988 to 1994 period, 18.7% of children 2 to 5 years of age had untreated dental caries in their primary teeth, and 11.3% of 6- to 14-year-olds had untreated caries in their permanent teeth (USDHHS, 1999).

Substantiated and indicated cases of child abuse and neglect increased by 20% between 1990 and 1994 but then fell by 6% between 1994 and 1997 to slightly under 1 million. But the National Incidence Study of Child Abuse and

Neglect suggests that the number may be much higher, around 2.8 million in 1993. This study includes not only the substantiated and indicated cases, but also those known to community processionals but not necessarily reported. Black children are about 15% of the child population but experience about 27% of the substantiated and indicated cases of child abuse (USDHHS, 1999).

The rates of several chronic health conditions have increased in the last few decades. Asthma, the condition with the highest prevalence, increased 75% between 1980 and 1994. A slight decrease occurred between 1995 and 1996. Asthma is still another condition in which the rates are higher among black children and those from low-income families. Asthma is associated with indoor sources including house dust mites, cockroaches, and tobacco smoke and can be exacerbated by outdoor air pollution such as ozone, particulate matter, and sulfur dioxide (EPA, 2000). Increases were also reported between 1984 and 1996 for chronic bronchitis, chronic sinusitis, and migraine headaches (USDHHS, 2000).

Possibly as a result of these problems, the percentage of children younger than 18 years of age reported as having a limitation of activity because of a chronic condition increased from 5.0% in 1984 to 6.5% in 1997. Among children younger than 5 years of age the increase was from 2.5% to 3.4%, and among those 5 to 17 it was from 6.1% to 6.4%. The rates among those below the federal poverty level are almost double those for children at or above poverty. Rates for black, non-Latino children are higher than those for white, non-Latino children, which are higher than those for Latino children of any race (USDHHS, 2000).

Some increases in child abuse, activity limitation, and other measures may be partially due to changes in definitions, increased reporting, or differential reporting by ethnicity. For example, some increased reporting of activity limitation may be because of the availability of benefits for children with certain conditions under the Supplemental Security Income program for disabled children.

AIDS, a previously unknown disease, is being diagnosed in infants, children, and adolescents. During the period 1988 to 1993, CDC estimated that between 6,000 and 7,000 children were born each year to HIV-infected women and that between 1,000 and 2,000 of these children were infected annually. As a result of clinical trials showing the effectiveness of zidovudine (ZDV) therapy for pregnant women, the Public Health Service issued recommendations in 1994 for routine ZDV treatment to reduce perinatal transmission and in 1995 for routine HIV counseling and voluntary testing for all pregnant women. The CDC now reports a 43% decline in perinatally acquired AIDS cases from an estimated peak of 901 in 1992 to 516 in 1995. In 1997, 473 cases were reported. This decline is because of a reduction in the number of births to HIV-infected women and to increased testing and treatment (Stotoet al., 1998). To further reduce perinatal transmission, in 2000 the U.S. Public Health Service recommended that all pregnant women be tested for HIV—that is, that such testing be a routine part of prenatal care for all women. (The frightening increases in other STDs among adolescents are discussed in Chapter 11.)

*Risk factors.* Obesity has become a major problem for children and adolescents. In the 1963 to 1965 period, 5.0% of children ages 6 to 11 were overweight, but by 1988 to 1994, the percentage was 13.6. For those 12 to 17 years of age, the increase was from 5.0% in 1966 to 1970 to 11.4% in 1988 to 1994. (USDHHS, 2000).

Possibly related to problems with weight control is the decline in physical activity among adolescents. The percentage of 12th-grade students who report that they actively participate in sports or are exercising "almost every day" has remained relatively stable at around 45% between 1976 and 1999 (USDHHS, 2000). Although enrollment in physical education has remained unchanged during the first half of the 1990s, however, daily attendance in physical education has declined from approximately 42% to 25%. Moreover, the percentage of high school students who reported being physically active for at least 20 minutes in physical education classes declined from approximately 81% to 70% during the first half of the 1990s (President's Council on Physical Fitness and Sports, 1996). A sedentary lifestyle is more common among low-income than high-income adolescents, especially girls (NCHS, 1998).

On the positive side, use of automobile restraints (car seats and seat belts) by infants, toddlers, youth, and young adults increased between 1994 and 1998, although least for those 16 to 24 years of age. Also, the percentage of students in Grades 9 through 12 reporting having been in a physical fight within the past year decreased between 1991 and 1999, as did the percentage reporting carrying a weapon at least once within the past 30 days (USDHHS, 2000). (The CDC's [2000] *Youth Risk Behavior Surveillance—United States, 1999* includes data on many of the behaviors discussed here and others as well.)

The EPA reported declines in the 1990s in the percentage of children living in counties where one or more of six criteria air pollutants exceeded national air quality standards; in the percentage of children's days with unhealthy air quality; in the percentage of homes with children younger than age 7 in which someone regularly smokes; and in the percentage of children living in areas served by public water systems that had any violation of drinking water standards. Many children, however, still live in areas with potential cancer or noncancer health effects because of air pollution and pesticide residues in food (EPA, 2000).

## Children's Use of Health Services

Health services for children should be used to

- prevent diseases,

- diagnose and cure them when possible,

- treat injuries, and

- minimize disability if a condition cannot be cured.

The data on deaths, illnesses, and disabilities suggest that much ill health cannot be prevented or even cured by health services, narrowly defined; rather, improving child health requires changes in health behavior and in the physical and social environment. Nevertheless, health services play an important role in some areas of prevention, such as immunization, and in many areas of disability limitation, such as asthma control.

Unfortunately, fewer long-term data are available on uses of health services than on mortality. Ways of counting the use of health services has lagged behind the ways of counting deaths. Five types of data will be examined in this section: hospitalization rates, rates of use of physicians, indicators of access, immunization rates, and health insurance.

### Hospitalization

Hospitalization of children is relatively rare as compared with older individuals and usually indicates a severe problem, with the exception of hospitalization for pregnancy among adolescent females. Rates of hospitalization are declining overall as well as among children. In 1970, there were 66.8 discharges from short-stay hospitals per 1,000 children less than 15 years of age and in 1998, 38.3. Days of care also declined. The principal reasons for hospitalization of children younger than 15 in nonfederal, short-stay hospitals in 1998 were diseases of the respiratory system, especially pneumonia and asthma, injury and poisoning, and diseases of the digestive system (Hall & Popovic, 2000; Kozak & Lawrence, 1999).

The principal reasons for inpatient operations on children under 15 in nonfederal, short-stay hospitals in 1985 were tonsillectomy with or without adenoidectomy, myringotomy, and reduction of fracture (excluding skull and facial). By 1995, the rates for all causes were reduced, and the first two remained appendectomy and reduction of fracture (tied), followed by tonsillectomy and myringotomy (tied) (NCHS, 1998).

### Physician Use

The number of physician contacts (including consultations in person or by telephone for examination, diagnosis, treatment, or advice provided by a physician or a person working under the physician's supervision, but excluding inpatient care) for all causes has remained remarkably stable. In 1987 the rates were 6.7 per child younger than age 5 and 3.3 for children ages 5 to 14; and in 1996, they were 6.5 and 3.3. White children had more contacts than black children, and those with the lowest income had the most contacts (NCHS, 1999). The percentage of children less than 6 years of age with no physician contact during the past year decreased with income. The percentage of children younger than age 15 with an interval of less than a year since the last physician contact increased from 68.4% in 1964 to 85.6% in 1996, whereas longer intervals have declined (NCHS, 1999).

## Access Indicators

The 1993 access to care and health insurance questionnaires of the NHIS (Simpson et al., 1997) used two indicators of health care access: regular source of care and unmet health needs.

*Regular source of care.* In 1993, 96.3% of children birth through 4 years of age had a regular source of care, as did 92.6% of those ages 5 to 17. Whites were more likely to have a regular source of care than blacks and blacks more than Latinos. The likelihood of having a regular source of care increased with income. Insurance also influenced this indicator. Among uninsured children only 79% had a regular source of care, as compared with 94% of those with public insurance and 97% of those with private insurance. The major reason given for having no regular source of care was "lack of health insurance or can't afford" (34%), followed by "does not need a doctor" (32%). Between 1993 to 1994 and 1997 to 1998, the percentage of children younger than 6 years of age with no usual source of care declined slightly from 5.2% to 4.5%, and among those 6 to 17, it declined from 9.0% to 7.8% (NCHS, 1998).

The source of care is also important: 84% used a private physician's office, 11% a clinic, and 1% an emergency room. The proportion of black children using the emergency room as a regular source of care was eight times higher than that of white children. When compared with children with private health insurance, those with no health insurance were more than five times as likely to use the emergency room as a regular source of care, and children with public health insurance were approximately 10 times as likely (Simpson et al., 1997).

*Unmet health needs.* Among children from birth to 4 years of age, 6.2% were reported to have an unmet health need, and among children ages 5 to 17, 12.6%, or 7.3 million children, had an unmet health need. Almost 1.3 million children were unable to obtain needed medical care, 2.7 million delayed medical care because of worry about the cost of care, 4.2 million were unable to obtain dental care, more than 800,000 could not obtain prescription medicine or glasses, and more than 270,000 needed mental health services and could not obtain them. There were no major differences by race, but unmet needs declined as income increased. Uninsured children were more than three times as likely to have an unmet health need as insured children (Simpson et al., 1997).

## Immunization Rates

The 1989 to 1990 epidemics of vaccine-preventable diseases alerted this country to the weaknesses in its immunization programs. The federal government, foundations, states, and localities initiated new programs to improve immunization rates. The most recent report suggests that these efforts have been successful. In 1998, 79% of children 19 to 35 months of age had received the combined series of vaccines (four doses of diphtheria-tetanus-pertussis vaccine, three doses of polio vaccine, one dose of a measles-containing vaccine, and three doses of Haemophilus influenza Type B vaccine). This was a slight increase over 1994 and a much larger increase over the early part of the decade. Children from families below the federal poverty level are less likely to be immunized that those at or above it. White children are more likely to be fully immunized than black or Latino children (USDHHS, 2000).

## Health Insurance

Health insurance is crucial to obtaining adequate medical care. The coverage of children by Medicaid, the primary government health insurance program for poor families, has increased dramatically since its inception in 1965. In 1987, 15.5% of children were covered by Medicaid, and by 1993, the percentage had risen to 23.9. In 1999, it was 20.0%, probably because the expanding economy placed more parents in jobs that provided health insurance. Unfortunately, the percentage of children covered by private insurance, usually the employer-based insurance of an adult in the family, decreased from 66.7% in 1987 to 58.1% in 1994, although it rose to 61.5% in 1999. This has resulted in the percentage of uninsured children remaining relatively unchanged, at approximately 13% to 14%, except for 1997 and 1998, when it reached 15% (Fronstin, 2000).

## Concluding Summary

### Current Status of Child Health

America's children are, in general, healthy and getting healthier. Mortality rates are declining, and many illness and injuries are being prevented. Nevertheless, there is no reason for complacency. The differences in mortality and other indicators between poor and nonpoor and between children of color and white children remain substantial. (The chartbook in the NCHS [1998] edition of *Health, United States* is devoted to displaying these differences for all ages and many conditions.) Other countries have made greater strides in reducing deaths, illnesses, and injuries. Although the U.S. has reduced many financial and other barriers to medical care, many children are still not covered by health insurance and, for this reason and others, have difficulty in obtaining the care that they need.

## Time Trends

A review of trends suggests that the greatest improvements have been in the reduction of mortality in infants, children, and adolescents. Among infants, the reduction in mortality has been largely because of our ability to save infants born too soon and too small, but also to the reduction in birth defects and SIDS. Unfortunately, we have made no progress in reducing the percentage of infants born prematurely or at low birthweight. A great deal of clinical research is being focused on these problems and, it is hoped, some interventions will be found to reduce these problems. Although deaths from injuries remain entirely too high (and are the major cause of death from age 1 through adolescence), the mortality rate has decreased, indicating perhaps that education about health-risk behaviors and safety-oriented modifications of the physical environment have been at least partially successful. Immunizations have significantly reduced the burden of childhood disease, and new vaccines promise to make inroads into the remaining serious childhood diseases. Lead poisoning, although still a problem in some areas and in some populations, has declined substantially. Anemia and other nutrition-related conditions are becoming less of a problem. Dental disease, once one of the expected sources of childhood pain, has been brought under partial control by fluoridation and dental sealants.

But this country has not made significant progress in several areas, in addition to prematurity and low birthweight. Obesity is a growing problem and lack of physical activity may soon become one. Asthma rates are much too high. Suicide rates, although down from the excessively high rates in the late 1980s and early 1990s, remain stable and too high. Deaths from firearms and motor vehicle accidents are declining, but are still too high. And the rates of child abuse and neglect are unacceptable.

## Recommendations

What can be done to reduce the number of children dying, experiencing acute or chronic illness or injury, or having their parents or guardians report limitations of activity or less than excellent or very good health? The preceding sections should have made it clear that although medical care is very important for prevention of illness, treatment of the sick and injured, and care of the chronically ill and disabled, it cannot by itself prevent the major sources of death and disability. Other societal efforts are essential, as well as new medical discoveries in areas such as the prevention of premature birth and the prevention and cure of AIDS.

*Reduction in absolute and relative poverty*. Many experts would state that the single most important change necessary to improve child health is a reduction in absolute and relative poverty. All policymakers would not agree with this statement, but the significant effect of economic status on health has been explored and confirmed in many studies (see, for example, Duncan & Brooks-Gunn, 1997; Klerman, 1991). These studies have shown that poor children experience higher rates of mortality and of acute and chronic illnesses, injuries, and other health-compromising conditions than more affluent children. Moreover, the evidence is strong that the poorer health of children who are of color is usually not because of their race or ethnicity, but rather to the fact that the rates of poverty are higher among most of these groups than among whites as a whole. Certainly there is no proof that raising the standard of living of the poorest segments of our society by itself would improve the health of the children. But if raising their standard of living would make it possible for poor families to live in better housing and in better neighborhoods, for their children never to experience hunger, for their children to attend better schools, and for them to obtain health care for their children from the same providers as more affluent children, it would seem reasonable to expect that their children's health would improve.

Moreover, substantial evidence now exists that it is not only absolute poverty, but also relative poverty that influences mortality rates and possibly children's health. A series of studies from England has shown that the more dramatic the disparity between a nation's affluent and its poor, the higher are its mortality rates (Wilkinson, 1996). In the United States, the same has been shown for states; that is, the greater the difference between the rich and the poor in any state, the higher that state's mortality rates are. (Kawachi & Kennedy, 1997). The investigators believe that the greater the economic disparity in an area, the lower the social cohesion. They postulate that lower social cohesion leads to higher rates of deaths from homicide, suicide, certain injuries, and perhaps other causes.

*Behavior change through education.* The preceding sections should have made it clear that a second way to improve the health of children is through changing the behavior of the children and their parents. Parents and children need to be educated about what they must do to protect and improve their health. For example, the single most important cause of death is injuries. Many of these can be prevented by simple procedures such as using car restraints and stair guards, surveilling water hazards, following safe smoking procedures, not leaving children unattended, safeguarding poisons, locking firearms, and using bicycle and motorcycle helmets.

Education appears to have reduced the rate of death from SIDS. Health care providers and the media have cooperated in the Back to Sleep program, which urges parents to place their infants on their backs, rather than their stomachs, when they sleep. The prone position has been found to be associated with higher rates of SIDS.

If children and adolescents are to grow properly, they must be offered nutritious food. Women are taking folic acid supplements before and during pregnancy to reduce the possibility of bearing an infant with a neural tube defect. Exercise is important for good health among children and adolescents and can help prevent obesity.

Contraceptive use can prevent the births of unwanted children, who are at higher risk for child abuse and neglect regardless of the mother's age, and births of children to teenagers, who often are insufficiently mature to provide for the physical and emotional needs of their children. Education about HIV/AIDS appears to have positively affected the sexual behavior of adolescents, as shown by increasing use of condoms.

Low birthweight is a major cause of death and disabilities and one that can be reduced by the improving the behaviors of pregnant women. Smoking, excess drinking, and the use of illegal drugs all contribute to less than optimal pregnancy outcomes. Heavy drinking among pregnant women can produce fetal alcohol syndrome. Changing these sometimes addictive behaviors, however, requires more than standard educational techniques. It often requires counseling and behavioral modification techniques.

A recent study of adolescent health-risk behaviors found that race/ethnicity, income, and family structure were only weak explanations for these behaviors. More important predictors were problems with schoolwork and spending a lot of time "just hanging out" with friends, especially friends involved in risk behaviors. The most consistent protective factor was the presence of a positive parent-family relationship (Blum et al., 2000). And the list of ways that the behavior of parents and of children can affect their health could be extended.

***Legislation, regulation, and taxation.*** Public policies, as expressed in legislation, regulation, and taxation, can reduce health risks directly, as well as encourage individuals to change their behaviors. This country has not relied on mothers to provide their children with nutritious foods or with vitamin supplements, it has required the supplementation of bread, milk, and other staples with vitamins and minerals. Nor do we totally depend on education to ensure that women obtain a sufficient amount of folic acid; rather we require the fortification of grain products.

Similarly, it is unlikely that lead poisoning would have dropped significantly if this country had depended on parents watching children to make certain that they did not inhale an excess amount of automobile exhaust or ingest
paint chips. Legislation was necessary to remove lead from gasoline and from
paint. Unfortunately, landlords are still renting apartments with leaded paint to
families with young children. Communities have shown a reluctance to pass
and enforce abatement ordinances.

Legislation and regulations have raised immunization levels by requiring
immunization for school entry and child care, increased the use of automotive
restraints and motorcycle helmets, increased the number of pools that are
fenced, placed guards at railroad crossings, made children's sleepwear flame-
retardant. Again the list could be continued.

Many states have begun to use, or are considering using, a multitude of
methods to reduce underage smoking. These include, in addition to education
in schools and other contexts, laws prohibiting the placing of advertisements
in certain areas, reducing children's access to cigarettes through vending
machines, and increasing the taxes on cigarettes.

The alarming rate of firearm fatalities, both intentional and accidental, suggests another series of approaches to improving child health. Legislation to
restrict the sale of firearms is controversial. At least steps could be taken to protect children from firearms in the home by requiring that they be locked in a
secure place and that a device be placed on them that would make most children unable to fire them.

Although not directed at child health, the provisions of the welfare reform
law, the Personal Responsibility and Work Opportunity Reconciliation Act
(PRWORA), are expected to influence maternal and child health. PRWORA was
passed by Congress in 1996 and is being implemented in a variety of more or
less constructive or punitive ways by states. PRWORA's direct impact on child
health will be through its health insurance provisions. PRWORA provides for
the continuation of Medicaid benefits for most women and children who were
eligible under the previous system. Eligibility, however, is no longer automatic
for some, that is, the women need to apply for Medicaid benefits for themselves
and their children. There is concern that some women may not take advantage
of their Medicaid benefits either because they believe that they and their children are no longer eligible or because the application is too burdensome unless
someone is sick, potentially reducing the use of preventive services.

Welfare reform may also have indirect effects on the health of children. For
example, to become employed, mothers may need to place their children in
inadequate child care arrangements, or working in addition to caring for a
household including children may place mothers under excess strain. If mothers do not find employment and are not excused from the welfare reform pro-

visions for some reason, the children may suffer severe economic deprivation and become dependent on relatives or charity for their sustenance. On the other hand, it is possible that, if their mothers are employed, welfare reform may have a positive impact on children by improving their economic status (although most postwelfare jobs pay little more than welfare) and by providing a role model of economic self-sufficiency in adult life.

*Improving access to high-quality medical care.* Although medical care by itself is not the answer to improving the health of America's children, it is certainly a major component of a multifaceted approach. But the ability to obtain needed medical care is often hampered by low income, the absence of health insurance, the reluctance of some providers to accept Medicaid, the shortage of providers in some areas, and other access factors.

In 1997, the federal government took a major step toward reducing some of these barriers by offering health insurance to a large group of uninsured children through the State Child Health Insurance Program (SCHIP). Passed by Congress as Title XXI of the Balanced Budget Act of 1997, SCHIP provides states with funds to offer health insurance to uninsured children. Congressional intent was to make health care available to almost all poor children either through states expanding their Medicaid programs or other means. But improving child health through SCHIP will only be possible if the states continue active outreach to enroll uninsured children (expanding coverage to parents has been found to increase the coverage rates of eligible children) and are able to find clinicians willing to provide these children with high-quality services, regardless of where the children live. Perhaps some states will even use the program as a step toward eliminating the two-tier system of medical care prevalent in so many underserved areas, in which poor children receive their care from public facilities operated by city, county, or state governments and more affluent children seek care in the private sector. Although the public facilities often provide excellent care and show great sensitivity to the needs of poor and of people of color, they have difficulty in providing the continuity of care that most families desire and in providing 24-hour, seven-day-a-week service. Policymakers are closely watching what states are doing in these areas and the effects of SCHIP on access to health care. SCHIP will not cover all children—and the United States will remain one of the few countries without a universal health insurance program—but it should significantly reduce the number who are uninsured.

## Implications

Children in the United States, particularly those who are poor, are not as healthy as they have a right to be. Raising the health status of the poor to that of the nonpoor, or raising the health status of all U.S. children to that of children in other industrialized nations, will take major governmental and private initiatives. A program of universal health insurance for children and improved access to medical care would be a major step in a forward direction. But there is also a need to change health behavior through education combined with legislation, regulation, and tax policies. Finally, U.S. citizens should consider the health consequences for low-income children, as well as the inadequate housing, destructive neighborhoods, and inferior schooling associated with poverty. Changing these situations would be more expensive than health insurance, but in the long run, such policies may be essential to improving significantly the health of U.S. children.

## Author's Note

Preparation of this chapter was made possible, in part, by a grant from the Maternal and Child Health Bureau, Department of Health and Human Services (MCJ 9040).

Portions of this chapter were taken, with permission, from the chapter, "Recent Trends in the Health of Children" by Lorraine V. Klerman and Janet D. Perloff in *Health Care for Children: What's Right, What's Wrong, What's Next*, Ruth E. K. Stein, MD (editor), Phyllis Brooks (associate editor), New York, United Hospital Fund of New York, 1997.

## References

Blum, R. W., Beuhring T., & Rinehart, P. M. (2000). *Protecting teens: Beyond race, income and family structure*. Minneapolis, MN: University of Minnesota Center for Adolescent Health.

Centers for Disease Control and Prevention. (1998). *Pediatric nutrition surveillance, 1997 full report*. Atlanta, GA: U.S. Department of Health and Human Services.

Centers for Disease Control and Prevention. (2000). Youth risk behavior surveillance— United States, 1999. *Morbidity and Mortality Weekly Report, 49*(SS-5).

Centers for Disease Control and Prevention. (2001). *WISQARS data*. Retrieved December 17, 2001, from: http://www.cdc.gov/ncipc/wisqars

Children's Defense Fund. (1998). *Two million missing children*. (2000, March 22).Available from http://www.childrensdefensefund.org/listservs.php. Washington, DC: Children's Defense Fund.

Davis, H., Schoendorf, K. C., Gergen, P. J., & Moore, R. M. (1997). National trends in the mortality of children with sickle cell disease, 1968 through 1992. *American Journal of Public Health, 87,* 1317–1322.

Duncan, G. J., & Brooks-Gunn, J. (Eds.). (1997). *Consequences of growing up poor.* New York: Russell Sage Foundation.

Environmental Protection Agency. (2000). *America's children and the environment. A first view of available measures.* Washington, DC: Author.

Federal Interagency Forum on Child and Family Statistics. (2000). *America's children: Key national indicators of well-being 2000.* Washington, DC: U.S. Government Printing Office.

Fronstin, P. (2000). *Sources of health insurance and characteristics of the uninsured: Analysis of the March 2000 Current Population Survey.* Employee Benefit Research Institute (Issue Brief 228).

Hall, M. J., & Popovic, J. R. (2000). *1998 Summary: National Hospital Discharge Survey. Advance data from vita and health statistics* (No. 316). Hyattsville, MD: National Center for Health Statistics.

Kaste, L. M., Selwitz, R. H., Oldakowski, R. J., Brunelle, J. A., Winn, D. M., & Brown, L. J. (1996). Coronal caries in the primary and permanent dentition of children and adolescents 1-17 years of age: United States, 1988-1991. *Journal of Dental Research, 75,* 631–641.

Kawachi, I., & Kennedy, B. P. (1997). Social capital, income inequality, and mortality. *American Journal of Public Health, 87,* 1491–1498.

Klerman, L. V. (1991). *Alive and well? A research and policy review of health programs for poor young children.* New York: National Center for Children in Poverty.

Kozak, L. J., & Lawrence, L. (1999). National hospital discharge survey: Annual summary, 1997. *Vital and Health Statistics, Series 13*(144).

Lewit, E. M., & Kerrebrock, N. (1997). Population-based growth stunting. *The Future of Children, 7,* 149–156.

Maternal and Child Health Bureau. (2000). *Child health USA 2000.* Washington, DC: U.S. Government Printing Office.

Murphy, S. L. (2000). Deaths: Final data for 1998. *National Vital Statistics Reports, 48*(11).

National Center for Health Statistics. (1997). *Health, United States, 1996-1997 and injury chartbook* [DHHS Publication No. (PHS) 97-1232]. Hyattsville, MD: U.S. Government Printing Office.

National Center for Health Statistics. (1998). *Health, United States, 1998 with socioeconomic and health chartbook* [DHHS Publication No. (PHS) 98-1232]. Hyattsville, MD: U.S. Government Printing Office.

National Center for Health Statistics. (1999). *Health, United States, 1999 with health and aging chartbook* [DHHS Publication No. (PHS) 99-1232.] Hyattsville, MD: U.S. Government Printing Office.

National Center for Health Statistics. (2000). *Health, United States, 2000 with adolescent health chartbook.* [DHHS Publication No. 00-1232]. Hyattsville, MD: U.S. Government Printing Office.

President's Council on Physical Fitness and Sports. (1996). *Physical activity and health.* Atlanta, GA: U.S. Department of Health and Human Services.

Rivera, F. P., & Grossman, D. C. (1996). Prevention of traumatic deaths to children in the United States: How far have we come and where do we need to go? *Pediatrics, 76,* 567–573.

Simpson, G., Bloom, B., Cohen, A., & Parsons, P. E. (1997). Access to health care. Part 1: Children. National Center for Health Statistics. *Vital and Health Statistics,* (Series 10, No. 196).

Singh, G. K., & Yu, S. M. (1996). U.S. childhood mortality, 1950 through 1993: Trends and socioeconomic differentials. *American Journal of Public Health, 86,* 505–512.

Stoto, M. A., Almario, D. A., & McCormick, M. C. (1998). *Reducing the odds. Preventing perinatal transmission of HIV in the United States.* Washington, DC: National Academy Press.

U.S. Department of Health and Human Services, Office of the Assistant Secretary for Planning and Evaluation. (1999). *Trends in the well-being of America's children and youth: 1999.* Washington, DC: Author.

U.S. Department of Health and Human Services, Office of the Assistant Secretary for Planning and Evaluation. (2000). *Trends in the well-being of America's children and youth: 2000.* Washington, DC: Author.

Ventura, S. J., Martin, J. A., Curtin, S. C., Menacker, F., & Hamilton, B. E. (2001). Births: Final data for 1999. *National Vital Statistics Reports 49*(1).

Wilkinson, R. G. (1996). *Unhealthy societies: The afflictions of inequality.* New York: Rutledge.

# PART III
## FAMILY INDICATORS

# SEVEN

# Changing Family Circumstances

*Donald J. Hernandez*

## Overview

Family circumstances profoundly influence the current well-being and future prospects of children. The number of parents and siblings in the home and the educational attainments and work of family members largely determine both the economic resources available to children and the availability of family members to provide for their day-to-day care. This chapter portrays the revolutionary changes U.S. children have experienced historically in these family circumstances, key reasons for these changes, demographic projections for the future, and implications for public policy. In brief, this chapter explores and explains the following trends.

In 1860, the vast majority of U.S. children were whites living in families with a large number of siblings and with two parents who were literate but without advanced education, all of whom worked together to support themselves on the family farm. (The term *white* is used throughout this chapter to refer to persons who are white and who are not Hispanic or Latino.) Today, two-thirds of U.S. children are white, and one-third belong to racial or ethnic minority groups. Most children live in families with no more than three siblings, and most live with two parents who are much better educated than in the past and who both work for pay outside the home. But nearly one-third of children live with only one parent, usually their mothers, whose educational attainments are comparatively low by contemporary standards. Children in many racial and ethnic minorities are more likely than whites to have parents with limited education or to live in one-parent families. Most children spend much of their day in nonparental day care or in school.

Enormous increases occurred in family income and the standard of living since the 1860s, and family incomes doubled during the quarter-century following the Great Depression. But the final quarter of the 20th century brought large increases in child poverty and income inequality, with children in many racial and ethnic minorities especially likely to experience deprived economic circumstances.

It is projected that by 2040 a majority will be Latino, African American, or of another nonwhite race. Because most immigrants belong to racial or ethnic minorities, continuing immigration and comparatively high birth rates among immigrants imply that most population growth in the United States will occur as a result of immigration and births to immigrants and their descendants, and that in less than 40 years, white children will constitute a minority of children in the United States. Many immigrants come to the United States with the hope of finding well-paid work, and children in immigrant families have educational aspirations similar to or higher than children in native-born families. Many children in immigrant families live in poverty, however, because their parents have completed many fewer years of schooling than children in native-born families.

Current and future public policies will have a critical effect on the extent to which children in immigrant families and other children living in economically disadvantaged circumstances, especially racial and ethnic minorities, receive the education, health care, and economic resources required to ensure that they will become economically productive members of society during adulthood. The well-being, development, and future success of these children is of great importance not only to these children and their parents but also to the predominantly white baby-boom generation as a whole. The economic support for the baby-boom generation during retirement, beginning around 2010, will increasingly depend on the economic productivity of racial and ethnic minorities who are the children of today and of the years ahead.

## Why Family Circumstances Matter

Parents are the most important people in the lives of children, because they provide the day-to-day care and emotional nurturing children require, and because they obtain the economic resources essential to assure food, clothing, housing, education, and health care for children. But because parental time is strictly limited to 24 hours each day, children with two parents in the home have greater access, potentially, to parents as personal caregivers and as economic providers than do children living with one parent.

Because paid work by parents is the primary source of family income for most children, the number of parents who work for pay and whether they work part-time or full-time are key determinants of whether children live in poverty or in middle-class comfort or luxury. Of course, the time that parents devote to paid work is not usually available for personally monitoring or caring for their children. Hence, there is a trade-off for children between the value of economic resources and the amount of time available for parent-child interaction.

Children whose parents have comparatively high educational attainments also have relatively favorable economic prospects, both during childhood and when they become adults, because highly educated parents are more likely than parents who have completed fewer years of school to have well-paid jobs, and because children with highly-educated parents are more likely than other children to complete high school or college themselves.

Most children live not only with one or two parents but also with one or more brothers or sisters who are potential sources of lifelong companionship, but who also are potential competitors for the scarce time and economic resources parents can devote to their children. Although research has found the number of siblings to have little effect on a child's psychological well-being in adulthood, children in large families with five or more siblings do tend to complete fewer years of schooling than children from smaller families, and they are, therefore, less likely to enter high-status occupations with high incomes when they reach adulthood.

The current well-being and future prospects of children depend most immediately and directly upon the characteristics and the day-to-day decisions of parents and other family members. Parental decisions about marriage, divorce, and childbearing, about the amount of time to devote to paid work, and about what neighborhood in which to live, for example, influence parental availability to monitor and care for children, the quality of the school the child attends, the child's access to recreational facilities, and the child's exposure to possible physical assault from strangers or other dangers. But the effects of parental characteristics and the nature of parental decisions are shaped and constrained, sometimes severely, by social, economic, and demographic conditions, and by public policies beyond the control of individual parents.

Because public policies can enhance the well-being and development of children directly by providing critical resources, as well as by influencing broader social, economic, and demographic conditions, it is essential not only to track trends in family circumstances but also to understand causal processes that influence these circumstances. Public policies can seek to improve the lives of children by

- altering causal processes,
- augmenting positive outcomes, or
- ameliorating harmful consequences.

Consequently, regardless of whether family trends are helpful or harmful to children, public policies to enhance the well-being and development of children will be effective only if they are founded upon knowledge about both the trends and the reasons for the trends.

## Family Circumstances Measured Historically

The only sources of historical data on trends for a wide range of family circumstances and conditions for the era spanning the Great Depression to the present are the censuses that have been conducted every 10 years between 1940 and 1990. These trends can be extended to the present by national surveys, most notably the annual Current Population Survey conducted by the U.S. Bureau of the Census. Prior to 1940, the decennial censuses also provide uniquely valuable data, but for many fewer topics. Vital statistics on births and deaths are another source of valuable data for constructing historical trends on fertility and mortality.

This chapter draws on these data sets to present historical trends for children. Most of these trends were first constructed in *America's Children: Resources from Family, Government, and the Economy* (Hernandez, 1993a), pertaining to the number of parents and children in children's homes and to the educational attainments and labor force participation of parents, as well as other family conditions regarding income and poverty. These issues also have been explored by Hernandez (1993b, 1995). The chapter draws on the broader scientific literature to describe additional factors related to these trends, the range of public policies that might affect these trends, and projections for the future.

Selected studies presenting more detailed analyses historically include Elder (1974); for the more recent era in the United States, see the Federal Interagency Forum on Child and Family Statistics (1998) for a chart book of trends; for more detailed studies on this subject, see Brooks-Gunn and Duncan (1997), Cherlin et al. (1991), Haveman and Wolfe (1994), Huston et al. (1994), McLanahan and Sandefur (1994); and Phillips and Crowell (1994); and for an international perspective see Qvortrup et al. (1994).

## Historical Revolutions in Fathers' Work, Family Size, and Education

### The Explosion in Fathers' Nonfarm Work

Historically, the two-parent farm family was the primary form of economic production and family organization in the United States. Figure 7–1 shows that, once it began, the decline of the two-parent farm family occurred very rapidly. Between 1830 and 1930, the proportion of children living in two-parent farm families plummeted from 70% to less than 30%, whereas the proportion in nonfarm families with breadwinner fathers and homemaker mothers jumped from only 15% to a majority of 55%.

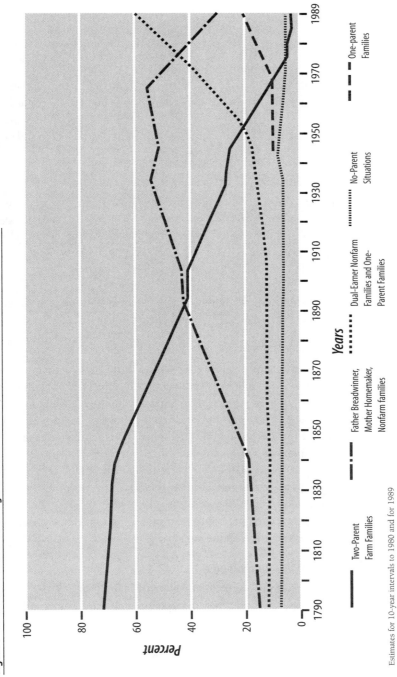

**Figure 7–1: Children from birth to age 17 in farm families, father-as-breadwinner families, and dual-earner families: 1790–1989.**

Two-Parent Farm Families

Father Breadwinner, Mother Homemaker, Nonfarm families

Dual-Earner Nonfarm Families and One-Parent Families

No-Parent Situations

One-parent Families

Percent

Years

Estimates for 10-year intervals to 1980 and for 1989.

Source: Hernandez, (1993a), p. 103. © Russell Sage Foundation; reprinted with permission.

This transformed the nature of childhood. In two-parent farm families, family members worked side by side to sustain themselves in small farming communities. But among two-parent families living in urban areas or in cities prior to 1940, fathers left the home for much of the day to work at jobs and earn income required to support their families, whereas most mothers remained in the home to care for their children and perform unpaid household labor.

One hundred years may seem like a long time, but most people in the United States today will live to be at least 75 years old. Thus, the revolutionary 100-year transformation to nonfarm work by fathers occurred in little more than one human lifetime, by today's standards.

## The Drop in Family Size

An equally revolutionary drop in family size accompanied the rise in urban living and fathers' nonfarm work. In the 65 years between 1865 and 1930, the median number of siblings in the families of adolescents plummeted from 7.3 to only 2.6 siblings per family. As a result, in 1865, a majority of adolescents had at least six additional siblings competing for their parents' time and economic resources, but by 1930, nearly 60% either were only children or had only one or two siblings in the home. This 65% drop in siblings in the home also occurred in less than a single human lifetime.

## The Expansion in Schooling

A third revolutionary change in children's lives during the same era was an enormous expansion in school enrollment and educational attainments. Between 1870 and 1940, school enrollment rates jumped sharply from only 50% for children ages 5 to 19, to 95% for children ages 7 to 13, and to 79% for children ages 14 to 17. Meanwhile, among students enrolled in school, the number of days spent in school doubled, jumping from 21% to 42% of the total days in the year. By 1940, therefore, school days accounted for about two-thirds as many days as a full-time adult work-year. This enormous expansion in schooling occurred in only 70 years, less than a single lifetime. Because the children of today are the parents of tomorrow, this led, in due course, to the enormous increases in parents' education.

## Explaining the Three Historic Revolutions

Why did these revolutions occur in fathers' work, family size, and schooling? One underlying cause motivated parents to choose all three courses of action, namely, the desire to maintain or improve the relative social and economic status of themselves and their children, or to keep from losing too much ground, compared with others who were taking advantage of emerging economic opportunities. During the first century of the Industrial Revolution, parents had three major ways to improve their relative social and economic status.

First, they could move off the farm so that fathers could take comparative-ly well-paid jobs in the expanding industrial economy. Second, they could limit their family size to a comparatively small number of children, so that available income could be spread less thinly. At a given income level, parents with fewer children have more money to spend on themselves and on each child than do parents with a larger number of children. Third, they could obtain higher edu-cational attainments, because higher educational levels became increasingly nec-essary to obtain jobs with higher incomes and greater prestige.

## The Recent Revolution in Mothers' Work

Two additional revolutions in children's families began after 1930. First was the explosion in mothers' employment outside the home. Figure 7–2 shows that, in 1940, only 10% of children lived with a mother who was in the paid labor force. By 1990, nearly 60% of children had a working mother—a sixfold increase in 50 years—and by 1995, 68% of children lived with working mothers.

Just as children in an earlier era had experienced a massive movement by fathers out of the family home to work at jobs in the urban-industrial economy, children since the Great Depression have experienced a massive movement by mothers into the paid labor force. The revolution in mothers' work is occurring twice as fast, however. The decline in the proportion of children in the two-parent farm family from 60% to 10% required the 100 years from 1860 to 1960. The corresponding increase in working mothers from 10% to 60% required only half as long—the 50 years from 1940 to 1990. It is no wonder that families and social welfare policies have only begun to adjust to this change.

## Explaining the Revolution in Mothers' Work

What caused this revolutionary increase in mothers' labor force participation? Much of the answer lies in the earlier historic changes in the family and econ-omy. As described above, between the early days of the Industrial Revolution and about 1940, many parents had three major avenues for maintaining or improving their relative economic standing. They could move off the farm and have the husband work in comparatively well-paid jobs in the growing urban-industrial economy, they could limit themselves to a smaller number of chil-dren, or they could increase their educational attainments.

But by 1940, only 23% of Americans lived on farms, and 70% of parents had only one or two dependent children in the home. Thus, for many parents, these two historical avenues for maintaining or improving their relative eco-nomic standing had run their course. Furthermore, because most persons achieve their ultimate educational attainments by age 25, additional schooling beyond age 25 is often difficult or impractical.

With these avenues to improving their family's relative economic status effectively closed for a large majority of parents after age 25, a fourth major

**Figure 7–2: Proportion of children with mothers in the labor force: 1940–1995.**

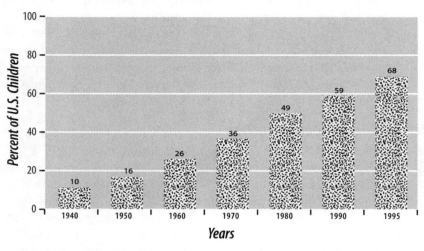

Source: Hernandez (1993a), p. 109; (1993b); (1997a). p. 155.

avenue to improving family income emerged between 1940 and 1960, name-ly, paid work by wives and mothers. Valerie Oppenheimer (1970) has shown that the traditional source of female nonfarm labor, namely unmarried women, was stationary or declining in size during the 1940s and 1950, whereas the demand for female workers was increasing.

Yet mothers were becoming increasingly available and well-qualified for paid work. Revolutionary increases in school enrollment had, by 1940, effec-tively released mothers from child care responsibilities for time periods equiva-lent to two-thirds of the hours in an adult workday, for about two-thirds of a full-time adult work-year, except for the few years before children entered elemen-tary school. Furthermore, many women were highly educated, because the edu-cational attainments of women had increased along with those of men.

Also, the historic rise in divorce, discussed below, made paid work increas-ingly attractive to mothers as a hedge against the possible economic disaster of losing access to most, or all, of their husbands' income through divorce.

Immediate economic insecurity and need due to fathers' lack of access to full-time employment also made mothers' work attractive. Figure 7–3 shows 40% of children in the Great Depression, year of 1940 lived with fathers who did not work full-time year-round. After the Great Depression this proportion declined but has since remained at high levels. Throughout the era since the Great Depression, despite the increase in one-parent families, at least one-fifth of children have lived with fathers who, during any given year, experienced part-time work or joblessness. This has been a powerful incentive for mothers to work for pay.

## Figure 7–3: Proportion of children living with a father who works less than full-time year-round: 1940–1995.

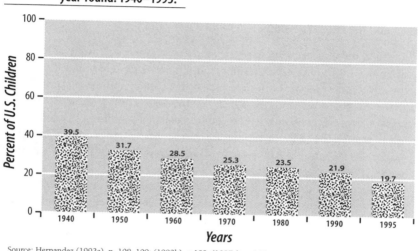

Source: Hernandez (1993a), p. 108–109; (1993b), p.192; (1997a), p. 155.

## The Recent Revolution in Mother-Only Families

Twenty years after the beginning of the expansion in mothers' paid work, yet another family revolution began, an unprecedented increase in mother-only families in which the father was not present in the home. Children in mother-only families in 1990 were about twice as likely to live with a divorced or separated mother as with a never-married mother. Thus, two-thirds of children in mother-only families lived with separated or divorced mothers, and one-third lived with never-married mothers.

Figure 7–1 shows only 6% to 8% of children lived in mother-only families between 1940 and 1960. This percentage increased to 20% in 1990 and to 24% in 1995. Of course, the total proportion of children who have ever lived without both parents is substantially higher, because some children live with their fathers only, or neither parent, in the home. Also, some one-parent families become two-parent families when the parents marry or remarry, but these families are replaced by one-parent families newly formed through widowhood, divorce, or out-of-wedlock childbearing. Thus, the total proportion of children who have ever lived with fewer than two parents before they reached age 18 has been enormously higher, historically and today.

Among white children born in the decades spanning the 1860s and 1960s, between one-fourth and one-third lived in families with fewer than two parents before reaching age 18, and this increased to one-half by the 1980s. Proportions among black children have been much higher historically, with one-half living in families with fewer than two parents before reaching age 18, and, for those born since 1980, four-fifths having experienced this situation.

## Explaining the Recent Revolution in Mother-Only Families

Why did a revolutionary increase in mother-only families occur after 1960? Between the 1860s and 1960s, a remarkably steady eightfold increase occurred in the divorce rate, with only three short-lived interruptions in conjunction with the World Wars and the Great Depression. During these 100 years, increasing divorce rates effectively counterbalanced declining mortality as a source of marital dissolution, and the increase in one-parent families was about proportionate. Much of the increase in divorce grew out of historic transformations in the family.

The economic interdependence of husbands and wives sharply constricted as fathers obtained jobs in the nonfarm economy. On preindustrial farms, it was economically necessary for fathers and mothers, and for older children, to work together to sustain the family. But a father with a nonfarm job could leave the family home and take his income with him. Simultaneously, in moving to urban areas, husbands and wives left behind rural small-town social controls that once censured divorce.

More recently, revolutionary post-1940 increases in mothers' paid work further weakened the economic interdependence of husbands and wives, because a mother with a nonfarm job could, if she desired, depend on her work alone for her income. She could separate or divorce the father and take her income with her.

Economic insecurity and need also contributed substantially to rising separation and divorce, at least after 1970. Elder, Conger, and their colleagues (1974, 1992, 1994) have shown instability in husbands' work, drops in family income, and a low ratio of family income to family needs lead to greater marital hostility, decreased marital quality, and increased risk of divorce.

Of the increase in mother-only families for white children between 1960 and 1988, 70% is accounted for by rising separation and divorce. Between 1940 and 1960, however, black children experienced much larger increases than white children in mother-only families with divorced or separated mothers. And, especially since 1970, black children also have experienced extremely large increases in mother-only families with never-married mothers.

The same factors leading to increased separation and divorce among whites were important for blacks. But the higher proportion of black children than white children living in mother-only families between 1940 and 1960 may also be due to the startling drop in blacks living on farms—from 44% in 1940 to only 11% in 1960—and by the extraordinary economic pressures faced by black families during these years.

Research by Wilson (1987) focuses on the extent to which young black men aged 16 to 24 experience greater joblessness than corresponding white men. Almost no difference existed in 1955, but by the late 1970s and 1980s, the gap had expanded to 15 to 25 percentage points. This represents a large and rapid reduction in the availability of black men who might economically support a family, and this reduction occurred during the main family-building ages. Thus, the data suggest that many young black women have decided to forgo temporary and unrewarding marriages in which a jobless or poorly paid husband might act as a financial drain.

## Poverty and Economic Inequality Since the Great Depression

As these revolutions in family life proceeded, how did income and poverty among children change? Median family income more than doubled in the 26 years from 1947 to 1973. But by 1993, median family income was at exactly the same level as in 1973, despite the enormous jump in mothers' paid work.

Turning to poverty, enormous increases in real incomes and standards of living between 1940 and 1973 led to corresponding increases in social judgments about what counted as a "normal" or "adequate" income. The relative nature of such judgments has been known for 200 years. In *Wealth of Nations*, Adam Smith emphasized poverty must be defined compared with contemporary standards of living. He defined *economic hardship* as the experience of being unable to consume commodities that "the custom of the country renders it indecent for creditable people, even of the lowest order, to be without" (*Alternative Measures*, 1989, p. 10).

More recently, in 1958, John Kenneth Galbraith argued:

> *People are poverty-stricken when their income, even if adequate for survival, falls markedly behind that of the community. Then they cannot have what the larger community regards as the minimum necessary for decency; and they cannot wholly escape, therefore, the judgment of the larger community that they are indecent. They are degraded for, in a literal sense, they live outside the grades or categories which the community regards as respectable.* (pp. 323–324)

Drawing upon these insights and additional literature, Hernandez (1993a) developed a measure of relative poverty using poverty thresholds set at 50% of median family income in specific years and adjusted for family size. Using this general approach to measuring income, families are classified as living in (a) relative poverty, (b) near-poor frugality, (c) middle-class comfort or prosperity, and (d) luxury. Specifically, according to this classification, a family's income level is described as "relatively poor" if it is less than one-half as large as the median family income, as "near-poor" if it is above the relative poverty level but less than three-fourths of the median income, as "middle class comfort" if it is above the near-poor level but less than 50% more than the median, and as "luxurious" if it is 150% percent of the median or more.

Figure 7–4 shows that the relative poverty rate among children dropped sharply after the Great Depression from 38% in 1939 to 27% in 1949. The 1950s and 1960s brought an additional decline of four percentage points, but by 1988, the relative poverty rate for children had returned to the comparatively high level of 27% that children had experienced almost 40 years earlier in 1949. By 1994, this had increased further to 28%. Relative poverty rates have been much higher for major racial and ethnic minorities. For example, the relative poverty rate for children in 1990 was 18% for whites but 50% for blacks and 45% for Latinos.

Figure 7–4 also shows changes in middle-class living and in luxury living. Income inequality declined between 1939 and 1969, especially immediately after the Great Depression, but then it increased substantially, both because relative poverty increased from about 23% to 28% between 1969 and 1994, and because the proportion of children in families with luxury-level incomes increased from 15% to 26%. Thus, the proportion of children living in middle-class families decreased from about 42% to 33% during the last quarter of the 20th century.

## Explaining the Quarter-Century Increase in Poverty

Why did childhood poverty increase? An important but sometimes overlooked change has been large declines in the incomes of working men, especially those in the prime ages for fathering and rearing children. Large increases have occurred since the early 1970s, and especially since 1979, in the proportion of those with "low earnings," that is, annual earnings below the official poverty threshold for a four-person family. After 1979, earnings declines were especially large among men who worked full-time, year-round and fell within the age range most likely to have children in the home.

Among full-time, year-round workers, the proportion of men ages 18 to 24 with low earnings dropped from 35% to 17% between 1964 and 1974, but then jumped to 40% by 1990; the proportion of men ages 25 to 34 with low earnings dropped from 12% to only 5%, but then jumped to 15%; and the proportion of men ages 35 to 54 with low earnings dropped from 13% to 5%, but then jumped to 9%.

Given the steep declines during the late 1960s, and the especially sharp increases since 1979, it is not surprising that trends in relative (and official) poverty rates followed a similar pattern during the past quarter-century; that is, children experienced large increases in relative (and official) poverty after 1969

**Figure 7–4: Children age 0 to 17 years by relative income level: 1939–1994.**

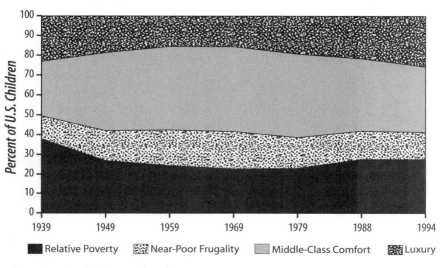

Source: Hernandez, (1993a), p. 245; (1997a), p. 155.

but especially since 1979.

Of course, the amount of income available to children from their fathers is substantially less for children living in mother-only families than for children living with both parents. However, the best available evidence indicates that approximately one-third of the increase in child poverty during the 1980s is accounted for by the increase in mother-only families, but the remaining two-thirds of the increase is unrelated to the rise in mother-only families and is directly accounted for by declining income (Hernandez, 1997b).

In other words, aside from the increase in mother-only families, childhood poverty rates and trends have been affected directly by historic trends in the proportion of children living with fathers who work full-time but have low incomes or who experience part-time work or joblessness in any given year. These features of fathers' work also have important indirect effects on childhood poverty, however, because of their historic influence on divorce and out-of-wedlock childbearing, that is, because of their role in fostering the increase in mother-only families and because of their influence on mothers' labor-force participation.

In short, economic and employment experiences of fathers and mothers are the central driving forces in determining levels and trends in childhood poverty. Today, as was the case 50 years ago, childhood poverty trends are not occurring mainly in response to trends in mother-only families that are inde-

pendent of economic factors; instead, these trends mainly respond to the economic and employment experiences of fathers and mothers.

## Demographic Projections: Immigrants and Minorities

Demographic projections suggest that issues of immigration and of race and
ethnicity will become increasingly important for the well-being and development of children in the United States during the next few decades. These issues
are tightly linked to current trends and future possibilities for public policy.

With U.S. fertility at or below the level needed to replace the population,
and with the baby-boom generation moving beyond childbearing ages, future
growth in the U.S. population will occur primarily through immigration and
through births to immigrants and their descendants. From the U.S. perspective, most immigrants are members of racial and ethnic minorities.

The proportion of children who are Latino, black, or of another nonwhite
race is expected to expand steadily and rapidly from 30% to 50% between 1990
and 2030, whereas the proportion who are white will decrease from about 70%
to only 50% (see Figure 7–5). Thus white children, the historical majority, will
become a minority in approximately 30 years. It will become increasingly necessary to focus on the lives of immigrant children and their descendants, most
of whom belong to racial and ethnic minorities, to adequately monitor the well-
being and development of children, and to understand key processes of family
and economic change in the United States during the coming decades.

The aging of the U.S. population provides another reason for increased
attention to immigrant and minority children and their families. The U.S.
Bureau of the Census projects that between 1990 and 2040, as children are
becoming more racially and ethnically diverse, their share of the total population will decline from 26% to 23%. The percentage of Americans who are
working-age adults 18 to 64 years old will also shrink, from 65% to 62%.
Meanwhile, people older than age 65 will expand from 12% to 21% of the total
U.S. population.

Consequently, future decisions about the resources devoted to children,
including spending on health care and education, will be made in a demographic context in which a declining working-age population will be called on
to support two dependent populations. These two populations, children who
represent a shrinking share of the population, and the elderly who represent an
expanding share of the population, have very different needs.

Furthermore, increased racial and ethnic diversity will occur at all ages, but
especially at younger ages. Projections for 2030 indicate that 75% of the elderly
will be white, compared with 59% for working-age adults, and only 50% for children. Thus, the experience of U.S. children during the coming years increasingly will be the experience of minority children, whereas the growing elderly pop-

## Figure 7–5: Percent of children who are Black, White (non-Latino), or Latino.

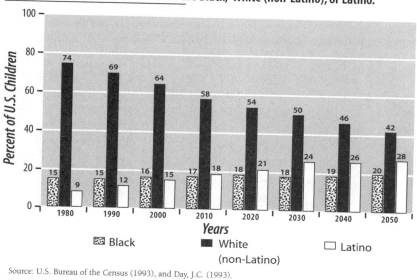

Source: U.S. Bureau of the Census (1993), and Day, J.C. (1993).
Estimates for 1980 to 1990, projections for 2000 to 2050.

ulation will increasingly depend for their economic support on the productive activities of working-age adults who are members of racial and ethnic minorities.

Hence, economic support for the future elderly, namely the baby-boom generation as they age, will become more and more dependent upon the quality of education, training, and health care received by members of minority groups when they are children. In other words, the health and adjustment of immigrant children and families, and of ethnic and racial minorities more generally, and the extent to which these children become productive members of society as adults, will have increasingly important consequences for the white population of the baby-boom generation during the next 30 years.

Recent reforms to the welfare system represent another reason for increasing focus on immigrant children and families. The welfare reform bill of August 22, 1996, rewrote the social contract between the U.S. government and the U.S. population regarding the nature of the safety net for persons in need. The revisions were most dramatic for legal resident immigrants, eliminating their eligibility for many programs, until and unless they become U.S. citizens. One important set of policy questions for children concerns the consequences, if any, of welfare reform and the associated reduction in government transfers to immigrant children and families.

A final reason for increasing focus on immigrant children and families is found in many U.S. schools today. In 49 of the largest 100 school districts, more than 50% of all students are black, Latino, or Asian American. In many of the schools in these districts, students speak a multitude of languages. It is not known what conditions lead to a successful educational experience for these children, or what barriers stand in their way. It also is not yet known how schools can develop programs and work effectively with parents from many diverse countries and cultures to achieve education goals.

For all these reasons, statistical indicators and research on consequences of public policies are needed for immigrant children. But there is a similar need for the broader population of children, including native-born racial and ethnic minorities, and the current white majority (see Hernandez, 1998; Hernandez & Charney, 1998; Hernandez & Darke, 1998, for detailed discussions of existing knowledge and recommendations for new research needed on children in immigrant and native-born families).

## Public Policies for Children: Planned and Possible

### Cutting Welfare Benefits

Reducing or eliminating welfare benefits for one-parent families has been viewed as a possible means of reducing economic incentives to bear children out of wedlock. This is a major thrust of recent welfare reforms. Despite the plausibility of this approach, scientific evidence to date suggests that welfare programs have had little effect in fostering single parenthood.

This conclusion emerges both from research in the United States and from international comparisons that show, despite the more generous welfare programs in western Europe, that these countries generally have less divorce and out-of-wedlock childbearing than the United States. Nevertheless, because recent welfare reforms will reduce benefits for one-parent families, it is essential that the consequences be monitored and studied to ascertain the effects, if any, that reducing benefits has on reducing divorce and out-of-wedlock childbearing. Because out-of-wedlock childbearing is especially common among certain ethnic and racial minorities, this calls for research that focuses on social, economic, or cultural processes that maybe unique to specific groups.

### Increasing Child Support from Noncustodial Fathers

A second approach to discouraging the formation of one-parent families is to require that noncustodial fathers make larger child support payments. The underlying idea is plausible, namely, that some fathers will be discouraged from divorce or out-of-wedlock childbearing if economic costs to noncustodial fathers are increased. Of course, it is extremely important to note that, from the perspective of mothers, increased child support payments from absent fathers represent an increased economic incentive to divorce or to bear children out of wedlock, because the mothers will have greater claims on fathers' incomes. It is not yet clear whether the Child Support Enforcement Act of 1984 and the Family Support Act of 1988, which are designed to increase these payments, will have such effects on divorce and fertility behavior.

Increased child support payments also are seen as a way to increase the income available to children in one-parent families. How much additional child support can noncustodial fathers afford to pay, and which children would benefit? Sorensen (1995) recently estimated that noncustodial fathers could pay much more as of 1990, $34 billion more than the actual payments of $14 billion, for a total of $48 billion.

But many noncustodial fathers have little or no earnings available for child support payments, because they work for only part or none of the year. Because men with limited education, restricted work opportunities, and low incomes tend to be divorced from, or to bear children out-of-wedlock with, women who have similar disadvantages, children in mother-only families who are most disadvantaged economically will also often have fathers who have little or no income to pay in child support.

For this reason, and because approximately 50% of officially poor children live in two-parent families in which the child already has access to the fathers' entire income, Sorensen's estimates imply that with a perfect child support system in 1993, the official poverty rate for children might have been reduced from about 23% to approximately 21%, that is, by only two percentage points. Instead of improving the economic situation of poor children, much of the potential increase in child support payments would improve the economic situation of nonpoor children with comparatively high incomes. Sorensen estimates that $27 billion of the additional $34 billion that noncustodial fathers can afford to pay, that is, 78% of the total, would be paid by fathers in the top 50% of the income distribution of noncustodial fathers.

Increased child support payments would bring many additional billions of dollars into the homes of children in mother-only families, but because children in the most economically disadvantaged families would receive only a small portion of these payments, a policy of increased child support payments will have comparatively little effect in reducing childhood poverty.

## Increasing Parents' Work and Earnings

A second policy approach to raising family income involves increasing either the amount of time that parents work or their earnings per hour of work.

Public policies might act to increase parents' paid work by providing resources that facilitate work, such as subsidized child care or access to transportation, as is planned within the national welfare reform. Presser and Baldwin (1980) have found that many minority mothers with young children would seek employment, or work more hours, if child care were available at a reasonable cost. Because a lack of affordable child care limits mothers' employment most among mothers who are young, black, single, and have low education and little income, additional public support for child care for young children may act to raise the amount of income available to many children who are especially disadvantaged. Policies to expand the number of available jobs, either directly or through subsidy programs, might also improve work opportunities for parents of economically disadvantaged children.

Public policies focusing less on the amount of work and more on increased earnings per hour of work include those to increase the minimum hourly wage, or to increase the work skills of parents through education and training programs. Raising the legal minimum hourly wage can immediately increase the income available to children in some families with parents earning the very lowest wages, whereas education and training programs can enhance the marketability and value of parents' work skills.

Officially poor children are split about equally between one-parent and two-parent families. Consequently, policies to increase parental employment and earnings could reduce economic disadvantage in one-parent families by increasing income both for custodial parents and for noncustodial parents; the latter could then afford to make larger child support payments. Such policies might also reduce poverty in two-parent families by increasing the earnings of both fathers and mothers.

### Increasing Government Income Transfers

A third policy approach to raising family income involves government transfer programs. A wide variety of public programs effectively transfer income from the government treasury to economically disadvantaged children by providing either cash payments or noncash benefits or services. Examples include the former Aid to Families with Dependent Children program, which has become the Temporary Assistance for Needy Families block grant; public assistance; food stamps; child nutrition; the Supplemental Food Program for Women, Infants, and Children; public housing and subsidized rent payments; foster care; Head Start; and the Earned Income Tax Credit.

Taken together, such cash and noncash benefits substantially reduce official childhood poverty. By one accounting approach used by the Census Bureau, the official poverty rate for children would have been 26% in 1993, if there had been no government income transfers, but these transfers acted to reduce childhood poverty by about 7.5 percentage points. All told, then, government income transfers reduced official childhood poverty by about one-fourth in 1993, from about 26% to about 19%.

Despite the important role government transfers play in reducing childhood poverty, children in the United States are much more likely to live in poverty than children in many other developed countries. For example, Smeeding and Torrey (1988) have used the Luxembourg Income Study (LIS) to develop estimates with a measure similar to the relative poverty rate, setting the poverty threshold at 50% of median disposable family income.

As of the mid-1980s, the poverty rate for children using this measure was 27% in the United States, compared with 10% to 16% in France, the United Kingdom, and Canada; 7% in Germany; and 3% in Sweden. The same pattern held true for children in one-parent families. The poverty rate among U.S. children in one-parent families was 63% compared with 55% in Canada, but only 30% in Germany, 22% in France, 16% in the United Kingdom, and 4% in Sweden.

What accounts for these differences in poverty? Another study (Hobbs & Lippman, 1990) reported that only 73% of poor families with children in the United States received government transfers; 27% received none. In several other major developed countries, namely Australia, Canada, Germany, Sweden, and the United Kingdom, nearly all poor families with children—99% or 100%—received government transfers.

## Government Income Transfers and the Working Poor

Many poor families with children in the United States do receive government transfers, but most are working-poor families with at least one family member who earned wage or salary income sometime during the year. In 1990, 60% of officially poor families with children were working-poor families who earned at least some wage or salary income, at 78% for two-parent families, and 49% for one-parent families. Thus, many children live in official poverty despite parents' work, and many live in families that receive government assistance that is not enough when combined with income earned from work to lift the family out of poverty.

## Immigration Policy: Ethnic and Racial Diversity

Another major potential policy goal might be to reduce immigration to the United States, which would reduce future growth in ethnic and racial diversity among children. Many nonwhite and Latino children may have health and educational needs (and related social needs) that differ from white children because of differences in poverty, language barriers, or cultural isolation. As described previously, population projections indicate that, because of trends in immigration and differential birthrates, the nonwhite and Latino proportion is likely to grow. Although public policy discussion has not focused explicitly on slowing the increase in the racial and ethnic diversity of children, substantial discussion is directed toward policies to reduce the flow of immigrants into the United States.

If such a policy were adopted and were effective, it would slow the increase in nonwhite and Latino children as a proportion of the total population during coming decades. Of course, large incentives to emigrate from third world countries to the United States result from enormous differences in both population growth rates and income levels. So a policy, for example, to close the borders to immigrants might be extremely difficult to implement. But even if immigration were stopped immediately, it must be remembered that about one-third of U.S. children today are nonwhite or Latino, and this proportion will continue to grow somewhat during coming years because of differential birthrates. In lieu of stricter immigration laws, racial and ethnic minorities will, together, account for approximately 50% of all children only 30 years from today.

## Child Care and Education

Child care and education play a critical role in the well-being and development of children. Hence, another major policy goal might be to expand child care and education opportunities. How would the need for nonparental child care change if welfare reform was successful in achieving central goals?

First, insofar as public policies successfully reduce divorce and out-of-wedlock childbearing, and thereby encourage the formation or maintenance of two-parent families, these policies would increase the potential availability of parents themselves to care for their children, and hence reduce the need for nonparental child care.

Acting in the opposite direction, however, insofar as public policies successfully encourage increased parental work outside the home, they increase the need for nonparental child care. Furthermore, because nonstandard work schedules are especially common for low-paying jobs, increased work among parents of economically disadvantaged children may increase the need for nonparental care during evenings, nights, early morning hours, or weekends.

If increased work leads to increased income, additional resources will be available to pay for child care. The new welfare reforms also provide for increased government support for child care. If increased access to child care were combined with increased opportunities for well-paid jobs under the new welfare reform, the result could be improved educational opportunities for children and reduced economic disadvantage. On the other hand, if child care costs increase more than income, then overall economic resources to pay for expenses not related to child care will not increase, and increased parental work will simply shift child care from parents to nonparental caregivers. Also, if the overall package of public policies, including government transfers, leads to increased parental work, but to decreased family income, the overall effect will be to increase poverty among children.

Taken as a whole, plausible changes in public policies do not appear likely to reduce the need and the demand for nonparental child care. Instead, these policies are more likely to increase the need and demand for nonparental child care. Furthermore, public policies do not appear likely to reduce most, if any, of the sources of demographic diversity or economic inequality for children, except by influencing poverty. But it appears most likely that recent welfare reforms will lead to increased childhood poverty.

Hence, there is a potentially increasing need for policies focusing on the different educational needs of diverse children, and there is an increasing potential for public child care and education policies to enhance the well-being and developmental outcomes of children. The first child care revolution in the United States required children older than 6 to spend much of their day in school. This revolution was mandated and paid for by governments as a social good in the public interest. Free public education through elementary school, and later through high school, led to revolutionary increases in educational attainments, and in the knowledge and skills of both children and workers. These advances contributed greatly to the historic economic expansion associated with the Industrial Revolution, and hence to broad increases in family income levels.

Partial government support for higher education has had the same effect. Jorgenson and Fraumeni (1995) have estimated that about 26% of total U.S. economic growth over the postwar period from 1948 to 1986 was the direct result of increasing investments in human capital, that is, increases in educational attainments. Today, with new productive technologies and increased global competition, the need is growing for workers who are still more highly trained and educated if the economic standard of living in the United States is to be maintained compared with other countries. As global economic competition increases, the United States is in the midst of a second child care revolution—one affecting children younger than 6 whose parent or parents work. From this perspective, both preschool child care and higher education are valuable, perhaps even essential, to society at large.

## Parental Leave

One additional public policy relevant to the very youngest children merits attention: parental leave from work for parents to care for newborn and young children. Although the amount of parental leave available to mothers and fathers does not directly affect family composition, it does influence the amount of time that parents can spend with newborn children. Many European countries have parental leave policies that are generous both in the time they allow parents to spend with young children and in the economic resources provided to families of young children. Parental leave policy in the United States is quite limited in both regards.

## The Mythical "Ozzie and Harriet" Family

Social welfare policies and programs are often viewed as being for someone else, for the families or children of other people. This is not the case and has not been the case for at least the past 50 years. Figure 7–6 shows the proportion of children in so-called Ozzie and Harriet families, in which the father works full-time year-round, the mother is not in the paid labor force, and all the children were born after the parents' only marriage.

Figure 7–6 shows that, even among children younger than age 1, it has never been the case since at least the Great Depression that a majority of children were born into such families. More than 50% of children were born into families in which the father did not fulfill the cultural ideal of a full-time, year-round breadwinner, or the mother did not fulfill the cultural ideal of a full-time homemaker mother, or at least one parent was previously divorced, or at least one child was born before the parent's current marriage. In short, the Ozzie and Harriet family may have been a cultural ideal, but it has been an empirical myth since at least 1940.

Insofar as the full range of social welfare policies and programs is aimed at helping those families that in various ways do not conform to the mythical Ozzie and Harriet ideal, these policies and programs are aimed at helping a majority of U.S. children.

## The Past and the Future

Different trends in family circumstances have different consequences for children. Historically, children benefited from the decline in the number of siblings in the home, from the increase in their own schooling and in parents' educational attainments, and from the shift to nonfarm work by fathers, because these changes tended to increase the availability of family members to provide for their day-to-day care and to increase economic resources available during both childhood and adulthood. Fathers became less available to children, but after age 6, children spent increasing amounts of time in school.

The more recent increase in mothers' paid employment further increased family income and provided a financial basis for many children to receive non-parental day care as a partial substitute for parental care while mothers and fathers were engaged in paid work away from home. The rise in one-parent, mainly single-mother families acted to reduce the availability of parents to personally care for their children and tended to reduce income available to children in such families. Increasing family income and decreasing poverty rates after the Great Depression benefited children, but poverty and income inequality have increased greatly during the past 25 years, mainly because of trends in parental earnings and the availability of work.

## Figure 7–6: Children in "Ozzie and Harriet" families at ages 0 and 17 for 1920s–1980s birth cohorts.

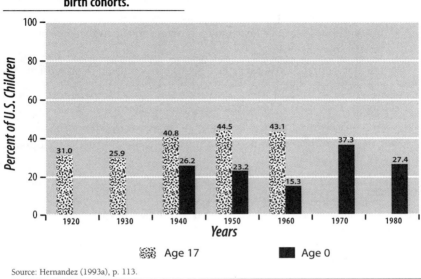

Source: Hernandez (1993a), p. 113.

Because most children with employed mothers live in families in which mothers' paid work is essential for the family to survive or to live in middle-class comfort, a decline in mothers' labor force participation is unlikely. Because non-farm work by fathers and mothers sharply reduced their economic dependence on each other, one-parent families are likely to remain common.

Future immigration will result in increasing racial and ethnic diversity, especially for children, and by about 2030, current racial and ethnic minorities will become a numerical majority. As the proportion of children who are Latino, black, or of another nonwhite group grows, the baby-boom generation will become increasingly dependent for economic support during its retirement on the productive capacity of minority workers, and hence upon the quality of health care and education received by minorities when they are children.

Racial and ethnic minorities tend to be concentrated in the inner cities of the United States, and most immigrants settle in urban areas. If future public policies are not successful in meeting the needs of children in immigrant families and of other minority children in economically distressed urban areas, the future of these children, as well as the economic security of the baby-boom generation during retirement, will be in great jeopardy. These children must become productive workers to support themselves and to sustain the economy on which the baby-boom generation, which consists mainly of whites, will depend when it reaches retirement.

Given the nature of the forces that have led to the rise of mother-only families and the increase in child poverty, policies most likely to be effective in improving the family circumstances of children are those that

- improve opportunities for parents to obtain stable and reasonably well-paid employment,

- transfer economic resources directly to economically deprived families with children, and

- improve the care and education received by children.

Such policies would reduce economic stress, encourage the formation and maintenance of two-parent families, and foster the well-being and development of children.

## References

Alternative measures of poverty. (1989, October 18). A staff study prepared for the Joint Economic Committee of the U.S. Congress.

Brooks-Gunn, J., & Duncan, G. J. (Eds.). (1997). Consequences of growing up poor. New York: Russell Sage Foundation.

Cherlin, A. J., Furstenberg, F. F., Chase-Lansdale, P. L., Kiernan, K. E., Robins, P. K, Morrison, D. R., et al. (1991). Longitudinal studies of effects of divorce on children in Great Britain and the United States. Science, 252, 1386–1389.

Conger, R. D., & Elder, G. H. (1994). Families in troubled times: Adapting to change in rural America. Hawthorns, NY: Aldine de Gruyter.

Day, J.C. (1993, November). Population projections of the United States, by age, sex, race, and Hispanic origin: 1993 to 2050. Current Population Reports, Series P-25, No. 1104. Washington, DC: U.S. Government Printing Office, p. xxi.

Elder, G. H., Jr. (1974). Children of the Great Depression: Social changes in life experience. Chicago: University of Chicago Press.

Elder, G. H., Jr., Conger, R. D., Foster, E. M., & Ardelt, M. (1992). Families under economic pressure. Journal of Family Issues, 13, 5–37.

Federal Interagency Forum. (1998). American's children: Key national indicators of well-being. Washington, DC: U.S. Government Printing Office.

Galbraith, J. K. (1958). The affluent society. Boston: Houghton Mifflin.

Haveman, R., & Wolfe, B. (1994). Succeeding generations: On the effects of investments in children. New York: Russell Sage Foundation.

Hernandez, D. J. (1993a). America's children: Resources from family, government, and the economy. New York: Russell Sage Foundation.

Hernandez, D. J. (1993b). The historical transformation of childhood, children's statistics, and social policy. Childhood, 1, 187–201.

Hernandez, D. J. (1995). Children's changing access to resources: A historical perspective. Social Policy Report, Society for Research in Child Development, 8, 1–24.

Hernandez, D. J. (1997a). Child development and the social demography of childhood. Child Development, 68, 149–169.

Hernandez, D. J. (1997b). Poverty trends. In J. Brooks-Gunn & G. Duncan (Eds.). (pp. 18–34). New York: Russell Sage Foundation.

Hernandez, D. J. (Ed.). (1998). *Children of immigrants: Health, adjustment, and public assistance.* Washington, DC: National Academy Press.

Hernandez, D. J., & Charney, E. (Eds.). (1998). *From generation to generation: The health and well-being of children in immigrant families.* Washington, DC: National Academy Press.

Hernandez, D. J., & Darke, K. (1998). The well-being of immigrant children, native-born children with immigrant parents, and native-born children with native-born parents. In *Trends in the well-being of America's children and youth: 1998.* Washington, DC: U.S. Department of Health and Human Services.

Hobbs, F., & Lippman, L. (1990). *Children's well-being: An international comparison. U.S. Bureau of the Census, international population reports* [Series P-95, No. 80]. Washington, DC: U.S. Government Printing Office.

Huston, A. C., McLoyd, V. C., & Garcia-Coll, C. (Eds.). (1994). Children and poverty: [Special issue.] *Child Development, 65*(2).

Jorgenson, D. W., & Fraumeni, B. (1995). Investment in education and U.S. economic growth. In D. W. Jorgenson (Ed.), *Postwar U.S. economic growth* (pp. 371–388). Cambridge, MA: MIT Press.

McLanahan, S., & Sandefur, G. (1994). *Growing up with a single parent: What hurts, what helps.* Cambridge, MA: Harvard University Press.

Oppenheimer, V. K. (1970). *The female labor force in the United States* (Population Monograph Series, No. 5, Institute of International Studies). Berkeley: University of California Press.

Phillips, D. A., & Crowell, N. A. (Eds.). (1994). *Cultural diversity and early education.* Washington, DC: National Academy Press.

Presser, H. B., & Baldwin, W. (1980). Child care as a constraint on employment: Prevalence, correlates, and bearing on the work and fertility nexus. *American Journal of Sociology, 85,* 1202–1213.

Qvortrup, J., Bardy, M., Sgritta, G., & Wintersberger, H. (Eds.). (1994). *Childhood matters: Social theory, practice and politics.* Aldershot, UK: Avebury.

Smeeding, T. M., & Torrey, B. B. (1988). Poor children in rich countries. *Science, 424,* 873–877.

Smith, A. (1776). *An inquiry into the nature of and causes of the wealth of nations.* London: W. Strahan and T. Cadell.

Sorensen, E. (1995). *Noncustodial fathers: Can they afford to pay more child support?* Washington, DC: The Urban Institute.

Wilson, W. J. (1987). *The truly disadvantaged: The inner city, the underclass, and public policy.* Chicago: University of Chicago Press.

# EIGHT

# Child Maltreatment: Past, Present, and Future Perspectives

*Dante Cicchetti and Sheree L. Toth*

Societal views on the rights of children have long exerted an effect on what is considered to be maltreatment, as well as on how society responds to instances of child maltreatment. A lack of respect for children's rights throughout history has been reflected in cultural practices that, according to our contemporary Western perspective, would be considered brutal or damaging to the welfare of children (Aries, 1962). Historically, infanticide, ritualized sexual practices with children, extreme corporal punishment, and the selling of children are examples of activities that have been viewed as acceptable. During early American times, Puritans advocated severe corporal punishment as a necessity that would instill moral character in children; the avoidance of such practices was regarded as maltreatment (Giovannoni & Becerra, 1979). The case of Mary Ellen (Lazoritz, 1990) graphically illustrates the limited options that were historically available to children who were mistreated. Mary Ellen was regularly beaten by her adoptive parents, yet there was little concerned citizens could do legally to intervene in behalf of the child. In the mid-1800s, child welfare was church-based, and therefore few governmental resources were mobilized for children who were not cared for adequately (Gelles, 1996). Eventually, Mary Ellen was removed from her home when, after extensive coverage in daily newspapers, the court chose to review the case because they determined that the child needed protection (Robin, 1982). It was as a result of this case that the Society for the Prevention of Cruelty to Children was founded in New York City in 1874. Despite the fact that, throughout history, the need to protect vulnerable children has been recognized, society has failed to address this problem adequately.

Over the course of the 20th century, political ideologies regarding parental authority and rights to privacy versus society's role in ensuring the welfare of children have impacted policies regarding the treatment of children. It seems fair to state that the current political climate in our country has placed precedence on the rights of parents over the welfare of children. The minimization of the need for addressing the stark reality of child maltreatment, in part, may stem from the fact that families in which child maltreatment is most prevalent often are not active participants in political and social organizations. Moreover, in general, children in our society lack a clear political constituency. This state of affairs is particularly true for children from disadvantaged families. For example, in the most recent (1996) National Incidence Study of child abuse and neglect, it was discovered that children from families whose incomes were less than $15,000 annually were 22 times more likely to experience some form of abuse or neglect than were children from families whose annual incomes exceeded $30,000. Relatedly, children from single-parent families were at increased risk for suffering abuse or neglect than were children residing in two-parent families (27.3 versus 15.5 per 1,000 children, respectively; USDHHS, 1996). Because maltreated children often reside in families characterized by economic disadvantage and social isolation, factors such as ethnic discrimination, racism, oppression, social class bias, sexism, segregation, and social inequities all influence the development of a national agenda to protect maltreated children (National Research Council [NRC], 1993).

In this regard, it is important to note that it just over 40 years ago that C. Henry Kempe and his colleagues (1962) identified the "battered child syndrome," thereby calling attention to the plight of abused children. It was not until 1974 that a national legislative agenda, P.L. 100-294, was instituted. The so-called Child Abuse Prevention and Treatment Act (CAPTA) mandated that suspicions of child maltreatment be reported to authorities if observed by a variety of professionals, including medical personnel and educators, among others. Noteworthy are the limitations of this legislation to professionals in many states, thereby abrogating citizens more broadly from responsibility for ensuring the welfare of this nation's youngest and most vulnerable members. This state of affairs has continued to the present day. As a component of CAPTA, the National Center on Child Abuse and Neglect also was begun and charged with obtaining an estimate of the occurrence of child maltreatment nationally. This initiative resulted in the compilation of three National Incidence Studies (NIS) of child abuse and neglect, beginning in 1979.

Whereas efforts to prevent the occurrence of child maltreatment and to treat its correlates and sequelae have grown (Toth & Cicchetti, 1993), the reality that we must confront as a nation is that the numbers of children who have experienced some form of maltreatment have escalated over the past several decades. This is demonstrated most graphically by referring to the statistics compiled in the NIS. The NIS provide an important perspective on the magnitude, gravity, and pervasiveness of child maltreatment. Because these studies utilized a nationally representative design, data obtained were not restricted to cases investigated by Child Protective Services (CPS) agency workers, but also reflect information provided by other community professionals that was not reported to CPS or that was screened out by CPS without investigation. Changes over time in the NIS for children identified by harm and endangerment standards are depicted in Figure 8–1. Because only the harm standard was utilized for the first NIS (NIS–1), endangerment statistics are not available for comparison purposes.

The U.S. Department of Health and Human Services conducted the first National Incidence Study (NIS-I) from 1979 to 1980, guided by the belief that the cases of maltreatment reported to authorities greatly underestimated the true rate of occurrence. Therefore, reports of maltreatment received by child protective authorities were supplemented with information gathered from professionals from community institutions and law enforcement officials. NIS-1 employed a definitional standard referred to as the *harm standard*, a relatively stringent criterion that requires that an act or omission result in demonstrable harm to the child to be classified as abuse or neglect. Data from child protective agencies indicated that the incidence was 17.8 per 1,000 children, with 42.7% of these reports being substantiated, resulting in a substantiation incidence rate of 7.6 per 1,000 children per year. When the NIS-1 criterion requiring moderate or severe harm was factored in, the incidence rate was 3.4 per 1,000 per year. This rate increased to 10.5 per 1,000 children, however, when data from non-CPS sources were taken into account.

Using the same design and criteria as that of NIS-1, NIS-2, which was completed in 1986 (USDHHS, 1988), found an estimated 14.8 per 1,000 children to have experienced substantiated maltreatment. However, when a definition of endangerment—a more conservative definition that subsumes a lesser degree of demonstrable harm and allows children who have not yet been seriously harmed to be included—was added to the study, the reported incidence rate was 22.6 per 1,000 children, a 66% increase over the NIS-1 estimates (USDHHS, 1988).

The most recent data from NIS-3 reveals that 1 out of every 43 children in the United States has experienced some form of maltreatment at the hands of a parent or primary caregiver (USDHHS, 1996). Using the harm standard, this reflects a 67% increase over NIS-2 estimates, and a 149% increase over NIS-1 estimates. Of special concern is the substantial increase in the incidence of children who were seriously harmed. The estimated number of seriously injured children rose from 141,700 to 565,000 in the seven years between NIS-2 and NIS-3, an increase of 299%!

When the definition of maltreatment is expanded to include children identified through the endangerment standard, estimates increase to more than 2.8 million cases nationwide, an increase of 98% over figures obtained in NIS-2. When using the harm standard, 1,500 children died because they had been

## Figure 8–1: Trends in rates of child maltreatment across the National Incidence Studies (NIS)

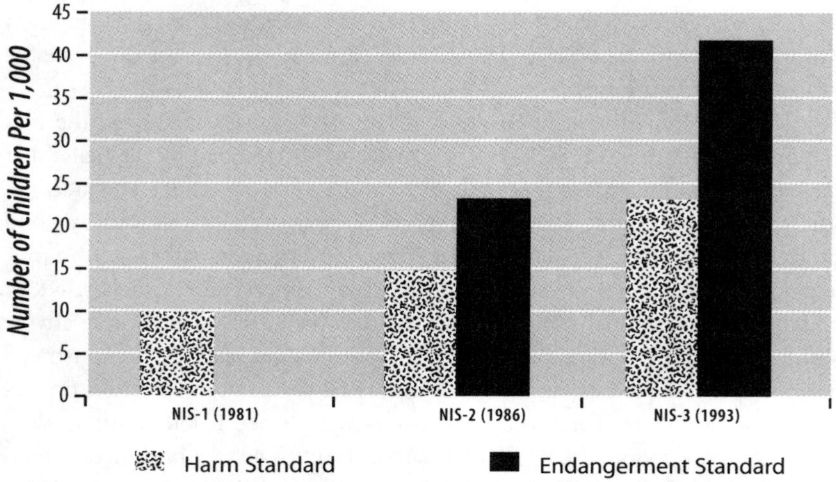

The data are from NIS-3 (USDHHS, 1996).

inflicted with fatal wounds and more than 36% of children identified by the harm standard experienced serious injuries (e.g., loss of consciousness, cessation of breathing, broken bones, and/or third degree burns).

In addition to increases in the overall incidence of child maltreatment across the three national studies, some other important trends also are apparent. In using the harm standard, both physical and sexual abuse rose significantly during the 13-year interval between NIS-1 and NIS-3. In 1993, a child in the United States had an 84% higher risk of being harmed from physical abuse than in 1980. NIS-3 also reported that, during the same time interval, more than five times the number of children were victims of sexual abuse, an increase of 407%. Emotional abuse showed a marginal incidence increase of 43% (USDHHS, 1996). Neglect also increased between 1980 and 1993, with emotional neglect being 4 1/3 times higher in 1993 than in 1986, and with physical neglect doubling during the same time period. Significant differences were not evident with respect to educational neglect.

Given these epidemiological estimates, one might readily begin to question whether these incidence and prevalence rates are reflective of a nation's commitment to the protection and promotion of its children's safety and well-being. As a society, we are faced with an increasing number of children who are suffering the deleterious effects of having been maltreated. It has been estimated that more than $500 million annually is spent on the array of services necessitated for children who have experienced abuse or neglect, including therapy, foster care, special education, and medical care. Furthermore, the future lost economic productivity of severely abused children is likely to prove to be expensive for society, with estimates ranging as high as nearly $150 million per year (NRC, 1993).

Since the identification of the battered child syndrome (Kempe et al., 1962), diligent efforts have been made to comprehend the causes and consequences of child maltreatment, as well as to prevent and provide intervention for this human tragedy. A unified, comprehensive plan of action capable of addressing the complexity of child maltreatment will emerge and be implemented in our society only through

- continually refining our definition of child maltreatment,
- enhancing our understanding of the etiology of child maltreatment, and
- building on our knowledge of the consequences of maltreatment on developmental processes.

Therefore, after describing epidemiological and definitional issues related to child maltreatment, we examine etiological considerations and developmental consequences of maltreatment. We conclude by discussing issues pertaining to prevention and intervention. Throughout each of these sections, we critically examine the state of the knowledge and propose strategies that are needed to continue to improve our understanding of, and subsequently, our ability to address the tragedy of child maltreatment. Because a significant component of this solution rests with modifications in current social policies toward impoverished children and families, we integrate recommendations for a social policy agenda.

## Epidemiological and Definitional Issues

Incidence and prevalence rates of child maltreatment in the United States are integrally related to criteria that are used to define an act as maltreatment. Therefore, it is important to examine how definitional decisions have affected epidemiological estimates of maltreatment. Historically, legislative officials have struggled over whether the government has the right to dictate parenting practices and determine what is and is not considered abusive behavior toward children. Shifts between liberal and conservative views with regard to appropriate government involvement have had a significant impact on decisions and policies regarding definitions of child maltreatment (Barnett et al., 1993), as well as on service availability. Typically, those with liberal philosophies have maintained that it is the responsibility of the state to protect minors from being oppressed by their families. This philosophical orientation results in a broad definition of child maltreatment. Conversely, those having more conservative persuasions have advocated for restricted definitions of maltreatment, arguing for the families' right to privacy and parental authority (Goldstein, et al., 1973).

The NIS-3 provides some sobering information (USDHHS, 1996). Although significant increases in the number of children who have been maltreated as defined by both the harm standard and the endangerment standard occurred from NIS-2 to NIS-3, CPS investigated approximately the same number of cases of child maltreatment in 1993 as in 1986. Thus, although the number of cases of child maltreatment increased dramatically, the percentage of children whose maltreatment was officially investigated by CPS declined significantly (e.g., 33% of children whose maltreatment met the endangerment standard in 1993 were investigated, compared with 51% in NIS-2), as shown in Figure 8–2.

The decrease in reports being investigated may reflect the realities of limited resources being allocated to support investigative efforts. In effect, this may result in only the most severe reports of maltreatment being addressed. Because extant data do not support the conclusion that more severe maltreatment is more detrimental to children's development (Manly, Cicchetti, & Barnett, 1994), this practice may jeopardize many children.

The issue of "unsubstantiated" reports of child maltreatment has been addressed by Drake (1996), who discusses the heterogeneity contained among unsubstantiated reports of maltreatment and cautions against adopting the belief that *unsubstantiated* means that maltreatment has not occurred. In fact, studies that have compared psychosocial outcomes among children with substantiated versus unsubstantiated maltreatment reports suggest that significant psychosocial maladjustment accompanies both unreported and unsubstantiated instances of child maltreatment. Therefore, the fact that fewer reports of maltreatment are being investigated suggests that greater numbers of children are not receiving necessary services to prevent the emergence of negative developmental sequelae and possible mental disorders.

Much research conducted in the area of child maltreatment has been hampered by problems related to definitional considerations. In fact, in their report on the status of research in the area of child maltreatment, the NRC (1993) concluded that "the variation in existing definitions and inadequate instrumentation impede high-quality research, inhibit the comparison of studies of related phenomena, and restrain the development of good evaluations of intervention efforts" (p. 344).

Because the field of developmental psychopathology provides an overarching framework that advocates interdisciplinary, multicultural, and multicontextual approaches to the study of developmental processes and outcomes (Cicchetti, 1993; Cicchetti & Toth, 1991; Garcia-Coll et al., 2000; Toth & Cicchetti, 1999, it allows various perspectives and viewpoints on defining mal-

**Figure 8–2:  Changes from NIS-2 to NIS-3 in percentage of children meeting endangerment standard who were investigated by Child Protective Services.**

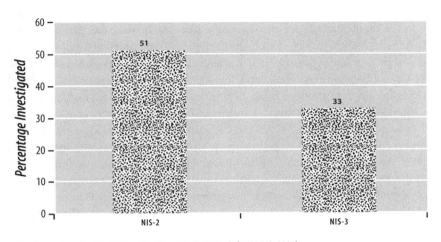

The data are from the third National Incidence Study (NIS–3). [USDHHS, 1996].

treatment to be integrated. According to the developmental psychopathology perspective, the developmental and contextual aspects of maltreatment must be considered if the causes and consequences of maltreatment are to be understood. As each of the components involved in child maltreatment, including the parent, child, and environment, are considered to be transacting over time (Cicchetti & Rizley, 1981) and across multiple ecological systems (Cicchetti & Lynch, 1993), an adequate definition of maltreatment must be able to capture these myriad influences. Definitional considerations related to child maltreatment are discussed more fully by Barnett et al., (1991). In general, four categories of child maltreatment are generally designated, including physical abuse, sexual abuse, emotional maltreatment, and neglect. These subtypes are subsumed under the harm and endangerment standards contained in the NIS.

### Etiological Considerations

An understanding of the complex array of factors that may eventuate in child maltreatment is important to understanding societal trends that may affect the occurrence, continuance, or worsening of child maltreatment. Media portrayals of child maltreatment fail to convey the complex interplay of multiple risk factors that influence the unfolding of abusive and neglectful behaviors. Despite prior historical beliefs that single risk factors such as parental psychopathology, a history of maltreatment in one's own childhood, poverty, and temperamental-

ly difficult children could, in isolation, eventuate in the occurrence of child maltreatment, careful research unequivocally reveals that there is no overriding cat-
alyst for child abuse and neglect (Cicchetti & Toth, 1995; NRC, 1993). As
sophistication in our knowledge has grown, so, too, has our recognition that
none of these single-factor models can explain adequately the genesis of maltreatment. Rather, in accord with the ecological-developmental framework proposed by Bronfenbrenner (1979), in which equal emphasis is placed on the role
of environmental, contextual, and familial factors, a consensus has emerged
regarding the contributions made by a variety of transacting factors operating at
various levels of the individual, familial, and societal ecologies.

Along these lines, Belsky (1980) drew on Bronfenbrenner's (1979) theory of
human development to conceptualize an ecological model as a framework for
understanding the broader context in which maltreatment occurs. (Figure 8–3)
In this model, the individual's environment is conceptualized as being composed
of several well-defined ecological levels. Some distal levels of the environment
exert influences that can be perceived by the individual, although they are more
remote than other levels. The two most distal levels of the environment are the
macrosystem, which includes the beliefs and values of the culture, and the
exosystem, which includes aspects of the community in which families and individuals live. Cultural beliefs such as social acceptance of violence, unequal distribution of resources resulting from racism, and tolerance of an economic condition in which one-fifth of preschool-aged children live below the poverty line
(Children's Defense Fund, 1991) are examples of macrosystem influences that
may contribute to the occurrence of child maltreatment and affect children's
developmental outcomes. Exosystem influences include the formal and informal
social structures that create a context for the family, such as factors in the neighborhood and community, and they include stressors associated with decreased
economic opportunity, unemployment, and violence within the community.

Other levels of the environment exert more direct influences on individual
development and adaptation. For example, the microsystem includes the
immediate setting in which the individual exists, most notably the family.
Factors in the family that play a role in the initiation of maltreatment and that
also influence children's development include family dynamics and parenting
style. In addition, domestic violence and family poverty are examples of stressors at the microsystem level.

Another highly proximal level of the environment, introduced by Belsky
(1980), is referred to as ontogenic development. This level includes factors within
the person connected to developmental history as well as to the person's current
development and adaptation. It is at the ontogenic level that the effects of maltreatment can be seen. The ontogenic level also includes characteristics that can
make the individual more vulnerable or more resilient to adverse circumstances.

## Figure 8–3:  An ecological-transactional model of child maltreatment.

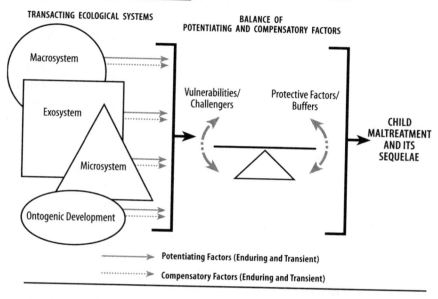

Cicchetti and Lynch (1993) integrated transactional and ecological models to examine the processes by which maltreatment occurs and development is shaped as a result of potentiating and compensatory risk factors present at each level of the ecology. Child maltreatment does not result in inevitable dysfunction, but its effects are considered within a broader context of risk and protective factors operating across different levels of the social ecology. In their model, Cicchetti and Lynch theorize that the balance among risk and protective factors and processes both determines the likelihood of maltreatment occurring and influences the course of subsequent development. Potentiating factors and processes increase the probability of maltreatment, whereas compensatory factors and processes decrease the probability of maltreatment. Similarly, negative developmental consequences occur when an individual's vulnerabilities outweigh his or her protective factors. In contrast, resilient outcomes occur when protective factors outweigh vulnerability factors (see Figure 8–3).

Risk factors within a given level of the model can influence outcomes and processes in surrounding levels of the environment. These transactions are mutually influencing and determine the amount of risk that the individual faces. At higher, more distal levels of the ecology, such as the macrosystem and the exosystem, potentiating factors increase the potential of conditions that support maltreatment, whereas compensatory factors decrease the potential of such conditions. Risk factors within the microsystem also contribute to the presence or absence of maltreatment and to the adaptiveness of family functioning. Because it is the level of the ecology closest to the child, characteristics of the microsystem have the most direct effects on children's development. It is at this proximal level that spousal abuse and child maltreatment are likely to have a direct effect on the development of children's adaptive or maladaptive functioning.

The manner in which children handle the challenges presented to them by family, community, and society is seen in their own individual development. An increased presence at all ecological levels of the risk factors associated with different forms of maltreatment and violence represents a deviation from the conditions that promote normal development and makes the successful resolution of stage-salient developmental issues problematic for children. As a result, children who have been maltreated have a greater likelihood of negative developmental outcomes and psychopathology (Cicchetti & Toth, 1995). On the other hand, an ecological-transactional developmental approach also should help to account for resilient outcomes in some children. The presence of enduring protective factors and transient buffers at any level of the ecology may promote adaptation and may help to explain why some children display successful outcomes in the face of poverty, violence, and maltreatment (Cicchetti & Rogosch, 1997).

Clearly, there are no simple solutions that can be applied to the causes and consequences of child maltreatment. Rather, it is apparent that far-reaching social policies are needed that will address all levels of children's ecologies.

## Developmental Correlates and Consequences

Although the thought of a maltreated child conjures up images of head trauma, bruises, broken bones, malnutrition, and the like, it appears that emotional damage, not physical damage, may exert the most long-term harmful effect on the psychological and biological development of abused and neglected children (Aber & Cicchetti, 1984; Garbarino et al., 1986). Curiously, the investigation of the effect of maltreatment experiences on children's psychological and biological development took a long time to capture the attention of researchers interested in child maltreatment. Although maltreatment has been recognized as a grave, pervasive, and serious problem in our society for nearly 40 years, the investigation of the developmental sequelae of child abuse and neglect is a relatively recent phenomenon. Previously, research and treatment were focused on the maltreating parent, with the guiding assumption being that if the parents could be successfully treated, then, provided any physical sequelae were handled medically, the children would require no psychological treatment or close empirical scrutiny to ascertain whether the maltreatment experiences had eventuated in deleterious psychological and biological harm (see Cicchetti &

Aber, 1980). Fortunately, the past quarter-century has witnessed a major upswing in the investigation of the psychological and, more recently, the biological developmental consequences of child maltreatment.

In 1984, Aber and Cicchetti highlighted investigations of the sequelae of maltreatment as essential for enhancing the quality of clinical, legal, and policymaking decisions for abused and neglected children. They conjectured that decisions concerning such issues as whether to report a child as maltreated, whether to coercively remove a child from the home, how to develop services to meet the specific psychological needs of maltreated children, and how to evaluate these services would all profit from a more elaborate and sophisticated database on the consequences of child maltreatment on developmental processes. In this section, we provide an overview of what is currently known about the sequelae of child maltreatment.

Although membership in low-income families has been linked to a variety of poor outcomes for children, including an increased likelihood of academic failure, emotional distress, mental disorder, and unwanted pregnancy (Duncan & Brooks-Gunn, 1997; Huston et al., 1994), child maltreatment has been shown to exert negative influences on development over and above the effects of poverty (Cicchetti & Carlson, 1989; Cicchetti & Toth, 1993). When compared with groups of nonmaltreated children from comparable socioeconomic backgrounds, children who have experienced maltreatment consistently have demonstrated significantly greater maladaptive functioning on the stage-salient developmental tasks of infancy and childhood (Cicchetti & Toth, 1995). Specifically, physiological and affective regulation, the development of a secure attachment relationship with the primary caregiver, the emergence of an autonomous and independent sense of self, the formation of effective peer relations, and successful adaptation to the school environment all pose serious problems for maltreated children. In addition, these children are at increased risk for developing an array of behavior problems and mental disorders (see Cicchetti & Toth, 1995, for an in-depth review of the sequelae of maltreatment).

Whereas there can now be no dispute that experiencing maltreatment greatly compromises psychological and biological development, children are not uniformly affected by their maltreatment experiences. In fact, research has shown that some maltreated children may function in a competent or resilient fashion despite their ignominious treatment.

A longitudinal investigation of the processes that contribute to resilient functioning in high-risk disadvantaged nonmaltreated and maltreated children illuminates our understanding of the pathways to resilient adaptation in the face of extreme psychosocial and biological adversity. Cicchetti and Rogosch (1997) examined the adaptation of a group of more than 200 school-age maltreated and nonmaltreated socioeconomically disadvantaged children over three consecutive years. Not surprisingly, given the extant literature on the cumulative risks that maltreatment experiences add to the experience of poverty on developmental processes, a higher percentage of nonmaltreated than of maltreated children were found to be resilient according to clearly operationalized indicators. Moreover, a higher percentage of maltreated than nonmaltreated children were shown to exhibit functioning in the lowest range of adaptive functioning throughout the three years of investigation.

However, resilient maltreated children were identified and differential predictors of resilience were found for maltreated and nonmaltreated children. Based on their findings, Cicchetti and Rogosch (1997) suggested that because personality resources and self-confidence were the major predictors of resilient adaptation in maltreated children, interventions might do well to focus on enhancing self-system processes such as autonomy, mastery, and self-determination in these youngsters.

Finally, we wish to underscore that understanding the consequences of child maltreatment and ameliorating its negative sequelae are made more complex by the fact that maltreatment is a multidetermined phenomenon that also frequently occurs in conjunction with a myriad of associated risks such as poverty, community violence, parental mental disorders, and substance abuse. Consequently, it can be difficult to isolate the source of influence. For example, findings of maladaptive developmental outcomes, behavior problems, and/or psychopathology in abused and neglected children may be the result of their maltreatment experiences, witnessing domestic violence, parental psychopathology, or some combination of these (and other) risk factors.

Perhaps most distressingly, there has been a dearth of policy-relevant research that might be able to address some of the issues associated with parent versus child rights (Cicchetti & Toth, 2000). Consequently, the bulk of policy decisions in the area of child maltreatment is made based on political and often affectively laden views on what is "in the best interests of the child." Research findings that are called upon to support a given decision frequently were not designed to answer the question being asked, and the findings are taken out of context and misapplied.

An example to support this point can be drawn from the area of attachment theory. Early research with institutionalized infants who were separated from their parents and found to be doing poorly (Spitz, 1965), as well as Bowlby's (1988) descriptions of the importance of maintaining secure affectional bonds between parent and child for the prevention of later psychopathology, have been portrayed as providing support for family preservation efforts. This work was not developed, however, to determine whether residing within a maltreating environment with one's birthparents was preferable to being moved to a nonmaltreating environment where birthparents were not present. In fact, although unwilling separation from parents certainly can give rise to emotional distress, so, too, can the insecure attachment patterns that research has found to characterize children's relationships with maltreating parents.

Although the guidelines included in the seminal trilogy, recently published as a compendium titled *The Best Interests of the Child* (Goldstein et al., 1996), argue that the continuity of a child's relationship with his or her adult caregiver is a universal essential to a child's well-being, and therefore conclude that avoidance of intrusions by the state into the family is critical, these conclusions are not based on empirical research. Similarly lacking empirical data is the argument made by Gelles (1996), who, after spending many years as a vocal advocate for family preservation in cases of child maltreatment, has now called for a change to a "child-centered" social policy. Toward this goal, Gelles (1996) offers a number of suggestions, including modifying the priority of the social services system away from family preservation and toward child safety. The views presented by Goldstein and colleagues (1996) and by Gelles (1996), although argued eloquently and framed with the goal of protecting children and fostering positive child development, both suffer a lack of empirical support for the conclusions drawn.

In view of the importance of decisions regarding family preservation versus removal in cases of child maltreatment, one may wonder, rightfully, why so little empirical research has been brought to bear on this issue. One of the most widely recognized efforts to examine home versus foster placement was initiated by Wald et al. (1988). These investigators enlisted the support of state and county protective services agencies to compare children in two jurisdictions who were placed in home or foster care. Children's development was assessed on a wide range of measures, including

- physical development and health status,
- cognitive development,
- academic performance,
- behavior problems,
- emotional problems,
- social behavior,
- parent-child relations, and
- children's satisfaction with self, peers, and school.

The report focused on the outcomes for white children because, although African American and Latino children were enlisted in the investigation, an unequal distribution between home and foster care limited the investigator's ability to evaluate the effect of alternative placements on functioning of non-white children.

Although by no means definitive due to methodological limitations, Wald et al. (1988) concluded that in most domains of development, foster children were showing improved functioning at the end of the two-year evaluation when compared with home-care children. These investigators concluded:

> *Although there was relatively little major change among the children in either group, there is some indication that foster care was more beneficial to the children most at risk, at least with regard to improving physical health, school attendance, and academic performance and preventing deterioration in social behavior at school. Both situations—remaining at home and placement in foster care—involved emotional stress for the children, but the stress caused by the conflict and chaos in their home environments may have had a more negative impact on the home children than the stress that separation, movement, and adjustment to new parents had on the foster children. (p. 183)*

Interestingly, although the provision of services to families was determined to be effective in helping to keep maltreated children with their birthparents, children in both home- and foster-care settings were found to show signs of emotional stress and adjustment difficulties. Unfortunately, this suggests that although the interventions were somewhat effective at achieving some modicum of family unity, children in both home-care and foster care settings who had been maltreated continued to experience significant difficulties. Insightfully, in evaluating the findings and conduct of this two-year investigation, Wald and his colleagues concluded that the question of relevance is not whether foster care is better than home care, but rather under what conditions, for which children, and with respect to which aspects of development might one setting be better than another.

## Prevention and Intervention

There can be no doubt that research on the efficacy of prevention and intervention approaches to child maltreatment is complicated by ethical, legal, and logistical problems, as well as by difficulties in isolating factors specifically associated with child abuse and neglect from a host of other factors present in multiproblem families (NRC, 1993). These challenges notwithstanding, it is nonetheless disconcerting that the NRC (1993) report concludes that, in general, the evaluation of interventions in the area of child maltreatment continues to be characterized by problematic methodological limitations, including limited sample size, lack of controlled experiments, the use of questionable measures, and assessment strategies that cannot be shared across interventions. To this list of problems that plague intervention research in the area of maltreatment, we add

- the paucity of random assignment to treatment conditions,
- the lack of standardized and accessible intervention protocols,
- variability associated with families that are willing to receive services, and
- impediments in gaining the cooperation of departments of social services, the gatekeepers of the system, in order to conduct methodologically sound evaluations of intervention effectiveness.

Cohn and Daro (1987) reviewed four multisite studies of program evaluations funded by the federal government since 1974. These studies involved an investment over a 10-year period and included 89 different demonstration treatment programs, for which the federal government spent approximately $40 million. In general, these authors concluded that treatment efforts were "not very successful" (p. 440), with one-third or more of the parents served maltreating their children while in treatment and more than one-half continuing to be viewed by treatment staff as likely to maltreat their children after their termination from intervention. Just as disheartening, despite repeated calls for the criticality of providing therapeutic services directly to child victims (Cicchetti et al., 1978), the NRC report concluded that the majority of treatment programs do not provide services directed at the psychosocial problems of the abused child. This finding echoes the conclusions of Wald and colleagues (1988), who found that the focus of intervention services in the majority of children that they observed were directed toward the parent. "Unless the child exhibits significant behavioral problems, most agencies do not evaluate the child's academic or social development" (p. 192). Moreover, Wald et al. (1988) note that in more recent years, social service agencies have been encouraged to provide interventions that are of limited duration. The push for time-limited treatment can only become worse as managed care, with its emphasis on cost-effectiveness, becomes more and more prevalent. Equally alarming, the NRC (1993) reports that one national survey found that more than one-third of confirmed cases of child maltreatment received no therapeutic or support services. Thus, we are faced not only with the fact that treatments for maltreated children have generally not been evaluated so as to show their effectiveness, but also with the grim reality that many children still do not even receive services when they are discovered to be maltreated.

Unless the gatekeepers of the system, specifically the child protective assessment and intake teams, recognize the importance of treating the child as well as providing concrete services and addressing family support needs, multitudes of maltreated children will fail to receive the services that could help them to achieve more adaptive functioning. Historically, the "services" provided by many child protective agencies have consisted almost solely of investigative activities, with little effort directed toward the amelioration of the effects of maltreatment. Unfortunately, in addition to a possible lack of knowledge regarding treatment needs, limited child protective resources have required a focus on the identification of maltreatment. With increasingly fewer resources, many states are unable even to fulfill legislative mandates. In fact, as mentioned earlier, there has been a national trend to screen maltreatment reports and to prioritize investigative activities as a function of the severity of the report. Not surprisingly, a reduction in services provided has also occurred.

Rather than moving forward toward more comprehensive services for maltreated children, we appear to be falling further behind in our efforts to combat the heinous problem of child abuse and neglect. Because the nature of the maltreatment experience cuts across the discrete areas traditionally associated with each of the agencies that are involved with child maltreatment—the child welfare system, the legal system, and the special education system—an integrated system of intervention has not emerged. Thus, rather than providing a comprehensive program of support to children who have been maltreated, intervention efforts often work at cross-purposes. Separate funding streams and difficulties in accessing services across these divisions exacerbate this problematic situation. We believe that the development of a federally mandated, integrated policy for the identification, assessment, and provision of follow-up intervention services to children and families in which maltreatment has occurred is an essential step in providing a comprehensive system of services for maltreated children.

Although impediments to the provision and evaluation of interventions to maltreated populations must be acknowledged, one must grapple with the assumptions that have impeded progress in this area. Why is it that, more than 20 years after the importance of providing services directly to maltreated children was voiced, surveys continue to show that at least one-third of maltreated children do not receive therapeutic intervention? Why is it that, despite the recognition that child abuse and neglect have become a "national emergency" in the United States (U.S. Advisory Board on Child Abuse and Neglect, 1990), resources available for necessary, large-scale, intensive interventions continue to be so limited?

To begin to address questions such as these, we must reexamine the beliefs and attitudes that initially informed approaches to addressing child maltreatment and consider whether their influence may still be present, despite an empirical knowledge base that should have challenged certain assumptions. Because the medical model that guided early conceptualizations of child maltreatment cast the parent in the role of "being ill" and in need of treatment, efforts were targeted at the perpetrator of maltreatment rather than at the victim.

Similarly, because a sound base of research regarding the impact of maltreatment on child development was lacking, it was assumed that by ending the maltreatment, either through treatment of the parent or removal of the child, all would be well. Such approaches continue to be prevalent, as evidenced not only by the number of maltreated children who do not receive therapeutic intervention, but also by the fact that, historically, the majority of children in foster care have received no therapeutic services. More recently, to examine predictors of the utilization of mental health services among children in foster care, Garland et al. (1996) found that 56% of the children had received mental health services. Overall, children who had been physically or sexually abused were more likely to receive services than children who had been neglected. In view of the maladaptive outcomes that often accompany foster care placement, even a 56% utilization rate suggests that there may be significant unmet needs for mental health services in the foster care population.

A number of issues may be contributing to the continuance of this situation. For example, those responsible for determining the service needs of maltreated children

- may not believe that these children are in need of services directed toward them specifically,
- may not consider services for children to be effective,
- may not have read the relevant literature and therefore may not be aware of the importance of service provision to maltreated children, or
- may have access to insufficient resources to provide services to children and parents, and, because of political pressures regarding the importance of family preservation, must choose between providing services to children or to parents.

To determine how best to move beyond the continued failure to provide for the treatment needs of maltreated children, issues such as these, as well as others of which we may be unaware, need to be examined.

Although in the area of child maltreatment, prevention generally is associated with the need to provide services directed toward stopping the occurrence or reoccurrence of maltreatment (i.e., primary and secondary prevention), we believe that resources also must be directed toward the prevention of the adverse consequences of maltreatment in children who have been abused or neglected. Because statistics show that a large number of children suffer severe maltreatment prior to the age of 5, it is especially important that services be made available for this group of youngsters. In the area of mental health, there often is a perception that prior to school age, children do not need to be involved in therapy unless they are evidencing significant developmental delays. However, a developmental psychopathology approach argues that early insults may exert much more severe and deleterious consequences over time, thereby suggesting that young maltreated children are at extreme risk for future mental and emotional disorders. In addition, findings of the delayed appearance of sequelae in some maltreated children further argue for the importance of early intervention for maltreated children. Although we concur that more traditional preventive efforts are necessary, until the rate of the occurrence of maltreatment is zero, we believe that the provision of therapeutic services for the maltreated child is an area that cannot be disregarded. In achieving this goal, it will be important that increases in treatment funding not occur at the expense of funding for prevention programs. Rather, we want to emphasize the importance of providing adequate support for both of these areas (Toth & Cicchetti, 1993).

As alluded to in our efforts to explain why maltreated children are not receiving sufficient therapeutic services, funding issues and their role also must not be minimized. The availability of funding, or lack thereof, enters into the equation both with respect to monies available to foster methodologically sound evaluation of service effectiveness, as well as with regard to numbers of personnel available to engage in initial investigations of child maltreatment and the person power needed to make and follow-up on service referrals for children and parents. Because caseloads of state social workers are often beyond their capacity, any additional responsibilities, even if in the best interest of a child or family, may fall through the cracks of the system in the midst of an array of more immediate demands.

Limitations inherent in the mental health service delivery system also may be entering into the failure to meet the needs of maltreated children. Currently, the majority of mental health facilities are center-based and require that those in need of services travel to the center for treatment. Despite a growing belief that home-based outreach may be needed with maltreating parents (Kitzman et al., 1997; Olds et al., 1997), mental health policies and reimbursement structures (e.g., reimbursement based on time involved with conducting a home visit) have not been modified to meet this need. Therefore, maltreating parents and their children are expected to have sufficient resources (emotional as well as logistical) to travel to a facility to receive treatment. More often than not, frequent failed appointments result in the decision to "close" the case due to parental "disinterest in treatment" or "resistance to treatment." The maltreated child, who has no ability to deal with this process, often is a victim once again, this time of a system that fails to respond adequately to his or her needs.

Finally, disconcerting as it is to consider, we must examine society's commitment to meeting the needs of disadvantaged, disenfranchised members of society, many of whom have been recipients of welfare and many of whom are people of color. Modifications to the welfare system serve to highlight some of the views that currently pervade our societal response to such children and families (Knitzer & Bernard, 1997). Despite the fact that federal welfare legislation, P.L.104-193, the Personal Responsibility and Work Opportunity Act of 1996, is likely to exert a major effect on the health and development of young children living in poverty, changes in welfare policies are typically driven by adult-focused goals (Collins & Aber, 1997). For example, in an effort to decrease welfare roles, stipulations such as "lifetime" financial assistance limits have been implemented. In addition, it has been estimated that welfare reform laws will put an additional 1 to 1.5 million children into poverty as well as cut approximately $3 billion over 6 years from child nutrition programs. Policies such as these cannot help but call into question society's willingness to invest in groups that are impoverished and struggling to survive. When one considers resources that are expended on less stigmatized conditions, such as childhood cancer, even though the numbers of children affected are far fewer than those confronted by child maltreatment, one cannot help wondering whether at least some of the impediments to progress in the area of maltreatment are linked to an unwillingness to invest in this sector of society.

## Conclusions

Although much important work remains to be conducted, we presently possess more knowledge about child maltreatment than any prior generation. Scientists have been more successful in enhancing our knowledge of the incidence and prevalence of child maltreatment, its causes, and its developmental consequences than at any previous time in history. Yet, paradoxically, our nation has been comparatively unsuccessful in profiting from this progress. Incidence rates of maltreatment have escalated dramatically over the last two decades, but authorities have not commensurately increased their investigations of suspected maltreatment. Consequently, a significant number of youngsters are failing to be identified and services that might combat the sequelae of maltreatment are not being made available. For example, our clinical experiences, as directors of a center whose primary focus for nearly 20 years has been child maltreatment, have demonstrated that parental acts that would have been considered to be indicated acts of maltreatment by CPS in the late 1980s are currently being designated as too minor to warrant the time and money required for investigation. This constitutes one simple yet powerful example of how economic and political shifts can paralyze and turn back progress that has been achieved in the fields of social science and public health. Moreover, similar limitations in funding of research have hampered the rate of progress in this area as well. In fact, when factoring in the effect of inflation, real dollars allocated toward research by the National Center on Child Abuse and Neglect (now named the Office on Child Abuse and Neglect), the federal agency responsible for more than one-third of total federal funding available for child abuse and neglect, decreased by 44% between 1981 and 1995 (Thompson & Wilcox, 1995).

In reflecting on the important relations among psychological science, public service, and the political context, including the availability of sufficient funding, Schneider (1996) concluded:

> Tension is unavoidable in the complex worlds of science, academia, and government. If psychology concentrates on its "almost connectedness" with the big questions that affect people's lives and presents what it learns in ways that people can understand and use, we will be able to deal creatively and productively with the tension. (p. 720)

In evaluating the goal attainment that resulted from the National Plan for Research on Child and Adolescent Mental Disorders (Institute of Medicine, 1989), members of the committee concluded:

> NIMH has thus far missed the opportunity to engage...in a well-organized effort to inform the public concerning the magnitude and consequences of child and adolescent mental disorders and to convey in appropriate media settings the results of empirical research and the need to take advantage of advances in related scientific disciplines (Members of the Committee, 1995, p. 720).

This conclusion becomes even more significant for child maltreatment. The failure to effectively disseminate research findings in the area of child maltreatment is a pervasive problem that must be rectified. Although a great deal of research on child maltreatment possesses policy implications, far too little actually reaches the policy arena. Rather, the results from many investigations are buried in scientific journals, and they subsequently never reach the desks of those who are in positions to institute change. Consequently, inadequate information is disseminated to policy advocates or to the lay public more generally, and services and funding allocations may be hindered by public views associated with negative conceptions of maltreating parents, families, and children.

In addition, to continue to broaden our knowledge of child maltreatment and to inform our efforts to remedy this abhorrent social problem, our research efforts must be strengthened. Specifically, it is critical that increased research dollars be allocated to investigations of the complex factors that contribute to the occurrence and perpetuation of child maltreatment, as well as to the diversity in outcome among maltreated youngsters. Toward this end, longitudinal investigations, despite their costliness and the difficulties associated with their implementation, must be conducted. With regard to intervention research, we must develop and test competing models of intervention in which children and families are randomly assigned to various treatment approaches. To achieve this important scientific goal, service providers and social service personnel must recognize the extreme importance of answering questions such as what children benefit from what type of services. As a society, we must commit the resources that will result in the training of young professionals who have the skills and the passion to implement this time-intensive work. We believe that such a commitment is obvious and an easy choice to anyone who has seen the face of a child who has suffered years of abuse, yet it is our challenge to communicate the importance of such initiatives.

In view of the failure of society to stem the increase in the occurrence of child maltreatment, we must critically examine policies and practices that are currently in existence. The continued focus on parental rights, with a concomitant emphasis on maintaining family unity and associated family reunification efforts, often jeopardizes the welfare of the children that, theoretically, the system is striving to protect. These policies must be evaluated with children's rights at the forefront of such decisionmaking processes. In addition, as a society we must decide if the welfare of our children is sufficiently important to warrant increased resources being allocated to the social services arena. Unless dollars are made available for improved training of personnel involved in the investigation and determination of cases of child maltreatment, opportunities for necessary intervention will be missed. Moreover, even the most skilled professional cannot address the magnitude of child maltreatment unless sufficient numbers of staff are available to handle the escalating number of reports received.

In addition to evaluating the policies and procedures that are initiated following the occurrence of maltreatment, we also must grapple with our failure to prevent the occurrence of maltreatment. Perhaps the implicit belief that all individuals have an innate capacity to parent needs to be revisited. Even the most well-educated, affluent parent readily acknowledges the challenges associated with being a parent. When added stressors of poverty, single parenthood, and social isolation are present, it is not surprising that the capacity to care for a child may be subverted. As welfare reform efforts are implemented and expectations for employment of single mothers carried forth, we also must be sensitive to the effects of these policies on child rearing. Unless resources are directed toward helping single mothers to manage potential stress associated with work demands, the trends of the last two decades with respect to escalating rates of child maltreatment will worsen.

Finally, as a society we must contemplate the responsibility of individual citizens in helping to eradicate child abuse and neglect. One cannot help shuddering at media accounts of children who have died as a result of abuse or neglect. We are less prone, however, to contemplate how a child could be subjected to prolonged and severe maltreatment, culminating in death, in the absence of someone trying to help the child. In reality, many cases of severe abuse are never brought to the attention of authorities until it is too late to save the victim. Where are we, as concerned citizens, in this process? It appears that the integrity of parental rights again prevails, causing otherwise compassionate individuals to not respond to the cries in the adjoining apartment, for example. Perhaps our laws regarding mandated reporting of suspected maltreatment need to be broadened to ensure that all members of society assume responsibility for protecting children from abuse and neglect.

As our nation moves forward in the new millennium, demographics concerning family structure, income level, and parental education are rapidly shifting in a direction known to be associated with enhanced susceptibility to child maltreatment. Thus, unless investments in children are made an explicit national priority, child maltreatment and its insidious causes and consequences will continue to increase at epidemic proportions. Protecting our nation's children and promoting their optimal development is clearly a humanitarian endeavor; it also is an essential investment in our nation's economic future, however. Preventive and protective efforts during infancy and childhood will translate directly into dollars saved through decreasing maladaptation and psychopathology and increased productivity when these children reach adulthood. To confront the challenge of maltreatment triumphantly, efforts to understand and address factors that are perpetuating child maltreatment must be strengthened. It is only through collaborations among researchers, practitioners, child welfare personnel, legal professionals, and social policy formulators that the cries of our children will be heard and addressed.

## References

Aber, J. L., & Cicchetti, D. (1984). Socioemotional development in maltreated children: An empirical and theoretical analysis. In H. Fitzgerald, B. Lester, & M. Yogman (Eds.), *Theory and research in behavioral pediatrics* (Vol. 2, pp. 147–205). New York: Plenum Press.

Aries, P. (1962). *Centuries of childhood*. New York: Vintage Books.

Barnett, D., Manly, J. T., & Cicchetti, D. (1991). Continuing toward an operational definition of psychological maltreatment. *Development and Psychopathology, 3*, 19–30.

Barnett, D., Manly, J. T., & Cicchetti, D. (1993). Defining child maltreatment: The interface between policy and research. In D. Cicchetti & S. L. Toth (Eds.), *Child abuse, child development and social policy* (pp. 7–74). Norwood, NJ: Ablex.

Belsky, J. (1980). Child maltreatment: An ecological integration. *American Psychologist, 35*, 320–335.

Bowlby, J. (1988). *A secure base*. New York: Basic Books.

Bronfenbrenner, U. (1979). *The ecology of human development: Experiments by nature and design.* Cambridge, MA: Harvard University Press.

Children's Defense Fund. (1991). *The state of America's children.* Washington, DC: Author.

Cicchetti, D. (1993). Developmental psychopathology: Reactions, reflections, projections. *Developmental Review, 13,* 471–502.

Cicchetti, D., & Aber, J. L. (1980). Abused children—Abusive parents: An overstated case? *Harvard Educational Review, 50,* 244–255.

Cicchetti, D., & Carlson, V. (Eds.). (1989). *Child maltreatment: Theory and research on the causes and consequences of child abuse and neglect.* New York: Cambridge University Press.

Cicchetti, D., & Lynch, M. (1993). Toward an ecological/transactional model of community violence and child maltreatment: Consequences for children's development. *Psychiatry, 56,* 96–118.

Cicchetti, D., & Rizley, R. (1981). Developmental perspectives on the etiology, intergenerational transmission and sequelae of child maltreatment. *New Directions for Child Development, 11,* 32–59.

Cicchetti, D., & Rogosch, F. A. (1997). The role of self-organization in the promotion of resilience in maltreated children. *Development and Psychopathology, 9,* 799–817.

Cicchetti, D., Taraldson, B., & Egeland, B. (1978). Perspectives in the treatment and understanding of child abuse. In A. Goldstein (Ed.), *Prescriptions for child mental health and education* (pp. 301-378). New York: Pergamon.

Cicchetti, D., & Toth, S. L. (1991). The making of a developmental psychopathologist. In J. Cantor, C. Spiker, & L. Lipsitt (Eds.), *Child behavior and development: Training for diversity* (pp. 34–72). Norwood, NJ: Ablex.

Cicchetti, D., & Toth, S. L. (Eds.). (1993). *Child abuse, child development, and social policy.* Norwood, NJ: Ablex.

Cicchetti, D., & Toth, S. L. (1995). A developmental psychopathology perspective on child abuse and neglect. *Journal of the American Academy of Child and Adolescent Psychiatry, 34,* 541–565.

Cicchetti, D., & Toth, S. L. (2000). Child maltreatment in the early years of life. In J. D. Osofsky & H. E. Fitzgerald (Eds.), *WAIMH handbook infant mental health* (Vol. 4, pp. 257–294). New York: John Wiley & Sons.

Cohn, A., & Daro, D. (1987). Is treatment too late: What ten years of evaluative research tells us. *Child Abuse & Neglect, 11,* 433–442.

Collins, A., & Aber, J. L. (1997). *Children and welfare reform: How welfare reform can help or hurt children, Issue Brief 1.* New York: National Center for Children in Poverty.

Drake, B. (1996). Unraveling "unsubstantiated." *Child Maltreatment, 1,* 261–271.

Duncan, G., & Brooks-Gunn, J. (Eds.). (1997). *Consequences of growing up poor.* New York: Russell Sage Foundation.

Garbarino, J., Guttman, E., & Seeley, J. W. (1986). *The psychologically battered child: Strategies for identification, assessment, and intervention.* San Francisco: Jossey-Bass.

Garcia-Coll, C., Akerman, A., & Cicchetti, D. (2000). Cultural influences on developmental processes and outcomes: Implications for the study of development and psychopathology. *Development and Psychopathology, 12,* 333–356.

Garland, A., Landsverk, J., Hough, R., & Ellis-MacLeod, E. (1996). Type of maltreatment as a predictor of mental health service use for children in foster care. *Child Abuse and Neglect, 20,* 675–688.

Gelles, R. (1996). *The book of David: How preserving families can cost children's lives.* New York: Basic Books.

Giovannoni, J., & Becerra, R. M. (1979). *Defining child abuse.* New York: Free Press.

Goldstein, J., Freud, A., & Solnit, A. (1973). *Beyond the best interests of the child.* New York: Free Press.

Goldstein, J., Solnit, A., Goldstein, A., & Freud, A. (1996). *The best interests of the child: The least detrimental alternative.* New York: Free Press.

Helfer, R. E., & Kempe, C. H. (Eds.). (1968). *The battered child.* Chicago: University of Chicago Press.

Huston, A. C., McLoyd, V., & Garcia-Coll, C. T. (Eds.). (1994). Children and poverty [Special issue]. *Child Development, 65*(2).

Institute of Medicine. (1989). *Research on children and adolescents with mental, behavioral, and developmental disorders.* Washington, DC: National Academy Press.

Kempe, C. H., Silverman, F. N., Steele, B. B., Droegemueller, W., & Silver, H. K. (1962). The battered child syndrome. *Journal of the American Medical Association, 181,* 17–24.

Kitzman, H., Olds, D., Henderson, C., Hanks, C., Cole, R., Tatelbaum, R., et al. (1997). Effect of prenatal and infancy home visitation by nurses for pregnancy outcomes, childhood inquiries, and repeated childbearing: A randomized controlled trial. *Journal of American Medical Association, 278,* 644–652.

Knitzer, J., & Bernard, S. (1997). *The new welfare law and vulnerable families; Implications for child welfare/child protection systems: Children and Welfare Reform* (Issue Brief 3). New York: National Center for Children in Poverty.

Lazoritz, S. (1990). What happened to Mary Ellen? *Child Abuse & Neglect, 14,* 143-149.

Manly, J. T., Cicchetti, D., & Barnett, D. (1994). The impact of subtype, frequency, chronicity and severity of child maltreatment on social competence and behavior problems. *Development and Psychopathology, 6,* 121–143.

Members of the Committee for the Study of Research on Child and Adolescent Mental Disorders. (1995). Report card on the National Plan for Research on Child and Adolescent Mental Disorders. *Archives of General Psychiatry, 52,* 715–723.

National Research Council. (1993). *Understanding child abuse and neglect.* Washington, DC: National Academy Press.

Olds, D., Eckenrode, J., Henderson, C., Kitzman, H., Powers, J., Cole, R., et al. (1997). Long-term effects of home visitation on maternal life course and child abuse and neglect: Fifteen-year follow-up of a randomized trial. *Journal of the American Medical Association, 278,* 637–643.

Robin, M. (1982). Historical introduction: Sheltering arms: The roots of child protection. In E. Newberger (Ed.), *Child abuse* (pp. 1–41). Boston: Little Brown.

Schneider, S. (1996). Random thoughts on leaving the fray. *American Psychologist, 51,* 715-721.

Spitz, R. (1965). *The first year of life.* New York: International Universities Press.

Thompson, R., & Wilcox, B. (1995). Child maltreatment research: Federal support and policy issues. *American Psychologist, 50,* 789–793.

Toth, S. L., & Cicchetti, D. (1993). Child maltreatment: Where do we go from here in our treatment of victims? In D. Cicchetti & S. L. Toth (Eds.), *Child abuse, child development and social policy* (pp. 399–438). Norwood, NJ: Ablex.

Toth, S. L., & Cicchetti, D. (1999). Developmental psychopathology and child psychotherapy. In S. Russ & T. Ollendick (Eds.), *Handbook of psychotherapies with children and families* (pp. 15–44). New York: Plenum Press.

United States Advisory Board on Child Abuse and Neglect. (1990). *Child abuse and neglect: Critical first steps in response to a national emergency.* Washington, DC: U.S. Department of Health and Human Services.

United States Department of Health and Human Services. (1981). *Study findings: National Study of Incidence and Severity of Child Abuse and Neglect* [DHHS Publication No. OHDS 81-30325]. Washington, DC.: Author.

United States Department of Health and Human Services. (1988). *Study findings: National study of incidence and prevalence of child abuse and neglect* [DHHS Publication No. OHDS 20-01099]. Washington, DC.: Author.

United States Department of Health and Human Services, National Center on Child Abuse and Neglect. (1996). *The third national incidence study of child abuse and neglect.* Washington, DC: U.S. Government Printing Office.

Wald, M., Carlsmith, J., & Leiderman, P. H. (1988). *Protecting abused and neglected children.* Stanford, CA: Stanford University Press.

# NINE

# Trends in the History of Child Care and Family Support: 1940–2000

*Emily D. Cahan and Juliet Bromer*

A series of changes in the social fabric of this country occurred during the 19th century that profoundly affected family life. Largely under the combined effects of urbanization, industrialization, and immigration, a domestic ethic in the United States arose in the mid-19th century. As families migrated away from farms and toward the new and tempting cities, men left the homestead to work in the new industries. Most women stayed behind and cared for the children. Thus was born the doctrine of "separate spheres" that stipulated that men and women be separated and their responsibilities divided between "work" and "child care." Alongside of this separation was the designation of maternal child care as optimal for child development and nonmaternal care as a last (and dangerous) resort for poor families for which maternal employment was required for survival. The resulting day nursery was, in its inception, a welfare program intended for families who had "failed" to uphold the domestic ethic. Thus, the domestic ethic is closely related to American traditions of individualism, self-sufficiency, and the primacy of mothers for child development (Kessen, 1979).

Since the mid-19th century, Americans have held attitudes toward nonmaternal child care outside of the home that can be characterized as ambivalent at best. The legacy of domesticity echoes throughout the history of child care just as the primacy of mother as child-minder runs through the history of child psychology. But the ethic, with all of its associated programs, policies, and public attitudes, especially in the last 50 years, has cracked. Public attitudes toward child care have changed as increasing numbers of mothers work outside of the home. As women have moved out of their historic roles as "keeper of the hearth and home," the public has voiced its demands for adequate care for all young children.

From the beginning of the welfare state in the first quarter of this century, child care was linked to the needs of poor children whose mothers were compelled to work. Later in this century, child care was viewed as either therapy for troubled families or as compensatory education for culturally deprived children. With the recent and enormous entry of middle-class mothers into the workforce, we now recognize child care as a need that cuts across traditional lines of social class, race, and ethnicity. Across these lines, the percentage of preschool-age children without a parent at home full-time increased from 13% to 52% between 1940 and 1989 (Hernandez, 1993, p. 150).

Three very recent events have solidified changes in American approaches to child care and family support. First, a 1997 study, sponsored by the National Institute of Child Health and Development (NICHD), found no main effects of child care on children. Instead, reports from these studies suggest that child care may have indirect effects on children resulting from an interaction between the quality of care and the quality of the child's home environment. High-quality child care can, in fact, enhance aspects of children's emotional, social, and cognitive development, especially for those children who may not have responsive or sensitive home environments. Conversely, poor-quality child care may have negative effects for children who do not experience secure relationships at home. Second, during a spring 1997 White House conference on young children, speaker after speaker reaffirmed the importance of the first three years of life. Armed with brain scans from young children who did and did not enjoy a rich early environment, conferees lent new technological evidence to longstanding convictions of developmental psychologists. Third, an October 1997 White House conference on child care reiterated the need for greater access to high-quality child care for more families. These three recent events symbolize and may perhaps mobilize new efforts to provide high-quality child care and family support to a wider range of families than ever before in U.S. history. The tide has changed.

The following pages take the reader through a sketch of the history of child care and family support since 1940. We believe that historical patterns of analyses can illuminate current practices and public policies.

## World War, Child Care, and Family Support

We begin our story by considering child care services sponsored by the federal government during an extraordinary time of crisis for Americans—World War II. In 1940, mobilization for war involved the unprecedented large-scale employment of women in war-related industries. These new levels of maternal employment created an equally unprecedented need for child care. When labor needs in defense required the employment of 1.5 million mothers with preschool children, the federal government responded by sponsoring child care. The variety of child care programs created to meet those needs still stands as a model for innovation in child care and family support.

When America entered the war, fewer than 1 out of 30 mothers with preschool-age children worked. By the war's end, nearly one mother out of eight with a child younger than 6 was employed (Chafe, 1972). Hundreds of thousands of newly employed mothers thus experienced firsthand the problems associated with working outside of the home, running a household, and raising children. With the increase in maternal employment, absenteeism and job turnover quickly became significant problems in the workplace. A survey made at a Michigan defense plant revealed that 15% of the working mothers missed work periodically because of problems arranging child care (Tank, 1980, p. 372). In addition to contributing to absenteeism and turnover, the lack of child care facilities prevented thousands of nonemployed mothers from joining the domestic war effort. The need for child care during the war was acute; newspaper and magazine accounts detailed stories of young children who were left with unstable guardians, in parked cars, or who were injured in accidents in unsupervised homes (Tank, 1980, p. 374). The United States responded with an astonishingly innovative set of initiatives.

During the war, working mothers, in concert with families, schools, corporations, and the federal government, devised a variety of solutions to meet their child care needs. Almost one-fifth of all families were headed by women, and many mothers worked—some worked to supplement low family incomes, some to boost a family's standard of living, and some out of patriotism for the war effort. At the beginning of the war, mothers of children younger than 2 years of age who worked had little choice in child care. Some relief would come in 1942 when, in the context of a national emergency, federal support for child care sprung forth. During the war, four kinds of child care arrangements were carved out:

- private arrangements made by the families themselves,
- federally sponsored child care centers created under the Lanham Act,
- child care centers operated by private businesses, and
- the hugely successful but largely forgotten Extended School Services (Tuttle, 1995).

Private arrangements for child care included care by fathers and other relatives. So many grandmothers filled the void that "if anyone should ask for a name for this war, it's Grandmother's War" (Tuttle, 1995, p. 96). Fathers working on different shifts served as the second most frequent source of child care.

In July 1942, Congress signed the Lanham Act into law The act provided federal funds to serve the community needs of war-impacted areas. These benefits included child care facilities as well as various other civic facilities. The provision of these federal funds for child care was contentious from the beginning. The controversy that surrounded the wartime federal support for child

care surely reflected the still-dominant domestic ethic and its attendant separation of spheres for men and women. The Federal Works Agency that controlled
the funds urged the expansion of group care for young children but only for
the duration of the war. As one agency official put it, funds were allotted

> solely as a war emergency measure in order to facilitate the employment of
> women needed in the war. We are not substituting an expanded educational
> program nor a Federal welfare program, but we are making money available
> to assist local communities in meeting a war need for the care of children
> while their mothers are engaged in war production. (Tank, 1980, p. 386)

Similarly, Francis Perkins, Secretary of Labor, observed in 1942 that:

> In this time of crisis...mothers of young children can make no finer contri-
> bution to the strength of the nation and its vitality and effectiveness in
> the future than to assure their children the security of home, individual
> care, and affections" (Tank, 1980, p. 380). The Chief of the Children's
> Bureau continued to assert that during the war, as during peacetime, a
> "mother's primary duty is to her home...no matter what the emergency.
> (Chafe, 1972, p. 164)

In the same spirit, a journalist observed that "no informed American needs
a psychologist to tell him that children separated from their home ties and
without constant care...are the troublemakers, the neurotics, and the spiritual
and emotional cripples of a generation hence" (Chafe, 1972, p. 164).

Many mothers felt reticent to send their children to existing day care centers. When asked in a Gallup poll in 1943 whether they would accept a job in
a war plant if their children were to receive child care free of charge, only 29%
of the mothers polled replied "yes," whereas 56% replied "no" (Chafe, 1972,
p. 381). One mother commented that "child care centers are all right for charity cases; but my children belong at home" (Chafe, 1972, p. 381). Older arguments about the dangers and the threat to the mother-child relationship posed
by out-of-home care persisted. Clearly, the federally funded child care centers
were an answer to a war problem and in no way indicated an eclipse of traditional ideological commitments.

By 1944, middle-class cooperative nursery schools and federally funded
child care programs coexisted alongside of a handful of initiatives made by private industry. As an example of corporate initiatives, Douglas Aircraft
announced plans to open a nursery within four miles of the plant but "out of
range as a target for the enemy" (Tuttle, 1995, p. 100). The most well-known of
these corporate programs, that of the Kaiser Shipbuilding Company in Portland,
Oregon, established 24-hour child care centers for children from 18 months to

6 years of age with the aid of $750,000 of federal funds. These high-quality centers offered long and flexible hours of operation, skilled and well-paid staff, close proximity to the production plants, and provision for take-out meals (Tank, 1980, p. 375). The Kaiser centers remained as exemplars of what was possible given "the necessary ingredients of priority, leadership, and professionalism" (Tuttle, 1995, p. 101). Last was the hugely successful but largely forgotten Extended School Services program for children ages 6 to 13, which was dubbed by one author as "one of the biggest success stories of the war" (Tuttle, 1995, p. 102). In a little-noticed move in August 1942, President Franklin Roosevelt allocated $400,000 to the U.S. Office of Education and the Children's Bureau "for the promotion of and coordination of [Extended School Services] programs for the care of children of working mothers" (Tuttle, 1995, p. 102).

The Lanham Act centers were a "win-the-war" program and not a "save-the-child" program (Steiner, 1976). Funds were withdrawn shortly after the war's end. After the war, women were laid off from manufacturing jobs "in droves," despite polls indicating that some women preferred to work outside the home (Coontz, 1992, p. 160). Between 1944 and 1947, the proportion of women in the labor force decreased from 36.5% to 30.8%. Many female workers were downgraded in their jobs to clerical and service positions. An ideological return to normalcy once again idealized the home environment and maternal care as the norm. Most mothers, particularly those of the middle class, returned home from work to care for their children as fathers returned home from war to work outside of the home.

## The Postwar "Return to Normalcy"

The war experience demonstrated women's capability to perform a wide assortment of tasks traditionally associated with men's work. The war also made it possible for large numbers of women to combine motherhood and work. Many women preferred this pattern after the war ended. Other women, especially those of the working class, continued to work as they had always done to support their families.

By the late 1950s, 2.9 million mothers with preschool-age children were employed and confronted with the problem of child care. These families continued to rely on traditional sources of child care—relatives, friends, or neighbors in a family setting. A 1958 Children's Bureau study revealed that 94% of these children were cared for either in their own or someone else's home while their mothers worked. One percent looked after themselves, and only 4% received group care in a day nursery, day care center, settlement house, or nursery school (Tank, 1980, p. 414).

Group child care during the late 1940s and 1950s remained unpopular. Willard Waller, a Barnard sociologist, argued that because working mothers during the war were not able to fulfill their maternal responsibilities, the children were neglected and the very survival of the home was threatened (Cahan, 1989). For Waller and many others as well, the solution was to restore the traditional nuclear family. Dr. Benjamin Spock added his voice to the charge and urged mothers to forgo employment during the preschool years for the sake of the children and the family. In both the 1947 and 1958 editions of *Baby and Child Care*, Spock declared that "useful, well-adjusted citizens are the most valuable possessions a country has, and good mother care during the earliest childhood is the surest way to produce them" (as cited in Grubb & Lazerson, 1982, p. 34). Spock was to change his attitude toward child care and maternal employment in later editions of his popular book.

In the field of child development, observations made of children in hospitals and orphanages who were severely deprived and neglected were generalized in the popular press as a warning against maternal neglect. René Spitz had observed babies in orphanages who suffered from grossly inadequate care, spent much of their time staring vacantly at the ceiling, were apathetic, and showed high rates of morbidity. Spitz (1945) concluded that the anomalous development of these babies was due to the lack of attachment to a specific caretaker. Other aspects of the babies' experiences were ignored, and generalizations about the effects of day care on normal children were made from the literature on this group of severely deprived children. Despite these limitations, many psychologists (Cahan, 1989), supported by an American culture hostile to child care, generalized Spitz's findings to family settings and concluded that young children should not be separated from their mothers.

Day care in the 1950s continued to be perceived and administered as a social welfare service reflecting trends established in the first quarter of this century. The task of welfare caseworkers was to coordinate child care with other social welfare services to help parents meet their "full parental rights and responsibilities" (Ruderman, 1968, pp. 12–17). Publicly supported day care that survived the termination of Lanham Act funds was sponsored by social welfare agencies. Centers established with public funds in the District of Columbia, for example, "were established for the exclusive use of children of low-income employed parents in the hope that they would enable poor mothers to get off of welfare rolls and onto payrolls" (Steiner, 1976, p. 18).

Thus, in the years following the end of the war, child care programs were used as a means of substituting workfare for welfare. Gil Steiner commented that in California where Lanham Act centers survived, the program "has been sustained through most of its life as a way of freeing low-income mothers from actual or potential dependence on welfare assistance" (Steiner, 1976, p. 20). As in the prewar years, most working mothers with preschool-age children made informal child care arrangements with relatives, friends, or neighbors. Few families in the U.S. mainstream relied on group care—regarded by most as appropriate only for "problem" children from "marginal" homes (Tank, 1980, p. 422). New York State's brief experiment with publicly funded child care ended in 1947 when Governor Dewey terminated state support for day care and called those who protested the decision "communists."

## The Coming-of-Age for Child Care and Family Support

Beginning in the 1960s and continuing through the 1970s, changes in child care for the preschool-age child reflected transformations in social, economic, and intellectual trends. In the early 1960s, the Social Science Research Council sponsored a series of three conferences on thinking in the young child. These conferences were landmarks and served, by reintroducing the work of Jean Piaget and others, to redirect a moribund child psychology into a vigorous investigation of children's cognitive development.

In the 1960s, new ideas about early child development led to a series of changes in content and a rapid growth in interest in early childhood education. Aside from the short-lived programs in "infant education" in the early 19th century (see Beatty, 1996), early childhood educators had traditionally placed little emphasis on intellectual development. Middle-class nursery schools were considered supplements to children's experiences at home and had traditionally emphasized social and emotional development. Traditional beliefs in the fixity and genetic determination of intelligence remained strong and helped to maintain the indifference to cognition.

Research conducted in the 1950s and 1960s challenged the immutability of intelligence by suggesting that certain kinds of experiences may affect the rate of early cognitive development. In 1961, J. McVicker Hunt published the extremely influential *Intelligence and Experience*. Hunt argued that the early years play a significant role in providing the foundation for later learning and cognitive development. Hunt's book was followed in 1964 by Benjamin Bloom's book *Stability and Change in Human Characteristics*—the result of his efforts to synthesize 50 years worth of longitudinal studies of cognitive development. Bloom concluded that a large number of cognitive skills—especially verbal ability, so-called general intelligence, and school achievement—revealed a pattern of rapid development in the early years followed by a slower rate of development. Bloom concluded that early childhood education can profoundly affect "the child's general learning pattern" (Bloom, 1964, p. 110). The work of Hunt, Bloom, and others might well have been ignored had it not been for the social context surrounding their publications. Initiated by President Kennedy and continued by President Johnson, early childhood education quickly became an important component in the war against poverty.

For the first time since the Progressive Movement 60 years earlier, social scientists wrote about poverty in the United States. "When we started the War on Poverty," reflected the Honorable Sargent Shriver, who directed the new Office of Economic Opportunity from 1965 to 1968, "there was nationwide ignorance about poor people; who they were, where they were, what their problems were, and so on. There was a fantastic lack of fundamental knowledge" (Zigler & Valentine, 1979, p. 49). Michael Harrington (1962) wrote about the legacy of what he called the "other America" in terms of increasing crime rates and declines in the number of qualified industrial and military workers. Half of military draftees were found unfit to serve because of poor health or inadequate education. It was suggested by some that poor living conditions and deviant social behavior characteristic of the poor were passed on from generation to generation in a cycle of poverty. The concept of the economically deprived as somehow "culturally deprived" gained force. Education, it was thought, could compensate for this so-called cultural deprivation by providing training in cognitive and social skills that would lead the poor out of poverty. "The naive optimism of this view is apparent in hindsight, but when the War on Poverty was designed in 1964, it embodied a basic belief in education as the solution to poverty" (Zigler & Valentine, 1979, p. 5). Discussions about child care merged with those about early education as well as those about community development, thus fusing together historically separate institutions for the care and education of the young child and the support of families in communities.

In late 1964, a panel of pediatricians, child development researchers, educators, and psychologists recommended to the Office of Economic Opportunity that comprehensive preschool programs be implemented so that poor children would be able to develop to their full potential. They argued that children in poverty lacked the kinds of experiences and opportunities from which children in more prosperous homes typically benefit. Furthermore, by the time the poor child gets to public school, too often the child is already unable to take full advantage of schooling, because the child's preschool years were deprived. Early compensatory education seemed to hold the promise for breaking the cycle of poverty.

Early in 1965, the Office of Economic Opportunity created Project Head Start. Motivated both by political considerations as well as a genuine concern for the effects of poverty on child development, Project Head Start sought to reach not only the "whole child," but parents and community as well. Medical and psychological services were combined with educational enrichment programs in an effort to improve the poor child's physical health, cognitive development, social skills, and emotional development. Socialization efforts increased the child's sense of dignity and self-worth as well as the child's capacity to relate positively to family and society (Steiner, 1976, pp. 26–29).

In addition to providing for child care and preschool education, Head Start programs sought to involve parents in such a way as to facilitate community organization and political action. The mandate for "maximum feasible participation" called for parents of Head Start children to be deeply invested in this children's program in a way that was both personal and political. Parents of Head Start children were involved in the hiring and firing of personnel; many became Head Start teachers themselves. Family support suffused this model of community development and early childhood education.

Project Head Start was launched as a summer program in 1965, with 561,359 poor children enrolled in 11,068 Head Start centers located in 1,398 communities. At the end of the summer, the administration expanded Head Start into a year-long program. A total of 171,000 poor children from 3 to 6 years of age were enrolled that fall in a program of social and cognitive enrichment, medical care, and nutrition that has been called "the country's biggest peace-time mobilization of human resources and effort" (Tank, 1980, p. 435).

Early education for the disadvantaged, broadly and not always consistently defined, crystallized into programs of compensatory education and became a central component of President Johnson's war against poverty. Demands for weapons in this war stimulated new research in child development and prompted new recommendations for public policy. There was a reciprocal influence between ideas in child development and social reform that, in many ways, echoed connections from early in this century between the child study movement and progressive reform (Siegel & White, 1982; White & Phillips, 2001).

The lessons and legacies of Head Start are many. After a century of institutional separation, programs for the care and education of the young child merged. Furthermore, family support reemerged as a mandate in the design of Head Start and similar programs. With a legislative mandate for maximum feasible participation, poor families and communities mobilized in behalf of their children. Surely, the empowerment given to families in the Head Start era contributed to the reemergence of family support as a model of social service. In so doing, Head Start challenged the prevailing American norms of self-sufficiency and self-reliance. Family support, the idea that families do not need to stand alone in the world, is as old as family life itself in the United States. The notion that families have been individual and self-sufficient units is a misleading myth. "The fact is...depending on support beyond the family has been the rule rather than the exception in American history....Americans have been dependent on collective institutions beyond the family, including the government, from the very beginning" (Coontz, 1992, p. 69–70).

During the course of the 19th and 20th centuries, in Europe and in the United States, a series of social movements served to create institutions and institutional models for family support. The roots of this modern institutionalization of family support are many and include movements such as those for early childhood education, parent education, self-help, and settlement houses. The infant schools in Boston, for example, during the 1820s and 1830s were designed both to educate the young and help poor parents rise out of poverty. The parent education movement began with the 1815 formation of maternal associations by mothers collectively seeking to find ways of "breaking the will of the child." Much later, and in secular scientific form, the parent education movement was institutionalized in the 1920s and 1930s with the largesse of the Laura Spelman Rockefeller Memorial. College-level parent education programs enabled parents (especially mothers) to teach other parents (especially mothers) about parenting while incorporating the newest findings in child development (Cahan, 1991). Settlement houses early in this century were committed to helping immigrant parents and their children find their way in the new world. During the 1960s and 1970s, family support had all the markings of a major social movement. The social turmoil of the 1960s, the civil rights movement, the war against poverty, and the women's movement all helped to broaden, deepen, and further institutionalize family support.

## Child Care and Family Support After Head Start

### Federally Funded Child Care Rejected

The years after the creation of Head Start could be characterized by the withdrawal of federal support for early child care and education programs, an increase in state control over programs, and an increase in enrollment of young children in early childhood programs across economic lines. Although Congress considered three child care legislative initiatives (the Comprehensive Child Development Program Act, the Child and Family Services Act, and the Child Care Act) between 1971 and 1979, all three acts failed to pass. Fears similar to those voiced during the 1950s that universal access to child care would undermine the American family blocked the approval of these national child care acts (Mitchell et al., 1989). President Nixon, in his veto of the 1971 act, went so far as to argue that "for the Federal Government to plunge headlong financially into supporting child development would commit the vast moral authority of the National Government to the side of communal approaches to childrearing over [and] against the family-centered approach" (as cited in Steiner, 1976, p. 115).

The lack of federal support required a shift in power to each individual state to build an infrastructure for child care. This shift from proposed federal to state funding and control for child care presaged a more general move in the 1980s from federal to state control over domestic policy. Although in the past, the government assisted families with young children during a national crisis, "in the early 1980s...the federal government stepped out, creating a crisis by leaving a void that states are now attempting to fill" (Kagan, 1988).

Several states passed legislation during the 1980s to create state-funded prekindergarten programs. By 1989, more than half of the states had established prekindergarten programs and most of these were administered by state departments of education and housed in the public schools (Mitchell et al., 1989, pp. 28–44). The programs served either 3- to 5-year-olds or only 4-year-olds, and a majority of the programs targeted service to low-income children. A few of these programs incorporated some kind of family support, including social services and nutrition and health services, as well as parent education. Although some programs—modeled on Head Start and influenced by the parent cooperative movement—succeeded in reaching out to parents as part of their mission, many programs took a more traditional stance in public education and focused their programs solely on children (Mitchell et al., 1989, p. 259).

Some of these state-initiated programs implemented sound early childhood practices and developmental curricula, yet many of the programs reflected a continued cultural emphasis on early academic subject matter and didactic teaching methods. Traditional public school practices, characterized by structure and formal instruction, trickled down to the preschool programs that were now becoming part of the public school domain. This cultural trend toward academic and formal instruction for young children, as opposed to play-based programming, has continued to fuel debates about appropriate programming for young children.

Edward Zigler (1987) has suggested that many parents and policymakers have looked toward preschool programs as possible remedies to the perceived problem that children are not "ready" for school. Zigler suggested this may be a result of the perceived failure of many public schools to adequately prepare children for academic success. Other possible factors contributing to this interest in early academic instruction might be found in the lingering cultural emphasis on cognitive development over social and emotional development prevalent during the 1960s. Some middle-income parents viewed the slight but positive evaluations of Head Start that showed children's gains in cognitive abilities and IQ scores as a rallying call to give their own children a similar academic boost in early schooling (Weissbourd, 1987, p. 41).

Many proponents of early childhood programs continued to reassert the importance of play as a response to the push for early academics. Play had been a central feature of early childhood programs since Froebel's invention of the kindergarten in 1837. In more recent years, new research about the importance of play during the early childhood years and in later school success has once again brought the subject of play back into the professional literature.

Cultural enthusiasm for or anxiety toward early academic instruction seems to fluctuate with political, social, and economic changes.

## Current Issues: Child Care Demand, Quality Improvement, and Professionalism

Changes in the American family and workforce have created an increasing demand for nonparental child care. As more women with young children at all income levels and across cultural and ethnic groups enter the labor force, child care is becoming an integral part of family and community life. Women with very young children are working in unprecedented numbers. According to a recent government survey, 57% of women with children younger than 3 and 51% of women with infants younger than 1 year are employed (U.S. Bureau of Labor Statistics, 2000). These figures are unprecedented, as is illustrated in a recent report showing that between 1976 and 1998, the proportion of women with infants in the labor force doubled from 31% to 59% (Bachu & O'Connell, 1998). A national survey (National Center for Education Statistics [NCES], 1996) reported that 60% of all children age 5 and younger are in some kind of regular child care arrangement.

Working parents of infants and toddlers have an even greater difficulty finding available, affordable, and reliable child care than do parents with pre-school-age children. The high caregiver-child ratio makes infant care more expensive than preschool programs, and the labor-intensive nature of infant care is a barrier to finding qualified staff. Despite efforts such as Early Head Start, targeted to children ages 0 to 3, many low-income mothers of young infants have fewer choices than middle-income parents in finding high-quality, reliable infant child care at an affordable cost.

As Figure 9–1 demonstrates, nonparental child care takes place in a variety of settings. Programs such as public and private preschools, Head Start, and nursery schools are referred to as center-based care. Care in the provider's home or in the child's home is referred to as home-based care. Although center-based care has received the most research attention, more children are in home-based forms of care. Most of home-based care (both relative and nonrelative) is offered in the provider's own home. A higher proportion of infants and toddlers receive care in home-based programs than in center-based child care programs—41% of infants in child care are in home-based care compared with only 7% in center-based care (NCES, 1996). Many center-based programs do not accept children younger than age 2 and many parents prefer the family-like setting of home-based care (Ehrle et al., 2001). Child care settings may also be categorized by the relationship of the provider to the children in care. Nonrelative care in the provider's home is referred to as family child care. Relative care takes place in either the provider's or the child's home and is often referred to as "kith and kin" care.

**Figure 9–1: Primary child care arrangements for children younger than age 5.**

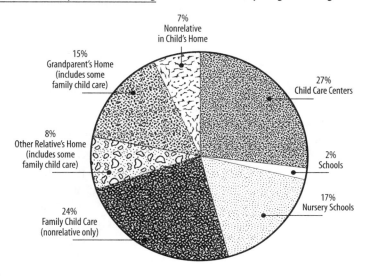

7%
Nonrelative
in Child's Home

15%
Grandparent's Home
(includes some
family child care)

27%
Child Care Centers

8%
Other Relative's Home
(includes some
family child care)

2%
Schools

17%
Nursery Schools

24%
Family Child Care
(nonrelative only)

Source: "Child Care Costs and Arrangements," (Fall 1993), by U.S. Bureau of the Census, 1995. Data recalculated to exclude care by father, mother, or relative in the child's home.

Despite the apparent variety of choices for child care, options are limited for many families due to limited spaces, high costs, and low levels of quality in many programs that offer custodial care at best.

In response to the growing demand for child care and the failure of many state initiatives to provide universal access, a few corporations have once again become involved in funding and supporting child care. The concept of child care as a work-related benefit to families echoes the social service aspects of the wartime Lanham Act child care centers. Employer-sponsored child care centers today continue to provide the conveniences of an on-site location, allowing working parents to visit their children during the day as well as providing flexible hours.

Despite this demand for and growing public awareness of the importance of high-quality environments for children, the quality of care and education for children in both child care centers and family child care homes across the country continues to be alarmingly low and in many cases threatens children's well-being. Recent national studies (Galinsky et al., 1994; Helburn et al., 1995) have found that only 14% of child care centers and only 12% of regulated family child care homes were rated to be good quality. Most centers and homes were rated as mediocre to poor in quality or even harmful to children's healthy development. Infant and toddler centers were found to have even lower ratings of quality—only 8% overall were rated as good. There is some indication from studies of infant care alone that relative and family child care offers a higher degree of responsive, positive caregiving to infants than center-based infant care (NICHD Early Child Care Research Network, 1996).

Although the outcome of prolonged infant care is still uncertain, these studies suggest that responsive child care, sensitive to children's individual needs, can contribute to positive developmental outcomes. Good child care, regardless of the setting, does not negatively affect the mother-child relationship. Poor child care, however, has detrimental effects on children's development. These negative outcomes may include disruptions in attachment as well as other social, emotional, and cognitive difficulties (Galinsky et al., 1994; Helburn et al., 1995; NICHD Early Child Care Research Network, 1996).

Although there is growing awareness about the need for higher quality child care, no federally regulated standards for all child care programs exist. State regulations are minimal and usually focused on physical safety and the prevention of physical and psychological harm to children. Although most states require first-aid training of some kind at the preservice level, many do not require any additional training for child care teachers or providers (Azer & Eldred, 1997). All states have some form of regulations for child care centers, and all but three states regulate family child care. Many state regulations exempt certain types of child care, such as church-based programs. Relative or kith and kin care is often unregulated, although states vary in how they define child care settings.

Training and education for teachers and providers are also essential components of high-quality child care programs. Several studies have documented that the levels of teacher and provider training and education are the most predictive indicators of quality in child care, especially for preschool- and school-age children (Galinsky et al., 1994; Helburn et al., 1995; Ruopp et al., 1979). Small group size is another strong indicator of quality, allowing the teacher or provider to form a stable meaningful relationship with each child, especially for very young children (NICHD Early Child Care Research Network, 1996).

*Defining quality.* Throughout this discussion, we have referred to high and low quality in programs for children and families. But "quality" is an elusive concept, and its definition is shaped by cultural values and constrained by available technologies for assessment. Despite the difficult task of defining quality in a wide array of child care settings, many national projects have attempted to do so. In 1987, the National Association for the Education of Young Children (NAEYC) published a document that defined high-quality programs for young children in terms of "developmentally appropriate practice" (Bredekamp, 1987; Bredekamp & Copple, 1997). The authors define *developmentally appropriate practice* as the consideration of typical development in the context of individual, cultural, and gender differences. In this model, teachers plan curriculum based on their knowledge of typical child development as well as through observations of individual children's interests, needs, and learning styles. The authors make clear that quality early childhood programming is not determined by the type of setting, but rather by the knowledge, training, and practices of the caregivers. Prior to the work of Bredekamp (1987) and her colleagues (Bredekamp & Copple, 1997), there had been no shared operational definition in the field for high-quality early childhood education. Grounded in child development research, this work has given early childhood practitioners a professional language and knowledge base on which to stand and stimulated the recent quality-improvement movement.

A growing sensitivity to cultural differences in child-rearing values has challenged definitions of high-quality child care based on Western ideals of development. Early childhood professionals must have "knowledge of the social and cultural contexts in which children live to ensure that learning experiences are meaningful, relevant, and respectful for the participating children and their families" in addition to knowledge of child development and individual children (Bredekamp & Copple, 1997, p. 9). Respect for diversity and for a range of cultural values is a requisite component of both high-quality child care and family support programs.

Focus on the quality of relationships and learning environments alone, however, will not lead to improved child care options for families. Quality is inextricably linked to compensation for caregivers and providers as well as affordability for parents. This relationship of quality, compensation, and affordability has often been referred to as the child care "trilemma."* Still seen as traditional women's work, child care has historically been characterized by low salaries and inadequate benefits. Many of the educators in the kindergarten and nursery school movements felt their work to be vocational, voluntary, and in some instances, social welfare work (see Beatty, 1990). Monetary compensation for caring and nurturing was seen as a contradiction to the altruistic motivations of the women doing the work. Private gain or, in many cases, self-reliance, was not a traditional goal for many of these women. This legacy of voluntarism continues to haunt the early care and education profession and indeed presents a significant barrier to the full professionalization of the field.

To achieve the goal of a high-quality early care and education system, the needs of child care workers (teachers and providers) must be considered, as well as the needs of children and families served. Low compensation, lack of benefits, long hours, and hard work lead to high turnover rates in child care settings. Child care teachers and providers are usually paid less than other workers with significantly lower levels of education and fewer skills. High

---

* We thank Gwen Morgan for calling attention to this "trilemma."

turnover rates in turn lead to a breakdown in the attachment between care-givers and children that is so central to the quality of care (Whitebook et al., 1989). At the same time, many parents cannot afford to pay the full cost of high-quality care. In fact, as Figure 9–2 shows, many low-income families spend a disproportionate amount of their income on child care compared with upper income parents (Figure 9-2).

The lack of any comprehensive investment in child care and the failure of market forces to provide adequate compensation for child care workers or high-quality care for families has left these two groups to bear the burden of this failure (Modigliani, 1993). Finding creative ways to finance the full cost of high-quality child care is currently a major topic among policymakers.

*The changing child care picture.* The emerging professional development movement among child care teachers and providers is one response to the problem of poor quality, low wages, and poor working conditions. Historically, the early care and education field has lacked the defining characteristics of pro-fessionals. Other professions and trades share public respect and recognition, national standards, training and education requirements, and opportunities for advancement. Toward this end, quality improvement initiatives for child care are leading to the development of an institutionalized career development sys-tem in many states. The purpose of these initiatives is to create a lattice of train-ing programs and incentives for people newly entering the field, as well as opportunities for advancement for those already in the field.

The concept of accreditation is also gaining momentum as a strategy for designating high-quality programs to parents and policymakers. Although state regulations can ensure a minimal level of safety for children, accreditation has the potential to improve the quality of child care and to fuel professional devel-opment and growth among providers. Center-based programs have a few vol-untary accreditation systems; the most widely recognized is sponsored by the NAEYC. The national professional organizations for both school-age child care and family child care have developed their own voluntary accreditation stan-dards. Growing awareness of these sectors of child care and the emergent pro-fessionalization of family child care and school-age providers represent prom-ising trends. Several states have started to offer tiered reimbursement rates for subsidized child care based on compliance with the high standards of accredi-tation. Some parents are starting to look for accredited programs and are often willing to pay more when they find one.

Throughout the history of programs for young children in the United States, trends in child care and family support have been inextricably linked with trends in social welfare programs. It is therefore no surprise that current trends in welfare reform are directly tied to child care initiatives. Welfare reform poses both an opportunity for improving the lives of families with young chil-

## Figure 9–2: Percent of monthly family income spent on child care by family income and poverty status.

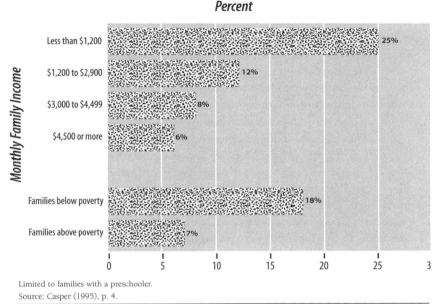

Limited to families with a preschooler.
Source: Casper (1995), p. 4.

dren as well as a potential threat to the well-being of low-income children and to quality improvement efforts of the child care field. The Family Support Act of 1988 allowed states to experiment with welfare reform by requiring Aid to Families with Dependent Children (AFDC) recipients to participate in training, education, or work. Under this act, welfare recipients would be entitled to child care while participating in job-related efforts. A 1992 Children's Defense Fund (CDF) survey of 50 states found, however, that initial welfare reform attempts had failed to address the needs of poor families and children. Inadequate funding for child care, lack of basic health and safety requirements for child care settings, and lack of parent choice were a result of "short-sighted policies that seek to minimize initial costs at the expense of essential long-term investments in AFDC children and families" (CDF, 1992, p. 9).

Welfare reform has triggered experiments in many states to train welfare recipients to become child care providers. Unfortunately, many proposals for training welfare recipients involve hasty recruitment into the child care field without sufficient supports to sustain new teachers or providers in their work or to ensure the quality and stability of care they will provide to children. High levels of motivation, the desire to work with children, ongoing training and education in child development, and economic incentives and support, including livable wages and benefits, are required to ensure the success of these initiatives.

Changing definitions of child care providers' roles is yet another challenge facing the improvement of quality in early care and education settings. Historically, professionals are seen as holding a body of knowledge not shared by their clients and therefore creating a relationship between professional and client that is formal, distant, and hierarchical. Caregivers have also conceptualized their role as serving only the child, without regard for the parents. Tensions in the teacher-parent relationship have prevented many teachers from embracing a partnership with parents and indeed, many teachers today define their responsibility toward parents in terms of their expert knowledge about children and the need to "educate" parents.

In the past decade, there has been a conceptual shift in thinking about family support in early childhood education among leaders and policymakers in the field. Child care programs are increasingly looked to as sources of family support and social services in addition to their caregiving and educational roles. The family support model in which parents and teachers are seen as having a shared knowledge base about children represents a shift away from a deficit model in which parents are seen as lacking in knowledge and skills related to child rearing and education. In a sense, child care as family support challenges the conventional concept of professionalism.

High-quality child care is necessarily caring, nurturing, supportive of families, and requires a cooperative partnership rather than a distancing between professional and client. This new conceptualization, however, has not yet taken hold among the majority of early childhood practitioners in the field. According to Powell:

> Day-care providers who wish to be responsive to families may need to revamp the traditional image of professionalism. In particular, the idea that the work of professionals should be relatively free of lay (parent) interference may need modification in the early childhood field. (Powell, 1987, p.129).

**Current efforts toward universal access.** Although universal funding and standards for child care are not on the horizon, the federal government and some states are showing signs of renewed interest in increasing access to early childhood education. In 1995, the Clinton administration commissioned the Child Care Bureau to administer federal child care programs to states for low-income children. Among their initiatives is a national newsletter on current trends in child care for advocates, policymakers, providers, and program directors. The U.S. military offers another potential model for child care quality improvement in the general population. Long recognized as having an exemplary early care and education system, the military is increasingly being looked to as a potential model for child care in the civilian world.

Some states, such as Connecticut and New York, have led the way toward universal access to early childhood education through public school mandates (G. Morgan, November 1997, personal communication). Despite these efforts, such wide-reaching plans often do not succeed in serving the target numbers of children and families. During the 1980s, a program called Project Giant Step in New York City was publicly funded to create access for all 4-year-olds to preschool programs. At fully funded levels, however, the program failed to meet the needs of all 4-year-olds in the city (Mitchell et al., 1989). Even Head Start serves only 38% of the eligible population (White & Phillips, 2001). It is hoped that public programs such as Head Start will expand and continue to influence and motivate states and the private and corporate sectors to make a similar commitment to young children and families.

## Conclusions

Child care and family support are not new facets of American life. Children have always required care, and families have never been the sole providers of such care. Kenneth Keniston wrote for the Carnegie Council on Children that "recognizing that family self-sufficiency is a false myth, we also need to acknowledge that all today's families need help in raising children" (1977, p. 23). It is reasonable to predict that the demand for child care will continue as ever more mothers with young children enter the workforce.

With new demands, sweeping changes in social programs, knowledge about child development, and policy initiatives have sprung forth a dizzying array of programs for young children. Welfare reform, in particular, has already precipitated a crisis for many single mothers unable to find or afford high-quality child care for their children. Despite crisis-driven past efforts and an emerging awareness of the importance of child care, a coherent system of service delivery still does not exist. The lack of a coherent child care system leaves many families with few choices and resources. Some experts have characterized the child care delivery system as a "nonsystem," failing to meet the needs of families and children from all economic backgrounds (Kagan & Cohen, 1997). The concept, however, of universal access to early care and education may never be fully embraced by a society that remains ambivalent about working mothers, nonmaternal child care, and the value of early education.

Possible solutions to the current child care crisis include trends toward collaboration between historically separate sectors representing child care and early education as well as increased public awareness and support for early care and education programs. Another development that has aided parents in negotiating the maze of child care services and venues has been the emergence of child care resource and referral agencies. Started in the 1970s, these agencies help parents find and choose child care and become more knowledgeable consumers of child care. Many of these agencies also educate the general public about the importance of high-quality child care, provide training to providers and teachers, expand child care availability, and work with employers to increase private resources for child care. The work of these agencies combined with state and national initiatives offers hope for a more integrated and seamless child care system in the future.

Alongside the problem of child care availability, the lack of quality programming will continue to challenge policymakers and parents. As researchers and practitioners reach consensus on the components of high-quality programs for children, the problem of finding and keeping qualified professionals to care for and educate the next generation will continue. The professional development movement provides promising possibilities for this dilemma.

Although the needs for child care and family support persist, the social, intellectual, and economic contexts in which these familial needs are embedded have changed. The kinds of programs designed to support families and young children look different today than they did in the past. Both child care and family support programs have had to adapt and respond to changes in family styles and a growing diversity of cultural values among those served in their programs. As the population served becomes increasingly diverse, definitions of quality programming, service delivery, and professionalism must change. The challenge of the next century will be finding ways to meet the needs of families and children while creating programs that are responsive, sensitive, and respectful of those served.

In conclusion, although we are unlikely in current times to see the kind of national commitment made to child care during the Second World War, recent debates and White House conferences on national child care legislation offer some hope for increased public support for early care and education. Policymakers and parents recognize the importance of available and affordable high-quality child care for the well-being of future generations as well as for the productivity of the current workforce. Older debates about whether or not child care is good for children have given way to more sophisticated and more complicated questions of how to make child care work for our children and families.

## References

Azer, S., & Eldred, D. (1997). *Training requirements in child care licensing regulations.* Boston: Center for Career Development in Early Care and Education.
Bachu, A., & O'Connell, M. (1998). *Fertility of American women* [Current population reports P20-526]. Washington, DC: U.S. Census Bureau.
Beatty, B. (1990). A vocation from on high: Kindergartening as an occupation for American

women. In J. Antler & S. K. Biklen (Eds.), *Changing education: Women as radicals and conservators*. New York: State University of New York Press.

Beatty, B. (1996). *Preschool education in America: The culture of young children from the colonial era to the present*. New Haven, CT: Yale University Press.

Bloom, B. (1964). *Stability and change in human characteristics*. New York: Wiley.

Bredekamp, S. (Ed.). (1987). *Developmentally appropriate practice in early childhood programs serving children from birth through age eight*. Washington, DC: National Association for the Education of Young Children.

Bredekamp, S., & Copple, C. (Eds.). (1997). *Developmentally appropriate practice in early childhood programs serving children from birth through age 8*. Washington, DC: National Association for the Education of Young Children.

Cahan, E. D. (1989). *Past caring: A history of U.S. preschool care and education for the poor, 1820-1965*. New York: Columbia University, School of Public Health, National Center for Children in Poverty.

Cahan, E. D. (1991). Science, practice, and gender roles in early American child psychology. In F. Kessel, M. Bornstein, & A. Sameroff (Eds.), *Contemporary constructions of the child: Essays in honor of William Kessen* (pp. 225-249). Hillsdale, NJ: Lawrence Erlbaum.

Casper, L. M. (1995). What does it cost to mind our preschoolers? *Current Population Reports* P 70-52, p.4. Washington, DC: U.S. Department of Commerce, Census Bureau.

Chafe, W. H. (1972). *The American woman*. New York: Oxford University Press.

Children's Defense Fund. (1992). *Child care under the Family Support Act: Early lessons learned from the states*. Washington, DC: Author.

Coontz, S. (1992). *The way we never were: American families and the nostalgia trap*. New York: Basic Books.

Ehrle, J., Adams, G., & Tout, K. (2001). *Who's caring for our youngest children? Child care patterns of infants and toddlers* [Occasional paper 42]. Washington, DC: The Urban Institute.

Galinsky, E., Howes, C., Kontos, S., & Shinn, M. (1994). *The study of children in family child care and relative care*. New York: Families and Work Institute.

Grubb, W. N., & Lazerson, M. (1982). *Broken promises: How Americans fail their children*. New York: Basic Books.

Harrington, M. (1962). *The other America: Poverty in the United States*. New York: Holt, Rinehart, and Winston.

Helburn, S., Culkin, M. L., Howes, C., Bryant, D., Clifford, R., Cryer, D., et al. (1995). *Cost, quality, and child outcomes in child care centers. Executive summary*. Denver: University of Colorado at Denver.

Hernandez, D. (1993). *America's children: Resources from family, government and the economy*. New York: Russell Sage Foundation.

Hunt, J. M. (1961). *Intelligence and experience*. New York: Ronald Press.

Kagan, S. L. (1988). Current reforms in early childhood education: Are we addressing the issues? *Young Children, 43*, 27–38.

Kagan, S. L., & Cohen, N. (1997). *Not by chance: Creating an early care and education system for America's children* [Abridged report]. New Haven, CT: Bush Center for Child Development and Social Policy.

Keniston, K., & the Carnegie Council on Children. (1977). *All our children: The American family under pressure*. New York: Harcourt, Brace, and Jovanovich.

Kessen, W. (1979). The American child and other cultural inventions. *American Psychologist,* 34, 815–820.

Mitchell, A., Seligson, M., & Marx, F. (1989). *Early childhood programs and the public schools: Between promise and practice.* Dover, MA: Auburn House.

Modigliani, K. (1993). *Child care as an occupation in a culture of indifference.* Boston: Wheelock College Family Child Care Project.

National Center for Education Statistics. (1996). *Child care and early education program participation of infants, toddlers, and preschoolers* [Report 95-824]. Washington, DC: Author.

National Institute of Child Health and Development Early Child Care Research Network. (1996). Characteristics of infant child care: Factors contributing to positive caregiving. *Early Childhood Research Quarterly, 11,* 269–306.

Powell, D. (1987). Day care as a family support system. In S. L. Kagan, D. R. Powell, B. Weissbourd, & E. F. Zigler (Eds.), *America's family support programs: The origins and development of a movement* (pp. 99–132) New Haven, CT: Yale University Press.

Ruderman, F. (1968). *Child care and working mothers.* New York: Child Welfare League of America.

Ruopp, R., Travers, J., Glantz, F., & Coelen, C. (1979). *Children at the center: Final report of the national day care study.* Cambridge, MA: ABT Books.

Siegel, A. W., & White, S. H. (1982). The child study movement: Early growth and development of the symbolized child. *Advances in Child Development and Behavior, 17,* 233–285.

Spitz, R. (1945). *Hospitalisation: An inquiry into the genesis of psychiatric conditions in early childhood. The psychoanalytic study of the child* (Vol. 1). New York: International Universities Press.

Steiner, G. (1976). *The children's cause.* Washington, DC: Brookings Institution.

Tank, R. M. (1980). *Young children, families, and society in America since the 1820s: The evolution of health, education, and child care programs for preschool children.* PhD dissertation, University of Michigan (University Microfilms No. 8106233).

Tuttle, W. (1995). Rosie the Riveter and her latchkey children: What Americans can learn about child day care from the second world war. *Child Welfare, 74,* 92–114.

Weissbourd, B. (1987). A brief history of family support programs. In S. L. Kagan, D. R. Powell, B. Weissbourd, & E. F. Zigler (Eds.), *America's family support programs: The origins and development of a movement.* New Haven, CT: Yale University Press.

White, S. H, & Phillips, D. (2001). Designing Head Start: Roles played by developmental psychologists. In D. L. Featherman & M. Vinovskis (Eds.), *Social science and policy making.* Ann Arbor: University of Michigan Press.

Whitebook, M., Howes, C., & Phillips, D. (1989). *Who cares? Child care teachers and the quality of care in America.* Oakland, CA: Child Care Employee Project.

Zigler, E. F. (1987). Formal schooling for four-year-olds? No. *American Psychologist, 42,* 254–260.

Zigler, E. F., & Valentine, J. (1979). *Project Head Start: A legacy of the war on poverty.* New York: Free Press.

# PART IV
## BROADER CONTEXTUAL AND POLICY ISSUES

# TEN

# Indicators of Children's Well-Being in a Community Context

*Tama Leventhal & Jeanne Brooks-Gunn*

During the last half-century, social scientists as well as policymakers have been concerned about the negative effects of residence in a poor community on children and youth. At the scholarly level, interest in neighborhood poverty has been most pronounced among urban researchers and developmental psychologists who operate largely independently of each other. Just recently have these lines of research converged, providing more policy-relevant implications for children and families. Early research on community-level indicators of child well-being can be traced to the urban sociologists Shaw and McKay (1942), who linked community social disorganization to juvenile delinquency. Social disorganization theory posits that structural factors of communities, such as poverty, residential instability, single parenthood, and ethnic heterogeneity, are integral to understanding behavior by means of their ability to thwart or promote community organization, in particular the formation of formal and informal neighborhood institutions.

More recently, the publication of Wilson's (1987) *The Truly Disadvantaged* led to a resurgence of interest in community contexts. Wilson's seminal work drew attention to increasing concentrated poverty at the neighborhood level in urban centers during the 1960s and 1970s, and the adverse effects of concentrated poverty and associated conditions for children and families residing in these communities. At this time, sociologists and other urban scholars were renewing appreciation of community social disorganization theory as a framework for understanding the plight of many poor, urban communities (see Sampson & Morenoff, 1997, for a review). Whereas much of the research tradition on community indicators of child well-being came from understanding how growing up in a poor community might limit children's chances, there is also a more broad-based literature that considers the possible effects of residing in affluent neighborhoods (Jencks & Mayer, 1990). This research explores how living in an affluent community could confer costs as well as benefits (costs due to relative deprivation and competition for resources).

In developmental psychology, the acceptance of more contextual (or eco-logical) models, as outlined by Bronfenbrenner (1979), ignited interest in com-munity effects on children and adolescents. Bronfenbrenner's theory of human development highlights the multiple contexts (e.g., schools/child care, peers, communities) in which individuals live and the resultant need for researchers as well as policymakers to consider their influence, both independent and jointly, on children and families. A related advancement was the recognition that not only do contexts shape individuals, but also individual characteristics may affect or form the contexts in which individuals interact (Aber et al., 1997; Bronfenbrenner, 1989).

A growing interest among developmental psychologists in so-called risk (e.g., absence of community resources) and protective factors (e.g., presence of community resources) further fueled attention to community contexts. A grow-ing body of research suggests that it is not just single risk or protective factors but the accumulation of such factors that is likely to result in negative or pos-itive child and family outcomes (Liaw & Brooks-Gunn, 1994; Rutter, 1987; Rutter et al., 1995; Sameroff et al., 1993; Sameroff et al., 1987; Werner & Smith, 1982). Risk and protective factors occur at multiple levels—individual, family, peer group, school, and community. The effects of each may vary for specific subgroups of children or families (Caspi & Moffitt, 1991; Graber & Brooks-Gunn, 1996).

Together, these theoretical and empirical lines of research from urban soci-ology and developmental psychology have shaped the growing body of research on community indicators of children's well-being over the past decade. Figure 10–1 presents a framework for examining community indicators on child well-being by integrating the macrostructural factors of urban sociology and the more microsystemic influences of developmental psychology (Aber et al., 1997; Gephart & Brooks-Gunn, 1997).

To understand the communities in which children live, we focus on two different lines of inquiry—the first considers potentially relevant dimensions of neighborhoods drawn from the theoretical social science traditions discussed thus far, and the second draws from the community development and service-use literature. This two-pronged approach reflects our belief that indicators of children's well-being should reflect conditions within communities as well as the services offered in communities. In this chapter, therefore, we first examine the dimensions of community life that are theoretically linked to the well-being of children and youth. We will outline potential methods for assessing com-munity indicators, as well as the dimensions thought to be important. Next, we ask whether community characteristics are associated with indicators of child well-being. Our conclusions are tempered by the paucity of relevant data on

**Figure 10–1: Community indicators in child well-being: A conceptual model.**

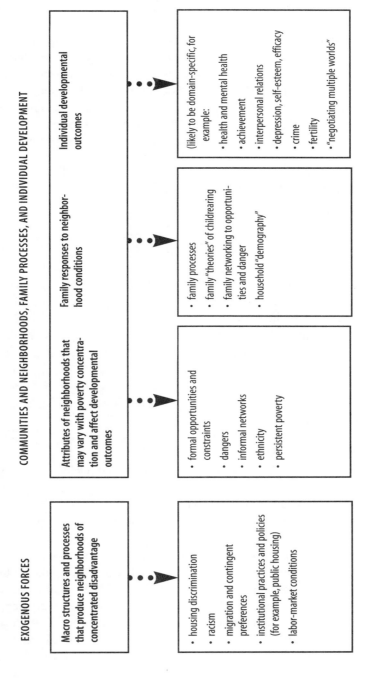

COMMUNITIES AND NEIGHBORHOODS, FAMILY PROCESSES, AND INDIVIDUAL DEVELOPMENT

EXOGENOUS FORCES

Macro structures and processes that produce neighborhoods of concentrated disadvantage

- housing discrimination
- racism
- migration and contingent preferences
- institutional practices and policies (for example, public housing)
- labor-market conditions

Attributes of neighborhoods that may vary with poverty concentration and affect developmental outcomes

- formal opportunities and constraints
- dangers
- informal networks
- ethnicity
- persistent poverty

Family responses to neighborhood conditions

- family processes
- family "theories" of childrearing
- family networking to opportunities and danger
- household "demography"

Individual developmental outcomes

(likely to be domain-specific, for example:
- health and mental health
- achievement
- interpersonal relations
- depression, self-esteem, efficacy
- crime
- fertility
- "negotiating multiple worlds"

Source: Gephart and  Brooks-Gunn (1997), p.xvii. © 1997 by Russell Sage Foundation. Reprinted with permission.

children. We draw heavily from work by the Social Science Research Council's Working Group on Communities and Neighborhoods, Family Processes, and Individual Development. Two volumes were published titled *Neighborhood Poverty*. The first volume focuses on context and consequences for children and the second volume on policy implications in studying neighborhoods (Brooks-Gunn et al., 1997a, 1997b; see also Leventhal & Brooks-Gunn, 2000, for a comprehensive review). Following a discussion on whether communities matter, we examine the relevant literature on designing and measuring community indicators based on services for children and families (health, education, and social welfare).

## What Dimensions of Communities Are Studied?

### What Is a Community?

There are several approaches to defining the community-level unit of analysis. The most common strategies employed are census information, health districts, school districts, or local knowledge of boundaries in cities. In these instances, communities or neighborhoods are defined in terms of previously constructed bureaucratic units. Other studies rely on participant ratings of communities to define the neighborhood unit of analysis, in which case boundaries are typically not specified. Based on local knowledge, ethnographers, on the other hand, may investigate a single community, yet tend to suggest that residents have different perceptions of neighborhood boundaries. The next section of this chapter will consider conceptual differences in community definitions in more depth; thus, in this section, we concentrate on methodological approaches to defining community indicators.

### Data Collection Techniques

In this section, we cover the most widely used methodologies employed by social scientists for studying community indicators. The data collection techniques are (a) census data, (b) systematic social observations, (c) community surveys, (d) participant ratings, and (e) key community leader surveys.

*Census data.* Among social scientists, census data are the most prevalent strategy for examining community contexts. Census tract boundaries are delineated by Census Bureau guidelines with the advice of local communities and typically reflect prominent physical features that define neighborhoods (e.g., major streets, railroads) as well as important social and ethnic divisions. Data provided by the decennial census about neighborhoods come from the census forms the population fills out on April 1 of the first year of every decade. Census data provide information on economic and sociodemographic characteristics and allow social scientists to characterize communities according to a number of key dimensions, such as extent of neighborhood poverty, single-parenthood, public assistance receipt, and unemployment. To access census tract data, the participants' addresses must be geocoded (coded for census tract) and then tract-level data can be appended to the data set. Alternative neighborhood units that are smaller (e.g., blocks or block groups) or larger (e.g., county) than census tracts are also available from the census.

*Systematic social observations.* A less widely used data collection technique that is still in relatively formative stages is systematic social observations, or windshield surveys (Barnes-McGuire & Reiss, 1993; Perkins & Taylor, 1996). Systematic social observations entail having trained observers use a structured format to characterize communities; this approach has been used in local as well as national studies (Kohen et al., 2000; Sampson & Raudenbush, 1999; Spencer et al., 1997). Another strategy is videotaping neighborhoods and then coding community dimensions subsequent to data collection. Typically, the focus of the observation is the block or street on which the participant's residence is located, but adjacent streets are often observed as well. Unlike census data, these observational techniques provide information on communities' physical features (e.g., presence of graffiti and litter, housing conditions) and social organizational features (e.g., characteristics of people on the streets, presence of public drinking and fighting).

*Community surveys.* A community survey entails interviewing community residents (nonstudy participants) about their neighborhoods. Thus, this type of survey is usually an "add-on" to existing studies of individuals and families. The information obtained from a community survey is similar to that of participant ratings without the problem of confounding indicators because community-level data are obtained from a separate source than individual-level indicators. A recent study, the Project on Human Development in Chicago Neighborhoods (PHDCN), interviewed approximately 9,000 residents randomly sampled from 343 neighborhood clusters in Chicago (on average, 25 residents per cluster). Data were collected on collective efficacy (a combined measure of informal social control and social cohesion), as well as on other dimensions listed under participant ratings (Sampson et al., 1997).

*Participant ratings.* Another commonly used strategy because of the ease of data collection is participant ratings. Because information on community social resources are not available from census data, valuable information on perceptions of safety, neighborhood cohesion, stressors and hassles, community attachment, social support, and availability of community resources can be obtained (Simcha-Fagan & Schwartz, 1986). This approach, although yielding a variety of valuable information, however, is less desirable than community surveys or key community leader surveys because community indicators are confounded with individual-level indicators that are also assessed by means of participant ratings.

*Key community leader surveys.* The final data collection technique is interviewing key community leaders, such as prominent religious, political, business, and social leaders in the community, to get ratings of community characteristics as noted above. This strategy may be particularly useful for learning about the social and political dimensions of communities. The PHDCN as well as the Yonkers Community and Family Project (Brooks-Gunn et al., 2000) used key community leader surveys.

Clearly, each of the data collection techniques discussed has strengths and weaknesses based on reliability, validity, accessibility, cost, and feasibility. These factors have contributed to social scientists' utilization of these methodologies. In the following section, we turn to a more detailed discussion of the type of information that is collected from these various strategies.

## Dimensions of Community Characteristics

In this section, we provide an overview of the community-level indicators that may be most relevant to children and adolescents (Brooks-Gunn et al., 1997). These dimensions are drawn from empirical and theoretical work and may operate directly on child well-being or indirectly vis-à-vis parents, peers, or schools. An important point to note is that many of the community dimensions discussed are interrelated.

*Income and socioeconomic status (SES).* Because residence in an impoverished community has implications for other important contexts, such as child care, school, and peer groups, neighborhood income has been the most widely studied community dimension. Neighborhood income is usually evaluated with census data and defined in terms of neighborhood poverty and neighborhood affluence. These separate indicators of income are used because the presence of poor and affluent neighbors may have differential associations with child well-being. In research based on 1980 census data, we have designated the fraction of families in the census tract with incomes less than $10,000 as low income, the fraction of families with incomes between $10,000 and $30,000 as middle income, and the fraction of families with incomes more than $30,000 as affluent (see, for example, Brooks-Gunn et al., 1993). A recent volume on neighborhood poverty showed factor analysis on census data from the Panel Study of Income Dynamics (PSID), which yielded separate factors for low SES and high SES (Brooks-Gunn et al., 1997a). Most of the other community dimensions discussed in this section are correlated with neighborhood income and SES.

*Human capital.* Human capital entails the skills, knowledge, and capabilities possessed by community residents (Coleman, 1988). The presence of employed and educated individuals (i.e., individuals with human capital) in the community is considered essential to building an economic foundation in the community. Such individuals also provide role models for children and youth. Measures of human capital are based on census data and are typically assessed with respect to the percentages of high school graduates, college graduates, unemployed individuals, and professionals in the tract. Neighborhood unemployment is usually specified in terms of the age and gender of residents, with the percentage of males (males 18 to 25 years old or males 18 to 64 years old) unemployed in the community as the most commonly used indicator.

*Racial/ethnic heterogeneity.* Ethnic heterogeneity involves the racial/ethnic makeup of the community; it is hypothesized to be associated with diffuse social networks and social isolation of people of color (Sampson, 1992; Wilson, 1991a, 1991b). There are several different approaches to assessing racial/ethnic heterogeneity; all entail the use of census data. In the first volume of *Neighborhood Poverty*, factor analysis on census data from the PSID yielded a factor for ethnic diversity that included, among other variables, the percentages of foreign-born individuals and Latinos in the tract (Duncan & Aber, 1997). Several studies (e.g., PHDCN) have incorporated measures of ethnic heterogeneity into their design and used ranges such as 10% to 20% to indicate low concentration of a particular racial or ethnic group, and ranges such as 50% to 70% to indicate high concentration of a particular group .

*Residential stability.* According to social disorganization theory, residential instability in the community is associated with a breakdown in community institutions and resultant diminished social control. Residential stability measures drawn from the census include the proportion of residents who have lived in the same house for the past 5 years, the proportion of residents who have lived in current home for less than 10 years, and the proportion of owner-occupied houses. These variables have been examined individually or as composite variables derived from factor analyses (Coulton et al., 1995; Duncan & Aber, 1997; Sampson et al., 1997). Study participants or community residents can also be asked about their perception of the amount of renters in the neighborhood. These latter approaches are less optimal because they entail individual perceptions rather than institutional records and, as such, may have questionable reliability.

*Age structure.* The age structure of the community is associated with the extent to which adults are present to supervise children and youth. For example, in a neighborhood with a low adult-to-child ratio, children may be more susceptible to injury and danger, and older children and youth may engage in more problem behavior. In *Neighborhood Poverty*, factor analysis conducted with census data from the PSID yielded a factor for family concentration composed of the percentage of individuals age 0 to 17, the percentage of individuals age 65 and older, and ratio of persons to occupied housing units (Duncan & Aber, 1997). Coulton and colleagues (1995) have referred to this dimension as *child-care burden* (ratio of children to adults, ratio of males to females, and percentage of the population that is elderly; see also Korbin & Coulton, 1997).

*Collective efficacy.* Collective efficacy is a term originally conceived of by Bandura (1986) and recently employed by the PHDCN to describe the extent of social connections in the community and the degree to which residents monitor the behavior of others in accordance with socially accepted practices (Sampson et al., 1997). Essentially, collective efficacy is a combined measure of informal social control and social cohesion obtained; it is composed of 14 items. Informal social control was assessed by items such as the likelihood that neighbors could be counted on to intervene in various situations, including (a) children skipping school, (b) a fight in front of their house, and (c) threat of the local fire station being closed down because of budget cuts. Social cohesion was evaluated by items such as how strongly residents agreed that people are willing to help neighbors, the neighborhood is close-knit, and residents share values. Participants in a community survey rated all of these items on a Likert-type scale.

*Social support.* Social support entails access to friendship and social connections within the community and is hypothesized to intervene between community economic resources and child outcomes (Brooks-Gunn et al., 1998). At the neighborhood level, for example, social support may be particularly important in terms of assistance with child care. In this context, social support is usually assessed by presenting participants with scenarios in which support is required (e.g., time or money) and ascertaining whether individuals who are listed as supports reside in the participant's neighborhood (Boisjoly et al., 1995; Klebanov et al., 1994).

*Physical and social disorder.* Physical disorder reflects the physical conditions of the community, and social disorder is characterized by the social interactions within the community as well as the content and consensus of values (Sampson & Morenoff, 1997). Both physical and social disorders are assessed through multiple methods. Social disorder has been operationally defined with census data by a number of community structural factors, such as residential instability, family concentration, crowded housing, and ethnic heterogeneity. In addition, interview data and systematic social observations are used to examine this dimension. Specifically, residents rate on a Likert-type scale how big a problem the following activities are in their community: fighting, gangs, loitering, public drinking, and drug use. Systematic social observation would entail having trained observers rate the presence of the specified activities. For physical disorder, residents rate the presence of graffiti, garbage, vacant housing, and abandoned cars. Again, trained observers can assess the presence of these attributes (as is being done in PHDCN).

*Safety/stressors.* Community-level stressors entail the prevalence of danger and violence in the neighborhood and the concomitant feelings of safety or physical threat that residents experience. The presence of these stressors and parents' resultant feelings of safety have implications for parenting and family management (Coulton, 1996; Furstenberg & Hughes, 1997). Participant ratings Susually assessed safety. Accordingly, residents are asked to indicate how worried they are about events such as being mugged, robbed, or shot. In addition, residents can rate the magnitude of these types of problems. A community survey could also obtain this information. Alternatively, systematic social observation can measure the lighting, police presence, community-watch signs, buildings with bars and barbed wire, and traffic. Finally, administrative data, such as uniform crime reports available from police departments, measure the incidence of violent crime in the community.

## Do Community Dimensions Matter for Child Well-Being?

In this section, we address the question, Do community dimensions matter for child well-being? We present a brief review of the findings on child indicators for each of the dimensions. We focus here on school achievement and readiness (IQ, verbal ability, grade failure, high school dropout rate, and years of schooling) and adolescent behavioral problems (sexual activity, teenage pregnancy, and juvenile delinquency). We discuss only direct neighborhood effects, although there is some evidence for indirect or mediated neighborhood effects on child and adolescent well-being (see Leventhal & Brooks-Gunn, 2000, for a review).

   *Income.* In a set of coordinated studies, Brooks-Gunn and colleagues (1993; Chase-Lansdale et al., 1997; Duncan et al., 1994; Klebanov et al., 1997; Klebanov et al., 1998) examined the effects of community income on young children's cognitive and verbal ability. Their findings indicate that 3- and 5-year-old children's IQ and verbal ability scores were positively associated with the presence of affluent neighbors (incomes greater than $30,000) compared with middle-income neighbors (incomes between $10,000 to $30,000), even when the researchers controlled for familial-level characteristics. Further, these outcomes were not associated with the presence of low-income neighbors (incomes less than $10,000), again, compared with middle-income neighbors. These results were replicated across two data sets—the Infant Health and Development Program (IHDP; a multisite intervention program for low birthweight, premature children) and the National Longitudinal Study of Youth-Child Supplement (NLSY-CS). In a sample of eighth graders in Baltimore, Entwisle, Alexander, and Olson (1994) also found that greater neighborhood income was associated with higher math achievement scores for boys. Furthermore, among older children and youth, neighborhood affluence has been found to be associated with high school completion and years of schooling completed (Brooks-Gunn et al., 1993; Duncan, 1994; Ensminger et al.,

1996; Halpern-Felsher et al., 1997). The benefit of affluent neighbors appears to extend to a reduced risk of adolescent childbearing (Brooks-Gunn et al., 1993). In addition, several researchers report negative associations between neighborhood SES and adolescent crime and delinquency (Loeber & Wikstrom, 1993; Peeples & Loeber, 1994; Sampson & Groves, 1989).

*Human capital.* The findings for human capital suggest stronger links with adolescent high school completion and behavioral problems than children's school achievement. A study by Crane (1991), using data from the Public Use Microdata Sample, found that when the percentage of professional or managerial workers in neighborhoods fell to an especially low level (or reached a "tipping point"), neighborhood effects were most pronounced for youths' chances of dropping out of high school. Not all studies report this nonlinear pattern, however. Several studies using alternative data analytic techniques to control for unexplained sources of variation found that the neighborhood dropout rate was positively associated with youth failing to complete high school (Aaronson, 1997; Foster & McLanahan, 1996). Other researchers have found that low numbers of professionals in the neighborhood and the percentage of unemployed residents in the community were positively associated with adolescent childbearing and sexual activity (Billy & Moore, 1992; Brooks-Gunn et al., 1993; Crane, 1991; Ku et al., 1993). In addition, several of the studies found that the percentage of full-time employed females was positively associated with these behaviors, but such findings probably have less to do with human capital and more to do with the monitoring and supervision of youth (Billy et al., 1994; Brewster, 1994a, 1994b).

*Ethnic heterogeneity.* In the IHDP and the NLSY-CS, family residence in an ethnically diverse community was negatively associated with young children's IQ and verbal ability scores, particularly for white children (Chase-Lansdale et al., 1997). Among adolescents, Duncan et al. (1994) found that the racial composition of neighborhoods only appeared to influence African American youth, most notably young men from advantaged families, such that living in a community with greater concentrations of African Americans had an adverse effect on their schooling. In addition, researchers have found that a high proportion of Latinos in the community was associated with reduced levels of adolescent sexual activity (Ku et al., 1993).

*Residential stability.* Residential stability primarily has been examined with respect to adolescent juvenile delinquency. Among researchers working within the community disorganization perspective, residential instability has been linked to adolescent juvenile delinquency (Sampson & Groves, 1989; Shaw & McKay, 1942).

*Age structure.* There is scant research examining community age structure on the selected indicators of child well-being. Among a sample of low-birthweight children, Chase-Lansdale and colleagues (1997) found that a greater concentration of families in the community (including the percentage of individuals age 0 to 17 and the percentage of individuals older than age 65) was negatively associated with preschool children's IQ and verbal ability scores. Among adolescents, Billy and Moore (1992) found that a high child-to-female-adult ratio in the community was associated with women's childbearing.

*Collective efficacy.* To date, the association between collective efficacy and community violence has been examined only at the community level; collective efficacy mediated the association between structural factors (concentrated poverty and residential instability) and community rates of violence (Sampson et al., 1997). A similar pattern may exist at the individual level, particularly for juvenile crime and delinquency.

*Physical and social disorder.* Few studies have examined the association between physical and social disorder and child and adolescent well-being, in part because of the dearth of studies employing systematic social observation. In a Canadian national study, neighborhood observations of disorder were negatively associated with children's verbal ability scores (Kohen et al., 2000). These measures were also associated with community-level crime and victimization rates (Sampson & Raudenbush, 1999). (Again, we acknowledge that this latter example is not a child indicator.) Several studies based on participant reports of disorder have found associations between reported community disorder (e.g., presence of vandalism, abandoned housing, burglary, loitering) and African American adolescents' grades and sexual activity (Gonzales et al., 1996; Lauristen, 1994).

*Safety/stressors.* Research on community safety/stressors has examined the association between this dimension and child and adolescent mental and physical health rather than the indicators discussed in this chapter. In general, these studies suggest that a majority of children and adolescents have been exposed to violence in the community by either witnessing an event, knowing a victim, or being a victim in events such as robberies, beatings, stabbings, shootings, or murders (Campbell & Schwarz, 1996; Martinez & Richters, 1993). This exposure has consequences for children's well-being.

## Choosing Community Dimensions for Indicators

In answering our original question, the most compelling evidence to date for neighborhood dimensions that matter for child well-being is for income/SES and human capital. Consequently, these dimensions are good investments for indicators. In our view, currently additional evidence exists that ethnic heterogeneity and residential stability are other potential indicators. Although collective efficacy is theoretically intriguing, it is a more problematic indicator of child well-being because it requires a community survey to collect reliable data. Insufficient evidence exists to determine the relative merits of age structure, social support, social and physical disorder, and safety/stressors as community indicators of child well-being.

## Community as Place, Face, and Space

Community indicators that are important for understanding child well-being also include the services available within a community. Here we define *services* as health, education, and social welfare services that have a child component. These would include services such as the Special Supplemental Food Program for Women, Infants, and Children (WIC), school lunch programs, and Head Start, as well as other educational, mental health, physical health, and welfare services. In the second volume of *Neighborhood Poverty* (Brooks-Gunn et al., 1997b), we examined four approaches to delivering services to children: (1) categorical programs, (2) family and community support services, (3) community development corporations, and (4) comprehensive community initiatives (Leventhal et al., 1997). The availability of appropriate child-oriented services is usually not listed by community or neighborhood, in part because of differences in how communities are defined by health, education, recreation, and crime institutions within cities and in part because families often cross into other communities for services. In addition, service delivery systems vary with respect to specificity, target, and funding sources.

Most services are typically delivered by means of categorical programs that are federally mandated, such as WIC, food stamps, school lunch programs, Medicaid, Head Start, housing programs, and Temporary Assistance to Needy Families (TANF, formerly Aid to Families with Dependent Children).[1] Recent legislation has shifted funding for some of these programs to block grants to states, which gives more local autonomy to programs. The second service delivery strategy, family and community support services, centers on integrating services for children and families in a community-based setting as well as building ties among community residents (Kagan, 1996; Schorr, 1991). The next approach to delivering services, community development corporations, concentrates on housing, job creation, and civic infrastructure (Briggs & Mueller, 1997). The final service delivery strategy, comprehensive community initiatives, integrates the first three approaches to delivering services by providing coordinated, integrated services in a community-based setting that frequently includes housing and community development (Brown & Richman, 1997; Kubisch, 1996). As evident from our description of these services, the degree to which children and families, rather than adults or individuals, are a focus of these services varies.

Building on the work of community researchers (Kubisch, 1996; Sullivan, in press), we have identified three different approaches for conceptualizing *community* to reflect on strategies for delivering services within communities: communities as place, communities as face, and communities as space. The first approach, defining communities as place, views communities as neighborhoods (geographic locales) and as bureaucratically defined catchment areas. Viewing communities as face highlights the psychological associations that communities comprise by focusing on relationships and social support. The third definition, communities as space, considers communities as physical and built environments for living, working, and political organizing. In this section, we extend these definitions of community to indicators of service use and delivery among children and families.

## Communities as Place

A place-based definition of communities suggests that communities are manageable units around which to organize and deliver services. This approach entails two main strategies for the provision of services to children and families: categorical programs and system reform. Although categorical programs are federally mandated, they are delivered at the community-level according to bureaucratically defined catchment areas. The intensity, quality, and availability of services vary by community. Unfortunately, no official registers or administrative data sources exist for measuring these aspects of service delivery or program efficacy, utilization patterns, and outreach efforts. The effectiveness of categorical programs may depend largely on how services are delivered and how families are recruited and informed. How families receive the available services, the extent to which an effort is made to provide high-quality services, and linkages with other services are also likely to play a role in effectiveness. Thus, it is critical to examine differences across communities in the provision and quality of services and recipient satisfaction in addition to variation in outcomes by community or catchment area. For categorical programs, these outcomes are rarely observed, yielding little information about the role of these programs in children's lives.

In thinking about measuring community indicators of categorical programs, we suggest directions for future research employing this service-oriented approach. Examining whether a child- or family-oriented service has delivery systems in a community could be one indicator, as well as how many services of a particular type exist in the community. The existence of outreach programs could be measured as well. Examining the number of eligible children and families served in a particular community (e.g., the number of WIC-eligible recipients and the percentage served) is an alternative indicator. Given that families often leave the immediate neighborhood for services, slightly larger definitions of communities as place than census tracts may be required.

Categorical programs use place-based (geographic) definitions of community, but not all categorical programs define community the same way (e.g., health districts, police precincts, school districts). This predicament has made service reform a popular place-based effort to enhance service delivery. Moreover, geographic definitions of communities may be more flexible than bureaucratic systems (categorical programs) because they represent the local community more precisely. The success of these system reform initiatives has been attributed to their (1) flexibility, comprehensiveness, and responsiveness; (2) child, family, and community orientations; (3) high quality staff; (4) effort to target the most at-risk families and provide appropriately tailored services; (5) high-quality management; and (6) theoretical perspectives rooted in client-centeredness and long-term prevention (Schorr, 1991). The attributes of these services contrast with the current ways that most bureaucratic institutions and systems deliver services, including categorical funding, standardized program operations, equitable distribution of services, and short-term planning and goals.

The criticisms of system reform efforts (and categorical programs for that matter), in general, are not specific to children. Thus, we offer potential indicators that may improve our analyses of these services for children and families. Assessing the number of programs that offer service coordination would be a useful indicator. Evaluating the number of children or families served by a cluster of services (or categorical programs) as a proportion of the number of families or children eligible for the services in the catchment area would be another valuable indicator.

## Communities as Face

In terms of service delivery, viewing communities as face entails a more integrated and holistic approach to delivering services to children, families, and communities than is offered in system reform (place-based initiatives). Typically, these services are composed of community-based, multiservice organizations dedicated to promoting the well-being of children and families; such programs are referred to as community and family support services. Like system reform, community and family support services require interagency coordination or the establishment of an umbrella agency (Kagan & Pritchard, 1996). Several relationships are highlighted by this approach: (a) relationships within families, (b) relationships between families and service providers, (c) relationships among service providers, and (d) relationships among members in the community. Relationships within families emphasize the need to acknowledge family functioning and relational systems within families when providing services to children and families. Relationships between families and service providers point to the need to integrate community-based services for family members and enhance the relationship between families and providers. The next component, relationships among service providers, is concerned with building a community among service providers. Building relationships within communities attempts to foster ties among community residents (see Leventhal et al., 1997, for further details).

Clearly, conceptualizing indicators of these relationships is difficult, particularly relations with families and relations between families and service providers. An indicator of relationships among service providers could be the presence of interagency organizations or umbrella agencies, similar to that proposed for service reform. To examine relations among community members, the presence of community-based organizations such as block groups, community watch groups, mentoring programs, and so on could be indexed. Alternatively, the proportion of people who participate in these organizations relative to the population at large could be assessed.

## Communities As Space

When communities are defined as space, the focus is on housing and economic development as well as political organizing as primary targets of service delivery. Community development corporations and initiatives such as empowerment zones and enterprise communities have implemented these activities. Housing development entails the creation and management of affordable housing, and economic development involves both job training and job creation. Organizational governance is another component of community development corporations, but it clearly has more distal effects on children. Although these community development initiatives influence children, they generally do not provide child-oriented services. Rather, the effect of housing and economic development on children is primarily indirect through altering families' financial circumstance. Many community development corporations often try to have an effect on community building (i.e., relationships within communities) and neighborhood safety as necessary conditions to improving housing and economic development and political organization, however. Thus, safety may be one of the most important direct benefits of community development corporations for children.

When thinking about community indicators of child well-being for communities as space, several potential alternatives arise. Researchers could examine the number of recreational services, parks, libraries, and job training programs available. Assessing residents' feelings of safety is another indicator.

## Conclusions

We have used a two-pronged approach to examine community indicators of child well-being. In the tradition of social scientists, we covered methodologies employed and relevant indicators for child well-being. Our review indicates that methodologically, researchers need to move beyond census data and participant ratings in order to adequately examine the range of community indicators that may be relevant for child well-being. The second perspective of community indicators drew from community development and service delivery researchers. Although the findings for these indicators were not reviewed, this approach to examining community indicators has had limited scope, suggesting that community-level analyses of services are needed.

We conclude by suggesting the community-level indicators of child well-being that researchers may seek to incorporate into their studies based on current research and data availability, and similarly, that policymakers and practitioners can use to evaluate the status of children and youth in a community context. Drawing from several sources, we present community indicators that tap different dimensions of community context relevant to children and youth. From census data, perhaps the best indicator of child well-being is SES (income or composite measure). The findings reviewed suggest the need to move beyond neighborhood poverty as a single indicator of community SES and to distinguish between poverty, middle income, and affluence. This renewed outlook is particularly important because some child and adolescent outcomes, most notably achievement, are associated with residence in affluent neighborhoods, whereas other family and adolescent outcomes, such as behavioral outcomes, are associated with residence in poor neighborhoods. Furthermore, other characteristics of census tracts are highly associated with SES, such as single parenthood, low education, low number of professionals, and unemployment, making SES the primary community indicator to consider for child well-being. At the census tract level, stability of residence is another important indicator of child outcomes, especially adolescent crime and delinquency.

The community indicators of child well-being for service delivery vary depending on the definition of *community* employed. These indicators, however, require new methodologies, because most of the specified indicators are not available from current data sources, the exception perhaps being city-level data on categorical programs. Such information would enrich our understanding of the role of communities vis-à-vis services in the lives of children and families.

The remaining indicators are also drawn from various sources other than the decennial census, some of which were not reviewed in this chapter but are discussed here for prescriptive purposes. Violence (safety and stressors) is a critical community indicator that can be monitored by police districts using uniform crime reports available from police departments. Community health indicators of child well-being can be measured for local health districts using data available from state and city health departments and include the percentage of low-birthweight children, infant mortality rates, and the percentage of children who have been immunized. The next important indicator is educational outcomes, such as school dropout rates, competency test scores, percentage of children failing, and percentage of children in special education, available by school district from state and city departments of education. Among older adolescents, unemployment rates are another valuable indicator that should be measured at the community-level but for units larger than census tracts, such as ZIP code, region, or city, or by aggregating across census tracts, because people often do not work in their neighborhood of residence. In addition, because census data are only available every 10 years, more current data sources are required to adequately reflect the employment circumstances of youth, which are highly variable and depend on local labor market conditions. In sum, all of these indicators rely on existing data sources that provide aggregate-level data and are good indicators of the environment in which children and youth are growing up. Most of these indicators are also appropriate from measuring change at the community-level because data are collected annually, unlike the census (Leventhal & Brooks-Gunn, in press).

Alternative indicators may be relevant, depending on the desired community intervention, especially if researchers, policymakers, and practitioners want to track change over time in communities (Berlin et al., 2001). For example, in Healthy Start, a community-based home-visiting program that targets child health, the percentage of low-birthweight babies and infant mortality rates may be measured over time with time series analyses conducted to see if these indicators increase or decrease within a particular catchment area where the program is administered. For community policing interventions, program evaluators could examine yearly crime reports for the community. For educational interventions, such as Beacon Schools, which use schools to provide an array of services to children and families in low-income areas, high school dropout rates could be monitored. In all of these instances, evaluators would need to find somewhat comparable communities without the community interventions and examine time trends to see if they are similar or different to the intervention communities. These analyses, although useful, are plagued by possible biases; it is impossible to equate communities, and it is difficult to know if innovations in intervention spread to surrounding communities that are not targeted by the intervention. Thus, it may be a challenge to discern whether control communities are influenced by the intervention under investigation or by some other intervention.

An alternative strategy to intervening at the community level, recently employed by the U.S. Department of Housing and Urban Development, entails providing families in distressed communities with opportunities to relocate to new neighborhoods. The Moving to Opportunity for Fair Housing Demonstration, conducted in five U.S. cities, used an experimental design in which families living in public housing in high-poverty neighborhoods were randomly assigned to one of three groups: (a) receive a housing voucher only in a low-poverty neighborhood and special assistance and counseling to move, (b) receive a voucher only and no relocation requirement, or (c) receive no voucher (i.e., remain in public housing; Goering et al., 1999). The goal of the program is to combat concentrated poverty and the diminished opportunities that accompany it. This study design also addresses some of the methodological problems encountered in examining community context. Following families over time who move from high-poverty to low-poverty neighborhoods will provide insight into how a dramatic change in neighborhood residence affects (positively and negatively) the lives of a particularly vulnerable group of children and families. In addition, tracking the well-being of families who move to new communities of their choice has direct relevance for current housing policy (or community-oriented policies), in which the creation of new public housing for the poor has been supplanted by mixed income housing coupled with the allocation of housing vouchers.

Another technique that is useful for looking at larger policies, such as categorical programs, is to examine communities within different states. For example, a recent study, Fragile Families, is selecting three more macroconditions—generosity of welfare benefits, child support enforcement, and unemployment rates—to see if the behaviors of family formation and paternal involvement (and, subsequently, child well-being) vary in 21 cities with different combinations of welfare benefits, child support enforcement, and unemployment rates (see Brooks-Gunn et al., 2000, for additional details on this study and other community-based initiatives).

These latter approaches to assessing community dimensions do not involve speaking with individuals in communities. Researchers and policymakers concerned with individual-level approaches have several options. First, a community survey, such as that used to measure collective efficacy, could be conducted, which entails obtaining ratings from residents within a community. This measure could be used in assessing community-based organizations. Specifically, do such endeavors alter collective efficacy in communities?

Addressing this question would require a community survey, not necessarily just interviewing those families or practitioners involved in the community-based organizations. In addition, the community survey needs to be conducted within a pretest and posttest design with parallel community surveys conducted in a comparable neighborhood without the community-based organization. Finally, individual surveys can be conducted with parents and children involved in a community intervention, in which these families are asked about community efficacy, safety of the neighborhood, and observed violence. All of these dimensions represent indicators of the environment in which children are living.

In summary, we encourage social scientists to incorporate indicators of community context into studies of child well-being and policymakers and practitioners to consider more seriously community-level indicators of children's well-being. In this chapter, we have proposed alternative conceptions of community than those typically employed to stimulate thinking about ways to enhance our understanding of the role of communities in children's lives. At present, there are existing data sources that facilitate the use of community indicators in research on child well-being and that provide valuable information to policymakers.

## Authors' Note

The research presented here was made possible by support from the Foundation for Child Development; the National Institutes of Child Health and Human Development (NICHD); the Administration for Children, Youth, and Families; and the NICHD Research Network on Child and Family Well-Being.

## Endnotes

1. A brief review of the federal programs that provide in-kind (direct) benefits to low-income children follows. The Special Supplemental Food Program for Women, Infants, and Children provides vouchers for special supplemental food to low-income pregnant, lactating, or postpartum women; infants; and children up to 5 years old. The program also provides nutrition education and referral to health care and social service providers. The National School Lunch Program and the School Breakfast Program provide free and subsidized meals to low-income school-age children. The Food Stamp Program provides low-income households in need of food assistance with vouchers that can be used to purchase all food, except alcohol, tobacco, and hot foods prepared for immediate consumption. Medicaid is the main public health insurance program for low-income women and children. Head Start is an early educational intervention designed to serve low-income infants and children up to 5 years of age.

# References

Aaronson, D. (1997). Sibling estimates of neighborhood effects. In J. Brooks-Gunn, G. J. Duncan, & J. L. Aber (Eds.), *Neighborhood poverty: Policy implications in studying neighborhoods* (Vol. 2, pp. 80–93). New York: Russell Sage Foundation Press.

Aber, J. L., Gephart, M., Brooks-Gunn, J., Connell, J., & Spencer, M. B. (1997). Neighborhood, family, and individual processes as they influence child and adolescent outcomes. In J. Brooks-Gunn, G. J. Duncan, & J. L. Aber (Eds.), *Neighborhood poverty: Context and consequences for children* (Vol. 1, pp. 44–61). New York: Russell Sage Foundation Press.

Bandura, A. (1986). *Social foundations of thought and action: A social cognitive theory.* Englewood Cliffs, NJ: Prentice-Hall.

Barnes-McGuire, J., & Reiss, A. (1993, November). *Systematic social observation manual: Project on Human Behavior in Chicago Neighborhoods* (Report prepared for the Foundation for Child Development). Cambridge, MA: Foundation for Child Development.

Berlin, L. J., Brooks-Gunn, J., & Aber, J. L. (2001). Promoting early childhood development through comprehensive community initiatives. *Children's Services: Social Policy, Research and Practice, 4*(1), 1–24.

Billy, J. O., & Moore, D. E. (1992). A multilevel analysis of marital and nonmarital fertility in the U.S. *Social Forces, 70,* 977–1011.

Billy, O. Brewster, K. L., & Grady, W. R. (1994). Contextual effects on the sexual behavior of adolescent women. *Journal of Marriage and the Family, 56,* 387–404.

Boisjoly, J., Duncan, G. J., & Hofferth, S. L. (1995). Access to social capital. *Journal of Family Issues, 16,* 609–631.

Brewster, K. L. (1994a). Neighborhood context and the transition to sexual activity among young black women. *Demography, 31,* 603–614.

Brewster, K. L. (1994b). Race differences in sexual activity among adolescent women: The role of neighborhood characteristics. *American Sociological Review, 59,* 408-424.

Briggs, X. S., & Mueller, E. (with Sullivan, M. L.). (1997). *From neighborhood to community: Evidence on the social effects of community development.* New York: Community Development Research Center, Graduate School of Management and Urban Policy, New School for Social Research.

Bronfenbrenner, U. (1979). *The ecology of human development.* Cambridge, MA: Harvard University Press.

Bronfenbrenner, U. (1989). Ecological systems theory. In R. Vasta (Ed.), *Annals of child development—Six theories of child development: Revised formulations and current issues* (pp. 187–250). Greenwich, CT: JAI Press.

Brooks-Gunn, J., Berlin, L. J., Leventhal, T., & Fuligni, A. (2000). Depending on the kindness of strangers: Current national data initiatives and developmental research. *Child Development, 71,* 257–267.

Brooks-Gunn, J., Duncan, G. J., & Aber, J. L. (Eds.). (1997a). *Neighborhood poverty: Context and consequences for children* (Vol. 1). New York: Russell Sage Foundation Press.

Brooks-Gunn, J., Duncan, G. J., & Aber, J. L. (Eds.). (1997b). *Neighborhood poverty: Policy implications in studying neighborhoods* (Vol. 2). New York: Russell Sage Foundation Press.

Brooks-Gunn, J., Duncan, G. J., Klebanov, P. K., & Sealand, N. (1993). Do neighborhoods influence child and adolescent development? *American Journal of Sociology, 99,* 353–395.

Brooks-Gunn, J., Duncan, G. J., Leventhal, T., & Aber, J. L. (1997). Lessons learned and future directions for research on the neighborhoods in which children live. In J. Brooks-

Gunn, G. J. Duncan, & J. L. Aber (Eds.), *Neighborhood poverty: Context and consequences for children* (Vol. 1, pp. 279–297). New York: Russell Sage Foundation Press.

Brooks-Gunn, J., Rauh, V., & Leventhal, T. (1998). Equivalence and conceptually-anchored research with children of color. In H. E. Fitzgerald, B. M. Lester, & B. Zuckerman (Eds.), *Children of color* (pp. 25–51). New York: Garland Press.

Brown, P., & Richman, H. A. (1997). Neighborhood effects and state and local policy. In J. Brooks-Gunn, G. J. Duncan, & J. L. Aber (Eds.), *Neighborhood poverty: Policy implications in studying neighborhoods* (Vol. 2, pp. 164–182). New York: Russell Sage Foundation Press

Campbell, C., & Schwarz, D. F. (1996). Prevalence of impact and exposure to interpersonal violence among suburban and urban middle school students. *Pediatrics, 98,* 396–402.

Caspi, A., & Moffitt, T. E. (1991). Individual differences are accentuated during periods of social change: The sample case of girls at puberty. *Journal of Personality and Social Psychology, 61,* 157–168.

Chase-Lansdale, P. L., Gordon, R., Brooks-Gunn, J., & Klebanov, P. K. (1997). Neighborhood and family influences on the intellectual and behavioral competence of preschool and early school-age children. In J. Brooks-Gunn, G. J. Duncan, & J. L. Aber (Eds.), *Neighborhood poverty: Context and consequences for children* (Vol. 1, pp. 79–118). New York: Russell Sage Foundation Press.

Coleman, J. S. (1988). Social capital in the creation of human capital. *American Journal of Sociology, 95,* S95–S120.

Coulton, C. J. (1996). Effects of neighborhoods on families and children: Implications for services. In A. J. Kahn & S. B. Kamerman (Eds.), *Children and their families in big cities: Strategies for service reform* (pp. 87–120). New York: Columbia University School of Social Work, Cross-National Studies Program.

Coulton, C. J., Korbin, J. E., Su, M., & Chow, J. (1995). Community level factors and child maltreatment rates. *Child Development, 66,* 1262–1276.

Crane, J. (1991). The epidemic theory of ghettos and neighborhood effects on dropping out and teenage childbearing. *American Journal of Sociology, 96,* 1126–1159.

Duncan, G. J. (1994). Families and neighbors as sources of disadvantage in the schooling decisions of white and black adolescents. *American Journal of Education, 103,* 20–53.

Duncan, G. J., & Aber, J. L. (1997). Neighborhood models and measures. In J. Brooks-Gunn, G. J. Duncan, & J. L. Aber (Eds.), *Neighborhood poverty: Context and consequences for children* (Vol. 1, pp. 62–78). New York: Russell Sage Foundation Press.

Duncan, G. J., Brooks-Gunn, J., & Klebanov, P. K. (1994). Economic deprivation and early-childhood development. *Child Development, 65,* 296–318.

Ensminger, M. E., Lamkin, R. P., & Jacobson, N. (1996). School leaving: A longitudinal perspective including neighborhood effects. *Child Development, 67,* 2400–2416.

Entwisle, D. R., Alexander, K. L., & Olson, L. S. (1994). The gender gap in math: Its possible origins in neighborhood effects. *American Sociological Review, 59,* 822–838.

Foster, E. M., & McLanahan, S. (1996). An illustration of the use of instrumental variables: Do neighborhood conditions affect a young person's chance of finishing high school? *Psychological Methods, 1,* 249–260.

Furstenberg, F. F., Jr., & Hughes, M. E. (1997). The influence of neighborhoods on children's development: A theoretical perspective and research agenda. In J. Brooks-Gunn, G. J. Duncan, & J. L. Aber (Eds.), *Neighborhood poverty: Policy implications in studying neighborhoods* (Vol. 2, pp. 23–47). New York: Russell Sage Foundation Press.

Gephart, M. A., & Brooks-Gunn, J. (1997). Introduction. In J. Brooks-Gunn, G. J. Duncan,

& J. L. Aber (Eds.), *Neighborhood poverty: Context and consequences for children* (Vol. 1, pp. xiii-xxii). New York: Russell Sage Foundation Press.

Goering, J., Kraft, J., Feins, J., McInnis, D., Holin, M. J., & Elhassan, H. (1999, September). *Moving to opportunity for Fair Housing Demonstration Program: Current status and initial findings.* Washington, DC: U.S. Department of Housing and Urban Development.

Gonzales, N. A., Cauce, A., Friedman, R. J., & Mason, C. A. (1996). Family, peer, and neighborhood influences on academic achievement among African American adolescents: One-year prospective effects. *American Journal of Community Psychology, 24,* 365–387.

Graber, J. A., & Brooks-Gunn, J. (1996). Transitions and turning points: Navigating the passage from childhood through adolescence. *Developmental Psychology, 32,* 768–776.

Halpern-Felsher, B., Connell, J. P., Spencer, M. B., Aber, J. L., Duncan, G. J., Clifford, E., et al. (1997). Neighborhood and family factors predicting educational risk and attainment in African American and white children and adolescents. In J. Brooks-Gunn, G. J. Duncan, & J. L. Aber (Eds.), *Neighborhood poverty: Context and consequences for children* (Vol. 1, pp. 146-173). New York: Russell Sage Foundation Press.

Jencks, C., & Mayer, S. (1990). The social consequences of growing up in a poor neighborhood. In L. E. Lynn & M. F. H. McGeary (Eds.), *Inner-city poverty in the United States* (pp. 111–186). Washington, DC: National Academy Press.

Kagan, S. L. (1996). America's family support movement: A moment of change. In E. F. Zigler, S. L. Kagan, & N. W. Hall (Eds.), *Children, families, and government: Preparing for the twenty-first century* (pp. 155–170). New York: Cambridge University Press.

Kagan, S. L., & Pritchard, E. (1996). Linking services for children and families: Past legacies, future possibilities. In E. F. Zigler, S. L. Kagan, & N. W. Hall (Eds.), *Children, families, and government: Preparing for the twenty-first century* (pp. 378–393). New York: Cambridge University Press.

Klebanov, P. K., Brooks-Gunn, J., Chase-Lansdale, P. L., & Gordon, R. (1997). Are neighborhood effects on young children mediated by features of the home environment? In J. Brooks-Gunn, G. J. Duncan, & J. L. Aber (Eds.), *Neighborhood poverty: Context and consequences for children* (Vol. 1, pp. 119–145). New York: Russell Sage Foundation Press.

Klebanov, P. K., Brooks-Gunn, J., & Duncan, G. J. (1994). Does neighborhood and family poverty affect mothers' parenting, mental health, and social support? *Journal of Marriage and the Family, 56,* 441–455.

Klebanov, P. K., Brooks-Gunn, J., McCarton, C., & McCormick, M. C. (1998). The contribution of neighborhood and family income upon developmental test scores over the first three years of life. *Child Development, 69,* 1420–1436.

Kohen, D., Brooks-Gunn, J., Leventhal, T., & Hertzman, C. (2000). *Neighborhood income and physical and social disorder in Canada: Associations with young children's competencies?* Unpublished manuscript.

Korbin, J., & Coulton, C. J. (1997). Understanding the neighborhood context for children and families: Combining epidemiological and ethnographic approaches. In J. Brooks-Gunn, G. J. Duncan, & J. L. Aber (Eds.), *Neighborhood poverty: Policy implications in studying neighborhoods* (Vol. 2, pp. 65-79). New York: Russell Sage Foundation Press.

Ku, L., Sonenstein, F. L., & Pleck, J. H. (1993). Neighborhood, family, and work: Influences on the premarital behaviors of adolescent males. *Social Forces, 72,* 479–503.

Kubisch, A. C. (1996). On the term *community*: An informal contribution. In A. J. Kahn & S. B. Kamerman (Eds.), *Children and their families in big cities: Strategies for service reform* (pp. 256-260). New York: Columbia University School of Social Work, Cross-National

Studies Program.

Lauristen, J. L. (1994). Explaining race and gender differences in adolescent sexual behavior. *Social Forces, 72,* 859–884.

Leventhal, T., & Brooks-Gunn, J. (2000). The neighborhoods they live in: Effects of neighborhood residence on child and adolescent outcomes. *Psychological Bulletin, 126,* 309–337.

Leventhal, T., & Brooks-Gunn, J. (in press). Changing neighborhoods and child well-being: Understanding how children may be affected in the coming century. *Advances in Life Course Research.*

Leventhal, T., Brooks-Gunn, J., & Kamerman, S. (1997). Communities as place, face, and space: Provision of services to young children and their families. In J. Brooks-Gunn, G. Duncan, & J. L. Aber (Eds.), *Neighborhood poverty: Policy implications in studying neighborhoods* (Vol. 2, pp. 182–205). New York: Russell Sage Foundation Press.

Liaw, F., & Brooks-Gunn, J. (1994). Cumulative familial risks and low birth weight children's cognitive and behavioral development. *Journal of Clinical Child Psychology, 23,* 360–372.

Loeber, R., & Wikstrom, P. H. (1993). *Individual pathways to crime in different types of neighborhoods.* In D. P. Farrington, R. J. Sampson, & P. H. Wikstrom (Eds.), Integrating individual and ecological aspects of crime (pp. 169-204). Stockholm: National Council for Crime Prevention.

Martinez, J. L., & Richters, P. (1993). The NIMH Community Violence Project: II. Children's distress symptoms associated with violence exposure. *Psychiatry, 56,* 22–35.

Peeples, F., & Loeber, R. (1994). Do individual factors and neighborhood context explain ethnic differences in juvenile delinquency? *Journal of Quantitative Criminology, 10,* 141–157.

Perkins, D. D., & Taylor, R. B. (1996). Ecological assessments of community disorder: Their relationship to fear of crime and theoretical implications. *American Journal of Community Psychology, 24,* 63–107.

Rutter, M. (1987). Psychosocial resilience and protective mechanisms. *American Journal of Orthopsychiatry, 57,* 316–331.

Rutter, M., Champion, L., Quinton, D., Maughan, B., & Pickles, A. (1995). Understanding individual differences in environmental-risk exposure. In P. Moen, G. H. Elder, & K. Luscher (Eds.), *Examining lives in context: Perspectives on the ecology of human development* (pp. 61-96). Washington, DC: American Psychological Association.

Sameroff, A. J., Seifer, R., Baldwin, A., & Baldwin, C. (1993). Stability of intelligence from preschool to adolescence: The influence of social and family risk factors. *Child Development, 64,* 80–97.

Sameroff, A. J., Seifer, R., Barocas, R., Zax, M., & Greenspan, S. (1987). Intelligence quotient scores of 4-year-old children: Social environmental risk factors. *Pediatrics, 79,* 343–350.

Sampson, R. J. (1992). Family management and child development: Insights from social disorganization theory. In J. McCord (Ed.), *Advances in criminological theory* (Vol. 3, pp. 63–93). New Brunswick, NJ: Transaction.

Sampson, R. J., & Groves, W. B. (1989). Community structure and crime: Testing social-disorganization theory. *American Journal of Sociology, 94,* 774–802.

Sampson, R. J., & Morenoff, J. (1997). Ecological perspectives on the neighborhood context of urban poverty: Past and present. In J. Brooks-Gunn, G. J. Duncan, & J. L. Aber (Eds.), *Neighborhood poverty: Policy implications in studying neighborhoods* (Vol. 2, pp. 1–22). New York: Russell Sage Foundation Press.

Sampson, R. J., & Raudenbush, S. W. (1999). Systematic social observation of public spaces: A new look at disorder in urban neighborhoods. *American Journal of Sociology, 105,* 603–651.

Sampson, R. J., Raudenbush S. W., & Earls F. (1997). Neighborhoods and violent crime: A multilevel study of collective efficacy. *Science, 277,* 918–924.

Schorr, L. B. (with Booth, D.). (1991). Attributes of effective services for young children: A brief survey of current knowledge and its implications for program and policy development. In L. B. Schorr, D. Booth, & C. Copple (Eds.), *Effective services for young children* (pp. 23–45). Washington, DC: National Academy Press.

Shaw, C., & McKay, H. (1942). *Juvenile delinquency and urban areas* (Rev. ed.). Chicago: University of Chicago Press.

Simcha-Fagan, O., & Schwartz, J. E. (1986). Neighborhood and delinquency: An assessment of contextual effects. *Criminology, 24,* 667–703.

Spencer, M. B., McDermott, P. A., Burton, L. M., & Kochman, T. J. (1997). An alternative approach to assessing neighborhood effects on early adolescent achievement and problem behavior. In J. Brooks-Gunn, G. J. Duncan, & J. L. Aber (Eds.), *Neighborhood poverty: Policy implications in studying neighborhoods* (Vol. 2, pp. 164–181). New York: Russell Sage Foundation Press.

Sullivan, M. L. (1993). *More than housing: How community development corporations go about changing lives and neighborhoods.* New York: Community Development Research Center, Graduate School of Management and Urban Policy, New School for Social Research.

Sullivan, M. L. (in press). Local knowledge and local participation: Lessons from community studies for community initiatives. In J. P. Connell & A. C. Kubisch (Eds.), *Applying a theories of change approach to the evaluation of comprehensive community initiatives: Progress, prospects, and problems.* Washington, DC: Aspen Institute.

Werner, E. E., & Smith, R. S. (1982). *Vulnerable but invincible.* New York: McGraw-Hill.

Wilson, W. J. (1987). *The truly disadvantaged.* Chicago: University of Chicago.

Wilson, W. J. (1991a). Public policy research and "the truly disadvantaged." In C. Jencks & P. E. Peterson (Eds.), *The urban underclass.* (pp. 460–481). Washington, DC: Brookings Institution.

Wilson, W. J. (1991b). Studying inner-city social dislocations: The challenge of public agenda research. *American Sociological Review, 56,* 1–14.

# ELEVEN

# Children and the Changing Media Environment: From Plato's Republic to Hillary's Village

*Donald F. Roberts*

*Just turn on your television, any time of the day, any day of the week, and see what is competing for their attention. I'll bet that if a stranger came into your home and began telling your kids stories about the same kinds of characters and events, using the same kinds of words and pictures, you'd throw him out. You wouldn't wait for a surgeon general's report to validate what your instincts as a parent told you was a hazard to your children's mental and emotional health.*

—Clinton, 1996, p. 272

## Historical Concern with Media Messages

### Who Tells the Stories, Shapes the Child

The concern voiced by Hillary Clinton (1996) is neither new nor isolated. Her disquiet about the effect of media images joins a long line of warnings about how the stories children encounter influence their beliefs, attitudes, and behaviors. Anyone who has paid attention to the news media over the past several decades, however, probably senses a marked increase in the number and intensity of warnings about the negative effects on children of most contemporary communication media: television, motion pictures, music lyrics and videos, computer and video games, the Internet—all have come under scrutiny and attack. Those with a bit more gray hair may recall U.S. Senate hearings on comic books in the 1950s or debates in the early 1930s and the late 1960s over whether and how to rate motion pictures (precursors of recent discussions about rating TV content). Steven Starker's *Evil Influences* (1989) catalogs even earlier red flags waved over whatever medium was making stories available to youth during any particular historical period. From early 20th-century denunciations of silent films, to 19th-century attacks on the dime western and bowdlerizing of Grimm's Fairy Tales, through 18th-century forays against the novel, back at least to Plato's banishing of storytellers from the Republic (Plato, trans. 1941), media—or more accurately, media messages—have raised anxieties.

Some of the concern has been due less to evidence of harm to children than to fear of change and resistance to the idea that succeeding generations are as likely to adapt as to adopt parental beliefs and values. Nevertheless, caregivers have long correctly sensed that the stories children encounter influence their developing view of the world. Recently, scientific research has begun to disentangle anxiety over change from actual risk to children's development, as well as to identify potential benefits of the media and the messages they sometimes bring.

Among the reasons stories from "outside" engender so much angst, three of the most important are the perceived vulnerability of children, threats to parental control of information, and changes in communication technology.

## The Perceived Vulnerability of Children

Research supports the widespread perception that children are particularly vulnerable to messages from others. Young children lack experience and sophisticated thinking skills. They are prone to misinterpret messages. They have not developed criteria to make "good" decisions about what to believe, what to discount, what to ignore. In short, they are susceptible to messages in ways that, typically, adults are not. Hence, a case can be made that children merit special protections, one of the most important of which traditionally has been parental control of information.

## Parental Regulation of Information

During children's early years, parents function as gatekeepers, controlling much of the information reaching their offspring. An important aspect of growing up is a gradual erosion of such controls. Through the normal course of development, children move from the nursery to the neighborhood to the local school, encountering new sources of information at each step. As new sources introduce new ideas and information—stories from outside—parental control is attenuated and children begin to construct a more elaborate view of the world. In earlier times or more traditional settings, the move from nursery to neighborhood to school seldom brought large changes in the nature of information reaching children. Because neighbors and teachers typically viewed the world much like parents, they were more likely to reinforce than modify the parental view of the world.

Communication technologies, by their very nature, change the parent-child information relationship. Their function is to tell stories across time and space, to provide access to information far different from that likely to be filtered through traditional gatekeepers—to bring messages from outside. The more access children have to such messages, the greater the likelihood they will encounter information different from, even contradictory to, that of traditional socialization agents, information that helps shape a different view of the world. In short, media threaten the parental information monopoly almost by definition.

### The Revolution in Communication Technology

The spread of television heightened concerns about media effects on children. As late as the 1950s, traditional socialization agents remained the primary source of information for the first seven or eight years of a child's life, and influenced access to media even longer. Few children read for meaning until around age 7, and they interpret both print and radio symbols in terms of the image of the world they have already constructed—primarily from parental input. Moreover, 50 years ago, most children's movie attendance and print purchases required parental consent (at least until 11 or 12 years of age). Mid-20th-century parents still had relatively little competition in shaping their children's earliest impressions.

By the early 1950s, however, television began to crack the parental information monopoly in significant ways. In most households, television is on a great deal of the time, providing even the very young both physical and psychological access to stories from outside well before traditional socialization agents have established a baseline image of the world. Not only did television raise public concern about children and media to new levels, the more diverse and vivid television images became, the greater that concern. Recently, almost exponential increases in technology's ability to provide more stories to more children far more vividly than ever before have further increased society's concerns. As parents field questions about sexual innuendo in prime-time situation comedies, watch their children decapitate adversaries in bloody video games, and await the arrival of virtual reality media that promise to let children "experience" what they now only see and hear, they and others concerned with the welfare of children voice deep anxiety about the role of media in children's lives.

## The Changing Media Environment

Today's media environment differs remarkably from that of the 1960s. New media have proliferated: Cable television, music video, the Internet—all provide new levels of customization in content and delivery. Technological innovation has enhanced realism, fueled the quest for ever more extraordinary special effects, and provided the engaging feature of interactivity. The discovery and exploitation of a highly profitable youth market has motivated continuing escalation in the amount and intensity of content attractive to youth and in the means through which it can be accessed.

## Media Proliferation and Mass Customization

The first large-scale study of U.S. television and children (Schramm et al., 1961) described a media landscape consisting of print, motion pictures, radio, and the then "new" communication technology—broadcast television. By the beginning of the 1990s, the field had become much more crowded (Dorr & Kunkel, 1990). New technologies made information of all kinds more widely available, faster, in greater amounts, and more vividly than ever before. VCRs, personal computers, video game players, and personal audio systems were added to the media mix; cable and satellite vastly expanded the number of available TV channels; the video rental business was born; the emergence of FM radio, audiocassettes and CDs, and music videos reshaped the music industry; a trend from general to special interest publishing and the emergence of desktop publishing spawned numerous special interest magazines, many aimed at youth; the Internet and the World Wide Web offered access to almost unlimited (and often unvetted) information and opinion; virtual reality technology promised new ways to learn, to play, to "experience."

Important changes within media also enhanced their vividness and increased their impact. Digital technology raised special effects to new heights, imbuing symbolic sounds and sights with fidelity approaching reality. Today's audiences hear orchestras in their own living rooms with sound equaling the symphony hall; at local movie theaters, they experience space travel so real it can engender motion sickness; they witness mayhem and bloodshed so vivid it leaves viewers ducking to avoid splatters. We are only beginning to explore how such technological changes influence psychological responses to media, but early experimentation indicates that the impact can be dramatic (Reeves & Nass, 1996).

## Discovery and Exploitation of the Youth Market

As late as the 1950s, youth did not play a primary role in the economics of mass communication. Parents were seen as the primary purchasers; children were viewed largely as a means to motivate them. High quality children's content was a means to stimulate parents to purchase a TV set (or a movie ticket, or an encyclopedia) for their youngster's benefit; successful family programs were those that attracted parents to view with their children; effective commercials stimulated children to nag parents to purchase products. By the mid-1960s, however, a number of forces converged to change this view. Saturation of U.S. homes with television, steadily increasing demands for advertising time, the Kennedy administration's accent on youth, and children's growing economic clout all converged to make youth a valuable, specialized audience (Pecora, 1998). As demands for advertising time during periods of heavy adult viewing pushed children's programming to Saturday mornings, advantages to such a children's television ghetto became apparent. Production costs were lower for children's programs. Reruns could be shown more frequently. Twice as much time could be devoted to commercials. Commercials aimed specifically at children could be developed. In short, Saturday morning became a profit center. By 1967, youth had become a specialized niche market, and there was out-and-out network competition for the Saturday morning audience.

By 1968, U.S. children between 4 and 12 years old were spending $2 billion of their own money annually; the figure rose to $6 billion in 1989, and to more than $68 billion in 1995. Teenagers in 1999 spent $105 billion of their own (Wood, 2001). Moreover, children and adolescents either spend or influence the spending of additional tens of billions of their families' dollars. Little wonder that media respond to this market. Youth comprise more than 30% of our motion picture audience; they account for more than 40% of popular music purchases; the music video, invented for and often produced by them, has influenced audio-visual techniques in most other media. Youth have become much more than a niche market; they are at the core of contemporary popular culture, and much of the content of popular media is produced for them (Christenson & Roberts, 1998). They have become central players in a very different media environment than existed 40 years ago.

## Children and Youth as Media Consumers

### Children's Media Use

Children's media time has been increasing for several decades. It is difficult to obtain accurate measures of time spent with the various media because children do not estimate time very well and only television comes in convenient half-hour units. Nevertheless, numerous studies using different measures with widely varying samples converge enough to enable some reasonable approximations. Estimates from the beginning of the 1960s put the total media exposure (i.e., print, radio, film, and TV use) of the average sixth grader at between 35 and 40 hours per week (Schramm et al., 1961). From the late 1980s onward, estimates of middle school children's television viewing alone have ranged from 20 to 40 hours per week (e.g., Brown et al., 1990; Kaiser Family Foundation, 1998). If we add another two to three hours of music exposure (radio, recordings, music videos), plus additional time devoted to reading, using the computer, movie and video viewing, and playing video games, estimates of media exposure for today's average junior high school student run as high as 60 hours per week (Roberts, et al. 1999). Of course, much of this exposure occurs as a secondary activity. A good deal of television viewing and substantially more than half of all music listening accompany other activities ranging from housework to homework and even to other kinds of media use. Nevertheless, regardless of how divided their attention might be, it appears that contemporary U.S. youngsters spend as much as 35% of their time in the presence of one or more media.

Television dominates during preadolescence. Regular viewing begins as early as 2 years of age, peaks near the end of grade school, then declines as the academic and social demands of junior and senior high school cut into available time. Music media use—radio, recordings, and music videos—takes off at about age 10 and soon passes TV viewing, increasing to four hours per day by the midteens (some estimates, noting music's frequent role as background for many adolescent activities, place music exposure nearer to six hours daily; Christenson & Roberts, 1998). Print use climbs slowly from about the end of third grade, when reading for meaning begins, but nonschool reading seldom averages more than one-half hour per day.

Reliable data on time devoted to other media are scarce. Teenagers comprise 30% of the motion picture audience, but we lack information on how much time an average youngster spends at the movies. More than 40% of U.S. households with children have personal computers, but they tend to be higher income households. Recent estimates put 2- through 18-year-olds' computer time at just more than 20 minutes daily (an estimate that includes many youngsters who do not use a computer at all) (Roberts et al., 1999). VCR and video game use has been estimated to account for about 5% of 9- to 15-year-olds' total media budget, but again, measurement procedures do not allow estimates of media time per se (Nickelodeon, 1998; Wartella et al., 1990). There are, of course, large variations in children's media use. Some children watch little or no television, while others watch seven or eight hours daily; some children never read, while some seem happy only when buried in a book.

## Predictors of Media Use

Numerous factors in addition to age influence exposure. Children from lower socioeconomic levels tend to view television more, use print less, and have more limited access to personal computers than their counterparts from higher socioeconomic strata. Black youth spend more time with television than do their white peers; girls listen to music more than boys. Both music listening and television viewing tend to be higher in single-parent families. Children with few friends spend more time with media overall. By 7 or 8 years of age, brighter children and more creative children generally spend less time with television and somewhat more time reading.

Many of these factors make a difference because they locate conditions that influence access to media in terms of time, availability, or attractive alternatives. For example, children who spend more time within the household for whatever reason—girls with household chores, children from less safe neighborhoods, youngsters with few friends—all watch more television. Those from higher socioeconomic strata not only have more access to print media and personal computers, but also enjoy a wider array of attractive, alternative nonmedia activities to which they devote time. Children from two-parent families encounter more household demands and less unstructured free time; single-parent children with less supervision and companionship turn to TV more often. Because television is a family medium, children wishing to escape parents watch less of it. Bright and creative children tend to engage in many alternative activities, leaving less time for media. In short, differences in needs, interests, abilities, and access predict differences in whether, how, and why children use media. What remains constant across all such variations, however, is that contemporary U.S. children inhabit a world permeated by media and their messages.

## Children as a Special Audience

Much of our sense that children are particularly vulnerable to media stems from the perception that they comprise a special audience (Dorr, 1986). They are special in the sense that they think about the world and interpret new information in qualitatively different ways than adults. Research documents rapid and dramatic changes throughout childhood and adolescence in how children think, in what they think about, and in the kinds and levels of experience they bring to bear when interpreting new information (Flavell et al., 1993). Significant age-related changes occur in children's understanding of the basic nature of information, of messages, and of message and story conventions, all of which influence what information is attended to, how it is interpreted, and how it is responded to. Although 5-, 10-, and 15-year-olds may watch the same television program, listen to the same song, or play the same computer game, they typically focus on different kinds of information, think about it in different ways, and ultimately "understand" quite different messages.

Cognitive maturation and the accumulation of knowledge and experience both play important roles in this transformation. Obviously, a typical 12-year-old knows a good deal more about most things than does a kindergarten child; she has had seven or eight more years to glean information from direct experience and from messages originated by parents, friends, teachers, print materials, television shows, and even video games. What one knows about something—one's existing mental representation of the world—affects interpretation of subsequent information, including media content. Age makes a substantial difference, but it is not the only mediator leading to differential experience. For example, urban children are likely to develop a more detailed image of city life than rural children, who in turn probably map the rural landscape in more complex terms than do urban children. Such factors as gender, ethnic background, social class, personal interests, and so forth all influence what children know, hence, how they respond to media messages.

Age-related cognitive abilities also affect how children make sense of media. Very young children tend to think in highly concrete terms; they are perceptually bound, responding primarily to how things look. Gradually, children begin to make inferences that incorporate not only appearances, but also things below the surface—psychological states and social contexts. As cognitive development progresses, older children and young adolescents begin to deal with the abstract, the implied, and the hypothetical—with how things might be or ought to be. One way to think about developmental changes in how children interpret information is in terms of a move from the surface of things to the interior, from the immediate percept to the underlying concept, and ultimately to possible (and often implied) relations among all of these.

Such changes in cognitive functioning influence interpretations of media content. Studies of children's understanding of television demonstrate a progression from focusing on how characters look and what they say and do toward understandings that also encompass characters' feelings and intentions, why things happen, how things might be, and so on. When interpreting stories, young children typically do not use implicit information or draw inferences to connect scenes, actions, and characters; they have difficulty linking noncontiguous scenes and integrating bits of information from different parts of a narrative. As they grow older, however, children begin to perform such operations, developing a sense of message and story structure, learning to interpret successive scenes in light of what has gone earlier. Similarly, although younger children often confound reality and realism and fail to distinguish fantasy from reality, older children more easily distinguish between realism and reality and more readily compare media depictions of events and characters to real life (see Collins, 1983; Dorr, 1986).

Cognitive development also influences thinking about the very nature of information and messages. Adults usually interpret anything they perceive as a message at least partly in social terms, bringing to bear strategies that include making inferences about source, intent, social context, and so forth. Young children, on the other hand, are not as adept at making sign-symbol distinctions. They must learn that natural signs and shared symbols differ, that unlike directly experienced information, messages are social constructions, created by someone for some purpose, requiring different interpretative strategies. They often treat messages little differently from directly experienced information and overlook information intended by the writer or actor to shape audience perceptions of a symbolic character, attributing the same characteristics to the screen role that they have previously associated with real-life people or roles, making little allowance for the symbolic nature of the message (Worth & Gross, 1974).

Finally, children must learn that different kinds of messages require different kinds of interpretative strategies. Schramm (1971) contended that adults typically use culturally defined cues and contexts to classify messages as primarily serving one of four functions—information, education, persuasion, or entertainment—adjusting interpretive strategies accordingly. Whether they focus on a source's expertise or its credibility, whether they test message claims against some known truth or reality or choose to suspend disbelief, whether they rehearse and store parts of the message or merely note and pass over its components—that is, the relevance, validity, and value they assign to messages; the array of responses they identify as appropriate; and so forth—all such interpretation strategies depend on inferences about message intent. Preschoolers seldom make such distinctions. Rather, they view a *Sesame Street* segment teaching the alphabet, a commercial pushing the latest shape in sugared cornflakes, and an animated cartoon as if each was primarily informational in nature (Blosser & Roberts, 1985). Indeed, parental perceptions that young children often treat fictional entertainment or persuasive appeals in the same way that they process "legitimate" information is a major source of concern about the impact of media on children.

## Research on the Nature of Media Effects

Research on media effects has changed over the past 20 years, moving away from seeking powerful or massive effects on mass audiences toward a search for more limited, conditional effects. In addition, growing recognition of learning as the fundamental media effect has stimulated increased attention to cognitive outcomes.

### Conditional Effects

Many discussions of mass media at least implicitly characterize audiences as passive, conceive of influence as largely a function of exposure, and posit massive effects, assuming that large numbers of those exposed to a given message respond in highly similar ways. However, empirical research fails to support this view, leading some to posit minimal effects models and speculate that mass media are of relatively little importance to social behavior (McGuire, 1986).

Recently, communication researchers have begun to doubt both powerful and minimal effects models, questioning assumptions that people respond to a given message in similar ways and that important effects necessarily implicate large numbers. They argue that because such conditions as age, experience, social background, needs, interests, and circumstances lead individuals to interpret and respond to the same message in quite different ways, the likelihood of pointing to any one outcome as massive is greatly diminished. Not diminished, however, is the potential importance of each possible outcome. Importance does not require large numbers. Even though relatively few children may actually imitate karate kicks learned from a Saturday morning cartoon, such effects can be quite important—for example, to other children who share the same classroom. Importance is always a value judgment.

Much current media research, then, takes a more conditional approach. It conceptualizes responses to media as essentially constructive acts in which messages supply material out of which people construct meaning depending on individual attributes, social context, and so forth. People's abilities, interests, needs, and expectations influence responses as much as message form and content. Therefore, rather than infer effects based on changes in a small portion of large, undifferentiated audiences, conditional studies begin by theoretically defining subgroups and the conditions that should make them particularly responsive to a given message, then looking for effects within most of that limited group.

## Cognitive Outcomes

The kinds of media effects receiving attention have also shifted—from a focus on attitude and behavior change several decades ago to greater current emphasis on cognitive outcomes. The new emphasis views behavior as a function of an individual's "picture" of the world, variously labeled scripts, schema, knowledge structures, or mental representations. For instance, a child's "school schema," her mental representation regarding what schools are and how one behaves within them, significantly influences how she acts in school. To the extent that a message changes this schema, regardless of whether she has an immediate opportunity to act on the basis of the new mental image, it has had an effect. In other words, the fundamental effect of media messages is learning, conceptualized as any change in existing schema.

The distinction between learning and acting is important. Typically, we judge learning on the basis of performance. A student who performs what we have just taught has obviously learned. However, failure to perform does not necessarily mean failure to learn. Performance is a function of many factors largely independent of the message that produced learning: arousal, incentives, roles, social circumstances, and so forth. Learned beliefs and behaviors are manifested primarily when conditions call for them. Thus, although children may learn various courtship conventions, beer brand preferences, or aggressive behavior from media messages, most won't display what has been learned until an age or situation when dating, beer drinking, or fighting become possibilities and are perceived as appropriate. Because individuals make sense of messages by comparing incoming information to existing mental representations, attention to a message implies that some "effect" almost always occurs, even if only the most minuscule reinforcement of an existing schema. The question, then, is not whether media messages affect children, but which messages, under which conditions, in which ways.

## Conditions that Mediate Learning from Media

Following the first few laboratory studies of television and children in the early 1960s, attention turned from whether media messages had effects—clearly they did—to identifying factors that mediate differential outcomes: attributes of media content, of children, and of the viewing and performance situations that influence various responses.

Wilson and her colleagues (1996) reviewed a number of message-related contextual factors that influence the effects of exposure to media violence. These include whether violence is rewarded or punished, qualities of the perpetrator and the target, justification for the act, harm and pain cues, realism, humor, and the presence of weapons. Some contextual factors increase the likelihood of a given effect (e.g., attractive perpetrators increase learning), some decrease it (e.g., showing violence punished decreases fear), and some affect different outcomes differently (e.g., unjustified violence decreases learning and increases fear), but all influence how children incorporate media content into their knowledge structures. Although several factors in this list pertain primarily to portrayals of aggressive violence (e.g., presence of weapons), most operate regardless of the nature of the portrayal. Attractive actors or associated rewards increase learning of antisocial, prosocial, or relatively neutral behaviors.

Rewards and punishments associated with portrayed behaviors are particularly powerful contextual factors. Children learn very early to pay attention to rewards and punishments, whether directly or vicariously experienced, because they provide valuable information about what is worth learning and what is worth avoiding. Numerous studies demonstrate that portraying behavior as rewarded or punished influences children's responses (Bandura, 1986). Indeed, a case can be made that several other influential contextual factors are simply special cases of rewards and punishments: Harm and pain cues refer to long-term negative consequences; qualities of the actor may serve as a surrogate for positive or negative reinforcements (i.e., heroes are usually rewarded, villains punished). In short, portrayals of consequences or of cues that elicit inferences about consequences guide attention, memory, and expectations, and thus influence observers' subsequent responses.

Content attributes shown to affect children's responses represent one of three general dimensions: (1) efficacy (contextual cues indicating likelihood of reward/punishment, success, and so forth), (2) normativeness (contextual cues indicating acceptability, justification, frequency), and (3) pertinence (contextual cues indicating similarity to the viewer; Comstock, 1991). To the extent that either the substantive content or the formal characteristics of messages lead children to perceive acts as likely to be rewarded or otherwise elicit successful outcomes (efficacy), as manifestations of normal or typical beliefs or behaviors (normativeness), or as relevant to themselves and the world they inhabit (pertinence), to that extent media content affects children's mental representations of their world and the behavior such representations mediate.

Other content attributes also affect children's responses to media. Children understand and learn more from models perceived as similar to themselves, a finding that has been demonstrated for gender, race, and social class. Similarity in age is also important, with the caveat that children are especially interested in what lies ahead, so are particularly responsive to models just a few years older. Formal features of messages such as frequency, clarity, pace, music, humor, and salience of information all influence media effects.

Whether and how contextual cues are interpreted is not simply a function of message content. Perception of an actor as attractive or of the outcome of some action as rewarding also depends on the child. Prior experience shapes interpretation not only of portrayed behavior, but also of the contextual information that frames it. For example, children of different races, genders, ages, or social class, often have different conceptions of what constitutes attractiveness, or humor, or reward and punishment. Children from homes that avoid physical discipline may perceive a portrayal of a mild spanking as extremely punishing; those from families where physical discipline is common may see it as trivial. In short, interpretation of contextual factors is always the result of a kind of negotiated meaning—negotiated between elements of the message and the prior experience and expectations of the child.

## Specific Media Effects

Beginning with the Payne Fund research on motion pictures and youth in the early 1930s (Charters, 1933), more than 1,000 reports of empirical studies on media and children exist, far too many to review here. The following briefly catalogs only a few of the effects that have been demonstrated to follow from exposure to media content. Research areas selected because of their importance to social policymakers include violence, social stereotypes, sexuality, and prosocial behavior.

### *Violence*

Not surprisingly, effects of media portrayals of violence have received more attention than any other type of outcome in research on children and media. Hundreds of studies, encompassing surveys, time-series analyses, laboratory experiments, and field experiments, examine the impact(s) of media violence (Comstock, 1991).

Surveys find significant positive relationships between children's violence viewing and various indicators of aggression ranging from attitudinal inventories, to self-reports of delinquent behavior, to peer or teacher ratings of aggressiveness. These relationships typically survive controls for a variety of third variables. Although surveys fail to settle questions of causal direction, they leave little doubt that high exposure to media violence is associated with greater aggressiveness. Several longitudinal studies have addressed the causality issue by gathering data from the same children over periods ranging from several years to decades, and examining whether early viewing is more strongly related to subsequent aggressive behavior than the reverse. Longitudinal studies replicate the positive relationship between violence viewing and aggressiveness, and most find that early violence viewing relates to later aggressive behavior but that the reverse seldom holds, indicating that viewing more likely causes violence than the reverse (Huesmann & Eron, 1986).

Experiments, which control causal sequence, clearly demonstrate that viewing violence teaches children whether, when, and how to engage in aggressive behavior. Experiments consistently find that exposure to violent content increases children's subsequent aggressive responses on measures ranging from pen and pencil questionnaires, through manifested willingness to punish others, to aggressive behavior in free play situations. Effects have been shown with children ranging from 3 or 4 years old through the end of adolescence, with boys and girls, and with previously aggressive and nonaggressive youngsters. They have included direct imitation of new behaviors and elicitation of previously learned aggressive acts not specifically portrayed. Experiments have also shown that violence viewing can lead to increased levels of fear and decreased levels of sensitivity to violence and suffering.

Of course, these studies are open to criticism that laboratory experiments concerned with social behavior cannot be generalized. They have been questioned on grounds of artificiality and the willingness of researchers to generalize what may be short-term outcomes to long-term social behavior (e.g., Freedman, 1984). Partially in response to such attacks, the 1970s and 1980s saw several field experiments that attempted to shape real life to approximate the circumstances of an experiment. Over periods ranging from days to weeks, youngsters' television or film diets were manipulated in natural settings, and their behavior was observed and coded for aggressiveness. Although not free of internal flaws, the field experiments answered most challenges to external validity, and when considered in the context of the large body of survey and experimental findings, they further confirmed the causal relationship between viewing media violence and subsequent aggressive behavior (Comstock, 1991).

## Social Stereotypes

Media's role in the formation and maintenance of various types of social stereotypes has received sporadic attention since the early 1930s when Peterson and Thurston (1933) demonstrated that films such as *Birth of a Nation* negatively affected children's attitudes toward African Americans for as long as eight months after exposure. More recent work in which exposure to various portrayals of racial, ethnic, and national minorities was experimentally controlled confirms that both educational and commercial entertainment programs influence children's social attitudes. Not surprisingly, the effects reflect the nature of the content; positive portrayals produce positive changes and negative portrayals produce negative changes (Christenson & Roberts, 1983).

Research on gender stereotypes typically takes one of two approaches. The first presumes that current television fare offers a view of women largely conforming to traditional sex-role stereotypes, and uses surveys to document a relationship between viewing and traditional sex-role beliefs and attitudes. Such research typically finds that children who watch a great deal of television more readily accept traditional sex-role stereotypes than children who view less, and concludes that current television content "cultivates" traditional views of appropriate behavior for women. Unfortunately, correlational findings make causal inferences problematic.

The second approach seeks to demonstrate that "alternative" content—more egalitarian, nonstereotypical portrayals of women—can cultivate less traditional beliefs and attitudes. Largely experimental, this work demonstrates that children who see women portrayed in nonstereotypical occupations or traditionally male pursuits subsequently give less gender-stereotyped responses on measures of sex-role attitudes and beliefs. Effects tend to be greater for younger children and girls, but hold to some extent across most ages and both genders. For better or worse, then, information about others and about individual potential presented in media portrayals contributes to the worldview of the young audience. Although the long-term impact of such learning is unclear, this is a legitimate area for further study.

## Portrayals of Sexuality

Turning from sex roles to sex, recent concerns about the consequences for youth of increasing amounts, accessibility, and explicitness of sexual content in the media (Greenberg, 1994) have motivated several surveys relating adolescents' exposure to "sexy" television content to various sexual beliefs and attitudes. Teenagers say that they learn a great deal about sex and sexuality from television, and that television encourages sexual activity. Adolescents who frequently view programs in which sex plays a significant role (e.g., soap operas, music videos, selected prime-time dramas) give higher estimates of divorce rates and illegitimate births and believe that TV characters would not use contraception. Frequent viewers also express more permissive sexual attitudes and are more sexually active, but report less satisfaction with their own sexual experiences (or lack of experiences). Experimental work on the effect of sexual content finds that exposure to media content focusing on physical beauty—beauty commercials, programs such as the old *Charlie's Angels, Playboy* centerfolds—increases evaluations of the importance of physical attractiveness and decreases college males' satisfaction with their own girlfriends. Finally, controlled exposure to typical television programs containing sexual content resulted in 13- and 14-year-olds becoming less disapproving of nonmarital or extramarital sex, and viewing sexually explicit films led college students to report greater acceptance of sexual infidelity and promiscuity, less disapproval of rape, and less satisfaction with their intimate partners. It seems that media content may play a significant role in the sexual socialization of today's youth (Strasburger, 1995).

## The Emphasis on Negative Effects

The lion's share of research on children and media focuses on negative effects. This is largely a result of media's tendency to tell stories and portray behaviors that test norms, in combination with the field's orientation to policy-related, applied research. That is, a significant proportion of research on children and media has occurred in response to perceived "social problems," many of which are often depicted in media content. Not unreasonably, when violence, sexual permissiveness, drugs, social stereotyping, and so forth become social issues, the effects of media portrayals of these social issues on children elicit public attention. Given media's well-documented tendency to present content associated with such issues in amounts and ways highly likely to attract youngsters' attention and facilitate learning (e.g., Greenberg, 1994; Wilson et al., 1996), and given the kinds of public and parental concerns discussed at the outset of this chapter, it would be surprising if such "negative" effects of media did not receive intense scrutiny. It is important to note, however, that classification of any effect as negative or positive is fundamentally a value judgment and that substantial research has demonstrated that children obtain prosocial beliefs, attitudes, and behaviors from media messages if and when they encounter prosocial content.

## Prosocial Learning and Positive Effects

Although far fewer in number, effects studies have demonstrated that media content can influence such positive behaviors as sharing, friendliness, cooperation, helping, and altruism. So, too, for various positive cognitive effects. Children may learn anything from the alphabet, to basic reading skills, to occupational opportunities, to constitutional law from mass media. It is telling, however, that evidence for positive effects typically comes from experiments because of their inherent ability to ensure exposure to relevant kinds of prosocial content. That is, prosocial portrayals are either so infrequent or so non-salient in typical media fare that usually exposure must be carefully engineered to demonstrate prosocial outcomes.

To reiterate an earlier point, then, the issue is not whether children learn from media. The evidence indicates that children cannot *not* learn from the models they attend to, live or mediated. Rather, the issue concerns what they have an opportunity to learn. At bottom, the probability that media content will cause negative or positive effects largely depends on how much and how any particular kind of content is presented. If and when such things as cooperation, conflict resolution, or civility become frequent, salient, and attractive staples of media offerings, more children will learn such things as cooperation, conflict resolution, and civility.

### A Screen Is a Screen

The new communication media have engendered many calls for new research on effects, with the implication that earlier studies are no longer relevant. Although the preponderance of work on children's responses to media focuses on television, it is important to note that most factors that mediate learning and performance are not limited to the television screen. Obviously, between-media differences exist: Screen size, a large darkened room, and tiered seating make the movie experience different from watching television at home; the computer's interactive possibilities add potentially significant elements missing from film and television; print clearly requires different skills from audiovisual media. By and large, however, the many demonstrable similarities among media are more important than the differences. Children learn from successful, attractive models regardless of medium; the influence of frequency and salience of information and the impact of perceived consequences hold across all media. Thus, although some distinguish among media for various political or policy-based reasons, in the eyes of most viewers—especially children—a screen is a screen is a screen. Pending new evidence to the contrary, findings from research on children and television probably apply to other media as well.

## Summarizing Recent Trends

Although unease with the effects of messages reaching children from outside has a long history, recent increases in the number and nature of media and messages available to children, in the time children spend with media, and in scientific studies documenting media influences have given new urgency and legitimacy to the concerns of parents, educators, and policymakers.

The development of motion pictures and radio in the first half of the 20th century, the rapid growth of television following World War II, and the past decade's explosion in computers and the Internet have dramatically increased children's access to messages from outside. The emergence of cable and satellite television, FM radio, desktop publishing, and the Internet fragmented the mass audience and heightened competition for audience share, which along with emergence of youth as a significant market, seems to have increased various sources' willingness to make available to youngsters content of the kind likely to raise parental concerns.

As children's media options have grown, so too has the time they devote to media. Over the past several decades, the average junior high school student's media exposure has almost doubled, from 30 to 40 hours per week in the early 1960s to current estimates ranging as high as 60 to 70 hours per week, including time spent reading, viewing, listening, gaming, and Internet surfing. Although social and demographic variables locate large variations in exposure, there is no question that most U.S. children spend a significant part of their lives exposed to media messages (Roberts et al., 1999).

Concurrent with recent growth in children's media options, four decades of scientific research demonstrate that children incorporate information from media content into their developing mental representations of the world. Although any given message influences different subgroups of children in different ways, message attributes that implicate perceptions of efficacy, normativeness, or pertinence influence children's learning of portrayed content of all kinds. Media influences have been documented to affect beliefs, attitudes, and behavior in such domains as aggression; desensitization; fear; sexuality; and racial, ethnic, and sex-role stereotypes; as well as in various prosocial areas ranging from learning the alphabet to beliefs and behaviors associated with sharing, helping, and friendliness—to list only a few. Empirical studies leave little question that media messages play a significant role in children's socialization, suggesting that we must pay more attention to finding ways to help children become better consumers of information.

## Policy Implications

When media content is perceived as threatening children, government often is urged to "do something." The Federal Trade Commission has demonstrated some authority to limit the frequency and length of commercial messages in programs aimed specifically at young children, and the Federal Communications Commission has recently mandated a minimum weekly amount of "educational" programming for children. Attempts to control specific content, however, have been struck down repeatedly by U.S. courts.

Moreover, the newer technologies are increasingly capable of rendering censorship attempts futile. Content that youngsters cannot obtain in at least some video stores, they can probably find on the Internet. Protections that do not rely on censorship are needed. Rather than looking for ways to keep information from children, perhaps we should turn attention to helping children become better consumers of information.

Two assumptions underlie this approach. First, the education and socialization of children is one of the most important *shared* responsibilities of any society; second, in a democratic, pluralistic, information-based society such as ours, teaching children how to process and evaluate information critically and carefully and make informed decisions is central to successful socialization. The ability to decode and evaluate information from a wide array of media represents some of the most important training today's children can acquire, and parents, schools, and media all have roles to play and a shared stake in seeing that children acquire it. Given these premises, two interventions offer particular promise: (1) the introduction and implementation of comprehensive, wide-ranging media literacy programs for school-age children; and (2) adoption by all media of a uniform system of accurate, nonjudgmental content labeling.

## Media Literacy

Media literacy refers to a complex set of skills that help people construct meaning from, and think clearly about information from, all forms of symbols and media (Potter, 1998). It is the ability to process and evaluate information and information contexts carefully, critically, and efficiently to make well-informed decisions about any media content. Such decisions may range from acceptance or rejection of antismoking public service messages to evaluating whether a scene in a situation comedy warrants a smile or a frown. It includes judging the credibility of news encountered on the Internet and understanding the function of blood splatters in violent video games. Parents, schools, and the media themselves share responsibility for making media literacy skills an integral part of the socialization of all children.

## Parents

Parents provide important lessons about how to use media and how specific media content coincides with their own beliefs and values. Parents who watch soap operas tend to raise children who watch soap operas; parents who read a daily newspaper tend to raise children who do likewise. Equal in importance to their role as models, parents have unique opportunities to talk to their children about media, whether responding to a question about something in a storybook or television program or establishing rules and norms for media use in the home. Parental comments in response to children's media-related questions are particularly powerful. Educators refer to instances when events converge to make children raise a question as "teachable moments," when they are particularly sensitive to new information. Because such questions frequently occur in reaction to media content, to the extent that parents model critical thinking and respond in terms that include how media operate, media literacy training naturally occurs. Effective media literacy programs recognize the importance of helping parents to serve as early-childhood media literacy models, a task with which both schools and media can assist.

## Schools

Clearly, school-based media literacy programs are important. Guided discussion of media moves children beyond perceptual surfaces to more elaborated meaning, teaches them to think critically about information, and prompts the development of perspectives and insights they might not otherwise achieve. Unfortunately, although excellent examples exist, school-based media literacy programs are most notable for their absence. Limits on class time and resources explain part of the absence, but so too does an attitude that media literacy is just another frill. Not too many years ago, Senator William Proxmire took the Senate floor to ridicule the idea of "teaching children to watch television," giving a Golden Fleece award to developers of such curricula. And although many teachers claim to discuss media with students, they typically focus on news or other content with direct curriculum relevance: Television's *Roots* or interactive gaming's *Oregon Trail* warrant consideration as part of a history lesson, but there continues to be a strong norm against serious discussion of "pop" entertainment content. As the convergence of technologies makes the elements used to differentiate among media and types of content less important, it becomes even more imperative to make media literacy training a cornerstone of our educational system.

## Media

Media, themselves, need to assist parents and schools in developing media literate children. Media can provide resources to facilitate media literacy training, participating in the development and production of materials that explain how and why media operate and how intelligent consumers should approach them. They can establish forums at which media-related issues can be discussed. They can develop and distribute content that directly provides media literacy information.

Perhaps the most important action media could take would be to provide parents (and children) with basic information necessary for them to make informed media choices by introducing a universal system of content labeling. A debate is under way in many countries over whether and how to implement some kind of content labeling system for movies, television, video and computer games, and the Internet. Most who advocate content labeling view it as an informational strategy, a way to help parents make decisions about media content. Those who oppose the idea—in the United States, mostly representatives of the media industry and the American Civil Liberties Union—brand it as simply another form of censorship, arguing that establishing criteria necessary to label ultimately will have a chilling effect on content creators. Unfortunately, much of the discussion has used the term "rating" rather than "labeling," primarily because several plans offered for television and video games adopt the judgmental model of the existing motion picture rating system. Such rating systems are based on evaluative judgments of what is and is not appropriate for particular children, typically making a specified age the primary or only information provided. Labeling systems avoid such judgments, asking only that content producers describe the kinds and amounts of actions portrayed, much as food labels describe the content of a food package. The idea is that the more information one has, the better the decisions that can be made, a basic tenet of all media literacy training. Some critics claim there is no difference between ratings and labels, and that the distinctions necessary to describe different kinds and levels of content would be almost impossible to implement. However, at least one such informational system (used for computer games and the Internet) is in operation, and evidence continues to mount that parents prefer information to evaluation, and that both parents and children are better served by information than by either judgmental ratings or no advisories at all (Roberts, 1998).

## Coda

Whatever policies and procedures ultimately evolve, it is clear that pressures from parents, educators, and child advocates directed toward media and government are unlikely to subside in the near future. New communication technologies continue to make more information of more kinds available to more children. A substantial portion of available content is highly problematic when it comes to the child audience. Whether it is possible in this day to "protect" children from exposure to such content is questionable. The important issue, then, is whether we can find the means and the will to protect them simultaneously from potential negative effects of such exposure and from the negative effects of censorship.

## References

Bandura, A. (1986). *Social foundations of thought and action: A social cognitive theory.* Englewood Cliffs, NJ: Prentice-Hall.

Blosser, B. J., & Roberts, D. F. (1985). Age differences in children's perceptions of message intent: Responses to TV news, commercials, educational spots, and public service announcements. *Communication Research, 12,* 455–484.

Brown, J. D., Childers, K. W., Bauman, K. E., & Koch, G. G. (1990). The influence of new media and family structure on young adolescents' television and radio use. *Communication Research, 17,* 65–82.

Charters, W. W. (1933). *Motion pictures and youth: A summary.* New York: Macmillan.

Christenson, P. G., & Roberts, D. F. (1983). The role of television in the formation of social attitudes. In M. J. A. Howe (Ed.), *Learning from television: Psychological and educational research* (pp. 79–99). London: Academic Press.

Christenson, P. G., & Roberts, D. F. (1998). *It's not only rock and roll: Popular music in the lives of adolescents.* Cresskill, NJ: Hampton Press.

Clinton, H. R. (1996). *It takes a village and other lessons children teach us.* New York: Simon & Schuster.

Collins, W. A. (1983). Interpretation and inference in children's television viewing. In J. Bryant & D. R. Anderson (Eds.), *Children's understanding of television: Research on attention and comprehension* (pp. 125–150). New York: Academic Press.

Comstock, G. (with Paik, H.). (1991). *Television and the American child.* San Diego, CA: Academic Press.

Dorr, A. (1986). *Television and children: A special medium for a special audience.* Beverly Hills, CA: Sage.

Dorr, A., & Kunkel, D. (Eds.). (1990). Children in a changing media environment [Special issue]. *Communication Research, 17*(1).

Flavell, J. H., Miller, P. H., & Miller, S. A. (1993). *Cognitive Development* (3rd ed.). Englewood Cliffs, NJ: Prentice Hall.

Freedman, J. L. (1984). Effect of television violence on aggressiveness. *Psychological Bulletin, 96,* 227–246.

Greenberg, B. S. (1994). Content trends in media sex. In D. Zillman, J. Bryant, & A. C. Huston (Eds.), *Media, children and the family: Social scientific, psychodynamic, and clinical perspectives* (pp. 165–182). Hillsdale, NJ: Lawrence Erlbaum.

Huesmann, L. R., & Eron, L. D. (Eds.). (1986). *Television and the aggressive child: A cross-national comparison.* Hillsdale, NJ: Lawrence Erlbaum.

Kaiser Family Foundation. (1998). *Parents, children, and the television ratings system: Two Kaiser Family Foundation studies.* Palo Alto, CA: Kaiser Family Foundation.

McGuire, W. J. (1986). The myth of massive media impact: Savagings and salvagings. In G. Comstock (Ed.), *Public communication and behavior,* (Vol. I, pp. 178–207). Orlando, FL: Academic Press.

Nickelodeon. (1998, March). Kids and technology. *Inside Kids, 3.*

Pecora, N. O. (1998). *The business of children's entertainment.* New York: Guilford.

Peterson, R. C., & Thurston, L. L. (1933). *Motion pictures and the social attitudes of children.* New York: Macmillan.

Plato. (trans. 1941). *The republic of Plato.* (F. M. Cornford,trans.). New York: Oxford University Press.

Potter, W. J. (1998). *Media literacy.* Thousand Oaks, CA: Sage.

Reeves, B., & Nass, C. (1996). *The media equation: How people treat computers, television, and new media like real people and places.* Cambridge, UK: Cambridge University Press.

Roberts, D. F. (1998). Media content labeling systems. In R. G. Noll and M. E. Price (Eds.), *A communications cornucopia: Markle Foundation essays on information policy* (pp. 350-375). Washington, DC: Brookings Institution.

Roberts, D. F., Foehr, V. G., Rideout, V. J., & Brodie, M. (1999, November). *Kids & media @ the new millennium*. Menlo Park, CA: Kaiser Family Foundation.

Schramm, W. (1971). The nature of communication between humans. In W. Schramm & D. F. Roberts (Eds.), *The process and effects of mass communication* (pp. 1–53). Urbana: University of Illinois Press.

Schramm, W., Lyle, J., & Parker, E. B. (1961). *Television in the lives of our children*. Stanford, CA: Stanford University Press.

Starker, S. (1989). *Evil influences: Crusades against the mass media*. New Brunswick, NJ: Transaction Press.

Strasburger, V. C. (1995). *Adolescents and the media: Medical and psychological impact*. Thousand Oaks, CA: Sage.

Wartella, E., Heinz, K. E., Aidman, A. J., & Mazzarella, S. R. (1990). Television and beyond: Children's video media in one community. *Communication Research, 17,* 45-64.

Wilson, B. J., Kunkel, D., Linz, D., Potter, J., Donnerstein, E., Smith, S., Blumenthal, E., & Gray, T. (1996). Television violence and its context: University of California, Santa Barbara study. In National Television Violence Study: *Scientific Papers* (pp. 5-268). Studio City, CA: Mediascope.

Wood, M. (2001, January). Teens spend $153 billion in 1999. Teenage Research Unlimited. Retrieved from: http://www.teenresearch.com/PRview. cfm?edit_id=75.

Worth, S., & Gross, L. (1974). Symbolic strategies. *Journal of Communication, 24,* 27–39.

# TWELVE

# Historical Overview of Children and Childhood in the United States in the 20th Century

*Joseph M. Hawes & Kriste Lindenmeyer*

T his chapter is a broad overview of the major developments affecting children and the ideas inherent in the concept of childhood. It seeks to identify major developments in public policy affecting children and broad trends in thinking about children. The focus is on important events—such as the creation of the first juvenile court in Illinois in 1899 and the passage of the Sheppard-Towner Act (designed to promote maternal and child health and reduce infant mortality) in 1921—and on social issues such as child health, child labor, child abuse, and the increase of the scientific study of children. For convenience, the chapter is divided by decades, and the impact on children of major social developments such as the Great Depression or World War II is also included. In addition, the chapter discusses the rise of major social agencies such as the Federal Children's Bureau and the importance of social reform efforts such as those of the Progressive Era (which focused much of its attention on children), the New Deal of the 1930s, and the movement on behalf of children's rights in the 1970s. The chapter concludes with a look at the social improvements in children's lives that happened in the 20th century and an indication of problems remaining.

For the sake of convenience, historians commonly parse the 20th century into decades—with the exception of the first two decades, which by consent are lumped under the heading of the Progressive Era. Although this division by decades is necessarily arbitrary, it does allow for clear periodization and helps thereby to organize material pertaining to the history of childhood and to children's experiences as historical actors in the American story.

The distinction between the history of children and the history of childhood is, like periodization, both arbitrary and fuzzy. "Childhood" as a social construction makes no sense if children themselves are not a part of it. Childhood is a matter of attitudes and assumptions, whereas children, despite the tendency to stereotype them or generalize about them, are people, albeit smaller and less powerful people than the adults who attempt to shape and control their lives. Having said this, one of the themes that dominates the history of children and childhood in the 20th century is the tension between these two foci. Childhood certainly has a clear and well-documented history, and the history of children is one of interaction with the assumed norms and ideas of childhood. Children have had more influence over the concept of childhood than most historians have realized. At times, children created their own world and made their own rules even as adults strove vigorously to limit their freedom and autonomy. Adults not only sought to control children's lives, they also worked to improve those lives in a variety of ways. Thus, the history of children and childhood in the 20th century is a history of increasing complexity. Children gain more control over their own lives even as adults find new ways to impose their wills on the youngest citizens.

During the 20th century, the percentage of children in the population has actually declined. In 1860, 52% Americans were less than 19 years of age. By 1900 this cohort was only 45% of the total and by 1950 only 33%. According to the 1990 census, only 24% of Americans are children. Hence, politicians and reformers have increased their rhetoric about children as a special group in need of social protection as the percentage of young people in the total population has diminished. Adults have become child advocates and child protectors and worked to

- eliminate child labor,
- reform delinquents,
- improve children's health, and
- increase our understanding of children themselves.

They have even tried (with mixed results) to mitigate the effects of poverty and deprivation. And children were very much a part of the history of the 20th century. They attended segregated schools; they died in great numbers as their parents struggled to get ahead in industrial America. Children starved and died during the Great Depression; lost parents and siblings in the great wars of the 20th century; and suffered discrimination because of their race or their ethnicity, gender, physical handicap, or class. Thus, this history is not simply a story of greater and greater triumphs. It is also a story of gains and losses, of persisting discriminations even in the face of improvements.

## The Progressive Era

An age of reform and renewal, the Progressive Era encompasses the years from 1890 to 1920. Most historians regard this rising interest in reform as a response to the excesses of industrial expansion in the late 19th century and the recognition that America's resources were not inexhaustible. Labor unions challenged employers by calling for higher wages and improved working conditions. Reformers wanted to clean up slums, vice districts, and cities generally. They wanted to put an end to child labor and increase school attendance; they wanted playgrounds for city children and a chance for those children to spend some time in the country. They worked to regulate the excesses of business even as they celebrated business accomplishments. The reformers believed that "the American family" was in danger and that knowledge was the key; the more knowledge they brought to bear on an issue, the sooner the issue could be addressed (Cavallo, 1981; Zelizer, 1985).

No one typified the progressive reformer better than Florence Kelley, who served as a factory inspector in Illinois under Governor John Peter Altgeld. Altgeld lost his bid for reelection in 1896 and Kelley, now out of a job, moved to New York, where she became the corresponding secretary of the National Federation of Consumers' Leagues. Her efforts, in conjunction with those of many other reformers, led to the creation of the New York Child Labor Commission. The commission sought, with some success, to pass legislation aimed at the elimination of child labor in New York State. That in turn led to the 1906 creation of the National Child Labor Committee (NCLC), whose purpose was the elimination of child labor through federal legislation.

Kelley and other progressive reformers also sought the improvement of children's lives through other means. In Chicago and Denver, new, informal juvenile courts had appeared, accompanied by the hope that they might address the problems of juvenile crime and child neglect and thereby reduce or eliminate adult crime. The juvenile court idea quickly caught on, and most states had them before the progressive period ended. Between 1899 and 1920, 45 states enacted some form of juvenile court law. Even the exceptions (Connecticut, Maine, and Wyoming) passed special legislation dealing with some of the problems included in juvenile court law. The establishment of juvenile courts formalized and expanded the definition of childhood. In 14 states, the courts' jurisdiction included children 16 years of age and younger; in 13 states through 17 years of age; and in 17 states through 18-year-olds. In Maryland, the juvenile court's authority extended to 18 for girls and 20 for boys. California used 21 for both boys and girls. Overall, the Progressive Era expanded the years of childhood and reinforced the idea that these years were a special period of life with specific needs and protections.

In keeping with new ideas about childhood and growing confidence in the progressive strategy of fact gathering to effect change, Florence Kelley and other reformers advocated the creation of a federal children's bureau to investigate, report, and protect "a right to childhood" (Lindenmeyer, 1997). President Theodore Roosevelt's 1909 White House Conference on the Care of Dependent Children offered a national forum to promote the idea. A tradition followed by successive American presidents during each of the 20th century's decades, the 1909 White House Conference set three overarching themes for 20th-century child welfare policy:

- an emphasis on prevention, government regulation, and scientific investigation as the best means to reform;

- a declaration that poverty is not indicative of immorality; and

- the belief that every child had a right to a "normal home life," narrowly defined as the nuclear family consisting of a full-time, stay-at-home mother and a father acting as the family's sole breadwinner.

Although the White House conference popularized the children's bureau idea, it took three more years for the proposal to navigate through Congress. President William Howard Taft finally signed the act establishing the U.S. Children's Bureau on April 9, 1912. This new agency, for the first time, recognized federal responsibility for the nation's youngest citizens. The act mandated that the Children's Bureau, located within the Department of Commerce and Labor, "investigate and report...upon all matters pertaining to the welfare of children and child life among all classes of our people." In other words, the focus was to be upon the needs of the "whole child" (Lindenmeyer, 1997; Muncy, 1991).

Nonetheless, the agency's initial appropriation of only $25,640 made an extensive program impossible. Consequently, the Children's Bureau's first chief, Julia C. Lathrop, implemented a program of federal, state, and private cooperation that became the blueprint for 20th century U.S. child welfare policy. Her choice of infant mortality for the fledgling bureau's first subject of investigation also highlights Lathrop's political savvy. Despite the fact that many politicians found it difficult to openly oppose efforts to help America's needy children, congressional debates concerning the Children's Bureau's establishment revealed that some critics felt child welfare beyond federal authority and perhaps an invasion of parental rights. Others believed that a federal children's bureau simply duplicated the activities of already existing government agencies. Sensitive to such criticism, Lathrop chose infant mortality as the least controversial issue concerning the "whole child." Building on the popularity of the existing infant health movement, Lathrop noted that no branch of the federal government had investigated the causes and prevention of infant mortality. The U.S. Public Health Service (PHS) recognized infant mortality as a serious problem but had only focused on the connection between contaminated milk and babies' deaths. To the surprise of many, the Children's Bureau estimated that, of the 2.5 million babies born in the United States each year, perhaps 300,000, or approximately one of every eight, died before his or her first birthday. Emphasizing the problem's urgency, the Children's Bureau noted that this rate ranked far behind many other "modern" nations and meant that persons 75 to 84 years of age had a better chance of seeing their next birthday than did newborns. The Children's Bureau enlisted an army of volunteers to implement mandatory birth registration, encourage prenatal and postnatal care, and urged state and local governments to establish public health care for poor mothers and babies (Meckel, 1990).

Indeed, modern America seemed to pose a special threat to children's health. Many Progressive Era child welfare reformers rejected 19th-century beliefs about the inevitability of high death rates among children and instead proclaimed life and health the first right of the child. Rickets, tuberculosis, summer diarrhea, whooping cough, measles, polio, and many other diseases ravaged the nation's children. During World War I, the Children's Bureau and the Women's Committee of the National Council of Defense declared 1918 to be Children's Year, with the stated purpose of stimulating the "civil population [to do] all in its power to protect the children of this nation as a patriotic duty" (Lindenmeyer, 1997, p. 71). As their primary goal, sponsors of Children's Year worked to save the lives of the many children who died from preventable causes each year in the United States. The campaign included a national drive to weigh and measure the nation's children, a recreation drive intended to increase "physical vigor" among children, a hygiene drive urging education in health care and proper nutrition, and a back-to-school drive surreptitiously designed to remove children from the work force. As Children's Bureau physician Anna E. Rude noted, the campaign resulted in the "establishment of standards of prenatal, obstetrical and postnatal care, infant care, examination and supervision through the preschool period, [and] standardized periodic examinations throughout school life" (Lindenmeyer, 1997, p. 73). During the Progressive Era health became a significant aspect of scientific social work.

To many, children working on the nation's streets and in its mines, factories, and mills seemed the greatest threat to child health. As the Children's Bureau worked to reduce infant mortality and improve child health, NCLC continued its campaign to eliminate child labor by hiring Lewis Hine to photograph conditions in the mines, factories, and mills. NCLC had supported the establishment of the Children's Bureau, and after 1916, bureau staffers aided the campaign for a federal law against child labor. The campaign got a boost from the disastrous fire at the Triangle Shirtwaist Company in New York where 140 workers, most of them young women and girls, died. In 1916, Congress passed the Keating-Owen Act (an anti-child-labor law), and enforcement passed to the Children's Bureau. In 1917, the Supreme Court in the case of *Hammer v. Dagenhart* found the Keating-Owen Act unconstitutional. A second effort at federal regulation, the Pomerine Amendment (a tax on goods built with child labor), was struck down by the Supreme Court in 1922 in the case of *Bailey v. Drexel Furniture Co.* Congress did not succeed in passing a constitutionally acceptable child labor law until the Fair Labor Standards Act in 1938 (Felt, 1965; Hawes, 1991; Nasaw, 1985; Trattner, 1970).

## The 1920s: An Age of Standardization

Following Theodore Roosevelt's lead, President Woodrow Wilson called the second White House conference on children's issues for May 5–8, 1919. This meeting further glorified the middle-class family ideal, underscoring the powerful influence of the first White House conference. Above all, those present promoted the development of standards with respect to child welfare, a notion that became the keystone of so-called scientific child welfare efforts. For example, pointing to the successes of Children's Year, 1919 White House conference participants urged passage of a federal program designed to further reduce the nation's high infant mortality rate. The 1921 Sheppard-Towner Maternity and Infancy Act, administered by the U.S. Children's Bureau in cooperation with the states, was the United States' first federal experiment promoting national health care standards for mothers and children. Passed partly to appease an anticipated "women's voting bloc" expected as a result of the ratification of the 19th Amendment in 1920, the educational and diagnostic efforts funded through this seminal legislation reached more than four million American infants and preschool children, as well as 700,000 pregnant women. Although it is difficult to evaluate the direct effect, during the 1920s, the nation's infant mortality rate dropped from 75.6 per 1,000 live births to 67.9. In addition, Sheppard-Towner funds supported the salaries of state public health nurses, subsidized the operation of physician-run diagnostic clinics, paid for the training of midwives in rural areas, and promoted reliance on private physicians as the best means to good health. Whereas Sheppard-Towner established standards and raised public awareness about the importance of good health care, it also generally ignored the social and economic issues behind why so many babies and mothers died. Furthermore, although unintentional, the passage of Sheppard-Towner opened the door for criticism of the Children's Bureau's "whole child" philosophy. Although the effort promoted reliance on private physicians, the American Medical Association (AMA) denounced the Children's Bureau's supervision of Sheppard-Towner and called the effort "socialized medicine." A closer examination, however, reveals that AMA disliked the fact that the Children's Bureau, and not PHS, controlled the program. This criticism, coupled with the fact that the anticipated women's voting bloc never materialized, led Congress to refuse the Sheppard-Towner program's renewal, and it expired in 1929 (Ladd-Taylor, 1986; Lemons, 1973; Meckel, 1990; Muncy, 1991). Furthermore, President Herbert Hoover's association with the American Child Health Association

(ACHA) placed him firmly under the influence of AMA and consequently at odds with the Children's Bureau. Hoover was one of the founders of ACHA, an organization largely controlled by AMA physicians. In addition, Hoover's long-time friend, Secretary of the Interior and chief advisor, Ray Lyman Wilbur, MD, was a past president of the AMA who sought to wrestle all child health programs away from the Children's Bureau to give them to PHS. Such turf wars have continued to plague U.S. child welfare policy throughout the 20th century.

After World War I, the scientific study of children entered an era of great social acceptance and substantial funding from major philanthropic agencies. The focus of "child science" shifted from a concern with "problem children" to an emphasis on the normal child. The emphasis on the scientific study of the child was from the prewar progressive period. This focus gained added support when the nation became aware of the poor mental and physical condition of many young men drafted to serve in the war. The scientific study of children was one way to address that problem.

After the war, the focus on children also led to a national consensus that American youth were out of control and that the expertise of science should be applied to the social problem of juvenile delinquency. The Commonwealth Fund, directed by historian Max Farrand of Yale, established a series of child guidance clinics around the country, and they in turn hired psychiatrists to help them solve the problem of delinquency. But psychiatrists were not interested in delinquency per se, and they were aware of the prewar work of William A. Healy, which had shown that psychiatric disorders played only a small part in the causes of delinquency. Rather quickly, another focus—mental hygiene, a preventative approach to mental illness—replaced the focus of delinquency. As far as most psychiatrists were concerned, preventing mental illness and preventing juvenile delinquency were essentially the same; both were forms of "social psychiatry" and both were incorporated within the scope of a new professional organization, the American Orthopsychiatric Association, founded in 1924, which began the *Journal of Orthopsychiatry* in 1930 (Horn, 1989).

The child guidance clinics, reflecting this shift in interest, changed their emphasis from delinquents and delinquency to problem children and the problems of normal children and thereby changed their clientele from juvenile delinquents to ordinary children with ordinary problems. As the clinics moved in this direction, they became "medicalized," in that they now dealt (frequently through referrals from teachers and physicians) with children's routine emotional and psychological problems.

Like the clinics, the psychologists who were busy developing a science of the normal child saw themselves as functioning like doctors for a sick society. They would develop scientifically based expertise about children and from that derive sound child-rearing advice, which would, if properly applied, lead to profound social improvement. The key figure in this process was Lawrence K. Frank; he was not a scientist, but rather a promoter of the design for the development of child science. He held the purse strings for the growth of such areas as child development research and child psychology, serving as a director for both the Laura Spelman Rockefeller Memorial and the General Education Board of the Rockefeller Foundation (Cravens, 1993; Lasch, 1977).

Child science had three centers in the early 1920s—the Yale Psychology Clinic headed by Dr. Arnold Gesell, the Merrill Palmer School in Detroit, and the Iowa Child Welfare Research Station at the University of Iowa. Frank began sending money to Iowa in 1925, and he aided the development of centers at the University of Minnesota and the University of California, Berkeley. Across the bay at Stanford, the Commonwealth Fund had lent its support to the work of psychologist Lewis Terman, who had begun his project on the genetic study of genius. Meanwhile at Yale, Gesell, who also received some funds via Frank, was busy mapping the growth and development curves of normal infants. Psychologists at Iowa, Berkeley, Minnesota, and the Merrill Palmer School had begun to study the nature of intelligence in children, the basic element in the development of child science.

The goal of child science was standardization, the creation of reliable, scientifically based information that could be used to advise parents about the proper way to bring up healthy, intelligent children so that a repeat of the disappointments of the World War I draft could be avoided.

## The 1930s: Depression and Child Science

The Great Depression dominated American life in the 1930s, but people in the social sciences generally prospered. They were shielded from the effects of the depression because most held jobs with public agencies, and most agencies or educational activities hung onto their professional staff while cutting back everywhere else. Those who worked for institutes, schools, or colleges and universities continued during the 1930s, and the research projects in child science even increased their scope. Indeed, the Roosevelt administration worked with Congress to greatly expand the federal government's role in providing for the social welfare of the nation's citizens. The New Deal (a collective term for the Roosevelt administration's social and economic policies developed during the 1930s) actually created employment opportunities for those working in the social sciences.

The greatest single issue among social scientists during the 1930s was the controversy over the nature of intelligence. The controversy centered on research done at the Iowa Station. Beth Wellman reported that children who had enrolled in the station's nursery school showed a substantial gain in their IQ scores. In additional, psychologist Harold M. Skeels found that orphaned children placed in the state home for mentally retarded women showed significant, even spectacular gains in their IQs. No one knew why the IQ scores had improved, but the speculation was that the nurturing of the adult retarded women had had a positive influence. Such findings, stressing the impact of environmental factors on IQ, were not well-received by established scholars. The leading figure in the field, Lewis Terman of Stanford, along with several of his followers, attacked the Iowa findings, suggesting that the researchers had not followed proper scientific methodology in reaching these findings. The conventional wisdom about IQ died slowly. Findings from the Child Welfare Institute at the University of California, Berkeley, which were made public in 1939, confirmed the Iowa findings, and in the 1970s, research associated with Project Head Start clearly demonstrated that there was a strong environmental influence on IQ, thus confirming the findings of the Iowa Station in the 1930s (Cravens, 1993; Hawes, 1997; Lazar & Darlington, 1982).

If social scientists continued to work during the depression, a great many other Americans did not. In various efforts to address the social consequences of the depression, the New Deal included several programs and legislation that had important impacts on children's lives. The Social Security Act of 1935 included a section on Aid to Dependent Children, written by representatives from the Children's Bureau, which became the basis for government-supported welfare legislation after World War II, and the Fair Labor Standards Act of 1938 became the first permanent federal anti-child-labor law. The National Youth Administration established training programs for young people and set up work-study programs so that impoverished students could remain in high schools and colleges. The Civilian Conservation Corps put young men to work on a variety of socially useful projects and required them to send money home to their families. The Works Progress Administration set up nursery schools (to preserve teaching skills) that proved very popular.

Buoyed by the New Deal's attention to child welfare, the Children's Bureau called on President Franklin Roosevelt to sponsor a fourth White House conference on children. Held in Washington, DC, on January 18–20, 1940, and attended by health professionals, child welfare bureaucrats, and interested academics, the meeting's theme, Children in a Democracy, reflected attitudes held in the years just before United States' entrance into World War II. But specific topics were reminiscent of earlier White House conferences on children: Attendees lauded the establishment of the economic security of children as the primary insurance for America's future; they embraced the middle-class family ideal as the "threshold of democracy" (Lindenmeyer, 1997, p. 203), continued to call for ratification of the 1923 child labor amendment, and lamented juvenile delinquency rates, comparatively high maternal and infant mortality rates, and inadequate access to child health care. Although conference rhetoric was consistent with the past, however, the report also showed new trends in child welfare strategies developed or expanded during the 1930s.

First, the report praised the federal role in New Deal child welfare programs. Second, the Great Depression had revitalized Progressive Era arguments pointing to poverty as a threat to family stability and therefore child welfare. But, unlike the progressives, the meeting noted that poverty was as serious in rural America as in its cities. For example, participants pointed to a 1934 Department of Agriculture study that found of the 620,000 farm dwellings surveyed, 18% were more than 50 years old and very few had modern conveniences such as electricity, running water, and central heating. To deal with such low living standards, conferees suggested the continuation and further expansion of federal housing and home loan programs, a rising minimum wage, laws to safeguard the right to collective bargaining, higher public works spending to create jobs, and expansion of benefits under the Social Security Act. Third, the meeting placed a much greater emphasis on education than earlier White House conferences. And fourth, attendees linked children's emotional health to political rhetoric common to the prewar period and later to the cold war era.

The report argued that the fostering of self-respect and self-reliance, as well as respect for others and a cooperative attitude, were essential to democracy. Responsibility for maintaining the ideal did not fall wholly on the family, but instead also rested upon the community, state, and nation. Further supporting this agenda, the report included discussions about organized religion's proper role in the lives of children as a tool for securing emotional health and a means to encourage conformity to prescribed values. Those attending the meeting, perhaps unconsciously, opened the way for a future emphasis on the emotional rather than simply the economic needs of children (U.S. Children's Bureau, 1940).

## The 1940s: Wartime Politics

The general economic circumstances of Americans were improving at the time of the 1940 White House Conference. Beginning in late 1939, war production on behalf of the allies helped to lower the country's unemployment rate from a high of 25% during the worst years of the Great Depression to 14% by December 1941. Furthermore, the United States' entrance into the war after the Japanese attack at Pearl Harbor on December 7 quickly moved the nation to full employment. Wages rose, and American workers saved 25% of their disposable income from 1941 to 1945—an unprecedented rate at the time and never matched since. But the war highlighted other problems for the nation's children. Housing shortages and the greater mobility of families attracted to war production and military centers left many children in substandard and unhealthy homes. Overcrowding in schools, health centers, and recreation facilities led child welfare advocates to demand greater resources for children during the war. The emotional as well as the physical needs of children became the concern of child welfare policy advocates (Tuttle, 1993).

Among other concerns, many worried that the increasing number of women entering the paid-labor force was detrimental to the emotional and physical health of children. Like most of America, the Children's Bureau continued to reject the idea that mothers with young children should work outside of the home. During the 1930s, only 8% of mothers with children younger than 10 years of age worked for wages.

Beginning in 1934, Congress funded the Works Progress Administration's day nurseries. But this program was primarily a welfare measure designed to furnish jobs for unemployed teachers and other child welfare workers. The program's benefits for working mothers and their children were secondary or even nonexistent. Linking day care to poverty, most child welfare advocates concluded that only those mothers forced to work by economic necessity would put their children into day care.

The Lanham Act enacted in 1940 expanded day care during the war, but even as the wartime labor shortage intensified, the Children's Bureau continued to ignore reality and only reluctantly in 1944 endorsed family day care over institutionalized day care. In addition, the Bureau set 2 1/2 to 3 years of age as the minimum for children sent to group care facilities. Consequently, employed mothers most often avoided the issue by securing the services of a family member or neighbor, or by leaving the child unattended at home, or even in the family car parked in the factory lot. Children left at home were called "latch-key kids" or "eight-hour orphans" by the press (Lindenmeyer, 1997, p. 220). The few existing public day care centers were frequently overcrowded, substandard, and charged high fees. The Census Bureau estimated in 1944 that the 2.75 million mothers working outside of their homes had 4.5 million children under the age of 14. At the wartime employment peak in 1945, however, only 1.6 million children were enrolled in federally subsidized nursery schools and day care centers.

By the end of the war, the Lanham Act expired. Public fears intensified that working mothers neglected their children and thereby contributed to higher juvenile delinquency rates. Reports of "boisterous boys and girls" (Gilbert, 1986, p. 32) and rising instances of runaway children, higher numbers of high school dropouts, and high truancy rates frightened many. Young people also had more money to spend, as many them had found jobs because enforcement of child labor laws was relaxed during the war. Higher youth employment rates led to termination of the Civilian Conservation Corps and the National Youth Administration in 1943. But the hardships of the previous decade were evident. For example, from April 1942 through March 1943, the military rejected approximately 2 of every 100 white and 10 of every 100 black recruits due to "educational deficiency" (Lindenmeyer, 1997, p. 234). The negative social effects of the Great Depression and the war that followed reversed many earlier gains in education and child labor reform.

The federal government's most significant program impacting child welfare during the war was actually an effort designed to improve morale in the military. The Emergency Maternal and Infant Care Program (EMIC) expanded the Social Security Act's Title V maternal and infant health care provisions. Administered by the Children's Bureau, one of every seven babies born in the United States during the war years and demobilization was a "government baby." By late 1940, it became clear that enlisted men's salaries were inadequate to pay for up-to-date prenatal, delivery, and postnatal care for military wives. In addition, private charities were generally inadequate or absent for military personnel. Army and Navy commanders noted that this circumstance led to low morale. In response, Congress appropriated $130 million for EMIC from 1943 through demobilization in 1949. The program raised hospital standards; encouraged pregnant women to seek prenatal, delivery, and postnatal care from physicians; and gave many Americans their first experience with health insurance. Although EMIC was the most extensive maternal and infant care program to date, it had several fundamental limitations. Remarkably, even women contributing to the war effort as wives of defense workers, those employed in defense industries, those enlisted in the military, and unmarried mothers whose babies were fathered by men in the military were not eligible. EMIC was strictly a military measure instituted solely to improve the morale of men in the military (Lindenmeyer, 1997; Sinai & Anderson, 1948). Clearly, the Children's Bureau hoped that this would be a model for a postwar national maternal and infant health care program. The AMA and private insurance companies convinced Congress, however, that this was another version of socialized medicine, and the program ended amid cold war rhetoric. Overall, the war years focused attention on several children's issues, but resulted in no significant shifts in federal child welfare policy.

## The 1950s: The Age of Conformity

The booming wartime economy and financial successes of the postwar years provided a smoke screen camouflaging the poverty of many children and their families. For most Americans, economic hardship seemed a thing of the past. Consequently, in an age consumed with cold war rhetoric, child welfare policies emphasized conformity and anticommunism. By 1950, EMIC had ended, but wartime concerns about the rising delinquency rates and moral decline lingered.

As part of an overall effort to examine crime and possible links to communism, Senator Estes Kefauver of Tennessee held a series of hearings on delinquency and its causes. The Kefauver subcommittee heard testimony that linked comic books, movies, and television with delinquency. Although the committee reached no firm conclusions, calling instead in the time-honored tradition for more study, the hearings did arouse public concern that stimulated the development of a code for comic book publishers modeled on the motion picture code, which had been in place for that industry since the 1930s (Gilbert, 1986).

Perhaps the true cause of social concern about young people in the 1950s was the effort to create a single national model of family life based on an idealized nuclear family, a family with a successful bread-winning father and a subservient, stay-at-home mother and several conforming, complacent children. The model had existed since the Progressive Era, but became a symbol of capitalist success and anticommunist rhetoric in the cold war years. Between 1890 and 1940, only about 45% of Americans owned their own homes. By 1960 the rate had risen to 62%. The model was nothing new but became a reality for a majority of Americans for the first time in the postwar years. Promoters linked home ownership with anticommunism and what many believed to be America's moral superiority. William Leavitt put it this way in 1948, "No man who owns his house and lot can be a Communist. He has too much to do" (Rosenberg, 1992, p.142). Such families resided in the expanding suburbs around most American cities and there lived the good life as the husband/father climbed the ladder of success. There was just enough truth in this rosy picture to make most Americans believe that it was what life should have been for everyone; it certainly was the image of the typical, middle-class, suburban American family presented on television shows like "Ozzie and Harriet."

Youthful resistance to the powerful cultural directives of the 1950s seemed to be a serious social problem, but when compared with the more explosive 1960s, the 1950s look bland and conformist. Yet, during the 1950s, the Civil Rights crusade was gaining strength, and it was children who lived through the realities of school desegregation. Postwar optimism may have added to the Civil Rights movement's success. Americans wanted to believe, though, that they could secure an endlessly prosperous and expanding future for their children if the children would only buckle down and do what they were told. The 1950s were the last period when self-appointed experts could talk about a single, undifferentiated America, and even in that decade, the Civil Rights movement challenged the naiveté and arrogance of that view. Later, American pluralism could no longer be ignored, even among children (May, 1988).

## The 1960s: The Great Society

Michael Harrington's 1962 book, *The Other America,* estimated that 25% of Americans were not benefiting from the postwar era's prosperity. Partly in response to Harrington, Lyndon Johnson supported a number of landmark domestic measures—the Civil Rights Act of 1964, the Voting Rights Act of 1965, and the beginning of a national "war" on poverty. A keystone of the war on poverty was Project Head Start, a program designed to overcome the economic and cultural disadvantages poor children brought to school with them. The basic idea for Head Start was that disadvantaged children should be given compensatory education so that they could catch up with their more fortunate schoolmates. The idea that IQ scores could be boosted—a proposition first promoted nationally by researchers at the Iowa Child Welfare Research Station in the 1930s and later supported by psychologists at the University of California, Berkeley—lay at the center of Project Head Start, but the program included many nonacademic aspects such as health education, nutrition, and social competence. Head Start proved very popular and survived efforts by Presidents Richard Nixon and Ronald Reagan to scale it back. Studies of students enrolled in Head Start supported the earlier Iowa findings; with high-quality intervention, IQ and life chances could be improved (Lazar & Darlington, 1982; Zigler & Valentine, 1979).

Although Head Start is something of an exception, many of the other Great Society efforts impacting America's children were fashioned after New Deal programs. For example, during the New Deal years, the Federal Housing Authority offered low-cost, low-interest loans to encourage private home ownership. Beginning in 1944, the GI Bill of Rights further expanded this effort through Veteran's Administration loans. But many blacks, Appalachian whites, and Latinos found that discriminatory real estate and home mortgage practices kept them from taking advantage of such programs. Also contributing to the inequity problem, the New Deal had subsidized "slum clearance" and the construction of high-rise "projects" to house the urban poor. The postwar boom further worsened the concentration of poor black, Latino, and Appalachian whites and their children in the nation's cities as many middle-class whites fled to the rapidly growing suburbs. As a consequence, by 1967, more than 400,000 housing units had been torn down in city neighborhoods, whereas only 41,000 new units of federally subsidized individual houses had been built. The postwar fascination with private home ownership as a means to secure democracy did not apply to the urban poor.

In 1968, President Johnson addressed the problem in a special message to Congress, "The Crisis of the Cities." Looking to the New Deal's earlier model, Johnson asked for money to fund the construction of new housing units that would result in not only rental units, but also home ownership for 100,000 poor families. The program appealed to the old Progressive Era notion that a better environment would best benefit America's poor children. It was also a response to the growing demands for equal economic opportunity by civil rights activists such as Dr. Martin Luther King, Jr. Supporters of Johnson's Demonstration Cities Program (or what later became known as Model Cities) argued that the plan would help to eliminate the "disease, despair, joblessness and hopelessness, excessive dependence on welfare and the threats of crime, disorder, and delinquency" in America's cities. More important, such efforts would address the "culture of poverty" many believed existed among America's poor children.

The 1960s also saw renewed interest in preventing child abuse. Concern about the welfare of children has been a part of American public discourse since the colonial period, but like other social concerns, interest waxed and waned. The emergence in the 1960s of a new sensitivity to child abuse can be traced to the work of a pediatrician, C. Henry Kempe, who published a paper in 1961 on what he called "the battered child syndrome." In an article published in the *Journal of the American Medical Association*, Kempe (1961) and his associates described the syndrome and noted that "a marked discrepancy between clinical findings and historical data as supplied by the parents" (p. 17) was one of the key criteria for diagnosis. The media took up the syndrome and gave it national publicity, which in turn led to revised legislation requiring individuals to report cases of suspected child abuse. In 1973, under the sponsorship of Senator Walter Mondale of Minnesota, Congress passed the Child Abuse and Prevention Act, which was designed to improve the responses of state welfare agencies to cases of suspected child abuse (Gil, 1970; Gordon, 1988; Pleck, 1987).

The Job Corps was another of the Johnson War on Poverty programs emphasizing cultural change and environmental factors for improving the circumstances of America's children. Established under Title I of the Economic Opportunity Act, Job Corps was intended to provide vocational and social training as well as offer new life experiences for adolescents from poor rural and urban areas. The postwar economy demanded skilled workers. By the 1960s, the majority of Americans graduated from high school for the first time in our nation's history, but there were more poorly trained young people who could not find work than the program could accommodate. In addition, there were problems with recruits who had never before been away from home and were sent from rural areas to live in cities and vice versa. The underlying racial and ethnic prejudices present in American society did not escape Job Corps centers. Adolescents enrolled in the programs quarreled among themselves, and many communities complained of the rowdy and promiscuous behavior of recruits. Although modeled on the New Deal's Civilian Conservation Corps and lasting 20 years, the Jobs Corps was largely a failure, as few of the graduates found anything other than low-paying, dead-end jobs.

Other efforts had more mixed results. During the 1960s, Congress expanded the Social Security Act's Aid to Dependent Children program (renamed Aid to Families with Dependent Children [AFDC]) and removed the "morality tests." The "tests" eliminated benefits if there was any evidence that a family on AFDC had a relationship with an able-bodied male. The clause denied funding to most blacks and members of other ethnic minorities (Mink, 1995). The federal government also instituted the Supplemental Food Program for Women, Infants and Children (WIC) providing federal funds for milk, cereal, and other nutritious products for pregnant poor women and infants (Unger, 1996).

Although they were always controversial, programs such Head Start, WIC, and other parts of the War on Poverty enjoyed strong public support. Together with the publicity about child abuse, this support reflected a renewed national interest in children and childhood in the 1970s, and at this time a number of advocates for the rights of children appeared. These advocates fell into two groups—the protectionists who placed themselves in the *in loco parentis* role and the liberationists who thought that children should have the same rights as adults.

Probably the two best-known child liberationists were Richard Farson and John Holt. Farson argued that children needed the right to participate in society given the expanding role of institutions in children's lives. Holt questioned the very basis of the social construction of childhood, writing "the fact of being a 'child,' of being wholly subservient and dependent, of being seen by older people as a mixture of expensive nuisance, slave, and super pet, does most young people more harm than good" (Holt, 1974, pp.1–2). Both Holt and Farson argued for granting adult rights to children, including the right to equal treatment by the law and the right to vote (Farson, 1974; Holt, 1974).

Child protectionists were not willing to go quite as far as the liberationists, and they saw children's rights as claims on the larger society, not as entitlements to full citizenship. Farson and Holt believed that children should be empowered to be their own advocates, whereas the protectionists saw themselves as speaking out on behalf of children and their needs. The best known of contemporary child advocates is Marian Wright Edelman of the Children's Defense Fund, an agency modeled on the National Association for the Advancement of Colored People. The Children's Defense Fund focuses on the needs of retarded and handicapped children, on reform of the juvenile justice system, on child development and on the need for high quality day care and welfare programs (Edelman, 1992; Interview with Marian Wright Edelman, 1974).

As the end of the 20th century approached, conservatives began to attack some of the social programs of the New Deal and the Great Society; they argued that federal social programs undermined family values, promoted illegitimacy, and wasted taxpayers' money. Behind these attacks was a distorted view of the history of American families, an assumption that the quiet domestic life of millions of Americans in the 1950s represented the restoration of traditional American family life after the tumultuous decades of the 20th century, which included two world wars and the Great Depression (Murray, 1982). But the 1950s were a departure from history and a break with many long-term trends. Birth rates, which had been declining since the end of the 18th century, increased in that decade, creating the well-known baby boom. What made this possible was the unique nature of the period as the nation enjoyed enormous material prosperity that in turn provided cheap energy, government subsidized home loans, and steady employment. So people married early and had more children. Yet a number of Americans did not share in this prosperity. Nearly 25% of all Americans lived below the poverty level, including more than half of all older Americans. People of color also did not share in this prosperity, being confined to ghettoes and inferior schools by legal and de facto segregation.

## From the 1980s to the End of the Century

In the late 20th century, many conservatives, long disturbed by the rebellion of young people in the 1960s and 1970s, believed that more emphasis on sexual abstinence would return American society to the Eden of the 1950s. But a closer look at that decade reveals that the incidence of extramarital sex had already begun to increase in the years immediately following World War II. Furthermore, teenage pregnancy and motherhood was much more common in the 1950s—the rate was 97 out of 1,000 girls aged 15–19 in 1957—than in the 1980s (in 1983 the rate was 52 of every 1,000 girls). It is difficult to determine how many of the births in the 1950s were illegitimate, though the continued activity of agencies such as the Florence Crittenton Homes (which encouraged mothers of illegitimate children to put their babies up for adoption) suggests that many of the births were out of wedlock. Nevertheless, there is clear evidence that the highest rates of adolescent pregnancy in the history of the United States occurred in the 1950s and 1960s. In some respects, despite popular perceptions to the contrary, teen pregnancy rates since 1970 are more in keeping with the trends of the 1920s than the 1950s and 1960s. The difference is that since 1970, early marriages, so common in the early post-World War II years, are no longer advocated as the ideal. Consequently, many young mothers no longer give their babies up for adoption or quickly marry.

On December 22, 1987, in the midst of the growing controversy over federal responsibility for child welfare, President George Bush and Congress jointly created the National Commission on Children (NCC). Headed by Senator John D. Rockefeller (D-WV), the 32 members of the commission were mandated "to serve as a forum on behalf of the children of the Nation" (NCC, 1991, p. viii). The commission's final report, published on May 1, 1991, showed that although tremendous strides have been made in reducing the nation's infant mortality and improving child health, one of every five children is poor; many often fall below their peers in other countries when tested in math, reading, and science; and many others live in violent or exploitative circumstances.

The commission report cited several demographic changes it believed intensified the need to "invest in America's children" (NCC, 1991, p. viii). Perhaps the most dramatic change has been the increase in mothers working for wages outside of their homes. In 1990, 58% of mothers with children under age 6 reported that they were working or looking for work outside their homes. Mothers of school-age children were even more likely to be in the paid-labor force, with more than 74% of women whose youngest child was between 6 and 13 working for wages. Another important shift is the rise in the proportion of children living in single-parent households. In 1970 about 12% of children lived with only one parent, but by 1990 nearly 25% did. The nation's rising divorce rate is the largest factor contributing to this shift. But there has also been a significant increase in the number of births outside marriage. In 1960, only 5% of all births occurred to unmarried mothers. In 1990 almost 25% of all children were born to unmarried women. In addition, although the adolescent pregnancy rate has actually declined since the 1950s, in 1990 almost 40% of white babies and 90% of black infants born to females under 20 years of age had unmarried mothers. Indeed, the growing discontent with federal welfare programs often rests on the increase of unmarried AFDC recipients. But, as many scholars have shown, this negative sentiment expressed toward unmarried mothers is nothing new (Gordon, 1994).

The most controversial portion of the 1991 NCC report was its set of recommendations for improving health care for America's youngest citizens. Unable to agree on a final recommendation, the report includes two reports on health. Among other recommendations, the majority report calls for a universal health insurance system for pregnant women and children through age 18. The minority report instead describes a "public-private partnership" (NCC, 1991, p. 160) promoting "innovation, [which would] not adversely affect economic growth and stability, and promote the delivery of high-quality, cost-effective care" (NCC, 1991, p. 160). Both prescriptions include rhetoric familiar to those reviewing the debates over Sheppard-Towner and other proposals for national health insurance in the past.

Ultimately, the commission called for the "strengthening and supporting of families" (NCC, 1991, p. xxix). This, concludes the report, involves a better coordination of child and family policies, expansion of child welfare efforts on the federal level, uniform eligibility criteria, a streamlining of application processes, incentives to encourage demonstration projects at the state and local level, and a substantial increase in salaries for those working in child welfare and education. Using language reminiscent of Florence Kelley and other Progressive Era reformers, commission participants cautioned that "investing in children is no longer a luxury—or even a choice. It is a national imperative as compelling as an armed attack or a natural disaster" (NCC, 1991, p. xxxvii).

The decade of the 1990s saw conservatives win a greater number of elections and a move in the direction of drastically reducing government programs for children and youth, except those that exhort abstinence. Most notable among the conservative reforms has been the abandonment of AFDC in the Personal Responsibility and Work Opportunity Reconciliation Act of 1996 [P.L. 104-193]. As the law notes, "effective October 1, 1996, no individual or family is entitled by federal law to receive welfare help." Among other provisions, the law also places a five-year lifetime limit on aid, mandates that minor parents receiving aid must live with their parents or in another adult-supervised setting, requires minor parents receiving aid to attend high school or an alternative education or training program, and imposes work requirements in combination with child care subsidies for adult recipients (an abandonment of the earlier notion that even poor mothers should remain within the home to care for young children). The law also implements stricter enforcement of child support laws. As this is written, the implications of this welfare reform are still to be determined. What will happen to poor and disadvantaged children under the new law is still to be learned. If prosperity continues, many children will escape the unfortunate effects of poverty. If hard times return, the effects of this law could be drastic.

## Conclusion

At the beginning of the 21st century, we find the notion that the last century was the Century of the Child, as announced with great hope by reformers at the century's beginning, not fully sustained. The early part of the last century saw a new social emphasis on childhood and a new concern for America's young citizens, a concern that led to a number of efforts on behalf of children, but those efforts achieved only partial success. Today, the United States still lags behind other advanced industrialized nations because its infant mortality rates are high and because these rates for African Americans are higher than in many so-called third world countries. In 1990, the infant mortality rate was 9.1 deaths per 1,000 live births. But black babies died at more than twice the rate of whites (in 1990, the rate for African Americans was 16.9, whereas that for whites was 7.3), and the overall U.S. rate placed it 21st among industrialized countries. These data can be seen both as a national scandal and as indicators of great progress. In 1915, for example, the infant mortality rate for the United States as a whole was 99.9 deaths per 1,000 live births. For whites the ratio was 98.0 and for African Americans a stunning 181.2 (National Center for Education Statistics, 1993, p. 209). There are other indicators of progress. In 1900, for example, 72.4% of children aged 5–17 were enrolled in school. In that same year there were about 95,000 high school graduates, or about 6.4% of the population of 17-year-olds in the country. By 1990, 95.8% of the population aged 14–17 were in school, and by that same year 85.7% of Americans aged 25–29 had completed high school (National Center for Education Statistics, 1993, p. 209). At the end of the century, a smaller proportion of children lived in poverty than was the case at the beginning. These numbers do not tell the whole story, however. In 1920, for example, the divorce rate was 1.6 per 1,000 population; by 1988 the rate was 20.7 per 1,000 population (National Center for Education Statistics, 1993, pp. 58, 64). In 1900, the birthrate was 32.3 per 1,000 population and in 1910 the rate per 1,000 women aged 15–44 was 126.8. In 1950 (during the baby boom), the birth rate for women aged 15–44 was 106.2. By 1990 that rate had declined to 70.9. Among women aged 15–19, the birth rate in 1950 was 81.6 per 1,000 women of that age range. In 1990 the rate had declined to 59.9, clear evidence of the declining rate of teenage pregnancies (U.S. Census Bureau, 1995, p. 75). As noted at the beginning of this chapter, children now constitute a smaller percentage of the total population.

Taken together, these numbers indicate that children's lives have improved in a number of ways. They are more likely to survive infancy and attend and complete school than previous generations. Child labor, once commonplace in American society, has declined substantially. (This is not to say that children do not work for wages, but that very few children under the age of 16 are legally employed.) In countless other ways, children's lives are different from the lives of children in 1900. At the beginning of the 20th century, many children were likely to experience the death of family members: grandparents, parents, and siblings. Today, the death of even grandparents is a rare experience for children (Uhlenberg, 1985). More children today will have experienced the divorce of their parents than had the children of the earlier period, but the break-up of families happened in the early 20th century as well. Death broke up many families, and the desertion of families by fathers (without the benefit of divorce) was a common occurrence.

So the century can be seen as one characterized by many advances in science, including the science of the child; in medicine, which saw a dramatic drop in infant mortality; and in attitudes, as children were freed from the need to labor in mines and factories and as they were supposed to be freed from abuse and neglect. Still, children die (many now from gunshots and automobile accidents rather than epidemic diseases) and are abused (how many we may never know) and neglected or abandoned or grow up in chaotic or broken homes. At the beginning of the century, social compassion for the incapacity of children was on the rise; at the end of the century, compassion and concern for children seem to be in retreat. So long as good economic conditions persist, perhaps national social concerns are unnecessary. If the economy falters, the dismantling of the safety nets for children and their families in the 1990s may prove to have been unwise.

# References

Cavallo, D. (1981). *Muscles and morals: Organized playgrounds and urban reform, 1880-1920.* Philadelphia: University of Pennsylvania Press.

Cravens, H. (1993). *Before Head Start: The Iowa station & America's children.* Chapel Hill: University of North Carolina Press.

Edelman, M. W. (1992). *The measure of our success: A letter to my children and yours.* Boston: Beacon Press.

Farson, R. (1974). *Birthrights.* New York: Macmillan.

Felt, J. (1965). *Hostages of fortune: Child labor reform in New York state.* Syracuse, NY: Syracuse University Press.

Gil, D. (1970). *Violence against children: Physical child abuse in the United States.* Cambridge, MA: Harvard University Press.

Gilbert, J. (1986). *A cycle of outrage: America's reaction to the juvenile delinquent in the 1950s.* New York: Oxford University Press.

Gordon, L. (1988). *Heroes of their own lives: The politics and history of family violence in Boston, 1880-1960.* New York: Viking.

Gordon, L. (1994). *Pitied but not entitled: Single mothers and the history of welfare.* New York: Free Press.

Harrington, M. (1962). *The other America: Poverty in the United States.* New York: Holt, Rhinehart, and Winston.

Hawes, J. M. (1991). *The children's rights movement: A history of advocacy and protection.* Boston: Twayne.

Hawes, J. M. (1997). *Children between the wars, American childhood, 1920-1940.* New York: Twayne.

Holt, J. (1974). *Escape from childhood.* New York: Ballantine Books.

Horn, M. (1989). *Before it's too late: The child guidance movement in the United States, 1922-1945.* Philadelphia: Temple University Press.

Interview with Marian Wright Edelman. (1974). *Harvard Educational Review, 44,* 53-54.

Kempe, C. H. (1961). The battered child syndrome. *Journal of the American Medical Association, 181,* 17–19, 20–21, 23–24.

Ladd-Taylor, M. (1986). *Raising babies the government way: Mothers' letters to the Children's Bureau, 1915–1932.* New Brunswick, NJ: Rutgers University Press.

Lasch, C. (1977). *Haven in a heartless world: The family besieged.* New York: Basic Books.

Lazar, I., & Darlington, R. (Eds.). (1982). Lasting effects of early education: A report from the Consortium for Longitudinal Studies. *Monographs of the Society for Research in Child Development, 47,* 2–3.

Lemons, J. S. (1973). *Woman citizen: Social feminism in the 1920s.* Urbana: University of Illinois Press.

Lindenmeyer, K. (1997). *"A right to childhood": The U.S. Children's Bureau and child welfare, 1912-1946.* Urbana: University of Illinois Press.

May, E. T. (1988). *Homeward bound: American families in the cold war era.* New York: Basic Books.

Meckel, R. A. (1990). *Save the babies: American public health reform and the prevention of infant mortality, 1850-1930.* Baltimore: Johns Hopkins University Press.

Mink, G. (1995). *The wages of motherhood: Inequality in the welfare state, 1917-1942.* Ithaca, NY: Cornell University Press.

Muncy, R. (1991). *Creating a female dominion in American reform, 1890-1935.* New York: Oxford University Press.

Murray, C. A. (1982). *Safety nets and the truly needy: Rethinking the social welfare system.* Washington, DC: Heritage Foundation.

Nasaw, D. (1985). *Children of the city at work and at play.* Garden City, NY: Anchor Doubleday.

National Center for Education Statistics. (1993). *Youth Indicators 1993—Trends in the well-being of American youth.* Washington, DC: U.S. Government Printing Office.

National Commission on Children. (1991). *Beyond rhetoric: A new American agenda for children and families.* Washington, DC: U.S. Government Printing Office.

Pleck, E. (1987). *Domestic tyranny: The making of social policy against family violence from colonial times to the present.* New York: Oxford University Press.

Rosenberg, R. (1992). *Divided lives: American women in the twentieth century.* New York: Hill and Wang.

Sinai, N., & Anderson, O. (1948). *EMIC: A study of administrative experience.* (Bureau of Public Health and Economics, Research Series No. 3). Ann Arbor: School of Public Health, University of Michigan.

Trattner, W. (1970). *Crusade for the children: A history of the National Child Labor Committee and child labor reform in America.* Chicago: Quadrangle Books.

Tuttle, W. M., Jr. (1993). *Daddy's gone to war: The Second World War in the lives of America's children.* New York: Oxford University Press.

Uhlenberg, P. (1985). Death and the family. In N. Hiner & J. Hawes (Eds.), *Growing up in America: Children in historical perspective.* Urbana: University of Illinois Press.

Unger, I. (1996). *The best of intentions: The triumphs and failures of the Great Society under Kennedy, Johnson, and Nixon.* New York: Doubleday.

U.S. Census Bureau. (1995). *Statistical abstract of the United States.* Washington, DC: U.S. Government Printing Office. Available from http://www.census.gov/ prod/www/statistical-abstract-us.html

U.S. Children's Bureau. (1940). *Proceedings of the 1940 White House Conference on Children in a Democracy* (U.S. Children's Bureau Publication No. 266). Washington, DC: U.S. Government Printing Office.

Zelizer, V. (1985). *Pricing the priceless child: The changing social value of children.* New York: Basic Books.

Zigler, E., & Valentine, J. (Eds.). (1979). *Project Head Start: A legacy of the war on poverty.* New York: Free Press.

# THIRTEEN

# Policy Trends Affecting Children and Youth

*Brian L. Wilcox & Charles Barone*

"It was the best of times, it was the worst of times." Dickens' words could have been written about the well-being of America's children and youth in the latter part of the 20th century. The preceding chapters in this volume attest to the varied trends in the well-being of children and youth. Some indicators of well-being denote the tremendous strides that have been made over the past few decades, whereas other indicators suggest that little progress has been made in improving the welfare of children and youth. Many of the indicators reported in this volume paint a mixed picture: Often a step forward is followed by a step back. The most encouraging aspect of this volume from a policy perspective is that, over the past few decades, the amount and quality of indicator data available to help policymakers assess the well-being of America's children and youth has increased markedly. Although significant gaps in our ability to characterize the health and well-being of children and youth remain, we have a much better picture of the important trends than we did in 1980.

This chapter will summarize some of the important trends in the public policy arena that are affecting children and youth. We do not intend to describe changes taking place in each of the many policy domains, such as child care, public welfare, child welfare, and so forth, that affect the lives of children. Instead, we will look at much broader trends shaping the policymaking process, along with the policies themselves, that in turn affect the well-being of children and youth. We will look briefly at how these trends play out in particular policy debates, such as welfare reform, but our intent is to elucidate the broader trends shaping child and family policy rather than specific policies.

## Demography and Public Policy

To paraphrase Freud, demography is destiny, and there are many demographic trends that affect the U.S. policymaking context, but none more than the age

structure of our population. More specifically, the aging of the baby boom generation and the baby boom echo are two trends that hold enormous import for
the future of policies affecting children and youth. This latter group—the children of the baby boomers—has resulted in a new population bulge that has, in
turn, resulted in a new national record in school enrollment (51.7 million,
breaking the 24-year-old mark of 51.3 million). Despite this bulge, youth represent a declining proportion of the nation's population. Consequently, before
this cohort reaches adulthood, there will be a significant decline in the ratio of
wage earners to retirees as members of the baby boom generation retire in large
numbers. This ratio (wage earners to retirees) is expected to reach its low point,
2.6:1, in 2030. Although the changing age structure raises interesting political
questions, such as whether the retired baby boomers will support public
spending for the children of the baby boom echo, the clearest public policy
dilemma stems from the fact that working young adults will be hard-pressed to
generate the revenues needed to support existing entitlement obligations to the
elderly, such as Social Security and Medicare. The implications of the fiscal
pressures created by this situation are described below.

## Budget Policy as Social Policy: Effects of a Changing Fiscal Climate

It is an axiom among those who study the making of social policy that understanding policy means understanding the flow of funding. Dollars drive policy.
Stated more bluntly, budget policy is social policy. Less knowledgeable
observers of the policy process tend to focus on the passage of legislation as the
end point of this process, but it is not uncommon for legislative bodies, both
federal and state, to pass legislation only to let it die of starvation. Many a program has been authorized but never funded, or funded at a level that does not
permit adequate implementation of the program. The child and family policy
arena is replete with such examples. Funding shortfalls hamper the reach and
effectiveness of Head Start; the Supplemental Food Program for Women,
Infants, and Children (WIC) nutrition program; the Title X family planning
program; and the Title IV-B child welfare programs, just to mention a few.

The current fiscal climate is unique in the challenges it presents to policymakers. Heclo (1996) has provided a succinct analysis of three broad factors
precipitating the fiscal dilemma that will confront federal (and to a lesser
extent, state) policymakers over the next few decades. First, old sources of "fiscal slack" have dried up, making it far more difficult for policymakers to find
revenue for new social programs or for the expansion of existing ones. The so-
called peace dividend resulting from the end of the cold war had already disappeared by the end of the last century as defense spending fell to its lowest
level (as a percentage of total federal spending) since 1950. Despite the "hot

economy" of the mid-1990s, slowed economic growth since 1973 has reduced the growth rate in the public's incomes, resulting in a decrease in the number of people moving into higher income tax brackets and thereby reducing feder- al revenue growth. Finally, the 1981 legislation, which indexed tax brackets to inflation, means that increases in income below the rate of inflation no longer push one into a higher tax bracket. This "bracket creep," which was once a steady source of rising federal revenues, is now a thing of the past and a major reason for the decline in fiscal slack.

Second, deficits racked up over the past two decades, along with policy decisions obligating federal funds in future years, have placed strains on pres- ent and future spending choices. Although federal policymakers were able to balance the budget in 1997 and 1998, the prior-year deficits and resulting debt, which grew most rapidly during the 1980s, require that a growing portion of federal revenues be devoted to interest payments on the national debt. These interest payment obligations became the fastest growing portion of the federal budget in the late 1980s and utilized dollars that might formerly have been spent on various discretionary programs, including social programs serving children and youth. In addition to the growing interest payments on the debt, increasing middle-class entitlement spending has put tremendous pressures on the federal budget. By the mid-1990s, federal spending for retirement, disabil- ity, and health benefits alone equaled approximately 55% of federal revenues. The growth in entitlement spending, particularly for the most broad-based enti- tlement programs, has already forced significant reductions in other budget cat- egories, and especially in the nondefense discretionary category that includes most programs for children and youth.

Finally, Heclo (1996) notes that the worst news is yet to come. As men- tioned above, over the next few decades, the baby boom generation will enter retirement in enormous numbers. The various entitlement benefits due them will begin to be claimed, particularly Social Security and Medicare. Entitlement spending will expand rapidly and tax revenues will drop proportionately due to the smaller cohort of wage earners following the baby boomers. In the absence of changes in the tax rate or the entitlement benefits themselves, these benefits will consume more than 100% of federal revenues.

The federal budgetary crisis has already had significant effects on social spending for children and youth. Not surprisingly, before the end of the twen- tieth century, Congress focused its budget cutting on defense spending and programs serving low-income citizens and immigrants. Most programs that address the needs of children and youth have not received substantial cuts per se, but many have received no increases for many years, and inflation has taken its inexorable toll on these programs. Despite having balanced the budgets in

1997 and 1998, Congress will be faced with increasing pressures on the budget unless dramatic steps are taken to increase federal revenues and reduce entitlement obligations, or both.

It is important to recognize that at the same time, but for somewhat different reasons, many states are experiencing increased budget pressures.
Slowed economic growth over the past two decades has reduced fiscal slack.
Although the economic burst of the mid-1990s alleviated some pressure on
state budgets and actually resulted in many states running surpluses, counter-
vailing pressures to reduce the state and local tax burden on citizens have
negated any flexibility that might have arisen from these circumstances.
Virtually all states are required by law to produce balanced budgets, so running
a deficit when revenue shortfalls occur is not an option for most states.
Although some states have engaged in innovative policymaking benefiting children with the revenue windfalls of the past few years, many states have taken
a cautious stance and assumed that the circumstances giving rise to these windfalls will reverse in short order. The recent perturbations in the global economy are giving policymakers at all levels of government reason to be cautious
when obligating funds into the future.

Given this fiscal climate, it is reasonable to ask whether children fare worse
in the public policy arena than other segments of the population. Do children's
programs fare more poorly than other programs serving adults and the elderly? The answer is complicated; although several good analyses of federal spending on children's programs relative to other priorities exist (Sugarman, 1993;
U.S. House of Representatives, Committee on Ways and Means, 1993), there is
no comprehensive source of data on state spending for children's programs outside of education. In some policy domains, such as health care policy, children
fare somewhat better than adults but not nearly as well as the elderly; generally speaking, however, federal spending on programs for children and youth has
fared less well than that serving the elderly (Gold & Ellwood, 1994).
Considering state spending on children and youth does little to change the picture. The vast majority of state spending on children is for education, and this
level of funding has held relatively constant since 1970. State funding for other
children's programs varies dramatically from state to state, with most of the
funding attributable to welfare, foster care, and Medicaid (Gold et al., 1995).

Why might children fare relatively poorly in federal and state budgets? The
simplest answer is that children and youth lack effective political clout. They
are the one population group entirely dependent on others to advocate for their
interests. This would be less problematic if adults effectively represented the
interests of children and youth, but a recent survey of state legislators suggests
that they are not (State Legislative Leaders Foundation, 1995). In this survey,
state legislators had few positive responses when asked about child and family

advocates. Relative to advocates for other causes and groups, child and family advocates were seen as particularly naive about the policy process in general and effective lobbying methods in particular. Legislative leaders familiar with groups advocating on behalf of children report that these groups generally "lack a coordinated, manageable legislative agenda and well-defined goals" (State Legislative Leaders Foundation, 1995, p. 24). More often, child and youth advocates are invisible to legislators. As one unnamed legislator put it:

> In other areas of policy, there are powerful organized interests and individuals who will judge legislators and will keep them from oscillating so far. Not so much with children's issues. The number of people who walk the halls [in the state capitol] who even know these issues, much less care about them or are willing to advocate for them, is really depressing. (State Legislative Leaders Foundation, 1995, p. 24)

Another legislator, expressing his frustration regarding the naiveté of child advocates, commented, "Children's lobbyists must think I'm stupid. I'm on the Joint Fiscal Committee, but in six years as a leader, they've never come" (p. 30). Our own experiences as psychologists who have worked as legislative staff members are consistent with these characterizations of the representation of children. Among congressional staff, the "children's lobby" has a reputation for being disorganized, fractious, reactive rather than proactive, and relatively ineffectual.

The poor representation of children is compounded by the fact that poor children are especially underrepresented. Changing cultural attitudes, particularly toward the parents of poor and immigrant children, have further diminished the interest of politicians in addressing the concerns of low-income families. This represents a substantial change from the 1970s, when liberals and conservatives alike tended to support need-based programs serving low-income children.

## Public Versus Private Responsibility: Trends in Attitudes Toward the Role of Government

American social policy has always struggled with the fundamental issue of where responsibility for the well-being of children and youth resides. One strand of this debate has involved the degree to which responsibility should be ascribed, respectively, to government at the federal, state, and local levels. A second and more fundamental debate has centered on the role of government vis-à-vis nongovernmental entities, including business, charities, churches, community-based organizations, and, most significantly, families.

This section explores some of the key issues involved in such debates, describes current broad policy trends, and examines the assumptions of these different orientations against existing empirical knowledge and the historical record.

First, some historical context. In the 1960s and 1970s, the federal government assumed a much more active role with regard to social policies affecting children, youth, and families. This era can be characterized as one in which a more centralized approach to social policy predominated, grounded in the belief that a strong federal role was necessary to ensure an equitable distribution of power and resources and to guarantee coherency of U.S. policy for the nation as a whole. The federal role increased significantly in areas of social policy such as school desegregation (e.g., *Brown v. Board of Education*), health care (Medicare, Medicaid), nutrition (food stamps, school lunch, WIC), and the education of children with disabilities (P.L. 92-142), in which states and localities were perceived by many to have been failing until strong and decisive federal action was taken.

Beginning in the 1980s, the pendulum began to swing in the opposite direction, as there arose a combination of interrelated fiscal pressures and a changed political climate that resulted in dramatic changes in the national policy arena. The outcome of these changes is as yet unclear. They undoubtedly have significant implications, however, for policies and programs addressing the needs of children and youth.

In general, current trends can be described as being driven by at least three basic forces:

- *Philosophical.* The belief that social issues, particularly those affecting children, youth, and families, fall more appropriately in the domain of families, private charities, and state and local governments. In this view, government, especially the federal government, has overstepped its rightful reach and should play a lesser role in addressing the social issues affecting children and youth. This description generalizes across individuals such as "federalists," who accept a relatively strong governmental role but believe that power should be shifted from the federal government to states and localities, as well as those, particularly religious conservatives, who want to minimize government involvement at all levels and maximize the sovereignty of the family.

- *Administrative.* The concern that governments in general, and the federal government in particular, are overly bureaucratic and inefficient. Proponents of this position argue that those "closer" to the issues affecting children, youth, and families, such as local governments, private entities, and families themselves, know best what is needed for their particular communities and can operate most effectively and efficiently when unfettered by rules and regulations imposed by a centralized government.

- **Fiscal.** A third set of concerns is grounded in the philosophy and politics of fiscal conservatism. The central thrust here is that the growing cost of social programs has put an undue strain on federal and state budgets, resulting in increased deficits and higher taxes. Reducing the size and scope of government involvement in social policy is believed by these individuals to be a means to shrink the budget deficits, lower taxes, and, in doing so, allow families to address their problems in their own ways.

These broad policy trends, and the degree to which they represent very different approaches to social policy, can be illustrated by experience with two recent pieces of legislation. The first, a major overhaul of federal welfare programs, has been moving forward with increasing momentum over the last several years at the state, local, and, most recently, federal levels. The second, the "parental rights and responsibility" movement, although sounding a populist theme, has thus far been blocked by the U.S. Congress and by voters and legislatures in key states across the nation.

The changes in federal welfare policy represented in the Personal Responsibility and Work Opportunities Act of 1996 embody, to some degree, all of the forces outlined above. The changes were driven in large part by the widely-shared perception that welfare policy had not only been ineffective in reducing welfare rolls, but had actually contributed to the growth of those rolls by fostering dependency on welfare benefits and creating disincentives for recipients to seek and secure employment. State and local governments also complained that myriad federal regulatory and reporting requirements impaired their ability to effectively administer welfare programs in a way that best met the needs of their intended beneficiaries. In response to growing taxpayer resentment about the program's mounting costs, politicians increasingly felt pressure to cut welfare outlays and sought to do so by converting the program from an entitlement, in which funds flow out automatically to states and the end recipients according to the number of the poor and their estimated needs, to a block grant, under which benefits to individuals are time-limited and the allotment to states, which operate the program, would remain frozen regardless of social and economic circumstances. States and localities would also, in theory, be given greater flexibility in administering the program.

In the end, when President Clinton signed the federal welfare reform bill in August 1996, proponents of reduced federal involvement and greater state autonomy generally declared victory. What passed could be construed in the broadest sense as a successful attempt to transfer power from the federal government to state capitals and reduce the fiscal responsibilities of the federal government of ensuring a social safety net. In reality, the law was a patchwork representing greater flexibility in some areas and tighter Washington control in others, but the overall flow of power was seen for the most part as from the federal government to states and localities, and there were clear cost savings dedicated to reducing the federal budget deficit.

In contrast, another campaign designed to reduce the role of government—at all levels, in a wide variety of areas from child protection to education-has stalled at both the state and local level. Legislation generally described as reaffirming parental rights and responsibilities would establish in statute the family as the primary entity responsible for the "upbringing and education" of children. Although at first glance innocuous, the various legislative proposals designed to codify this policy were met with firm resistance from across the political spectrum. This resistance was due to fear that such legislation would undermine state and federal laws designed to

- facilitate government intervention in cases of child abuse and neglect,
- protect the confidentiality and privacy of youth seeking health and social services in clinical settings, and
- balance the interests of parents and the public in the development and administration of school curriculum and instruction.

The failure of the parental rights and responsibilities movement suggests that the public, at least presently, is generally not inclined to support the government's relinquishment of the role it has in protecting the welfare of children and youth. The failure of this movement is in part a repudiation of the more radical position supporting private over public responsibility for children and youth. Although policymakers have shown a willingness to transfer power from the federal to the state and local levels, they are showing greater reluctance to take actions that might prevent governments from assuming responsibility, at some level, for the well-being of children. Similar battles are being waged over such issues as school vouchers and the delivery of other social services with varying levels of success from community to community.

In summary, debates about intergovernmental responsibility, and the respective responsibility of the government and private sector, mirror a host of other issues involving political philosophy and social theory, concerns about program effectiveness and efficiency, and fiscal conservatism. The two examples above both generalize and simplify but connote broad themes. The shift in welfare policy indicates that, at least in some areas, there is a desire for decentralization and a heightened emphasis on the responsibility of individuals vis-à-vis taxpayer-funded programs. However, the outcomes, at least up to the present time, of the parental rights movement signal that there is also a desire to maintain a fundamental governmental role in protecting children and providing basic health services and education.

## Devolution, Deregulation, and Downsizing: The New Policy Environment

Most generally, policy changes in the new zeitgeist can be characterized as being accomplished through three broad mechanisms:

- *Downsizing.* Shrinking the size of government, particularly at the federal level.
- *Devolution.* Granting increased responsibility and decision-making power to the states and localities.
- *Deregulation.* Relaxing oversight and eliminating and simplifying rules for the administration of government programs to allow recipients greater flexibility.

The motivations and goals that drive policy positions on these issues vary across the political spectrum. At one end (which conventionally can be described as conservative) are those who see devolution and deregulation as the first step toward significant federal government downsizing. For these individuals, the ultimate goal is to decrease the federal role fundamentally, not just in terms of administrative or regulatory power, but in terms of the amount of resources the federal government dedicates to such endeavors. The ideal for some would be a very limited federal government with a very circumscribed set of responsibilities in defense and a few other key areas.

At the other extreme are the traditionally liberal forces that steadfastly resist any fundamental change in federal power, and who would indeed like to see an even stronger federal role in many areas. Those who hold this position would point to the conditions that predated federal intervention in various areas in warning that the current move to relinquish federal power over social programs will dilute their effectiveness and redirect resources away from the most needy who are their intended recipients.

At various points in between are those, probably representing prevailing opinion, who recognize the validity of points raised by those at either of the two extreme ends of the spectrum. They generally seek to maintain a federal government role in social policy, but for an array of practical and philosophical reasons, seek to modify it through various combinations of downsizing, deregulation, and devolution. Those in this group vary in how closely they are associated with either pole (liberal or conservative) of the political spectrum. Furthermore, examination of the variety of approaches and the underlying goals and assumptions suggests that there are real limits to a purely linear liberal/conservative characterization.

Thus far, recent efforts to downsize, devolve, and deregulate have met with mixed success. In 1995 to 1996, attempts by the newly elected congressional majority to downsize major programs such as federal student loans, compensatory elementary and secondary education, Medicaid, and Medicare were defeated (the funding for the latter two were reduced in 1997, albeit much more modestly than had been initially proposed). When the 104th Republican Congress adjourned in 1996, two of the three pieces of final legislation it passed actually strengthened the federal regulatory role in health and wage protections. On the other hand, the third piece of legislation, a major welfare overhaul, did generally embody the principles of federal government downsizing, deregulation, and devolution.

## Block Grants: Promises and Pitfalls

The most common vehicle for diminishing the federal role in social policy involves converting current "categorical aid" into what are known as "block grants." Block grants differ from categorical aid, mainly in that grantees have a greater degree of flexibility under block grants. Funds may be spent for a wider variety of purposes and targeted at a broader array of populations. Accordingly, fewer federal regulations are needed. A block grant approach may also involve converting a program from an entitlement to one that caps the allocation of funds and under which distribution to grantees remains fairly fixed over time. In truth, many programs defy simple categorization as block grant, categorical program, or entitlement, but the short-hand terms remain useful.

One set of arguments in favor of block grants, generally with a deregulatory thrust, is based on the assumption that the current system of categorical funding is too complicated and fragmented, resulting in national policy toward children and youth that is incoherent and inefficient. Gardner (1994) estimated that "in 1991 there were 557 federal grant programs...including 77 federal programs for children and families [each of] which are funded at a level of over $100 million per year" (p. 3). For example, over the last 30 years, separate federal categorical grant programs targeted at preventing high-risk behaviors among youth have been created and aimed at a variety of different problems including delinquency, violence, gang involvement, substance abuse, the high school dropout rate, and teen pregnancy.

The multiplicity of categorical programs has been cited as an obstacle to effective policymaking and service delivery at a number of levels. First, at the federal level, these programs fall under the jurisdiction of more than 20 congressional committees and are administered nearly impossible to establish a coordinated and coherent child and youth policy at the federal level. The problems created by the scope of the bureaucracy are compounded by the turf issues prevalent in legislative and administrative bureaucratic cultures. Turf battles frequently prevent congressional committees and federal agencies from working cooperatively to develop a comprehensive and coherent approach to problems affecting children and youth.

It should be pointed out that this criticism is by no means new. The U.S. General Accounting Office (1995) notes that a report by the Commission on the Organization of the Executive Branch in 1949 concluded that "a system of grants should be established based upon broad categories—such as highways, education, public assistance, and public health—as contrasted with the present system of fragmentation."

Second, given the level at which programs are implemented, both the research and intervention literature increasingly argue against a single problem-based approach and toward one that addresses the basic developmental needs of children and youth by targeting risk and protective factors that underlie multiple problem behaviors. Even for those who seek such integration, however,the plethora of categorical programs and the authorities who administer them make it extremely difficult for service providers at the local level to coordinate such programs and at the same time meet their respective regulatory guidelines. The funding sources, granting agencies, and funding cycles for services addressing pregnancy prevention, youth violence, services for runaways, mental health services, school failure, and drug, alcohol, and tobacco use vary considerably. Regulations involving age of recipients, eligibility criteria, appropriate uses of funds, and accountability and reporting requirements differ widely from program to program. It is difficult to construct a seamless web of developmentally appropriate services under such conditions.

The extent to which federal categorical requirements actually impede integration, however, is open to debate. Many providers achieve fairly good integration under the current system, albeit not without a good deal of hard work and maneuvering. Some argue that federal constraints are used as an excuse for inaction at the state and local level. For example, a recent offer by the U.S. Department of Education to waive current regulations for most federal elementary and secondary education programs resulted in a slew of requests for waivers of nonexisting regulations, representing 30% of all such requests. According to Larry Austin, spokesman for Oregon's education office, "there are a lot of 'phantom' rules out there. [In other words,] people were making excuses for why they could not implement innovative programs, which became evident when districts would apply for waivers that they didn't really need" (Education Week, 1997, p. 17).

Finally, some fiscal conservatives also argue that the consolidating programs can help reduce administrative expenses and overhead, resulting in the same level of services being delivered at a substantially lower cost.

On the other hand, some argue that there are a number of advantages to a categorical aid system. Gardner (1994) lists five:

- the targeted nature of categorical programming helps ensure that help gets to the populations that most need it;

- block grants are not as responsive to specific changes in need as categorical aid programs are;

- categorical funding systems are more conducive to focused lobbying efforts, whereas at the same time multiple programmatic funding pots lessen the probability that cuts to single programs will have a wide impact on a particular population, such as children;

- categorical programs may be more attractive to legislators, who can gain credit for activism in a specified issue area; and

- categorical aid focuses attention on particular problems, which mobilizes specific professional expertise.

Gardner's third point seems especially well-taken. Critics of the block grant approach have argued that block grants are often used as a tool to reduce expenditures, and that this fiscal function is true goal of block grants rather than the administrative advantages cited by supporters. As evidence, critics note that several major block grants, including the Social Services Block Grant, the Community Services Block Grant, and the Chapter 2 Education Block Grant, have all seen their funding decline significantly over the past two decades.

One of the most vexing issues regarding the move to block grants is the issue of accountability. The block grants established during the Reagan administration were frequently criticized because they dropped many reporting and accountability requirements along with the myriad regulations governing the use of funds under the old categorical programs that were folded into the block grants. The absence of sound accountability data hamstrung both Congress and federal program administrators, neither of which could determine whether these block grants were providing needed and useful services. Partly in response to this dilemma, Congress has recently attempted to impose greater accountability for outcomes on block grant recipients in exchange for a decrease in regulations and an increase in flexibility. This raises many problems, however, such as the comparability of data across states if no uniform standard is imposed and whether evaluation data can be collected, analyzed, and reported on a time scale consistent with the legislative cycle of reauthorization.

The block grant approach to funding social programs for children is currently ascendant, but it is important to recognize that even in the current climate, legislators have shown an unwillingness to block grant many programs. Efforts to block grant the Head Start program failed in 1998, as did similar efforts with respect to the Title X Family Planning program. If history is borne out, we are likely to see a mixture of block and categorical grants in place. The most dramatic change in recent years was the successful conversion of the federal welfare program from an entitlement program to a block grant. It is not clear that Congress will succeed in block granting other major federal programs in the near future.

## Bias Regarding the Role of Government Responsibility?

There is some evidence that attitudes about the role of government and the nature of child, youth, and family policy vary as a function of the populations toward which specific programs are targeted. For example, one of the most contentious issues in the debate over changes to the nation's welfare system involved whether benefits to welfare families encouraged recipients to have additional children. Generally, conservatives argued that tying benefits levels to the number of children in families receiving welfare acted as an incentive for recipients to have more children. Their solution: cap welfare regardless of family size.

An unusual alliance of liberals and faith-based groups argued against this policy change. Liberals contended that families with more children needed greater assistance, and that there was no logical or empirical basis for the assertion that the relatively modest additional amount of benefits per child—an average of $35 per month in 1996—was a significant factor in determining family size (Wilcox, et al. 1996). Faith-based groups, such as Catholic Charities, although not conceding the conservative argument that increased benefits caused families on welfare to have additional children, feared that the family cap still might be a factor in the decision of mothers on welfare who did become pregnant to terminate their pregnancies.

This mirrored other areas of debate in the welfare bill. For example, another contentious issue involved cash assistance to families with disabled children through the federal Supplemental Security Income Program (SSI). Critics of SSI argued, with little empirical evidence to support their case, that parents were coaching children to fake disabilities to qualify for benefits. Many suggested scrapping the program, scaling it back, or converting assistance to vouchers to ensure the parents spent the money in ways that directly benefited their disabled children.

Both the family cap and SSI debates, along with many other issues, were resolved through compromises. The final welfare bill encouraged, but did not require, states to impose family caps and rewarded states that showed both lower teen pregnancy rates and no corresponding increases in abortion. SSI remained as a cash entitlement, but with stricter standards for eligibility.

The point here is a general trend in the policy debate over the welfare bill. With regard to the welfare bill, politicians who generally argued for greater state and local flexibility advocated what, in some ways, was a much more prescriptive approach, which implied a fairly skeptical attitude about the ability of low-income parents to make wise decisions on behalf of their own children.

What is interesting is the marked contrast between the welfare debate and that which followed in other policy areas. Case in point: Many policymakers who argued for a family cap on welfare benefits also supported a yearly $500 per child tax credit for U.S. families (ultimately passed as part of the 1997 budget agreement), an amount slightly greater that the average yearly increase in benefits for welfare families which they had argued against. At no point in the consideration of the per-child tax credit did serious debate occur over whether this policy would cause families to have additional children, even though many of those families who would be eligible would have incomes only slightly above the poverty level. Nor, in contrast to the debate over SSI, did any serious question arise about whether families would spend this money wisely; in fact, one of the main arguments in support of the proposal was that families knew better than the federal government where best to direct this money on behalf of their children.

## The Scope of Child and Youth Policy

Despite continued calls from many quarters for a comprehensive child and youth policy in the United States, little progress toward this end has been made. The barriers to such a comprehensive approach are formidable. Most fundamentally, there is no consensus concerning what would be included in such a policy. For each issue that proponents might include in a comprehensive policy—guarantees of access to health care and high-quality child care, for example—there are opponents who argue that these policies undermine family autonomy and responsibility. The fundamental policy tension between public versus private responsibility that was discussed earlier plays out most clearly in the realm of child and youth policy issues. As Steiner (1983) has argued, child and family policy is an easy general rubric around which to unite, but the specific content is frequently divisive.

Another critical barrier to comprehensive policy is structural in nature. The federal policy process has been described as reactive, disjointed, and incremental. It is reactive in the sense that most policymaking is made in response to problems rather than in a more developmental fashion. Downs (1972) has described the resulting "issue attention cycle," in which important issues are constantly bumped from the legislative agenda as other problems requiring a reaction come to the attention of legislators. These "attention spasms" make comprehensive policy development difficult. The policy process is disjointed in the sense that responsibility for policymaking is divided across branches of government, and among federal, state, and local governmental entities. The Constitution limits the reach of the federal government with respect to many domestic policies, such as those regulating marriage and divorce. These factors,

along with the complex jurisdictions of the many House and Senate committees and subcommittees, result in a disjointed process that makes the development of coordinated, comprehensive policies more difficult. Finally, structural
features of our federal government, such as the separation of powers and the
considerable power given to individual members of the Senate to slow or stop
legislation, make incremental policymaking far more likely than comprehensive policymaking. Efforts to restructure vast areas of policy in a comprehensive fashion, such as the recent attempt to redesign health care policy, are very
rarely successful. Health care policy is an excellent example of a policy domain
that has been constructed in an incremental fashion.

If the development of a comprehensive child and youth policy is unlikely,
what goals should advocates for children and youth pursue? Our sense, as
longtime observers and participants in the federal policymaking process, is that
advocates for children and youth, as well as researchers concerned with their
well-being, have frequently missed important opportunities to inform and
influence policies affecting children and youth because of an overriding focus
on children and youth as individuals. This individualistic bias has translated
into advocacy efforts directed toward small classes of problems affecting children and youth, which in turn has led to disjointed efforts often placed in competition with one another.

Policy directed at the issue of child abuse and neglect offers a good example of this problem. The Child Abuse Prevention and Treatment Act (CAPTA)
was enacted in 1973 and was to be the centerpiece of federal activity directed
at the problems of abuse and neglect. A small state grant program was successful in encouraging states to develop mandated child abuse reporting laws, but
beyond this, the success of this legislation has been quite limited. Over the
years, advocacy organizations used the CAPTA reauthorization process as an
opportunity to lobby for provisions benefiting their particular constituencies.
Consequently, funding for demonstration projects would focus on children
with disabilities one year and drug-dependent mothers the next. Child abuse
policymaking degenerated into a contest over which subpopulations would
have their concerns addressed, and the larger issues of how to design an effective approach to the prevention of abuse and neglect became a tertiary concern.
In the end, the National Center on Child Abuse and Neglect was downgraded
to an Office on Child Abuse and Neglect, and now plays a fairly insignificant
role in this policy arena.

In recent years, research on children and youth has increasingly been
informed by a broader, developmental contextualism along the lines described
by Bronfenbrenner (1979), Lerner (1991), and others. Researchers have
extended their models of influences on the development of children to include
schools, neighborhoods, communities, and policies. The burgeoning research

supporting the importance of these developmental contexts suggests new
avenues for policy action and advocacy. A developmental contextual perspective focuses attention on issues such as neighborhood quality, structural characteristics of middle schools, residential racial segregation, and the economic
health of neighborhoods and communities.

Policymaking has tended to give limited attention to these contexts,
instead focusing on creating programs targeting the behaviors of children and
youth. A study panel of the National Research Council (1993) pointed out the
shortcomings of this approach and made an elegant case for shifting our policy and program attention to the contexts themselves and the transitions children make between the important contexts in their lives. Shifting our attention
from children and youth to the important contexts in their lives does not make
addressing the important problems confronting children and youth simpler,
but it is likely that efforts of this type will bear more substantial and long-
lasting results.

Child and youth policy advocacy efforts must take into consideration the
changed nexus of policymaking we have described here. The shift of power to
the state and local policymaking levels is real, yet advocacy efforts appear to be
slow in responding to this change. It is essential, however, that those concerned
with the well-being of children and youth recognize this change and respond
accordingly. Although federal legislators have access to considerable expertise
on the myriad issues they must address, there is a genuine dearth of high-
quality information available to state and local policymakers. Advocates must
refocus a major part of their efforts to the states. Researchers must attend to the
policy questions as state and local policymakers define them. There is some evidence that this is beginning to occur around issues raised by the state-level
implementation of welfare reform, but other areas of policymaking are still
largely ignored or addressed in an ineffectual fashion.

## References

Bronfenbrenner, U. (1979). *The ecology of human development*. Cambridge, MA: Harvard
    University Press.
Downs, A. (1972). Up and down with ecology: The issue attention cycle. *Public Interest, 26,*
    38–50.
Education Week. (1997, Aug. 8). *State officials seek flexibility, regulatory relief.* 17.
Gardner, S. (1994). *Reform options for intergovernmental funding system: Decategorization poli-
    cy issues.* Washington, DC: Finance Project.
General Accounting Office. (1995). *Block grants: Characteristics, experience, and lessons
    learned* (GAO/HEHS-94-4FS). Washington, DC: Author.
Gold, S. D., & Ellwood, D. (1994). *Spending and revenue for children's programs.*
    Washington, DC: Finance Project.

Gold, S. D., Ellwood, D., Davis, E. I., Liebschutz, D. S., Ritchie, S., Cohen, C., & Orland, M. (1995). *State investments in education and other children's services: Fiscal profiles of the 50 states.* Washington, DC: Finance Project.

Heclo, H. (1996). Coming into a new land: The context shaping American social policy. In S. B. Kemerman & A. J. Kahn (Eds.), *Whither American social policy?* New York: Columbia University School of Social Work.

Lerner, R. M. (1991). Changing organism-context relations as a basic process of development: A developmental-contextual approach. *Developmental Psychology, 27,* 27–32.

National Research Council. (1993). *Losing generations: Adolescents in high-risk settings.* Washington, DC: National Academy Press.

State Legislative Leaders Foundation. (1995). *State legislative leaders: Keys to effective legislation for children and families.* Centerville, MA: Author.

Steiner, G. Y. (1983). *The futility of family policy.* Washington, DC: Brookings Institution.

Sugarman, J. M. (1993). *Expenditures for children: Existing data and perspectives on budgeting.* Washington, DC: The Finance Project.

U.S. House of Representatives, Committee on Ways and Means. (1993). *Overview of entitlement programs: The 1993 Green Book.* Washington, DC: Government Printing Office.

Wilcox, B. L., Robbennolt, J. K., O'Keeffe, J. E., & Pynchon, M. E. (1996). Teen nonmarital childbearing and welfare: The gap between research and political discourse. *Journal of Social Issues, 52,* 71–90.

# About the Editors

*Carol Bartels Kuster* received her PhD in clinical/community psychology from the University of Maryland, College Park, in 1996. She is a former associate director of the Collaborative for Academic, Social, and Emotional Learning at the University of Illinois at Chicago (UIC). Most recently she served as supervisor of early childhood programs at Washburn Child Guidance Center in Minneapolis, providing therapeutic services for preschool-age children and their families. Her research and clinical interests include school- and community-based intervention and prevention programs and the effects of early childbearing and family violence on children's well-being.

*Mary Utne O'Brien* is associate director of the Collaborative for Academic, Social, and Emotional Learning at UIC. She has worked for more than 20 years on research, policies, and programs concerning the social fabric—including studies on poverty, homelessness, AIDS prevention, violence prevention, and racism. She consults with federal, state, and municipal governments; universities; and community-based organizations on the design and development of research on these and other issues.

O'Brien earned a PhD in sociology (focus on research methods and social psychology) in 1978 from the University of Wisconsin-Madison. She was Senior Survey Director at the National Opinion Research Center at the University of Chicago throughout the 1980s, where she was responsible for the design and management of complex federal surveys (e.g., William Julius Wilson's Study of Urban Poverty, Peter Rossi's study of the homeless, and a number of school-based Department of Education and RAND Corporation studies). From 1991 to 1996, she was Associate Professor of Epidemiology in the School of Public Health at UIC, where she developed and taught the school's first course on the epidemiology of HIV/AIDS. While at UIC, she was research director and codirector of the nation's largest research and service project for the prevention of HIV infection among injection drug users. In 1999, she wrote Chicago's five-year *Strategic Plan for HIV/AIDS Prevention.*

*Herbert J. Walberg,* research professor of education and psychology at UIC, was awarded a PhD in educational psychology from the University of Chicago and was formerly assistant professor at Harvard University. He completed a term as Founding Member of the National Assessment Governing Board, sometimes referred to as the "the national school board," because it has been given the mission of setting subject matter standards for U.S. students. He has written and edited more than 50 books and contributed more than 380 journal articles to educational and psychological research journals on such topics as educational effectiveness and productivity, school reform, and exceptional human accomplishments. He frequently writes for widely circulated practitioner journals and national newspapers, serves as an advisor on educational research and improvement to public and private agencies in the United States and other countries, and testifies before the state and federal courts and U.S. congressional committees.

A fellow of four academic organizations, he has won several awards and prizes for his scholarship and is one of three U.S. members of the International Academy of Education. He holds appointments in the UIC Center for Urban Educational Research and Development and the Mid-Atlantic Laboratory for Student Success. He currently serves on several not-for-profit boards and is Chairman of the Board of the Heartland Institute (www. heartland.org), which provides policy analyses for federal and state legislators and newspeople and publishes the magazine *Intellectual Ammunition* and two newspapers, including *School Reform News.*

*Roger P. Weissberg* is professor of psychology and education at UIC. He is chair of the psychology department's Division of Community and Prevention Research and directs a National Institute of Mental Health (NIMH)-funded predoctoral and postdoctoral prevention research training program in urban children's mental health and AIDS prevention. Professor Weissberg is the Executive Director of the Collaborative for Academic, Social, and Emotional Learning (www.casel.org), an organization committed to supporting the development and dissemination of effective school-based programs that enhance the positive social, emotional, academic, moral, and healthy development of young people. He also holds an appointment with the Mid-Atlantic Laboratory for Student Success funded by the Office of Educational Research and Improvement of the U.S. Department of Education. The author of more than 125 articles and chapters focusing on preventive interventions with children and adolescents, he has also coauthored nine curricula on school-based social-competence promotion programs to prevent drug use, high-risk sexual behaviors, and aggression. His research interests include school and community preventive interventions, urban children's mental health, and parental involvement in children's education. He received his PhD in clinical psychology from the University of Rochester in 1980 and from 1980 to 1982 was Research Director for the Primary Mental Health Project, a program for the early detection and prevention of school maladjustment.

Dr. Weissberg was a professor in Yale University's psychology department between 1982 and 1992 and also directed its NIMH-funded Prevention Research Training Program. He is past president of the APA Society for Community Research and Action and cochaired an APA Presidential Task Force on Prevention: Promoting Strength, Resilience, and Health in Young People. Dr. Weissberg is a recipient of the William T. Grant Foundation's five-year Faculty Scholars Award in Children's Mental Health, the Connecticut Psychological Association's Award for Distinguished Psychological Contribution in the Public Interest, and the National Mental Health Association's Lela Rowland Prevention Award. He was named a 1997-2000 University Scholar at the University of Illinois. In 2000, he received the APA Distinguished Contribution Award for Applications of Psychology to Education and Training.

# About the Contributors

*Joyce C. Abma* is a statistician/demographer for the National Center for Health Statistics. She received a PhD in sociology from The Ohio State University in 1993. She works on the National Survey of Family Growth, a periodic survey of pregnancy and childbearing among U.S. women aged 15–44. She participates in the design, administration, and public dissemination and analysis of the data. Her research interests and projects include interpretation of trends and differentials in sexual activity and contraceptive behavior among teenagers, causes of recent declines in pregnancy rates among teenagers, nonvoluntary sexual intercourse, voluntary childlessness among U.S. women, and women's childbearing intentions and their subsequent childbearing behavior. Her most recent publication focused on changes in patterns of sexual risk behaviors among teenage males and females: J. Abma and F. Sonenstein (2001), "Sexual activity and contraceptive practices among teenagers in the United States, 1988 and 1995," from *National Center for Health Statistics: Vital and Health Statistics*, 23(21).

*Charles Barone* is the Democratic Deputy Staff Director for the House Committee on Education and the Work Force. Previously, he was the legislative director for Congressman George Miller, serving as Miller's chief advisor on issues pertaining to children, youth, and families. He oversaw Congressman Miller's legislative work as the senior member of the House Committee on Education and the work force on education, child care, child nutrition, juvenile justice, work force training, and other issues.

His published research has centered on social-ecological approaches to understanding children and youth, with a particular focus on school transitions, prevention and positive youth development, adolescent sexual behavior, and urban violence.

Before working for Congressman Miller, Barone served as Senior Legislative and Federal Affairs Officer for the American Psychological Association and as

Legislative Assistant and Chief Education Advisor to Senator Paul Simon. Before coming to Capitol Hill, Barone was a Postdoctoral Fellow in the Children's Mental Health Prevention Research Program in the Department of Psychology at Yale University. He received his doctorate in clinical/community psychology from the University of Maryland at College Park in 1991.

*Juliet Bromer* is currently a doctoral student in the Committee on Human Development at the University of Chicago. She received her BA from Columbia University and her MS from Bank Street College of Education. She previously worked as a research associate at the Family Child Care Project, one of the Centers for Child Care Policy and Training at Wheelock College. Her work there involved the development of a national accreditation system for family child care providers. She has taught young children in a variety of urban settings and also worked as an instructor at Wheelock College. Her dissertation research focuses on the social support roles and neighborhood influences of child care providers in low-income communities.

*Jeanne Brooks-Gunn,* a developmental psychologist, is the Virginia and Leonard Marx Professor of Child Development and Education at Teachers College, Columbia University. She is the first Director of the Center for Children and Families, which was founded in 1992 at Teachers College, and is the Codirector of the Columbia University Institute of Child and Family Policy. She has been a visiting scholar at the Russell Sage Foundation, has served on three National Academy of Science panels, was president of the Society for Research on Adolescence, is coeditor of the Society for Research in Child Development's Social Policy Reports, and is on the Governing Council of that society.

 Author of more than 350 articles and 14 books, her specialty is policy-oriented research focusing on family and community influences on the development of children and youth. Her research centers on designing and evaluating interventions, programs, and policies aimed at enhancing the well-being of children living in poverty and associated conditions. She has received the Urie Bronfenbrenner Award for her lifetime contribution to developmental psychology in the areas of science and society (American Psychological Association [APA], Division 7), the Vice President's National Performance Review Hammer Award for her participation in the Federal Interagency Forum on Child and Family Statistics, the Nicholas Hobbs Award for her contribution to policy research for children (APA, Division 37), the John B. Hill Award from the Society for Research on Adolescence for her lifetime contribution to research on adolescence, and the Distinguished Contribution to Research in Public Policy Award from the Committee on Public Interest of the APA.

*Tama Leventhal* is a research scientist at the Center for Children and Families, Teachers College, Columbia University. She received her PhD with distinction in developmental psychology at Teachers College, where she was also a graduate fellow at the Center for Children and Families. She was a fellow in Putting Children First, a research fellowship program in child and family policy, and she held a Columbia University Public Policy fellowship. Her research interests are in linking developmental research with social policy regarding children, youth, and families, particularly low-income families. Her work examines individual-, family-, and community-level influences on child development, with a majority of her research focusing on understanding how neighborhood contexts affect child and family well-being. Selected publications on this topic have appeared in *Psychological Bulletin* (2000), *Neighborhood Poverty: Context and Consequences for Children* (New York: Russell Sage, 1997), and *Advances in Life Course Research* (2001). Additional lines of research consider the antecedents and consequences of adolescent employment and the effects of early intervention and service use on children's development.

*Brett Brown* is the director for Social Indicators Research at Child Trends, a nonpartisan, nonprofit research center that studies children and families. Dr. Brown holds a doctorate in sociology from the University of Wisconsin. He directs many of Child Trends' projects on social indicators of child, youth, and family well-being and does research on fatherhood and the transition to adulthood. He is a member of the Committee on Community-Level Programs for Youth, a member of the National Academy of Sciences, and was a member of the Federal Healthy People 2010 Adolescent Health Working Group.

*Emily Davis Cahan* is an Associate Professor of psychology at Wheelock College in Boston. She received her AB from Harvard University in 1978 and her PhD in developmental psychology from Yale University in 1987. While at Yale, she was a fellow at the Bush Center for Child Development and Social Policy and was awarded a Spencer Foundation postdoctoral fellowship from the National Academy of Education in 1988 to further her studies in the history of developmental psychology. Dr. Cahan has published numerous works on the social, intellectual, and institutional history of developmental psychology. These works include "Science, Practice, and Gender Roles in Early American Child Psychology," in *Contemporary Constructions of the Child: Essays in Honor of William Kessen*, edited by F. Kessel, M. Bornstein, and A. Sameroff (Lawrence Erlbaum, 2001); with S. H. White, "Proposals for a Second Psychology," in *Developmental Psychology* (1992); with H. Yeh, "Between Biology and History: Ruminations on Selfhood," in *Human Development* (1999); and with J. Feuser, "Remembering William Kessen (1925-1999)," in *History of Psychology* (2000).

*Dante Cicchetti* is the Shirley Kox Kearns Professor of psychology, psychiatry, and pediatrics at the University of Rochester and director of the Mt. Hope Family Center. He received his PhD from the University of Minnesota and accepted his first faculty position at Harvard University. He has published extensively in the area of emotional development, Down's syndrome, child maltreatment, childhood depression, and developmental psychopathology and has edited and contributed to many books, including *Attachment in the Preschool Years* (Chicago: University of Chicago Press, 1990); *Child Maltreatment* (New York: Cambridge University Press, 1989); *Risk and Protective Factors in the Development of Psychopathology* (New York: Cambridge University Press, 1990); *The Self in Transition* (Chicago: University of Chicago Press, 1990); and *Child Abuse, Child Development and Social Policy* (Norwood, NJ: Ablex, 1993). Most recently, Cicchetti coedited a two-volume set titled *Developmental Psychopathology* (New York: Wiley, 1995) with Donald Cohen. He also coedited *The Promotion of Wellness in Children and Adolescents* (Washington, DC: CWLA Press, 2000) with Julian Rappaport, Irwin Sandler, and Roger Weissberg. Cicchetti is also the founding editor of the journal *Development and Psychopathology*, published by Cambridge University Press and the Rochester Symposium on Developmental Psychopathology.

*Thomas J. Corbett* is Emeritus Professor of Social Work and an affiliate of the Institute for Research on Poverty (IRP) at the University of Wisconsin–Madison. He recently retired after serving two terms as associate director of IRP, including one year as acting director. Professor Corbett holds a doctorate in social welfare from the University of Wisconsin. His professional work includes extensive work on poverty and social policy issues at all levels of government—local, state, and national. He continues to facilitate a network of senior state welfare officials through the Midwest Welfare Peer Assistance Network and is involved in developing a West Coast equivalent called WEST-PAN. His scholarly work has focused particularly on the evolution of current welfare programs and attempts to reform them, topics on which he has written numerous papers and articles. In addition, he regularly speaks to various audiences on these issues. At the School of Social Work, Professor Corbett has been in charge of the social policy internship program and has taught various social policy and program evaluation courses at both the undergraduate and graduate levels. On leave from the university from June 1993 to May 1994, Professor Corbett served as a Senior Policy Analyst in the Office of the Assistant Secretary of Planning and Evaluation in the U.S. Department of Health and Human Services, where he worked on national welfare reform and other issues. More recently, he was a member on the Panel on Data and Methods for Evaluating Changes in Social Welfare Programs organized by the National Academy of Sciences.

*Joseph M. Hawes* is professor of history at the University of Memphis in Tennessee, where he has been since 1984. Prior to that he was professor of history at Kansas State University. His degrees are from the University of Texas at Austin (PhD, 1969), Oklahoma State University (MA, 1962), and Rice University (BA, 1960). His most recent publications include *Family and Society in American History*, coedited with Elizabeth Nybakken (Urbana: University of Illinois Press, 2001); *Children Between the Wars: American Childhood, 1920-1940* (New York: Twayne, 1997); and *The Children's Rights Movement: A History of Advocacy and Protection* (Boston: Twayne, 1991). Professor Hawes teaches courses on the history of childhood in the United States and on the history of American families. A current project is the Encyclopedia of the American Family (ABC-CLIO, forthcoming). Professor Hawes is a founding member and President elect of the Society for the History of Childhood and Youth.

*Donald J. Hernandez* is professor of sociology and affiliated with the Center for Social and Demographic Research at the State University of New York at Albany. Formerly, he was a special assistant with the U.S. Bureau of the Census. He also served as study director with the Board on Children, Youth, and Families of the National Academy of Sciences and the Institute of Medicine for their Committee on the Health and Adjustment of Immigrant Children and Families. That research is published by the National Academy Press in *From Generation to Generation: The Health and Well-Being of Children in Immigrant Families and Children of Immigrants: Health, Adjustment, and Public Assistance.* Dr. Hernandez formerly served with the U.S. Bureau of the Census as the senior subject matter expert for the Survey of Program Dynamics, which is designed to assess consequences of federal welfare reform, especially for children, and as chief of the Marriage and Family Statistics Branch, where he was responsible for many innovations in the collection, analysis, and reporting of Census Bureau data related to children, households, and family composition and change. He earned his PhD in sociology from the University of California, Berkeley. His book, *America's Children: Resources from Family, Government, and the Economy*, is the first national study using census and survey data with children as the unit of analysis to document the timing, magnitude, and reasons for revolutionary changes experienced by children since the Great Depression in family composition, parents' education, mothers' work, and family income.

*Lloyd Johnston* is a program director and distinguished research scientist at the University of Michigan's Institute for Social Research. A social psychologist by training, he received his formal education at Williams College, Harvard University, and the University of Michigan (PhD, 1973). For the past 27 years, he has served as the principal investigator on the Monitoring the Future study, which has provided the country some of its most reliable measures of trends in substance abuse and related factors among American secondary school students, college students, and young adults. These annual national surveys, which have been funded by the National Institute on Drug Abuse under a series of investigator-initiated research grants, have helped policymakers interpret the trends in young people's use of illicit drugs, cigarettes, and alcohol and have contributed to our knowledge of the effect of various environmental and role transitions on substance use. Johnston is also the principal investigator of the more recent Youth, Education, and Society Study, funded by the Robert Wood Johnson Foundation.

Dr. Johnston has published and lectured extensively on substance abuse among adolescents and young adults. Among his publications are *Drugs and American Youth* and the annual monograph series titled *Monitoring the Future National Survey Results on Drug Use*. He has advised six presidential administrations on drug-related matters and has testified before Congress on many occasions. He has served on the National Advisory Council on Drug Abuse, the White House Conference for a Drug-Free America, and the National Commission for Drug Free Schools.

*Lorraine V. Klerman* is a professor at the Heller School for Social Policy and Management, Brandeis University, Waltham, Massachusetts. At the time of writing, she was a professor in the Department of Maternal and Child Health, School of Public Health, University of Alabama at Birmingham. She has conducted research and published extensively in the areas of adolescent sexuality, pregnancy, and parenting; school absenteeism; prenatal care; unintended pregnancy; and support programs for underserved families. She has served on numerous federal and state expert panels and advisory groups and as a consultant to several foundations. She received a BA from Cornell University and both a master's and a doctoral degree in public health from the Harvard School of Public Health. She has served on the faculty of the Department of Epidemiology and Public Health, School of Medicine, Yale University. In 1996, she was awarded the Martha May Eliot Award of the American Public Health Association for distinguished service to mothers and children.

*Kriste Lindenmeyer* is associate professor of history at the University of Maryland, Baltimore County. From 1991 through 2000, she was in the history department at Tennessee Technological University in Cookeville. Lindenmeyer earned her PhD in history from the University of Cincinnati in 1991. She is the author of *A Right to Childhood: The U.S. Children's Bureau and Child Welfare, 1912-1946* (University of Illinois Press, 1997); editor of the anthology *Ordinary Women, Extraordinary Lives: Women in American History* (Scholarly Resources, 2000); and coeditor with Andrew Kersten of *Politics and Progress: American Society and the State Since 1865* (Greenwood Press, 2001). Professor Lindenmeyer teaches courses in U.S. social history and public history and specializes in the Gilded Age and Progressive Era. Lindenmeyer has also taught U.S. women's history at Vanderbilt University. Her current project focuses on American children and youth during the 1930s.

*Patrick M. O'Malley* is a senior research scientist at the Survey Research Center, Institute for Social Research, University of Michigan. He received a PhD in psychology from the University of Michigan in 1975. His principal research activity has been as a coinvestigator on the Monitoring the Future project, which has been funded through a series of research grants from the National Institute on Drug Abuse since 1975. The study, which involves annual national surveys of secondary school students in grades 8, 10, and 12, and of adults through age 40, provides the nation with annual reports on trends in the use of tobacco, alcohol, and illicit drugs. Dr. O'Malley is currently chair of the Social Sciences, Nursing, Epidemiology, and Methods Review Committee for the National Institutes on Health and is a past member (and past chair) of the Drug Abuse Epidemiology and Prevention Research Review Committee for the National Institute on Drug Abuse. He has served on four committees for the National Academy of Sciences and has published extensively on the epidemiology and etiology of use and abuse of psychoactive drugs, including the policy implications of the research. He is coauthor of three recent books: *Smoking, Drinking, and Drug Use in Young Adulthood: The Impacts of New Freedoms and New Responsibilities*, published by Lawrence Erlbaum Associates (1997); *Selecting Statistical Techniques for Social Science Data: A Guide for SAS Users*, published by SAS Institute (1998); and *The Decline of Substance Use in Young Adulthood: Changes in Social Activities, Role, and Beliefs*, published by Lawrence Erlbaum Associates (2001).

*Donald F. Roberts* is the Thomas More Storke Professor and director of the Institute for Communication Research in the Department of Communication at Stanford University, where he has also served as Department Chair. His research focuses on how children and adolescents use, interpret, and respond to media. He has published numerous empirical research papers and syntheses of the literature on children and media, including chapters in the *Handbook of*

*Communication*, the *Handbook of Social Psychology*, the *International Encyclopedia of Communications*, *Learning from Television: Psychological and Educational Research*, and the *Handbook of Children and the Media*. His books include *The Process and Effects of Mass Communication* (University of Illinois Press, 1971), *Television and Human Behavior* (Columbia University Press, 1978), and most recently, *It's Not Only Rock and Roll: Popular Music in the Lives of Adolescents* (Hampton Press, 1998).

Some of Roberts' recent activities include a large-scale examination of U.S. youth's media use for the Kaiser Family Foundation (*Kids & Media @ the Millennium*, 1999) and an ongoing project that examines the recent emergence of "teen television"—that is, programming created explicitly for the adolescent viewing audience. He is currently working on a chapter reviewing the research literature on adolescents, technology, and media for the new *Handbook of Adolescent Psychology*. Roberts recently chaired the Independent Advisory Council to the National Television Violence Study, and he helped plan and participate in former Vice President Al Gore's conference on families and the media. Roberts currently advises such companies as MGM Animation, DIC Entertainment, Nelvana, and ABC/Disney on the development of programming that meets Federal Communications Commission requirements for educational and informational broadcast television content for children.

*Lawrence C. Stedman* is associate professor at the State University of New York (SUNY) at Binghamton, where he teaches courses in educational research and policy. Prior to SUNY, he was a district policy analyst, secondary school teacher, and a Volunteer in Service to America. He received his PhD in educational policy studies from the University of Wisconsin–Madison. His research has focused on the condition of U.S. educational achievement and historical trends in general knowledge and cultural memory. He has written extensively on test score decline, literacy trends, and international assessments of education. His articles have appeared in *Educational Researcher*, *Educational Theory*, *Phi Delta Kappan*, *Reading Research Quarterly*, and other journals. His thesis and earlier publications were on effective schools research. He is one of the authors of *Literacy in the United States: Readers and Reading Since 1880*, which received the History of Education Society's biennial Outstanding Book Award.

*Sheree L. Toth* is associate professor of psychology at the University of Rochester and associate director of the Mt. Hope Family Center. She received her PhD in clinical psychology from Case Western Reserve University. Her research interests are broadly based in the area of developmental psychopathology. She has contributed to many journals and books in the area of child maltreatment, including *Developmental Psychopathology* (New York: Wiley,

1995) and the *Handbook of Developmental Psychology* (New York: Wiley, 1998). Toth is coeditor of *Internalizing and Externalizing Expressions of Dysfunction* (Hillsdale, NJ: Lawrence Erlbaum, 1991); *Developmental Approaches to Depression* (New York: Cambridge University Press, 1992); *The Self and Its Disorders* (Rochester, NY: University of Rochester Press, 1992); *Trauma: Perspectives on Theory, Research and Intervention* (Rochester, NY: University of Rochester Press, 1997); and *Child Abuse, Child Development and Social Policy* (Norwood, NJ: Ablex, 1993).

*Brian L. Wilcox* is currently director of the Center on Children, Families, and the Law, and professor of psychology at the University of Nebraska–Lincoln, where he is affiliated with the law/psychology and developmental psychology programs. He has published in a number of areas related to child, youth, and family policy, including adolescent sexual behavior and risk taking, child maltreatment, welfare reform, and children and media. He is currently conducting HIV/AIDS prevention research in Brazil and studying father involvement in the Early Head Start program. Wilcox is a member of the Research and Effective Programs Task Force of the National Campaign to Prevent Teen Pregnancy; past Chair of the APA Committee on Children, Youth, and Families; and President of the APA Division of Child, Youth, and Family Services. Prior to coming to the University of Nebraska, Wilcox served as Director of Public Policy for the APA, as a legislative assistant to Senator Bill Bradley, and as a member of the psychology faculty at the University of Virginia. He received his doctorate in community psychology from the University of Texas at Austin.

# Author Index

## A

Aaronson, D., 240
Aber, J. L., 190–191, 199, 232, 234, 236, 237, 239, 242, 247
Abma, J. C., 8–9, 103–125, 129, 321
Adams, G., 218
Aidman, A. J., 260
Akerman, A., 186
Alan Guttmacher Institute, 104, 106
Alexander, K. L., 239
Almario, D. A., 141
Altgeld, J. P., 279
Anderson, O., 288
Annie E. Casey Foundation, 4, 22
Aral, S., 104, 114
Ardelt, M., 164
Aries, P., 181
Austin, L., 309
Azer, S., 220

## B

Bachman, J. G., 78, 80, 81, 83, 95, 96, 98
Bachrach, C., 103, 106, 108, 124
Bachu, A., 218
Baldwin, A., 232
Baldwin, C., 232
Baldwin, W., 171
Bandura, A., 238, 265
Bardy, M., 158

Barnes-McGuire, J., 235
Barnett, D., 185, 186, 187
Barocas, R., 232
Barone, C., 14–15, 299–314, 321–322
Bauman, K. E., 259
Bearman, P., 110
Beatty, B., 213, 221
Becerra, R. M., 181
Belsky, J., 188
Bennett, W. J., 4, 17
Berlin, L. J., 236, 247, 248
Berliner, D., 54
Bernard, S., 199
Bestor, A., 53
Beuhring, T., 147
Biddle, B., 54
Billy, J., 116
Billy, O., 240, 241
Blane, H. T., 89
Bloom, B., 143, 144, 213
Blosser, B. J., 263
Blum, R. W., 147
Blumenthal, E., 265, 269
Boggess, S., 113
Boisjoly, J., 238
Both, D., 35
Botsko, C., 41, 44
Bowlby, J., 192
Bracey, G., 54
Bradner, C., 113

334

# Subject Index

*Page numbers followed by f and t refer to figures and tables, respectively.*

Family Support Act (1988), 171, 223
Farm families, 10, 155
Fashion industry, and drug use, 98
Fathers
    as breadwinners, 158, 159*f*, 160, 176, 207
    with low earnings, 166, 167
    nonfarm work of, 158–160
    paying child support, 170–171
    as source of child care, 209
    working less than full-time, 162, 163*f*, 167
Federal Communications Commission, 271
Federal government
    deregulation of, 307–308
    devolution of power from. *See Devolution*
    downsizing, 307–308
    goal-oriented programs launched by, 32
    measuring health of children, 131–132
    monitoring well-being, 30
    recommendations for, 43–45
    role of
        attitudes toward, 303–306
        bias regarding, 311–312
    sponsoring child care
        Head Start, 214–215, 216, 290
        lack of, 216–218
        during World War II, 208–211, 287
Federal Housing Authority, 290
Federal Interagency Forum on Child and Family Statistics, 3–4, 29–30, 47, 133
Federal Trade Commission, 271
Federal Works Agency, 210
Films, 260, 270
Firearms, injury by, 137, 148
First sexual intercourse, 9, 104
    before age 15, 114–117, 115*t*
    age at, 113–117
        and multiple sexual partners, 117, 118*t*
    and age of partners, 120–121, 122*t*
    contraceptive use at, 106

early, risks of, 104
long-term trends in, 114
voluntary or nonvoluntary, 118–120, 120*t*
Fiscal conservatism, 305
"Fiscal slack," 300–301
Folic acid supplements, 147
Foster care, 193–194
Foundations
    as consumers of social indicator data, 30
    measuring health of children, 132
    recommendations for, 46–47
Fragile Families, 248

## G

Gaming, 43
GED. *See General Educational Development*
Gender
    and illicit drug use, 95
    and media use, 260
    and mortality, 136
    and smoking, 85, 87
    and STDs, 109
Gender stereotypes, in media, 268
General Accounting Office, 66–67
General Educational Development (GED), 57
Genital herpes, 109
Genital warts, 109
Geography achievement
    historical comparisons of, 58, 70, 71
    NAEP findings on, 67*t*, 68
Goals 2000: Educate America Act (1994), 32
Goal-setting, social indicators used for, 31–33
Gonorrhea, 109
"Government baby," 288
Government transfer programs, 172–173
Grandmothers, as source of child care, 209
Great Depression, children in, 284–286
Great Society, 290–293

# H

goal-oriented programs launched by, 32–33

measuring health of children, 132

recommendations for, 46

responsible for social issues, 304, 305

Low birthweight infants, 135, 145, 147

LSD

availability of, 96

in counterculture movement, 98

disapproval of, 96

prevalence of, 84t, 93, 94f

Luxembourg Income Study (LIS), 173

Luxury, 165–166, 167f

# M

Macrosystem, 188, 189

Maltreatment. *See Child maltreatment*

Manipulation, 43

The Manufactured Crisis (Berliner and Biddle), 54

Marijuana

availability of, 96

in counterculture movement, 82–83, 98

disapproval of, 96

prevalence of, 81, 84t, 93, 94f

reasons for not using, 98

"stepping stone theory" and, 80

urbanity and, 95

Marketing. See Advertising

Marriage, average age at first, 103

Massachusetts, state-local initiatives in, 35

Maternal and Child Health Bureau, 133–134

Math achievement

community income and, 239

historical comparisons of, 57

international, 70

NAEP findings on, 59, 67, 67t

racial gaps in, 64f

Measles, 137

Media, 13–14, 255–274

censorship of, 272, 274

children and adolescents as consumers of, 259–263

and drug use, 82

portraying child maltreatment, 187, 202

portraying violence, 265, 266–267

public policies on, 271–274

sexuality in, 268–269

social stereotypes in, 268

Media environment, changing, 257–259

Media exposure, amount of, 259

Media literacy, 272

of parents, 272

school-based programs of, 273

training in, 273

Media messages

children interpreting, 261–263

effects of, 263–270

historical concern with, 255–257

recent trends in, 270–271

Medicaid, 144, 148

Medical discoveries, 130, 134

Medicare, 301

Mental health

child maltreatment and, 195, 197, 198

and juvenile delinquency, 283

Mental hygiene, 283

Merrill Palmer School, 284

Microsystem, 188, 189–190

Middle-class comfort, 165–166, 167f, 236, 239, 246

Milestones (Minnesota program), 32

Minimum hourly wage, increasing, 172

Minnesota, goal-oriented programs launched by, 32

Misrepresentation, 43

Model Cities, 291

Monitoring

health of children, 129, 130

social indicators used for, 30–31

Monitoring the Future Study, 83, 91, 98, 132

"Morality tests," 292